Shakespeare and
the Question of Theory

Shakespeare and the Question of Theory

Edited by

Patricia Parker and Geoffrey Hartman

New York and London

First published in 1985 by
Methuen & Co. Ltd

Reprinted 1990, 1991, 1993 by
Routledge
11 New Fetter Lane, London EC4P 4EE
29 West 35th Street, New York NY 10001

The collection as a whole © 1985 Methuen & Co. Ltd and Methuen, Inc.
Chapter 13 © 1984 Stanley Cavell
Other chapters © the respective authors

Photoset by Rowland Phototypesetting Ltd
Bury St Edmunds, Suffolk
Printed in Great Britain at the University Press, Cambridge

Library of Congress Cataloging in Publication Data
Main entry under title:

Shakespeare and the question of theory.

1. Shakespeare, William, 1564–1616 – Criticism and interpretation –
Addresses, essays, lectures.
I. Parker, Patricia, 1945–   . II. Hartman, Geoffrey H.
PR2976.S3373   1985   822.3'3   85–13835

British Library Cataloguing in Publication Data
Shakespeare and the question of theory.
1. Shakespeare, William – Criticism and interpretation
I. Parker, Patricia II. Hartman, Geoffrey H.
822.3'3   PR2976

ISBN 0 415 05113 4

Contents

PATRICIA PARKER

Introduction

Every major rethinking of literature and theory has a way of returning to particular texts, whatever the theoretical resistance to the very idea of a canon; and often to discover that what was canonical was not so much, or not just, the text in question but the received readings of it, its normalization as a cultural icon or familiar construct. The theoretical ferment which, in Stephen Greenblatt's phrase here, "has affected (some would say afflicted)" literary studies during the past decade has called into question traditional ways of thinking about, classifying, and interpreting texts. And so, perhaps, it was inevitable that a book such as this – which both begins with "theory" and questions it in turn – should be devoted to Shakespeare, arguably the most canonical and culturally pre-eminent of subjects. Shakespeare himself has been not just the focus of a variety of divergent critical movements within recent years but also, increasingly, the locus of emerging debates within, and with, theory itself, as Greenblatt's own simultaneous use and critique of deconstruction makes clear. Larger theoretical developments have had their echo in what is now amounting to a wholesale reconsideration of the Shakespearean corpus – from the controversy over what constitutes an authoritative "text" for plays which exist in so many versions, to the perception of a kinship between Derridean wordplay or Bakhtinian heteroglossia and Shakespeare's own inveterate punning, from the exploration by feminist critics of the differing roles of women in Shakespeare to the reopening of historical and ideological questions in ways other than a simple return to the static conservatism of Tillyard's long-influential *Elizabethan World Picture*.

This is a book, then, both for those interested in Shakespeare and for those interested more generally in the emerging debates within contemporary criticism and theory, since Derrida, Foucault and others first burst upon the consciousness of English-speaking readers almost a generation ago. It begins with what the label "theory" perhaps still most readily brings to mind – analyses of language and figure, deconstructive strategies of reading, but also a broader engagement with what Joel Fineman here highlights as the "rope-tricks" of rhetoric to which modern theory has been so influential in returning critical attention. Howard Felperin starts from a tendency in Shakespeare criticism not unlike the kind parodied in L. C. Knights's classic "How many children had Lady Macbeth?" and argues in his discussion of representation in *The Winter's Tale* for Shakespeare's own sophisticated awareness of the inescapable mediacy of all language, of the instability of meaning and the radical uncertainty of interpretation. Elizabeth Freund illustrates her thesis that it is possible, in the wake of contemporary theoretical discourse, to show that "the Shakespearean self-reflexive forays of wit match, remarkably, the wit of the deconstructionist enterprise" by an examination of the ways in which *Troilus and Cressida*, like recent rhetorical analysis, questions the assumptions of unified meaning central to certain kinds of criticism and calls attention to its own intertextuality by foregrounding its highly literary *materia*. Geoffrey Hartman, reviewing the varieties of traditional Shakespeare scholarship, from G. W. Knight to Empson to Leavis, from historical scholarship to editorial gloss to biographical sleuthing, focuses on the ways in which Shakespeare's notorious punning and wordplay undo the hegemony of any single order of discourse, compelling us, as he puts it, to realize the radically social and mobile nature of the language exchange. My own essay attempts in turn to ground the language of *Othello* more historic-ally in the crossing of rhetorical and judicial, and the uncertainty of reference which Felperin describes as problematic for both audience and jealous husband in the link between rhetoric, representation, and the classic problem of this tragedy's supposed double time scheme.

Hartman's essay invokes Dr Johnson's famous, or infamous, remark on the pun or quibble as Shakespeare's "fatal Cleopatra" in order to explore the richness of precisely such punning play within *Twelfth Night*. But Johnson's very choice of phrase betrays the gender associations of his age – and not just his age – with the slippery and suspect deviance of figurative language itself. What is only implicit, then, in the essays in part I, in Hartman's pursuit of this "fatal Cleopatra" or the evocation in *Othello* of the often violent misogynist topos of women's troublesome speech or verbal *copia*, is in part II opened up for a debate which both continues recent feminist inquiries into the "woman's part" in Shakespeare and raises the question of the methodologies and assumptions appropriate to a genuinely historical feminist criticism. For Elaine Showalter, the "part" of the woman extends beyond that of the character within a single play – Ophelia, for instance, in *Hamlet* – to the representations which elide the boundary between dramatic and social, "art" and "life," between a role in a play dominated by the male character who gives it its name and the part played by this particular woman in the "living theater" of female pathology which so crucially informed the emerging discourse and practice of psychoanalysis. Nancy Vickers, whose well known essay on the *blazon* in *Writing and Sexual Difference* already sets out the ways in which the body of woman becomes, in Cixous's phrase, the "uncanny stranger on display," here focuses on both the Sonnets and *Lucrece*, a poem in which the *blazon*'s inventory of separate and reified parts is part of the motivated discourse of a rape, of a contest in which a woman's role, as Mary Jacobus has observed in another context,[1] is to figure the rivalry between men.

Jonathan Goldberg, in a discussion ranging over, among others, *The Merchant of Venice*, *Julius Caesar*, *Measure for Measure* and *A Midsummer Night's Dream*, polemically opposes what he sees as a tendency within certain recent feminist criticism of Shakespeare simply to identify genre and gender, or purely to oppose male and female. He employs a broadly Derridean and Lacanian language to investigate the discourse of power which for him complicates this question, returning to Simone de Beauvoir's insight that woman is a cultural construct in order to counter what he takes to be ahistorical constructions of the "woman's part." Joel Fineman, observing that at the end of *The Taming of the Shrew* things are as patriarchally inflected as at the beginning, investigates how it is that an apparent discourse of subversion manages to re-secure the very order to which it appears to be opposed, and whether it is finally possible to voice a language that does not speak sooner or later for the order and authority of man. In an argument which links his essay with those in part I as well as with Showalter's very different questioning of Freud and Lacan, Fineman also asks why the question of rhetoric should evoke from psychoanalysis the patriarchalism for which Lacan appears to be the most explicit mouthpiece, just as the same question provokes the anti-patriarchal gender deconstructions of a Derrida or the French feminism of a Julia Kristeva, Luce Irigaray, or Hélène Cixous. Fineman's essay suggests an intimate connection between rhetoric and the very placing of "woman," as indeed might a glance at those numerous Elizabethan rhetorical handbooks in which discussions of *ordo* and proper sequential "disposition" so frequently invoke the model of "man" first, "woman" second as the conventional example of a proper order both in discourse and in nature. Or as the reinstitution of patriarchy in as controversial a play for feminist analysis as *A Midsummer Night's Dream* suggests a rule associated with what is called the ordered "chain" of discourse.

All four essays in part II invoke questions of power, politics and history, in turn the explicit subjects of part III. Stephen Greenblatt, in a discussion which includes *The Comedy of Errors*, *Twelfth Night*, and *All's Well That Ends Well*, adopts what he terms a "cultural poetics" in order to explore the relation between *King Lear* and Samuel Harsnett's *A Declaration of Egregious Popish Impostures* – one not analogous to traditional source study or so-called historical "background," but rather closer to Brecht's "alienation effect" or to the dynamic of "internal distantiation" described by Althusser and Macherey. René Girard, whose theoretical writings figure in other essays in this volume, focuses by contrast not on power and politics in specific historical terms but on the underlying structure of "mimetic desire" which in a play such as *Troilus and Cressida* inextricably links the erotic and the political, the economy of masculine desire to that vicious circle of rivalry and imitation which is the Trojan war itself. Harry Berger, Jr, in a different way, links the political preoccupations of the *Henriad* with the psychological, focusing both on the problem of genealogical succession from father to son and on the debate between text-centered and stage-centered critics of Shakespeare, suggesting at once the power of theatrical performance and the Lacanian "discourse of the Other" it represses. Thomas M. Greene reads the Sonnets as calling into doubt both the representation of the bourgeois poet's aristocratic friend as the source of all value and an alternative economic system located in the value of the poetry itself, while Stanley Cavell – writing on the play which, especially after Brecht, has provoked radically divergent political responses – argues that *Coriolanus* is concerned not so much with a specific politics as with the very formation of the political.

The volume comes to an end with three essays on *Hamlet*, still the most discussed of all of Shakespeare's plays. East German critic Robert Weimann, whose analysis touches on *Lear* as well, outlines the critique of mimesis in recent deconstructive and Girardian theory – including that undermining of certain notions of representation and interpretation with which Howard Felperin began – but questions whether the methodologies of poststructuralism can provide a satisfactory framework for the complex question of mimesis in Shakespeare, suggesting instead an approach to this question through Marx's concept of *Aneignung* or "appropriation." Margaret Ferguson, observing that Shakespeare's tendency to blur generic lines has often been remarked but not related to the way in which Shakespearean tragedy seems often to imply a questioning of the casting of a given story *as* tragedy, approaches this broader problem by exploring both the techniques of wordplay within *Hamlet* – including the "fatal Cleopatra" of the pun – and a process of dramatic literalization associated with the impulse to kill. Terence Hawkes's *Telmah* – or *Hamlet* in reverse – raises, finally, larger cultural and political questions about the context of all theory and criticism by focusing on the anxious response of John Dover Wilson both to an unsettling reading of the play and to the contemporary specter of Bolshevism in Russia and of working-class unrest more close at hand. Appropriately for the ending to this volume, it situates the critic – here not just Matthew Arnold, Dover Wilson, E. M. W. Tillyard, F. R. Leavis, or promoters of a particular educational project for the English classics, but by implication any critic or theorist – as always, culturally and politically, *interested* readers in the full sense of the word. And it reminds us as well that "theory," that supposed recent development or baleful foreign influence, is in fact always with us, performing both its radicalizing and its normalizing functions, posing questions but itself always open to questioning in turn.

*

The division of the book into parts – with "the woman's part" deliberately and sardonically placed as part II – merely suggests one possible grouping or common focus: in reality, the concerns of the essays across these partitions greatly overlap. Berger's observation that genealogical succession in the *Henriad* betrays a latent ideal of male parthenogenesis expressed in the fear, scapegoating and repression of the feminine, like Greene's characterization of the unstable gender of poetry in the Sonnets or Girard's description of the laws of masculine desire and of rivalry among males, joins Showalter's and Vickers's feminist analyses of other texts, and attests, perhaps, to the growing influence of feminist criticism on the kinds of questions being asked of both literature and history; while Greene's description of the Sonnets' "rhetorical economics," like Cavell's highlighting of Marc Shell's discussion of "verbal usury" in *The Merchant of Venice*, suggests the metaphor of "increase" which pertains not just to husbandry but to the economy of language as well.

Felperin's characterization of the radical subjectivity of the listener in *The Winter's Tale* suggests the realm of affect which contemporary theory has termed affective stylistics, or reader response, the dimension of reception which might be said to have been included in the Renaissance within the implied psychology and manipulative power of rhetoric itself. But Girard also invokes the problem of affect: his argument that Shakespeare in *Troilus and Cressida* makes allowance for the male chauvinism of his audience just as in *The Merchant of Venice* he does for its antisemitism suggests that the only theory of response adequate to an understanding of the plays is one which acknowledges the gap between their restatement of the traditional clichés and the subtler message which subverts them, a particularly strenuous contemporary restatement of Milton's "fit audience though few," and clearly for Girard part of the vocation of the interpreter of an author such as Shakespeare.[2]

Together the essays raise for debate a whole range of central issues, both in the criticism of Shakespeare and in the larger field of thinking and theorizing about literature itself – from its formal and linguistic structures to its relations with power, politics, gender, and history. And no more clearly than when they differ sharply from one another. The influence of psychoanalysis – so pervasive in its impact on modern theory – emerges, but with very different conclusions, in Elaine Showalter's tracing of its ideologies of sexual difference, in Fineman's discussion of Derrida on Lacan, in Cavell's beginning from Janet Adelman's justly celebrated psychoanalytic reading of *Coriolanus*, in Berger's theorizing of the relation between textuality and performance, or in

Ferguson's extensions of Freud, Jones, and Lacan on *Hamlet*. Girard's critique of the blindness of readings of *Troilus and Cressida*, in which "Cressida has falseness and infidelity written all over her from the beginning," polemically engages the assumptions of Freund's deconstructive analysis of Cressida's text-determined condition as "always already sentenced" by citation, while Geoffrey Hartman's evocation of Shakespeare as the poet of a Keatsian Negative Capability – a celebrated touchstone of liberal criticism which Margaret Ferguson has elsewhere pointedly contrasted with more engaged approaches to Shakespeare, both Marxist and feminist[3] – is part of his defense of an interest more in "poetical character" than in its relations to "character" in the world (domestic or political), or in the concerns of what he calls "ideological critics." Robert Weimann's critique of the limitations of poststructuralist discussions of mimesis is by contrast paralleled by Stephen Greenblatt's argument that deconstructionist theory, though it has broken down the boundary between literary and nonliterary in ways useful to his own historical investigations, has also discounted the specific, institutional interests involved in local instances of undecidability: that though it is often accused of being a satanic doctrine, it is in fact, in this sense, by no means satanic enough. And both are joined by Terence Hawkes's concluding remarks on not just the omission but the active exclusion of politics from criticism.

Weimann's calling into question, finally, of the primarily textual basis of much recent theory – contrasting sharply as it does with Berger's argument for the priority of text over performance – indirectly leads us to one of the central issues in contemporary debates "for" and "against" recent theory, the contrast between a rhetoric of tropes and a rhetoric of persuasion. It might be argued that the incursion of printing and its own proliferation of writing and textuality – an incursion which Shakespeare himself frequently alluded to – already envisaged the possibility of such an apparent split, though rhetoric in Shakespeare's day still involved not just a scheme of tropes and figures but the whole armory of manipulation and response, in contexts which were traditionally not just literary or judicial but political. *The Winter's Tale*, like *Othello* and other plays of Shakespeare, depends crucially on the trope known as *enargeia*, that vivid and lifelike description which was as much the persuasive tool of an Iago or a Iachimo as of a Shakespeare, and which in the Renaissance was commonly and richly confused with *energeia*, the domain of "actuality" in metaphor. For those more familiar with contemporary theory than with the intricacies of Renaissance rhetoric, this very confusion might suggest something like what the late Paul de Man repeatedly emphasized as the sheer radical positing power of language itself, and its aberrations. And anyone interested in this aberrance, or in what Derrida and modern language theorists have investigated as the power of the copula, might do worse than to follow out the implications of so apparently simple a construction as "This is

Illyria" in *Twelfth Night*, the tragic consequences of Macbeth's "Is this a dagger which I see before me," or the subtleties of that curious debate in *The Tempest* over whether Tunis "is" or "is not" Carthage ("His word is more than the miraculous harp. . . . He hath rais'd the wall, and houses too"), in a play in which the constructive power of the word itself is so much at stake.

Shakespeare's own acute awareness of the construction of texts – as well as of persuasive discourses and dramatic productions – encourages in its very wit a self-conscious perception of the bases, and biases, of all constructions, including a volume such as this one. And so we pass, from this brief Prologue to the play itself, with the hope that "in such indexes, although small pricks / To their subsequent volumes, there is seen / The baby figure of the giant mass / Of things to come at large . . ."

Notes

1. "Is there a woman in this text?" (*New Literary History*, 14, 1 (Autumn 1982), 117–41).
2. For a similarly strenuous Girardian critique of traditional Shakespeare criticism, see his "Hamlet's dull revenge," in Patricia Parker and David Quint (eds), *Literary Theory and Renaissance Texts* (Baltimore, 1986).
3. "'Debate that bleedeth at our doors': recent criticism of Shakespeare" (*Yale Review*, 71, 3 (Spring 1982), 414–26).

I
Language, rhetoric, deconstruction

1

HOWARD FELPERIN

"Tongue-tied our queen?": the deconstruction of presence in *The Winter's Tale*

> Firstly, nothing exists; secondly, even if anything exists, it is unknowable; thirdly, even if anything can be known, it cannot be communicated by language.
>
> Gorgias, as reported by Sextus Empiricus

In the first issue of a new journal on Shakespeare, self-mockingly titled *The Upstart Crow*, the opening article offers a reinterpretation of *Othello*. Where past critics have gone wrong, it argues, has been in their failure to see that Desdemona has had an affair with Cassio before the beginning of the play. Indeed, her sexual appetite is, as her name clearly suggests, positively "demonic," and altogether too much for the aging Othello. Her passivity toward the end of the play, so the argument goes, has nothing to do with stoic self-dramatization, natural dignity, or the virtue that suffers long and is kind. It is simply a matter of her having realized that she has been found out, and that the game is up. The author of the article (who shall remain unnamed for reasons by now apparent) shows restraint in not specifying how many children Desdemona has had as a result of her liaison with Cassio, if indeed she has had any. Having set criticism of the play back on track, he is content to leave these and related questions to the rest of us to answer in due course.[1]

In introducing the present paper on *The Winter's Tale*, I cite this article not to follow its lead and pursue its method, but to raise through an extreme case a perennial problem of criticism. The problem I have in mind arises for the audience or interpreter whenever a work of literature makes reference to

3

prior or off-stage or, in the most general terms, unrepresented action. To what extent ought we to feel constrained in interpreting that which is not actually presented in the text, not actually "there," as we say, before us? To what extent may we reasonably entertain such speculation as part of our larger attempt to interpret the text within which the unrepresented action occurs or, as it were, fails to occur? What, so to speak, can one fairly make of an absence or a gap? There is no escape from this problem, in so far as the traditionally mimetic ambitions of literature in general and drama in particular encourage us to consider its characters and plots as if they were actions performed by human beings with past and ongoing lives no less "real" for being invisible or unavailable to us, and still in some sense "there" while remaining unrepresented. Does our neighbor cease to exist when he disappears behind his front door? Short of voyeurism, how can we re-create his activities behind that door, given other knowledge of him? In this respect, is our perception of literary characters very different from that of our next-door neighbors? Moreover, the strategic reference to a prior event or off-stage life is a repeated, characteristic, and highly effective device of that literature traditionally deemed "realistic"; of, that is, the nineteenth-century novel, or the drama of Ibsen and Chekhov. It may well be one of the devices by means of which the illusion of an actual world populated by actual people is achieved in Shakespearean drama as well – Maurice Morgann asserted as much in the eighteenth century, initiating that tradition of characterology which turns only too easily into the sort of criticism with which we began.[2] Hence we must ask how far we can pursue this mode of criticism before our enterprise becomes misguided, before we ought to stop and remind ourselves that the work with which we are dealing is, as we sometimes say, "only a play," only artificial personages in a fictive construct whose "life" consists only in representation. Did A. C. Bradley go too far? Or L. C. Knights not far enough? And how far do these same strictures apply to our speculations concerning the past or off-stage or invisible lives, even the inner or subjective lives in their ultimate opacity, of the people we know and gossip about in what we call – simply or simple-mindedly? – "real life" or "life itself"?

In *The Winter's Tale*, at least as much as *Othello*, we are faced in a stark and peremptory way with this problem of what to make of unrepresented events. For its action, as everyone knows, arises as a direct consequence of Leontes' wild surmise that his wife has been betraying him with his best and oldest friend during the nine months prior to the opening of the play. Shakespeare, that is, presents us with a principal character who stakes his reputation, his happiness, his realm, his selfhood – stakes nothing less than everything – on his interpretation of behavior partly available and partly unavailable to him, and partly represented and partly unrepresented to us. In the conviction with which he presents his interpretation of events, Leontes is not altogether unlike the author of the article on *Othello* with which I began, perhaps not altogether unlike ourselves in our own efforts at interpretation. Indeed, on what authority do we assume – and it is so confidently and unanimously assumed by critics of the play as never to my knowledge to have been raised as an issue – that Hermione is in fact innocent of Leontes' suspicions in the opening act of the play? Why do we take for granted, as if it were a fact of nature, what can never be proved but only denied: that a king's wife has not had an affair with his best friend and nine months later given birth to an illegitimate daughter? How can we know that what has not been shown has not happened? In reaching the conclusion that we have unanimously reached as critics of the play, we have proceeded, indeed, been forced to proceed, in the absence of ocular or empirical proof, for how could there be ocular proof of what has not taken place? We have proceeded on grounds delimited on the one side by Anglo-Saxon law (which presumes formal innocence unless guilt is proved) and on the other by Pauline Christianity (which is based precisely on the evidence of things not seen).

Let me reassure you at once that my purpose is *not* to contend that all commentators on the play until now have been wrong, and that Leontes is right in supposing his wife has betrayed him. It does seem worth pointing out, however, that in the negative nature of the case as Shakespeare has taken pains to set it up, neither Leontes nor we can ever know for sure, short of divine revelation. I mention divine revelation, only because that is precisely what is at last represented to us on stage, what forces Leontes to change his mind, and what has prevented critics from doing with *The Winter's Tale* what the aforementioned critic did with (or *to*) *Othello* – though this last point must remain only conjecture. God – or at least Apollo – does speak in *The Winter's Tale*, and he speaks unequivocally: "Hermione is chaste; Polixenes blameless; Camillo a true subject; Leontes a jealous tyrant; his innocent babe truly begotten; and the king shall live without an heir, if that which is lost be not found." How could the oracle have been any more explicit or unequivocal? After such knowledge, it would take a very wilful interpreter indeed to maintain Leontes' view of the matter. In the face of that divine pronouncement, not even critics of Shakespeare have been that foolhardy.

Now, I realize that I would be laying myself open to being considered more foolhardy than any critic of the play has yet managed to be, if I were not to let the matter rest there. But at the risk of bringing chaos into order, I want to question the definitiveness of the oracle's pronouncement and the basis for our happy consensus. Of course that is no more than Leontes himself does: "There is no truth at all in the oracle. The sessions will proceed." Leontes, that is, seems suddenly to fall back on a mistrust of oracular pronouncements familiar enough in literature, Renaissance as well as classical. Although this is the only point in the play where such a conventional mistrust is ever hinted at, it would seem that such mistrust is well-grounded. The fondness of pagan oracles for ambiguity, obscurantism, equivocation, and general verbal trickery is commonplace in Elizabethan literature. Shakespeare himself exploits the equivocations of pagan prophecy in *Macbeth*, although there the unreliability of the witches' pronouncements is emphasized by contrast with the play's Christian milieu. Closer to the present context, the riddle of *Pericles* and the prophecies of *Cymbeline* are wholly consistent with our literary expectation of trickery from pagan sources. Both require considerable ingenuity to tease out their sense, in the latter case an interpretive strenuousness verging on interpretive self-parody, a wilful over-reading comparable to anything in our learned journals. The editor of the New Arden *Winter's Tale*, for example, contrasting the message of Jupiter with that of Apollo, calls the former "Merlinesque," perhaps recollecting the similarly riddling and anachronistic prophecies of the Fool in *Lear*.[3] Yet here, in the deliberately pseudo-classical context of *The Winter's Tale*, Shakespeare presents us with a most plain-spoken and un-Delphic Delphic oracle: "Hermione is chaste; Polixenes blameless; Camillo a true subject; Leontes a jealous tyrant," etc. Only the last clause of the oracle's pronouncement could be said to be in the least Pythian or even pithy, and even there the meaning is, in context, clear to all concerned. It is significant, for example, that Coleridge has recourse to the more teasing language we expect from oracles in suggesting a supplementary phrase to adumbrate Hermione's destiny. He describes his addition – "Nor shall he ever recover an heir if he have a wife before that recovery" – as "some *obscure* sentence of the oracle."[4]

Given the pellucid prose in which this oracle pronounces himself – and Shakespeare makes even more explicit and unequivocal the already clear pronouncement of his source – given this unwonted clarity, surely the matter must be considered resolved, our belief in Hermione's innocence proved beyond any reasonable doubt. Our consensus on this point is based, then, on nothing less than what in the world of the play is an unquestionable divine authority. We have, if not ocular proof, oracular proof, which is at least as good. Or is it? I have already suggested that the clarity of the oracle does not deter Leontes from questioning and rejecting its validity in terms no less direct and absolute than the oracle's own: "There is no truth at all i' th' Oracle: / The sessions shall proceed: this is mere falsehood" (III. ii. 140–1). But surely such skepticism, despite the tradition warranting it, cannot be allowed much force; after all, the death of Mamillius follows hard upon this latest blasphemy, and it is this news that finally shocks Leontes into recognition. How could Mamillius's death, in its precise timing and dreadful efficiency, be taken as anything other than clear evidence of divine design? Yet even this apparent "proof," this strong sense of Mamillius's death as portentous or exemplary, as bearing the hallmark of the archer-god who strikes from afar (Homer's and Sophocles' *hekebolos* Apollo), is not binding. The play offers a naturalistic or coincidental explanation of Mamillius's death as the result of an illness already under way in the second act: "He took good rest to-night; / 'Tis hop'd his sickness is discharg'd" (II.iii. 10–11). If Mamillius dies of mumps or measles, it does weaken, though admittedly it does not rule out, the case for divine intervention. In fact, yet a third diagnosis of Mamillius's decline is twice offered to us, a diagnosis that mediates between the naturalistic and the superstitious or religious explanations; namely, that the boy's disease is psychogenic: "The prince your son, with mere conceit and fear / Of the queen's speed, is gone" (III.ii. 143–4; see also II.iii. 12–16). We are thus invited, at several points, to view Mamillius's death as the result of natural rather than supernatural causes. If we choose to do so, the foundation on which both Apollo's divine authority over the action and the divine authentication of Hermione's innocence are based begins to weaken.

Now just as Apollo's authoritative and authenticating presence within the world of the play is not quite so solidly "there" as we might wish — I shall return to this point shortly — so Leontes' jealous and destructive passion is not quite so flimsy and fanciful, so unfounded and "out of the blue" as is often casually assumed. Consider, for example, the tortured monologues in which Leontes discloses his jealousy to us. Since these are cast as commentaries on behavior taking place before his eyes, and in the first instance before our eyes too, there must be some empirical ground, as it were, for his suspicions, however slight. Are the gestures of friendship that pass between Hermione and Polixenes "too hot," or the paddling palms, pinching fingers, practis'd smiles, and heartfelt sighs enumerated by Leontes as evidence (I.ii. 108–18) as clearly adulterous as Leontes suggests? These questions are necessarily a matter of theatrical production; but unless we are ready to suppose a positively hallucinatory Leontes, gestures in some degree susceptible of such descriptions must take place in front of us. So too must Hermione's "Still virginalling / Upon his [Polixenes'] palm" (I.ii. 125–6) shortly thereafter. (The impossibility of rendering theatrically the suggestive force of the word "virginalling" must stand as a perennial caveat to those who maintain the primacy of performance over text.) Later in the scene, when his wife and friend have exited or are exiting, Leontes is presumably looking at *something* when he states: "Go to, go to! / How she holds up the neb, the bill to him! / And arms her with the boldness of a wife / To her allowing husband!" (I.ii. 182–5). And finally, the catalogue of evidence he cites to Camillo, while some of it may be the conventional stuff of literary or represented passion, also carries with it a direct appeal to observed behavior:

> Is whispering nothing?
> Is leaning cheek to cheek? is meeting noses?
> Kissing with inside lip? stopping the career
> Of laughter with a sigh (a note infallible
> Of breaking honesty)? horsing foot on foot?
> Skulking in corners? wishing clocks more swift?
> (I.ii. 284–9)

Leontes' suspicions, while they may end in speculation, do nonetheless begin in perception: "Ha' you not *seen*, Camillo . . . or *heard*? . . . or thought?" (I. ii. 267–71). This is why it is impossible to ascertain just what basis there is for Leontes' jealousy, the degree to which what he describes is a distortion of an enacted reality, or the relative proportions of perception and imagination in his account of what goes on. We see enough to know it has some basis, but not enough to say how much. We are from the outset in a world of interpretation – the producer's and our own – where nothing can be either wholly dismissed or wholly believed, and nothing can be known for certain.

The condition of interpretive uncertainty I have been trying to describe obviously arises, in the cases of both Hermione's conduct with Polixenes and Apollo's control over events, as a consequence of Shakespeare's choice to leave both actions unrepresented or, at most, only partly represented. In this respect, Apollo's status in the play as a kind of *deus absconditus* is paradigmatic and crucial. We have already seen that he is not really or fully "present," that is, not presented to us at all, and only represented in the world of the play through the mediating forms of a written pronouncement and a descriptive account by Cleomenes and Dion. Despite its extraordinary clarity and definitiveness, the pronouncement turns out, as we have begun to realize, to be disturbingly difficult to verify or validate. Since it is supposed to be itself a validation, there is nothing left to fall back on when its validity is questioned, other than Cleomenes' reported awe. The god's language without the god to back it up is a bit like paper currency without any gold behind it. It becomes unstable, subject to the vagaries of special interests and private speculation, with all their devaluing effect. Once cut off from the presence of their divine speaker, with his univocality of meaning and intent, Apollo's words enter the realm of the human, the fallible, the ambiguous, in sum, the interpretable, where they can be contradicted or dismissed, for all we know, with impunity. The point seems to me worth emphasizing, because Shakespeare's divorcing of the god's words from the god's presence is a marked change from his dramatic practice in the two earlier romances, *Pericles* and *Cymbeline*, both of which include theophanies. (Even in Greene's *Pandosto*, Apollo speaks, whereas in *The Winter's Tale* his speaking is only reported.) By separating Apollo's words from their sacred and authenticating voice, Shakespeare adumbrates a larger problem of interpretation, one that bedevils the world of the play from the outset.

The problem to which I refer might be termed the problem of linguistic indeterminacy. If the language of the oracle is remarkable for its clarity and explicitness – while still leaving the issue of divine control in doubt – the language of the Sicilian court is no less remarkable for its ambiguity and slipperiness. For example, it would be reassuring if the doubts Shakespeare has left attached to Hermione's behavior on and off stage – since they cannot be cleared away by looking closely at what she does – could be cleared away by listening carefully to what she says. In fact, the opposite is the case. The more carefully we attend to what she says, the more the verbal evidence, as much as the visual, seems inconclusive, and only increases our – and Leontes' – uncertainty:

> Th' offences we have made you do, we'll answer,
> If you first sinn'd with us, and that with us
> You did continue fault, and that you slipp'd not
> With any but with us.
>
> (I. ii. 83–6)

> cram's with praise, and make 's as
> Fat as tame things. . . .
> You may ride 's
> With one soft kiss a thousand furlongs ere
> With spur we heat an acre.
>
> (I. ii. 91–6)

> I have spoken to th' purpose twice:
> The one, for ever earn'd a royal husband;
> Th' other, for some while a friend.
>
> (I. ii. 106–8)

So much of what Hermione says may be construed either within or outside the bounds of royal hospitality and wifely decorum. Her emphasis on greater warmth in persuasion, that is, may signify flirtation; the indefinite antecedents of her royal pronouns, self-incrimination; her earthy wit, bawdry; and her rhetorical juxtapositions of "husband" and "friend," a fatal identification of the two. "This entertainment," as Leontes himself points out, "May a free face put on, derive a liberty / From heartiness, from bounty, fertile bosom, / And well become the agent" (I. ii. 111–14). Yet these same words – "entertainment," "liberty," "fertile bosom" – may refer, as Leontes also makes clear, to behavior anything but innocent. The more closely we attend to the language of Polixenes and Hermione, the more we may detect in it (like Leontes again) a whisper of sexual innuendo. Can Polixenes' comparison of himself to "a cipher / Yet standing in rich place" (I. ii. 6–7) be taken as a sniggering allusion to his "standing-in" for Leontes? So it seemed to Neville Coghill.[5] What about Hermione's comment that Leontes presses his friend "too coldly," or her reference to Polixenes' "limber vows" (I. ii. 46)? So, they seem on scrutiny – I am almost ashamed to confess it – to me. Once our suspicions are aroused – and there is at least some language in these scenes that cannot help but arouse them – they become, like Leontes' own suspicions, promiscuous and contagious, tainting with doubt and duplicity all that passes between Hermione and Polixenes.

For it is not only sexual innocence, idealized by Polixenes as a pastoral state belonging to childhood, that has been lost, but a kind of verbal innocence as well. This latter loss might be described as a fall into a condition of multivocality or equivocation, a new helplessness to avoid finding or including a certain duplicity in what is said, meanings that may or may not have been intended. This loss of verbal innocence is evident in all the courtly banter over the force of the word "Verily" (I. ii. 45–56); it appears again in Hermione's labored distinction between "saying" and "swearing"; in the compromising implications of subsequent guilt, picked up by Hermione, in Polixenes' monologue itself on childhood innocence; in Leontes' worried retraction of the word "neat" with the recollection that "the steer, the heifer and the calf / Are all call'd neat" (I. ii. 124–5); in his querying whether Hermione has "never" spoken to better purpose and, if not never, then when? It is to be heard again in the reluctant and riddling revelations of Camillo to Polixenes: "How, dare not? do not? Do you know, and dare not?"; "A sickness caught of me, and yet I well?" (I. ii. 376, 398). It would not be difficult to multiply examples, for this loss of innocence with its discovery of verbal duplicity permeates the linguistic fabric of the opening act, with its play of quibbles, intended and unintended: "Satisfy? / Th' entreaties of your mistress? satisfy?" (I. ii. 233–4); its circumlocutions: "Nine changes of the watery star" (I. ii. 1); its curious, archaic, and esoteric diction: "the *gest* / Prefix'd", "The *mort o' th' deer*" (I. ii. 41–2, 118); and its syntax contorted to the point where the principals themselves, not to mention the audience, sometimes have trouble understanding what is said or implied or meant (I. ii. 220 ff.). This is not the place to try to enumerate all the instances of extraordinary – even by Shakespearean and Elizabethan norms – tortuousness in the language of the opening scenes. Suffice it to say that Leontes' suspicion of the word thrives upon the verbal mannerism, sophistication, even preciosity that dominates the language of Sicilia from the play's initial dialogue, and that works to obscure as much as it reveals. From the moment Camillo refers to a longstanding affection between the two kings, "which cannot choose but *branch* now" (I. i. 23–4) – the most often noted of the scene's many *double entendres* – we are in a realm where a speaker's apparent meaning can turn or be turned into its antithetical sense, where the medium for defining human reality is so problematic as to render that "reality" precarious at best. In the linguistic milieu of the opening scenes of the play, nothing is but what, in a fundamental way, is not.

It is of course Leontes in whom this fall from verbal innocence, which I have been struggling (in the nature of the case) to describe, is most gravely figured. But it is also Leontes who displays the keenest insight into, and offers the nicest formulation of, his own unhappy condition:

> Affection! thy intention stabs the centre:
> Thou dost make possible things not so held,

> Communicat'st with dreams; – how can this be? –
> With what's unreal thou coactive art,
> And fellow'st nothing: then 'tis very credent
> Thou may'st co-join with something; and thou dost,
> (And that beyond commission) and I find it . . .
>
> (I. ii. 138–44)

The passage is itself a notoriously difficult one, termed by one critic the "obscurest" in Shakespeare, and having attracted no less than five pages of commentary in the Variorum edition. Leaving its own verbal difficulties aside for the moment, the speech raises two considerations that bear directly on the cluster of problems with which we are concerned. Leontes sees, as we have begun to see, that the instability of meaning and uncertainty of reference he is experiencing first-hand – what I have generally termed linguistic indeterminacy – is not simply a function of expression but of interpretation as well. It arises, that is, not only out of an imperfection in the medium or the speaker's use of it, but out of the radical subjectivity of the listener or interpreter. For this reason, it is doubly inescapable, a condition that prevents us from ever arriving at certain or complete understanding in human affairs. Leontes, that is, seems to be aware that all he sees and hears is filtered through his own affective state and is to that extent created by it. The imagination operating under "strong emotion" has the power to transform something into nothing, or nothing into something, a bush into a bear, or that which is subjectively felt into that which seems objectively there.

This poetics of self-projection is familiar enough from a number of Shakespearean contexts; and the Leontes of the opening scenes has more than a touch of the lunatic and lover, the roles with which Shakespeare most closely associates that engrossing subjectivity which prevents our arriving at unanimity in our interpretation of the evidence of our senses, or even at agreement as to what constitutes such "evidence." But Leontes' monologue on "affection" raises a further problem, one that bears as directly upon the process and meaning of the play as Polixenes' later, more familiar monologue on nature and art, and one that Leontes himself seems to be aware of, albeit in the perverse way of seeking a wilful and premature solution to it. I am referring to Leontes' assertion of the power of the imagination to "make possible things not so held," to create a world of its own that may or may not refer to any prior or primary reality. In this formulation, Leontes reveals as much a touch of the poet and critic as of the lunatic and lover. Of course his account of the matter, as has often been observed, is not quite logical. If an unfaithful Hermione may be imagined who does not correspond to any reality ("things not so held," "dreams," "what's unreal"), it is also possible that an unfaithful Hermione may exist. Indeed, it is plausible, "credent" as he puts it, that such an imaginative construct may correspond to something in reality; in fact, he goes on to conclude, such a creature does exist, and he has found her out. In these last illogical steps, the lunatic-lover has of course taken over from the poet-critic. Leontes' insistence that his subjective state has an objective cause – despite his awareness of the problems involved – dominates the first two acts, and culminates in his stunning self-contradiction at the trial:

> Hermione: You speak a language that I understand not:
> My life stands in the level of your dreams,
> Which I'll lay down.
> Leontes: Your actions are my dreams
> You had a bastard by Polixenes,
> And I but dream'd it!
>
> (III. ii. 80–4)

What begins as a just recognition of the autonomy of the imagination turns into a wilful insistence on its referentiality.

In his uneasy transition – by way of a psychological projection Leontes suspects but cannot escape – from a poetics of self-enclosure to a poetics of reference, Leontes enacts in a mad, parodic form a characteristic drift of European literary criticism. The tensions between poesis and mimesis, between the formal and referential functions of literary language, are already present in Aristotle. By the time of Sidney's *Apology for Poetry*, those tensions have developed into something verging upon outright contradiction:

> There is no art delivered to mankind that hath not the works of Nature for his principal object, without which they could not consist, and on which they so depend, as they become actors and players, as it were, of what Nature will have set forth. . . . Only the poet, disdaining to be tied to any such subjection, lifted up with the vigour of his own invention, doth grow in effect another nature, in making things either better than nature bringeth forth, or, quite anew, forms such as never were in Nature, as the Heroes, Demigods, Cyclopes, Chimeras, Furies, and such like: so as he goes hand in hand with Nature, not enclosed within the narrow warrant of her gifts, but freely ranging only within the zodiac of his own wit.[6]

On the one hand, poetry is like all human art in being bound to nature as its object; that is, it is mimetic or referential. On the other, the poet is endowed with the power to bring forth a rival nature by "freely ranging only within the zodiac of his own wit"; poetry, that is, is an autonomous system. To the extent that words are not things and language can never be nature, these are clearly in some degree incommensurate and incompatible functions. If language is autonomous, it can never quite be referential. The one hand does not seem to be fully aware what the other is doing.

Or is it? It could be argued that Sidney's language in this passage, unlike that of Leontes' monologue on "affection," is cool, sophisticated, and self-aware. To judge from the construction of the passage, Sidney, unlike Leontes, seems to know that he is verging on self-contradiction, and his language plays on that knowledge. To make something "better" than nature is not the same as to make something "other" than nature, since the former process idealizes nature while the latter replaces it. But it is Sidney himself who alerts us to this distinction, to the potential frustration of mimetic intent by the formal systems that mediate that intention. Then, too, Sidney repeatedly employs a vocabulary of presence to assimilate the poetic process to the natural. Such phrases as "*grow* another nature," "*set forth* the earth," "*deliver* a golden," "*delivering them forth* in such excellence" – such phrases lay claim, in the name of poetry, to nothing less than a fullness, presence, and immediacy analogous to that of the sensory world, a kind of ultimate or perfected mimesis in which the mediation of language disappears or is transcended. Yet all this "growing into," "bringing forth," "delivering," and "setting forth" is itself only a linguistic process of invocation and comparison, and is in this respect no more than a substitute or stand-in for the second nature being invoked. Moreover, that second, golden nature is identified with a world of religious myth and poetic fiction, a world of dream and desire which is in a fundamental sense not there, no longer or never existent. Sidney's language of presence is motivated by, and oriented toward, a world of absence, a paradise lost that can be represented but not regained through poetic language, "figured forth" but not literally delivered. The large claims Sidney makes for poetry are thus qualified by the very language in which they are made. As if this continuous qualification were not enough, there is the framing anecdote of the horseman Pugliano on horsemanship with which Sidney begins *The Apology*, a caveat that puts the entire work into parentheses by warning us "that self-love is better than any gilding to make that seem gorgeous wherein ourselves are parties."[7] Beware the power of subjective self-interest to distort the object under scrutiny; in sum, beware of poets on poetry.

We find at play in Sidney's *Apology*, then, the tendency to endow airy nothing not only with a local habitation and a name, but with an objective existence as well – a tendency not unlike the one we have seen at work in Leontes' tortured speeches in *The Winter's Tale*. As a recent commentator puts it, Sidney offers a vision of poetry as "the direct representation of the best," and "the creation . . . of a world of golden presence."[8] Yet Sidney, as we have also seen, simultaneously implies that this present perfection toward which poetry longs cannot, in the nature of the linguistic case, be attained. The actual language of *The Apology*, that is, is in tension with the theory it expresses, but not because it is written in a self-deceived language of presence. If anything, it is written in the self-aware language of absence we know as fiction, but which we habitually, almost compulsively, wish to make over, in our reflections on it, into a language of presence. What simultaneously emerges from *The Apology* is the nostalgic or wishful longing for poetry to become a second creation, at least as full, as present, as immediate as the fallen and brazen first, and the cool awareness that its very secondariness as representation, mediation, and artifice prevents poetry from ever achieving this status. The idea of a restored poetic perfection is imaginatively entered into and entertained by Sidney; but it is not unequivocally affirmed – "the poet, he nothing affirms, and therefore never lieth" – entertaining being to affirming what representation is to presence. The very idea of "direct representation" is recognized by Sidney, if not by his latest commentator, as oxymoronic, as self-consciously so as the "absent presence" he invokes in Sonnet 106 of *Astrophil and Stella*.

How, then, do these observations bear upon the particular interpretive problems with which we have been concerned in *The Winter's Tale* or, indeed, upon the more general and theoretical problem of unrepresented action with which we began? To take up the latter question first, I would suggest that the example of Sidney serves to remind us of something obvious and familiar to us all, yet something that we – like Sidney himself, not to mention his recent commentator – seem only too ready to ignore or repress in our dealings with literature: namely, that all literature – not just the off-stage events of *The Winter's Tale*, or Cassio's negotiations with Desdemona, or the domestic history of the Macbeths, but *all* literature – is, in an important sense, unrepresented or, rather, *under*-represented action. "Under-represented," in the sense that in its very nature as *re*presentation, as figurative language, literature is never really "there" or fully present, but is always mediated action, action estranged by the linguistic medium in which it has its existence. I realize that to say this is to say something as self-evident as that fiction is not history and words are not things; indeed, I may well be saying only that. The discovery that language is a formal, self-contained system of arbitrary signs, or that literature is a system based upon the prior system of language – a representation, that is, of the reality of language rather than of a language of "reality" – these characteristically "modern" discoveries in no way negate the power of the sign to refer, to constitute a world of reference. Yet this world of reference, as we have seen in *The Winter's Tale*, finally has no objective reality or ontological stability, but recedes into an infinite play of signs and deferral of affirmed or authoritative meaning. Poetic reference is saved, but only at the high cost of interpretive incertitude. The referential dimension of language, of poetic or literary language *a fortiori*, changes its nature to be sure, but does not suddenly disappear when we realize that language is fundamentally problematic. Reference is never quite presence, yet it is not quite absence either. The world of the text and the text of the world, once securely because dogmatically defined, now become indeterminate because over-determined. And once having occurred, this fall into textual instability cannot be reversed or restored – since it is not the text but our perception of the text that has radically altered – despite the impatience of some to regain the security of a lost certitude by identifying literary reference with one form of presence or another. Thus, L. C. Knights tried to pull us back from that which certainly cannot be known – the inner and off-stage lives of Shakespeare's characters – to that which he contended could be known – the dramatic world of "the words on the page" – when neither can be known with any assurance.

When Sidney wrote in 1580, poetry stood in need of defense against the attacks of those who would have crudified it into a form of lying. Since then, it seems to me, it has more often needed defense against its would-be defenders, those who also violate poetry's tantalizing reserve in order to crudify it into a more or less outspoken form of truth-telling. *The Winter's Tale*, with a self-understanding extraordinary even for Shakespeare, dramatizes not only the precariousness of its own linguistic enterprise but the unhappy consequences of our positive incapability of accepting such precariousness as the condition of fiction. "Is it true, think you?" (IV.iv.267) asks Mopsa of Autolycus's ballad of a usurer's wife "brought to bed of twenty money-bags at a burden." "Very true, and but a month old," the balladeer replies; "Why should I carry lies abroad?" "True," too, is his ballad of a woman transformed into a fish "for she would not exchange flesh with one that loved her," at least according to Autolycus:

> *Autolycus:* The ballad is very pitiful, and as true.
> *Dorcas:* Is it true too, think you?
> *Autolycus:* Five justices' hands at it, and witnesses more than my pack will hold.
>
> (IV.iv.282–5)

Autolycus's ballads re-enact in a comic or surrealistic form not only Leontes' opening fantasies of illicit pregnancy and condign punishment, but his – and our – eagerness for verification, for grounding what must forever remain linguistic and poetic possibility in historical fact or empirical truth. Autolycus resolves the problem of truth of reference – "Is it true, think you?" – by appeal to the testimony of a midwife named "Mistress Taleporter, and five or six honest wives that were present," as well as the authority of "Five justices' hands at it, and witnesses more than my pack will hold." That parody of judicial, indeed oracular, authentication may be enough to satisfy the naive realism of the rustics, but no such simple confirmation – or disconfirmation – is to be found for Leontes' sophisticated fantasies, not even, as we have seen, in the Delphic oracle itself. In Leontes' case, validation is unavailable, a resting-point for reference repeatedly deferred and finally lost in the precariousness of language and the absence of an authoritative divine voice. The simple act of referring has turned into an endless process of deferral.[9]

Yet paradoxically it is this very deferral of reference, this problematization of language, on which the relative "realism" of *The Winter's Tale* depends. By foregrounding the fallen nature of human speech and backgrounding any divine or redemptive "reality" to which it refers, Shakespeare dramatizes, in linguistic terms, the condition of secularity within which we all, wittingly or not, inescapably dwell; language being, in Heidegger's phrase, the house we live in.[10] In *The Winter's Tale*, the backgrounding of the divine referee – in *Pericles* and *Cymbeline*, we should recall, it had been foregrounded – becomes the condition for a new and extraordinary realism, a realism with which Shakespeare has been increasingly credited in this play, as distinct from the earlier romances, by critics as diverse in outlook as F. R. Leavis and myself.[11] It is worth noting too, as a corollary of our argument and a condition of the play's "realism," that the linguistic problems foregrounded in the opening act of *The Winter's Tale* are never, because they cannot be, solved – not even in the exquisite transfigurations of the last. There, the language of art employed by Paulina is every bit as incommensurate and incompatible with the "nature" it attempts to define as was the language of presence employed by Leontes to identify what was imagination. The problem of language has been resolved only in the sense of having been accepted and transcended, resolved, that is, by fiat or on faith. Paulina's description of the "resurrection" of the last scene repeatedly adopts the language of miracle, magic, and madness at the same time that it repudiates miracle, magic, and madness.

Yet the superstition of the word that Mopsa and Dorcas exemplify in the sheep-shearing scene, and that lingers on in Paulina's account of Hermione's "resurrection," is only the other side of the suspicion of the word exemplified in the first act by Leontes, much as Leontes' jealousy had been, not the absence, but the dark side of his faith. Because suspicion and superstition, jealousy and faith, thrive alike on the evidence of things not seen, they depend alike on the distancing and darkening property of language. The very opacity that had been such a problem in the language of the opening act becomes, in the closing act, the means of resolving that problem. If we cannot know except through the dark glass of language, we might as well accept what is a necessary limitation on our knowledge. Like Leontes yet again, we may even relax and enjoy it, and come to welcome this uncertainty as the ground for belief: "If this be magic, let it be an art / Lawful as eating"; "No settled senses of the world can match / The pleasure of that madness." The faith Paulina appeals to us to awaken, like the applause Prospero in his epilogue to *The Tempest* implores us to give, is the outcome of a sophisticated, as distinct from a naive, realism. Such a sophisticated realism understands and accepts the inescapable mediacy of language, the radical difference between presence and reference, and the ultimate subjectivity of all interpretation; in sum, the fallen and irredeemable nature of language as a medium for defining human reality – of which the casual duplicity of the pun, Shakespeare's fatal

Cleopatra, is only the most familiar symptom. The sophisticated realism of Shakespearean art accepts the defects of language and foregrounds them. This foregrounding of linguistic difficulty in *The Winter's Tale* also suggests that the larger relation between poetic and ordinary language is one of figure to ground, poetic language – whether that of Renaissance drama or modern lyric poetry – emerging as a problematics of ordinary language, a making explicit, indeed conspicuous, of the undeclared difficulty of everyday speech.[12]

Notes

1. I am grateful to *The Shakespeare Newsletter*, XXIX, 2 (April 1979), ed. Louis Marder, for having brought this inauspicious inaugural to my attention.

2. Morgann writes: "He boldly makes a character act and speak from those parts of the composition which are *inferred* only, and not distinctly shown. This produces a wonderful effect; it seems to carry us beyond the poet to nature itself, and gives an integrity and truth to facts and character, which they could not otherwise obtain." Quoted from the *Essay on the Dramatic Character of Sir John Falstaff* (1777) by L. C. Knights in his now faded classic, "How many children had Lady Macbeth?" in *Explorations* (London, 1963), 12.

3. *The Winter's Tale*, ed. J. H. P. Pafford (London, 1966), lix. All quotations in my text are from this edition.

   Among the ancients, Cicero mentions a lost collection of dubious oracular replies, or *kledones* (*Of Divination*, II, lvi). Shakespeare's older contemporary, Robert Greene, author of *Pandosto, or The Triumph of Time* (1588), Shakespeare's source for *The Winter's Tale*, puts just such a *kledon* into the mouth of the brazen head in *Friar Bacon and Friar Bungay* (1590). There, the head's pronouncements – "Time is"; "Time was"; "Time is past" – are clearly of demonic inspiration. Milton shares Thomas Hobbes's lively contempt for "the ambiguous or senselesse answers of the Priests at *Delphi, Delos, Ammon*, and other famous oracles" (*Leviathan*, I, xii), though on religious rather than rationalist grounds:

   > What but dark,
   > Ambiguous and with double sense deluding,
   > Which they who ask'd have seldom understood,
   > And not well understood as good not known?
   > Who ever by consulting at thy [Satan's] shrine
   > Return'd the wiser, or the more instruct
   > To fly or follow what concerned him most,
   > And run not sooner to his fatal snare?
   > (*Paradise Regained*, IX, 434–41)

   For an introduction to the elusive subject of oracles and their language, see H. W. Parke, *Greek Oracles* (London, 1967), and Joseph Fontenrose, *The Delphic Oracle* (Berkeley, 1979).

4. *Coleridge on Shakespeare*, ed. Terence Hawkes (Harmondsworth, 1969), 277.

5. In "Six points of stage-craft in *The Winter's Tale*," in *Shakespeare Survey*, 11, ed. Allardyce Nicoll (Cambridge, 1969), 33: "Who can fail to wonder whether the

man so amicably addressing this expectant mother may not be the father of her child? For what other possible reason can Shakespeare have contrived the conversation so as to make him specify nine changes of the inconstant moon? These things are not done by accident."

6. Reprinted, with modernized spelling, in *Criticism: The Major Texts*, ed. W. J. Bate (New York, 1970), 85.

7. Ibid., 83.

8. Murray Krieger, "Poetic presence and illusion: Renaissance theory and the duplicity of metaphor" (*Critical Inquiry*, V, 4 (Summer 1979)), 603.

9. The astute reader will have recognized a certain resonance between my reading of *The Winter's Tale* and Jacques Derrida's critique of western logocentricity. Derrida might almost have been commenting on this play when he writes that "the center could not be thought in the forms of a being-present ... but a function, a sort of non-locus, in which an infinite number of sign-substitutions came into play. This moment was that in which language invaded the universal problematic; that in which in the absence of a center of origin, everything became a system where the central signified, the original or transcendental signified is never absolutely present outside a system of differences. The absence of the transcendental signified extends the domain and the interplay of signification *ad infinitum*" ("Structure, sign, and play," in *The Languages of Criticism and the Sciences of Man: The Structuralist Controversy*, ed. Richard Macksey and Eugenio Donato (Baltimore, 1970), 249).

10. See Martin Heidegger, "Letter on humanism," in *Basic Writings*, ed. David Farrell Krell (London, 1978), p. 193.

11. See "The criticism of Shakespeare's late plays," in *The Common Pursuit* (London, 1952), 175ff. My own earlier view of the play, radically revised here, is set out in *Shakespearean Romance* (Princeton, 1972), 211–45.

12. For a valuable working out of this view in the case of modern poetry, see Gerald L. Bruns, *Modern Poetry and the Idea of Language* (New Haven, 1974).

2

ELIZABETH FREUND

"Ariachne's broken woof": the rhetoric of citation in *Troilus and Cressida*

In Book VI of *The Metamorphoses* Ovid tells the story of Arachne, a subtle weaver of Lydia, too skillful for her own good. She dared to rival Pallas Athene with her superior artistry at the loom. Mortal and goddess engaged in a competition in which each wove splendid scenes into her tapestry. Athene represented the Immortals (including herself) as all-powerful figures of authority, while Arachne chose to weave tales of divine erotica into her web. When the work was done not even Athene's envy could deny the superior quality of Arachne's art. In her jealous rage the goddess struck through Arachne's loom and tore the tapestry. The girl, shamed and humiliated, hung herself, but the goddess restored her to life as a spider.

Arachne makes a single, abbreviated appearance in the Shakespearean canon, and even then her provenance is doubtful. Her tale of ill-fated rivalry with divine artistic power is curtailed to a rather obscure simile in V.ii of *Troilus and Cressida*.

> *Troilus:* Within my soul there doth conduce a fight
> Of this strange nature that a thing inseparate
> Divides more wider than the sky and earth;
> And yet the spacious breadth of this division
> Admits no orifex for a point as subtle
> As Ariachne's broken woof to enter.
>
> (V.ii. 146–51)[1]

By what devious detours of the imagination does this apocryphal "Ariachne" find her way into the texture of *Troilus and Cressida*? How subtle is "a point as subtle as Ariachne's broken woof"? What are we to make of this pointed figure, sharp enough to penetrate the impenetrable, yet obstructed by break-age and division? How *Ariadne*, who provided Theseus with the clue of a thread to guide him out of the Cretan maze, came to be enmeshed in *Arachne*'s web, whether by a printer's carelessness or an author's slip of the pen or daring of the imagination, is probably beyond conclusive recovery.[2] "Ariachne" may be an "original," a felicitous neologism spun spider-fashion out of the creator's own gut; or she may be no more than the accidental issue of a typesetter's clumsy fingers. In either event she is a new creation who also carries incontestable traces of prior origins.

The conflation or confusion in this marginal figure of "Ariachne," who is and is not Arachne, is and is not Ariadne, points the way into the major labyrinth of citation and the travesty of citation which is the "stuff" out of which *Troilus and Cressida* "make[s] paradoxes" (I.iii.184). Yet this frag-mentary clue proves also the very obstacle which thwarts the expectation of a safe conduct through the maze.[3] I hesitate to identify Shakespeare's muse in "Ariachne," but "Ariachne's broken woof" may be read as the aporetical figure in Shakespeare's tapestry of citations in *Troilus and Cressida*, allusively merging an image of the clue to the pattern with an image of the breaking and loss of the pattern. As in Troilus's contorted reasoning, a single signifier splits into the duality on which his tormented consciousness dwells: "This is and is not Cressid."

Here is the earlier part of Troilus's speech:

> This she? – No, this is Diomed's Cressida.
> If beauty have a soul, this is not she;
> If souls guide vows, if vows be sanctimonies,
> If sanctimony be the gods' delight,
> If there be rule in unity itself,
> This is not she. O madness of discourse,
> That cause sets up with and against itself!
> Bifold authority! where reason can revolt
> Without perdition, and loss assume all reason
> Without revolt. This is, and is not, Cressid.
>
> (V.ii.136–45)

"A supremely difficult speech," comments the play's most recent editor, "because although it attempts to use the language of logic and the methods of rhetoric, it is primarily (though not of course wholly) concerned to give utterance to an intolerable state of feeling."[4] Reasoning about reason here indeed proceeds by means of the language of logic and the methods of rhetoric, but is made difficult not because Troilus's intolerable state of feeling is unutterable (we don't know his state of feeling other than through its utterance), but because the nature of language itself strains against the rule of unity and the laws of non-contradiction to which the language of logic aspires. Troilus is recording with scholastic precision his response to a spectacle which causes his desires for a *self-same* Cressida to smash against "the attest of eyes and ears" (V. ii. 121) that "the self is not the same" (*The Phoenix and the Turtle*). The fabric of his proud dream is rudely violated by that which in the first instance wove it, namely, "the madness of discourse" – a phrase itself perplexed by the notorious ambiguity of genitives: has discourse gone mad and abdicated for the nonce from logic and reason, or does utterance itself exhibit the madness that discourse is? A bifold authority governs the utterance of Troilus, just as a bifold origin haunts Ariachne.

To the many reasons on account of which *Troilus and Cressida* has been claimed for modernity one could add its self-reflecting wit, its heightened language consciousness. The characters, for example, frequently scrutinize and judge each other like pieces of language. Cressida, described as "so glib of tongue," has "language in her eye, her cheek, her lip; / Nay her foot speaks!" (IV. v. 55–63); Achilles' "imagined worth / Holds in his blood . . . swol'n and hot discourse" (II. iii. 174); Hector notes that Achilles will "like a book of sport . . . read me o'er" (IV. v. 238); and Ajax, "languageless," is "a monster" (III. iii. 263). Shakespeare's identification of the nature of textuality with the textuality of nature is caught in the linkage of language and the body. But the world's body is not the only text. The play also persistently calls attention to its intertextuality, its anachronicity, its dependence upon a prodigious literary and rhetorical legacy. Within Shakespeare's dramatization of familiar legend, a vast encyclopedia of citation is embedded. The myth, the Matter of Troy, the classical topos, the set piece, the commonplace, the cliché, the name that has become a concept; references to books, texts, representations, figures of rhetoric – all these are on display as though to insist on the text's derivative status.

By foregrounding the necessary citationality of writing and reading, the Shakespearean text obliquely dramatizes the predicament of the Renaissance writer whose situation in history – in a particular moment of language use – exposes him to the hazards and pitfalls of belatedness. To be sure, drama is not the literary mode best suited to embody subjectivity, and this is one reason for which Harold Bloom excludes Shakespeare from *The Anxiety of Influence*. "Shakespeare is the largest instance in the language of a phenomenon that stands outside the concern of this book: the absolute absorption of the precursor."[5] Yet the case of *Troilus and Cressida* is a possible exception worth exploring; whether or not it proves the Bloomian rule remains to be seen. Homer and Chaucer are sufficiently rich fare to daunt the digestion of even as voracious a literary imagination as Shakespeare's; and one cannot overlook the rancid flavor of o'ereaten fragments, scraps and greasy relics dominating a text which abounds in food imagery. It is as though the play constructs a witty tropological fence to guard against its own heightened sense of the parasitism and rivalry of texts, recording the risks and adventures incurred in the project of absorbing, rewriting, reinterpreting, re-appropriating of origins.

The question of how to read a Shakespearean text with a rhetorical difference has barely begun to be opened up. Earlier mainstream critical commentary in the post-romantic shadow of Eliot relied heavily on a model of reading and a poetics which – begotten upon Eliot's theory of metaphysical wit – compels a heterogeneity of materials into unity. This model, by amalgamating and reducing disparate experiences to the will of a devouring mind, works to subdue and tame the radically subversive energies of wit to some kind of manageable order. In the climate of contemporary critical discourse, however, it is becoming possible to show how the Shakespearean self-reflexive forays of wit match, remarkably, the wit of the deconstruction-ist enterprise. Recent rhetorical analysis questions, as does Troilus, the rule of unity itself by examining the operations whereby language resists its own meanings and refuses to be contained in them. The question is one of the coincidence of language and meaning, and it has been pursued by shifting the focus of investigation to the apparently irreducible difference between them. Troilus's intense struggle to make sense of the contradiction and discontin-uity between what he knows and what he sees is an endeavor of "wit" – in the primal and antithetical sense of the word, which combines the elements of seeing and knowing, presence and cognition, the intuitive and the counter-intuitive – an endeavor analogous to the act of reading and interpretation which reports its knowledge of that which can only be negatively known. The problem thus is not merely one of spotlighting "witty" centers of energy and turbulence in language itself, but more generally a problem of witnessing: of how to stabilize the unstable relationship of knowing to known.

The question of wit seems to have been an issue for Shakespeare's audience too. I summon the earliest critic of *Troilus and Cressida*, the anonymous author of the advertisement entitled "A Never Writer, to an Ever Reader" (appended to the 1609 Quarto), who was perfectly confident with regard to the category of response appropriate to a play "passing full of the palme comicall" and who paid extravagant tribute to the Shakespearean power of wit: "All . . . haue found that witte there [in Shakespeare's comic representa-tions], that they neuer found in themselues, and haue parted better wittied then they came; feeling an edge of witte set vpon them more than euer they dreamed they had braine to grinde it on. So much and such sauored salt of witte is in his Commedies. . . . Amongst all there is none more witty then this." Despite the high esteem in which the Elizabethans held wit, they had no developed theory of the concept.[6] The term seems to have denoted "intellect" in general, and (before the seventeenth-century vogue of wit systematized and dualized the concept by splitting imagination between a false wit of fancy and a true wit of judgment) it covered a wide range of notions including humor, wisdom, understanding, invention, intellectual liveliness and dexterity of thought, an emphasis on ingenuity, and above all a contagious joy in the play of mind and language.

The likes of Feste, Rosalind or Falstaff – not only witty in themselves but the cause of wit in other men – spring to mind. Their wit defies containment or domestication: "Make the doors upon [wit], and it will out at the casement, shut that, and 'twill out at the keyhole; stop that, 'twill fly with the smoke out at a chimney" (*As You Like It*, IV.i.154–7). The wiser, the waywarder; for these masters of rhetorical manipulation (Feste calls himself a "corrupter of words") cannot claim to be entirely their own masters. In the design of Shakespeare's texts wit is not reducible either to subjectivity or to language alone; it leads a double and antithetical mode of existence. Lock it in the chamber of consciousness and it flies out of the chimney of language.

*

> What's in the brain that ink may character
> Which hath not figured to thee my true spirit?
> (Shakespeare, Sonnet 108)

Consider the witcraft[7] in the representation of Cressida. "Perchance, my lord, I show more craft than love," she says to her lover in the orchard scene (III.ii.151). She has but now confessed to loving Troilus secretly "night and day / For many weary months" (113–14), but also to playing a self-defensive role of "hard to seem won" (116). Then, alarmed by giving herself away, she backtracks: "In faith, I lie" (120). From such backtracking springs a series of inversions and reversals. The more she ventures to represent herself, the greater her misgivings. Perhaps she should have held her tongue. "Why have I blabbed? Who shall be true to us / When we are so unsecret to ourselves?" (123–4). This giving away of herself, with its double gestures of bestowing and retracting, creates a powerful sense of her sincere scruples and hesitations, but at the same time it only ensnares Cressida more surely in the impossibility of ever representing herself truly. Unlike Troilus, she has little confidence in the stable identity of selfhood or in the ability of discourse to represent it.

> *Troilus:* You cannot shun yourself.
> *Cressida:* Let me go and try.
>   I have a kind of self resides with you,
>   But an unkind self, that itself will leave
>   To be another's fool.
>   (III.ii.144–8)

23

The effect of a suffering persona is at once projected through the punning rhetoric and masked or hidden by it.

Such intermingling of craft and pathos in the verbal representation impales the interpreter's understanding on the dilemma of uncertainty. Even as – indeed, precisely because – we are persuaded that her love is stronger than her craft, we are made to realize that in being her rhetorical self (and there is surely no other) she can never be herself. For her love to be credible it must displace craft; but the illusion of credibility depends on the craft. To complicate this involution of rhetorized consciousness, we have also the verdict of history which has linked her name with falsehood. No representation of Cressida can slip away from this text-determined condition. Always already sentenced by tell-tale citation, she *must* play false, else she would not be herself: "As false as Cressida." No amount of "showing" of her honest intentions will allow her to wriggle off the cruel hook, and no extenuating "perchance" will redeem her from her original fall. The bifold effect of craft and pathos generates a shifting oscillation between two distinct experiences of the play. In one we are made aware of the derivative nature of the protagonists and their actions, indeed of their absence as characters, their nonexistence as other than citations from another text, inscriptions to be reinscribed and recontextualized. In the other, our awareness of citationality is displaced by the characters' mimetic allure, their power to move us, to persuade us of their dramatic presence and the quantity of felt life they represent.

The disjunction *and* continuity between character as schema or inscription and character as self-presentation or representation[8] is thrust upon us with the greatest insistence in the trysting scene (III. ii):

> *Troilus:* I am as true as truth's simplicity,
> And simpler than the infancy of truth.
> *Cressida:* In that I'll war with you.
> *Troilus:*   O virtuous fight,
> When right with right wars who shall be most right!
> True swains in love shall, in the world to come,
> Approve their truth by Troilus; when their rhymes
> Full of protest, of oath, and big compare,
> Wants similes, truth tir'd with iteration
> (As true as steel, as plantage to the moon,
> As sun to day, as turtle to her mate,
> As iron to adamant, as earth to th' centre)
> Yet, after all comparisons of truth,
> As truth's authentic author to be cited,
> "As true as Troilus" shall crown up the verse
> And sanctify the numbers.

Cressida: Prophet may you be!
            If I be false, or swerve a hair from truth,
            When time is old and hath forgot itself,
            When water-drops have worn the stones of Troy,
            And blind oblivion swallow'd cities up,
            And mighty states characterless are grated
            To dusty nothing – yet let memory,
            From false to false, among false maids in love,
            Upbraid my falsehood. When they've said, "As false
            As air, as water, wind, or sandy earth,
            As fox to lamb, or wolf to heifer's calf,
            Pard to the hind, or stepdame to her son" –
            Yea, let them say, to stick the heart of falsehood,
            "As false as Cressid."

                                             (III. ii. 167–94)

Not many texts lay bare the self-reflexive mechanisms of their rhetorical subterfuge, or loop back with such persistent disruption of our trust in the authority of words. What is represented is the taking of a vow of constancy, but the actual performative is glaringly absent. Instead of employing the more direct formula of "I promise to be true" – a speech act whose self-saying gesture is problematic enough[9] – the lovers resort to a duel of "literary" citation, whose purpose is to assert the original and nonderivative, the peerless and lasting nature of their identities as lovers. It is this very literariness which blocks and supplants the issuing of the intended promise, and predicts their canonization in the verbal clichés with which they are already associated: "As true as Troilus" and "As false as Cressida." Creatures of their word, their speech mimes purpose and conviction, but their being is predicated on the rhetoricity of the word.

Troilus's notion of truth is postulated on his sense of himself as an unwavering and self-identical source of fidelity. But the correlative construction on which Troilus founds his identity – "I am as true as truth's simplicity" – poses the question whether the simplicity of truth is like Troilus or Troilus like truth's simplicity, in a recursive gyre of figuration which triggers the deconstructive self-unraveling. On these uncertain grounds Troilus wishes to found a fresh and originating truth from within his fixed and stable selfhood, "as truth's authentic author to be cited," by discarding the stale comparisons of literary cliché, the "rhymes full of protest, of oath, and big compare . . . truth tir'd with iteration." But the strenuous embodiment of this consciousness in language destroys the subject; the very act of his authoring himself gives him away and splits the identity of author and word. His inaugurating gesture is altered in the act of utterance by the marks of non-originality and repetition: "'As true as Troilus'." The origin is already a citation,[10] and his

25

advertisement of himself as a source of singular and unique truth becomes a denial of this truth, identifying him as an inscription in somebody else's book.

Text giveth and text taketh away. Cressida's language exhibits an acute consciousness of this dilemma. Of course her legendary infidelity intensifies the *déjà lu* effect and stacks the intertextual cards more cruelly and ironically against her than against her faithful lover. In a sense she damns herself twice over. Her symmetrical and antonymous rejoinder to his *"When . . . then . . ."* prophecy is cast in the hypothetical and optative mode: *"If* I be false . . . *let* them say . . . 'As false as Cressida.'"* One might say that if the pathos of Troilus's vow consists in the way in which utterance denies him the truth he knows is his, the additional paradox which shadows Cressida's vow is its uncanny felicity. She speaks truer than she knows. But this "truth" is manifested in the mode akin to Cretan liars: if true then false, but if false then true. An "antic decorum" is Rosalie Colie's apt term for the "duplicitous intent, honestly proclaimed," of liar paradoxes.[11]

A self mediated by antic decorum braves the aporetical limits of language and gives a razor sharpness to the impasse in which all self-presentation is entangled. How can a character ever truly speak for himself without estranging himself, setting himself adrift, as we might say in the wake of Lacan and Derrida, in the symbolic order in which he is always already another, a self-alienated iterable citation? Whatever he says will divide him from himself, as must any verbal representation of consciousness. Hamlet's celebrated ordeal of consciousness, which exhibits at large the antic decorum of dismantling the self, is a Shakespearean paradigm for the "authenticity" of representation.

The intentionality of antic decorum is of course the crucial question. And Cressida's inherent duplicity is uncannily glossed by Derrida's remarks on the character of the sign:

> Every sign, linguistic or non-linguistic, spoken or written . . . can be *cited*, put between quotation marks; in so doing it can break with every given context engendering an infinity of new contexts in a manner which is absolutely illimitable. This does not imply that the mark is valid outside of a context, but on the contrary that there are only contexts without any center or absolute anchoring [ancrage]. This citationality, this duplication or duplicity of the mark is neither an accident or an anomaly, it is that (normal/abnormal) without which a mark could not even have a function called "normal." What would a mark be that could not be cited? Or one whose origins would not get lost along the way?[12]

We normally understand the durability of promises across time and space to be enabled by language, but this understanding entails the (abnormal) assertion that promises are always already empty, already a betrayal.

Cressida's image of time as oblivion ("When time is old and hath forgot itself ... And mighty states characterless are grated / To dusty nothing") may well record her particular consciousness of the merciless ravages and fluctuations which attend a senseless war of attrition; but these images also order a destruction of all consciousness, all contexts and origins. Such radical oblivion is the paradoxical condition for recycling and reiteration, the permanent renewal of promises. But the pathos of it is that all successive renewals of her own figure of duplication or duplicity will continue "to stick the heart of falsehood." It is a no-win situation for Cressida, strung perpetually between figurations of self-consciousness and self-obliteration. Even the comic increment of Pandarus's mediation which "seals" (closes – but also marks for reduplication) the lovers' pact contemplates the antitheses of infinite reiteration:

> Go to, a bargain made: seal it, seal it, I'll be the witness. Here I hold your hand, here my cousin's. . . . let all constant men be Troiluses, all false women Cressids, and all brokers-between Pandars.
>
> (III. ii. 195–202)

What more perfect instance of self-possession, one might think, than the coincidence of name and referent in the sign? But Pandarus's own identity is effaced and reconstituted in the infinite reiterations of his role. Perhaps the craftiest illusion of identity is the case of the eponymous subject, placing both subject and language in a *mise-en-abîme* of verbal mediation: pandar is a pandar is a pandar . . .

*

> "The question is," said Alice, "whether you can make words mean so many different things."
> "The question is," said Humpty Dumpty, "which is to be master – that's all."

A citation (from the Latin *citatio*, a command, p.p. of *citare*, to arouse, summon) is a summons to reading. Interpretation has traditionally responded to the summons by reflecting upon the strangenesses of texts or citations in order to reproduce as faithful an image as possible of the object of reflection. But the implication of disinterested thoughtfulness is already disqualified if an act of reflection is always *en abîme*. The following dialogue readily reveals that the discourse of politicians in *Troilus and Cressida* is as re-sourceful, as permeated with citationality, as unreliable as the discourse of lovers.

Achilles: What are you reading?
Ulysses: A strange fellow here
　　　　　Writes me, that man, how dearly ever parted,
　　　　　How much in having, or without or in,
　　　　　Cannot make boast to have that which he hath,
　　　　　Nor feels not what he owes, but by reflection,
　　　　　As, when his virtues aiming upon others
　　　　　Heat them, and they retort that heat again
　　　　　To the first giver.
Achilles: This is not strange, Ulysses.
　　　　　The beauty that is borne here in the face
　　　　　The bearer knows not, but commends itself
　　　　　To others' eyes; nor doth the eye itself,
　　　　　That most pure spirit of sense, behold itself,
　　　　　Not going from itself; but eye to eye oppos'd
　　　　　Salutes each other with each other's form;
　　　　　For speculation turns not to itself
　　　　　Till it hath travell'd and is mirror'd there
　　　　　Where it may see itself. This is not strange at all.
Ulysses: I do not strain at the position –
　　　　　It is familiar – but at the author's drift,
　　　　　Who in his circumstance expressly proves
　　　　　That no man is the lord of anything,
　　　　　Though in and of him there be much consisting,
　　　　　Till he communicate his parts to others.

                                        (III.iii.94–117)

Ulysses' citation extends a double summons: it enables reading by providing us with a theory of reading, according to which the object is reconstituted by careful reflection, but it also disables reading because, according to the theory, the object of reading is infinitely inaccessible, perhaps nonexistent. Citation, in other words, invites us to read the text (or scene), and also to read the notion of reading.

The drift of the text Ulysses is so "rapt in" concerns a perennial philosophical and literary critical topos:[13] we cannot step outside our own minds and must rely on reflection, echo, and mirroring otherness to constitute us. The "eye," organ of sight, cannot see itself but by reflection; the "I" cannot know itself with any immediacy, but must loop along strange courses of speculative mirroring which prohibit it from ever coinciding with itself. Achilles remains unperturbed by the prospect of a strange loop which puts in question the very existence of himself as subject, and he persists in believing that "speculation" (eyesight, insight, consciousness, the self) does eventually – even if indirectly – rise into view. But Ulysses pursues the more radical conclusion, that no man can ever be in full possession of himself, and continues to attack and undercut Achilles' confident self-possession until, by the end of the scene, Achilles is no longer so sure that he can see himself.

> My mind is troubled, like a fountain stirr'd,
> And I myself see not the bottom of it.
>
> (III. iii. 306–7)

Ulysses' intention in this scene has been, not to share his disinterested scrutiny of a philosophical text with Achilles, but to use it against him. The wily politician cites to incite, to arouse the moody and insolent warrior to rejoin the fighting by representing to him the idea that his "reputation is at stake" and his fame "shrewdly gored" by prolonged absence from the battlefield. Ulysses' rhetoric performs a double function: it suggests that representation is impossible (man cannot boast to have that which he hath) yet it nevertheless urges Achilles to represent himself (his reputation and his fame) with all the energy that he can muster. The impasse draws attention to the problematic and frequently asymmetrical relationship between the two functions of rhetoric as persuasion and rhetoric as representation,[14] a disjunction which time and again tangles the texture of Ulysses' speeches.

Consider the ways in which Ulysses' famous oration in I.iii on the "specialty of rule" – a *locus classicus* for Shakespeareans intent on reifying Elizabethan concepts of order – is an extraordinary feat of tropological reasoning and mystification. The commonplaces of order underlying his cosmology derive from a familiar tradition of writing and citation (Elyot, Hooker, the Homilies – to name only some of the best-known contemporary texts) which harks all the way back to Homer and Plato. Rhetorically speaking, however, the structure of the Ulyssean universe turns on a transumption of the central term "degree," and the causes of its failure. Basically, Ulysses' argument is that the authority of order has disappeared from sight, and that "Degree being vizarded, / Th'unworthiest shows as fairly in the mask" (83–4). The question is, under what conditions can the veiled figure of "degree" be unmasked?[15] Its concealment, after all, is not the source but the effect of the collapse of hierarchy in the Greek camp. As Ulysses' description suggests, degree as an ideology can be defined only by the presence of its effects. Yet Ulysses himself claims that it is manifest in cosmic order: "The heavens themselves . . . observe degree . . . And therefore is the glorious planet Sol / In noble eminence enthroned." But if natural order is the paradigm, then Ulysses' anthropomorphic description of the cosmos reverses the logical sequence of origin and copy, by implying that the heavens are an imitation of the social order. The cosmic model is thus authenticated "by way of fiction," as Puttenham puts it in glossing the figure of "Counterfait in personation" or metalepsis.[16] When the ideology of Degree is authenticated by rhetoric rather than reference (as Ulysses would like to pretend), it is no longer possible to identify what disrupts degree; and indeed Ulysses' noble analogies boil down to saying that when degree is disrupted it is disrupted. "But when the planets / In evil mixture to disorder wander, / What plagues and what portents, what mutiny . . . rend and deracinate / The unity and married calm of states" (94–100). According to his argument, degree is guaranteed by degree; if you take it away it isn't there, and the source of evil remains neatly unaccounted for, a blank which Ulysses' audience is invited to fill – in the event, with the name of Achilles. This blank is exactly the space from which the power of fiction and the fictions of power derive.

A similar process may be charted in Ulysses' representation in III.iii of calumniating Time to Achilles:

> Time hath, my lord, a wallet at his back
> Wherein he puts alms for oblivion,
> A great-siz'd monster of ingratitudes.
> Those scraps are good deeds past, which are devour'd
> As fast as they are made, forgot as soon
> As done.
>
> (III.iii.145–50)

Who is this personified Time? The context offers the notion of "oblivion" to ground the image, but it is unclear whether "Time" and "oblivion" are identical or differentiated. Is "oblivion" personified as the receiver of alms, or is it a property for whose sake (as with charity) alms are given? "Oblivion" could be identified as the destination of a mendicant vagrant, Time. But then Time, which endures long enough to forget itself (as in Cressida's image), is swallowed up by its own duration. The indeterminacies in turn make it impossible to tell whether the great-sized monster of ingratitudes is Time or oblivion. The scraps themselves are self-annulling objects which are devoured as fast as they are made, forgotten as soon as committed. These figures produce powerful effects of persuasion through connotations of beggary, monstrosity, cruel forgetfulness. But these effects derive from the absence of a stable referent.

Ulysses is persuading Achilles that he cannot expect to rest on his laurels; that his fame and honor are in a perpetual race against time and must be daily renewed in order to survive. But the rhetorical representation undercuts the persuasion by revealing that the race is already lost, because to perform the act in time on which fame rests is to leave it behind, already a devoured scrap. "To have done, is to hang / Quite out of fashion, like a rusty mail / In monumental mockery" (151–3).

It is not accidental that Ulysses plays the role of go-between. Spokesman, adviser, mastermind, self-appointed diplomatic envoy and interpreter – this pandar of politicians is also cast as inscribed reader and spectator. Within moments of Cressida's arrival in the Greek camp, he purports to read her like an open book:

> There's language in her eye . . .
> O, these encounterers, so glib of tongue,
> That give accosting welcome ere it comes,
> And wide unclasp the tables of their thoughts
> To every ticklish reader: set them down
> For sluttish spoils of opportunity
> And daughters of the game.
>
> (IV.v.55–64)

But the text he (mis)reads so acerbically is a transumption of the "character" of Cressida, who always exists only as a sign to be recontextualized. And if we cannot be sure that Ulysses has misread Cressida, the same uncertainty must inform the text of Ulysses.

The signs of theater are doubly mediated through the presence of an actor. The uses and abuses of actor-mediation are flaunted when Ulysses goads his fellow generals with a cruelly detailed account of Achilles' and Patroclus's mockery of them: the mimes which "pageant" these worthies are "stuff . . . to make paradoxes" (I.iii.142–84). Once again, the absent object of representation comes into view as an effect of rhetoric, an event straining to catch up with a referent from which it remains disengaged. To be sure, Ulysses' report of the caricatures may be taken (as it often is in productions) as a stage direction, and we get a strutting Agamemnon, a fumbling Nestor, etc. but it could be equally legitimate or effective for the actor on the stage to play *against* Ulysses' text. In either event, the fiction of "characters" is a structure of reflection; the mimes cite, or quote, the characters of Nestor and Agamemnon; or the actors playing these figures cite the mimes. Either perspective engenders the paradox which gives form to theater's mimetic art: we constitute character from the role, but the role is never the character. However far back we push, we never reach anything but mediation.

*

> How bootifull and how truetowife of her, when strengly forebidden, to steal our historic presents from the past postprophoticals so as to will make us all lordy heris and ladymaidesses of a pretty nice kettle of fruit . . . Hou! Hou! Gricks may rise and Troysirs fall (there being two sights for ever a picture) . . .
>
> (James Joyce, *Finnegans Wake*)

In re-imagining and re-citing the received narratives and commonplaces, Shakespeare plays every proleptic, analeptic, and metaleptic game possible with his counters. Thus the notion that "Helen must needs be fair / When with your blood you daily paint her thus" (I.i.90–1) transumptively substitutes the *casus belli* with desire for cause. Rhetoric leapfrogs diachrony, opening a multitude of alternative possibilities for reinterpretation, then foreclosing them. The repeated play with anachronicity compels us to read forwards and backwards in a strain against foreknowledge which briefly puts in doubt the authority of history, as if it were not determined but newly enacted.

Cressida in IV.ii desperately considers the possibility of a truly radical break with the scandal – the trap – of her inherited rhetorical being by refusing to be exchanged: "I have forgot my father; / I know no touch of consanguinity, / No kin, no love, no blood . . . I will not go from Troy" (99–112). But the poignancy of her rebellion depends on the fact that she "*must* be gone," that it is "so concluded." She may not "temporize with [her] affection" (IV.iv.6), in more than one sense. Hector must die, and is first slain by the word, in Cassandra's divinations ("Look how thou diest: look how thy eye turns pale: / Look how thy wounds do bleed at many vents" (V.iii.81–2)), and then in Achilles' savage "naming" of the atrocity he will later perform, a prediction which ominously shifts in the process of its enunciation from future to present to past tense:

> Tell me, you heavens, in which part of his body
> Shall I destroy him – whether there, or there, or there –
> That I may give the local wound a name,
> And make distinct the very breach whereout
> Hector's great spirit flew?
>
> (IV.v.241–5)

The primacy of the precursor reasserts itself, even threatening to put an end to speech and language. "Hector is dead: there is no more to say" (V.x.22).

I have argued that citationality, rhetoricity and anachronicity initiate us into a discourse which wittily braids and rends its own texture. The grafting of text upon text estranges the interpretive acts of mimetic retrieval which we familiarly perform on the Shakespearean (or any other fictional) text. Although self-referential, self-reflexive, metadramatic and metaleptic moments in a play can serve as the "stuff" for reconstituting identities, they are also moments of recoil. Metadramatic constitution of identity is as specular and as unnerving as the implication which Ulysses transmits to Achilles that he does not exist unless he outruns an image of his own reputation.

Can we construe Shakespeare's deconstruction of myths as an anxiety of identity? The elusiveness of identity permeates the play and confers a peculiar dimension of doubleness and doubtfulness on the casual requests for identification scattered throughout the play.[17] ("Do you know a man if you see him?"; "You know me, do you not?"; "What's Thersites?"; "What art thou?"; "Is this the Lady Cressid?"; "Is this Achilles?" and so forth.) The scene of Pandarus's ridiculous presentation of the warriors' parade in I. ii, for example, is structured entirely around this kind of inquiry ("Who's that? That's Antenor." "Who's that? That's Helenus . . ." "What sneaking fellow comes yonder? *Enter Troilus*"). An entire plot stretches between Troilus's rhetorical question, "Tell me, Apollo, . . . What Cressid is, what Pandar, and what we" (I. i. 98–9), and his "recognition" scene: "This is and is not Cressid" (V. ii. 145), a recognition thwarted by the disabling nature of cognition which it records:

> *Ulysses:* Why stay we, then?
> *Troilus:* To make a recordation to my soul
> Of every syllable that here was spoke.
> But if I tell how these two did coact,
> Shall I not lie, in publishing a truth?
> (V. ii. 114–18)

What then is the recognition scene of *Troilus and Cressida*? It is hard to select from the anatomy of wreckage, dissolution, savagery, fragmentation and disenchantment which the fifth act spreads before us.

> *Troilus:* . . . O false Cressid! false, false, false!
> (V. ii. 177)

> *Thersites:* Lechery, lechery, still wars and lechery!
> Nothing else holds fashion.
> (V. ii. 193–4)

> *Cassandra:* Behold! distraction, frenzy, and amazement
> Like witless antics one another meet.
> (V. iii. 85–6)

> *Troilus:* Words, words, mere words, no matter from the heart.
> (V. iii. 108)

> *Ulysses:* . . . great Achilles
> Is arming, weeping, cursing, vowing vengeance:
> Patroclus' wounds have rous'd his drowsy blood,
> Together with his mangled Myrmidons
> That noseless, handless, hack'd and chipp'd, come to him,
> Crying on Hector.
> (V. v. 30–5)

> *Hector:* Most putrefied core, so fair without
> (V. viii. 1)

Of the numerous and diverse exegeses which have been offered, Rosalie Colie's reading of *Troilus and Cressida* as a "monumental mock'ry" impresses me as being the most powerfully and persuasively argued. Her contention is that in this play Shakespeare travestied received forms, and indeed "attacked literature at its very source,"[18] and that, in doing so, Shakespeare reverses his more common practice "of animating his literary clichés into actual characters. . . . Shakespeare chose here to *reverse* that process, to show how human situations can be stripped of their personal and general meanings to be no more – and to deserve to be no more – than the clichés with which literature presents us."[19] Colie's account of the play thematizes "the danger in words, in their 'mereness,' their automatic substitution for real response and engagement"[20] by arguing that Shakespeare's puny anti-heroes are mocked and debased by the absence in their lives of the ancient originary ideals, the rich and solid presence of referents to substantiate the proud epideixis of yore.

What is too hastily resolved, however, (and indeed remains unresolvable) is the question of the drift of the mockery: precisely who is mocking whom? The argument could easily be turned around to claim that it is the ancient values themselves which are now exposed for what they may always have been: hollow verbiage, barely concealed duplicity, brutality and demagoguery, empty rhetorical pretenses parading as high idealism. I do not believe this debate can be settled, but I do believe that it is possible to move beyond it to a reflection, as I suggested in my opening remarks, upon *Troilus and Cressida* as a sustained meditation on the parasitism of texts and on the plight of a belated writer who knows that all the stories have already been told.

And so back to "Ariachne's broken woof." Ovid's tale of Arachne's metamorphosis handles the motif of divine emulation (imitation and rivalry) and artistic hubris with delicate irony. Arachne's source of inspiration is Athene, but the girl denies the divinity of art and challenges the goddess to the fatal contest. The presence of divine authority and power is represented by both weavers in their tapestries, magisterially and dogmatically by Athene, ironically by Arachne. Her depictions of divine metamorphosis and rape (Jove as bull, swan, satyr, shower of gold, flame of fire, etc.) concede the sheer power of gods even as they mock their waywardness, and therefore invite Athene's rage on scores both of superior artistry and of insult. The ironist can win the contest only by losing it. The violation of Arachne's loom and the girl's degradation signify both the recognition and the destruction of her superior skill as artist. The trace of this fable in "Ariachne's broken woof" allegorizes the antinomy of tradition and the individual talent in the composite figure of Ariachne, child of *écriture*.

I cannot here offer more than the briefest sketch of this thesis. Its premise is that the basic dilemma of the Renaissance writer lay in the necessity to define the relationship between the epoch's reverential reinvestiture of classical texts, and the new privileging of the values of originality; and the relationship between the authority of an artist's writ and that of his unique and matchless forerunner text. The Renaissance artist responded to the contradictory notion of originality (problematized in the very concept of "Renaissance") by means of a complex double gesture of homage and affront, acceptance and refusal, deference for and deferral of precursors in whose august shadows new writing subsists. We still await a Bloomian history of the Renaissance and such speculations must remain an unexplored background to any reading of *Troilus and Cressida*.

For the present I simply invoke my fable of Ariachne as Renaissance muse to gloss both the predicament informing the fiction and the plight of its maker. The "traces" of *Troilus and Cressida* are on display even before the curtain rises, in the very choice of plot. It is true that Shakespeare almost never bothers to invent new plots, but in no other play does he take on the redoubtable task of refashioning, decomposing, vulgarizing, declassicizing precursor texts quite so canonical and powerful, and nowhere does he strip *both* his sources *and* his own text of their "original" substance with such spirited iconoclasm. To dramatize yet again the all too familiar classics, and to plunder the relics of one's strongest literary forebears; to invoke the parental ghosts of Homer and Chaucer and then to travesty the prestigious modes of epic, tragedy, and romance is clearly to solicit a searing test of the writer's independent poetic powers, and to hazard a self-stigmatizing exhibition of the etiolated quality of these powers. *Troilus and Cressida* is probably Shakespeare's most daring experiment in defensive self-presentation, and perhaps his noblest failure. In that sense, the anomalous phenomenon which is *Troilus and Cressida* is all recognition scene, the recognition scene of Renaissance writing. It may yet come to be read as the period's paradigmatic text.

Notes

1. All references are to the Arden edition of *Troilus and Cressida*, ed. Kenneth Palmer (London and New York, 1982).
2. See New Variorum edition of *Troilus and Cressida*, ed. Harold N. Hillebrand (Philadelphia and London, 1953), 279–80, and Palmer, op. cit., 278.
3. I. A. Richards ("*Troilus and Cressida* and Plato," in *Speculative Instruments* (London, 1955), 210, singles out the image as a condensed gloss on Troilus's move to reconcile opposites which "come together and are indistinguishable – as Ariadne's clue and Arachne's web are merged in 'Ariachne's broken woof.' (As escape from a labyrinth containing a devouring monster, with an ensuing betrayal; a penalty for hubris with a horrible transformation.)" J. Hillis Miller comments on "Shakespeare's splendid portmanteau word 'Ariachne'" in a somewhat different vein: "to the dissimilarity of stories in the same mythical narrative line must be added the lateral repetition with a difference of distinct myths, here called attention to by the 'accidental' similarity of the names. This clashing partial homonymy perfectly mimes the relation between the two

stories" ("Ariadne's thread: repetition and the narrative line," *Critical Inquiry*, 3 (Autumn 1976), 66).

4. Palmer, op. cit., 276n.
5. Harold Bloom, *The Anxiety of Influence: A Theory of Poetry* (Oxford, 1973), 11.
6. See A. Stein, "On Elizabethan wit" (*Studies in English Literature*, I (1961), 75–91), who points out that "the neoclassical age enjoyed a superior critical vocabulary and the advantages of an advanced technical competence and consciousness; the Renaissance enjoyed a superior concept of wit. There are gains and losses on both sides" (78).
7. I gratefully acknowledge Geoffrey Hartman's coinage.
8. On the character of "character," see Joel Weinsheimer, "Theory of character: *Emma*" (*Poetics Today*, I (Autumn 1979), 185–211).
9. See Jacques Derrida, "Signature event context" (*Glyph*, I (1977), 172–97). Derrida's critique of Condillac's theory of writing and Austin's speech act theory has provoked some very interesting reflections on the nature of the performative. See, for example, Barbara Johnson, "Poetry and performative language: Mallarmé and Austin," in *The Critical Difference: Essays in the Contemporary Rhetoric of Reading* (Baltimore, 1980); Stanley E. Fish, "How to do things with Austin and Searle: speech act theory and literary criticism" (*Modern Language Notes*, 91 (1976), 983–1025), and "With the compliments of the author: reflections on Austin and Derrida" (*Critical Inquiry*, 8 (Summer 1982), 693–721).
10. For the logic which ties *iterability* to *alterity* see Derrida, op. cit., 179–80, and Fish, "With the compliments of the author," 702–4.
11. Rosalie L. Colie, *Paradoxia Epidemica: The Renaissance Tradition of Paradox* (Princeton, 1966), 5. On paradox in *Troilus and Cressida*, see also Tinsely Helton, "Paradox and hypothesis in *Troilus and Cressida*" (*Shakespeare Studies*, X (1977), 115–31).
12. Derrida, op. cit., 185–6.
13. See New Variorum edition, 411–15; the ideas are contemporary commonplaces, but many commentators (including I. A. Richards) identify "the strange fellow" as Plato.
14. See Paul de Man, *Allegories of Reading: Figural Language in Rousseau, Nietzsche, Rilke, and Proust* (New Haven, 1979).
15. "Degree" is amusingly vizarded in the dramatized encounter, immediately following, between Aeneas and Agamemnon, where Aeneas fails (scornfully?) to recognize the Greek general.
16. George Puttenham, *The Arte of English Poesie*, ed. Gladys Bridge Willcock and Alice Walker (Cambridge, 1963), 239.
17. Zvi Jagendorf has argued ("All against one in *Troilus and Cressida*," *English*, XXXI (1982), 199–210) that a polarity of "all" and "one" is at the root of the play's conception, and that Shakespeare's concern with the topic of character and identity "is a sceptical one, prejudiced against what is taken to be a sentimentally heroic sense of the independent self" (199).
18. Rosalie L. Colie, *Shakespeare's Living Art* (Princeton, 1974), 317.
19. Ibid., 322.
20. Ibid., 349.

3

GEOFFREY H. HARTMAN

Shakespeare's poetical character in *Twelfth Night*[1]

Writing about Shakespeare promotes a sympathy with extremes. One such extreme is the impressionism of a critic like A. C. Bradley, when he tries to hold together, synoptically, Feste the fool and Shakespeare himself, both as actor and magical author. Bradley notes that the Fool in *Lear* has a song not dissimilar to the one that concludes *Twelfth Night* and leaves Feste at the finish-line. "But that's all one, our play is done . . ." After everything has been sorted out, and the proper pairings are arranged, verbal and structural rhythms converge to frame a sort of closure – though playing is never done, as the next and final verse suggests: "And we'll strive to please you every day." Bradley, having come to the end of an essay on Feste, extends *Twelfth Night* speculatively beyond the fool's song, and imagines Shakespeare leaving the theater:

> the same Shakespeare who perhaps had hummed the old song, half-ruefully and half-cheerfully, to its accordant air, as he walked home alone to his lodging from the theatre or even from some noble's mansion; he who, looking down from an immeasurable height on the mind of the public and the noble, had yet to be their servant and jester, and to depend upon their favour; not wholly uncorrupted by this dependence, but yet superior to it and, also determined, like Feste, to lay by the sixpences it brought him, until at least he could say the word, "Our revels now are ended," and could break – was it a magician's staff or a Fool's bauble?[2]

The rhetoric of this has its own decorum. It aims to convey a general, unified impression of a myriad-minded artist. Shakespearean interpreters have a problem with *summing up*. Leaning on a repeated verse ("For the rain it raineth every day"), and more quietly on the iteration of the word "one" (*Lear:* "Poor Fool and knave, I have one part in my heart / That's sorry yet for thee"; *Feste:* "I was one, sir, in this interlude; one Sir Topas, sir, but that's all one"), Bradley integrates Shakespeare by the deft pathos of an imaginary portrait. Today's ideological critics would probably purge this portrait of everything but Shakespeare's representation of power-relations and hierarchy. Such critics might note that the portrait's final question serves only to emphasize the artist's marginality, his loneliness or apartness, as if by a secret law of fate being an artist excluded Shakespeare from social power in the very world he addresses.

The relation of "character" in the world (domestic or political) to "poetical character" (the imaginary relations to that same world which make up our image of a particular artist) is always elusive. Especially so in the case of Shakespeare, of whose life we know so little. A myth evolves, given classic expression by Keats, that the mystery or obscurity enveloping Shakespeare's life is due to the fact that a great poet has no "identity," that he is "everything and nothing" – as Bradley's evocation also suggests. John Middleton Murry's book on Shakespeare begins with a chapter entitled "Everything and Nothing" in which Murry explores his reluctant conclusion that "In the end there is nothing to do but to surrender to Shakespeare." "The moment comes in our experience of Shakespeare when we are dimly conscious of a choice to be made: either we must turn away (whether by leaving him in silence, or by substituting for his reality some comfortable intellectual fiction of our own), or we must suffer ourselves to be drawn into the vortex."[3]

The focus moves, in short, to the character of the critic, determined by this choice. Can *we* abide Shakespeare's question? Does the critic have a "character" of his own, or is he simply a bundle of responses accommodated to a special institution or audience: university students and dons, or other drama buffs, or the general public? Unlike Eliot, say, or Tolstoy, Murry has no body of creative writing to back up the importance of his interpretive engagements. There is, nevertheless, a sense that the critic's identity is formed by his selfless encounters with artists of Shakespeare's stature.

The "vortex" that threatens readers, according to Murry, includes the fact that Shakespeare delights as much in Iago as Imogen (Keats's words); and to shuffle off our ordinary conceptions of character – in Murry's phrase, the "mortal coil of moral judgment" – is both painful and necessary. Always, Murry claims, "when Shakespeare has been allowed to make *his* impression, we find the critic groping after the paradox of the poetical character itself as described by Keats." In an earlier essay, closer to Bradley's era, Murry had already put the problem of Shakespeare criticism in terms that showed how aware he was of reactions to the "vortex." He rejects the "'idea'-bacillus" that reduces Shakespeare to universal themes or the creation of character-types, yet he refuses to relinquish his rigorous quest for "the center of comprehension from which he [Shakespeare] worked." Programmatic as it is, Murry's statement of 1920 remains relevant:

> Let us away then with 'logic' and away with 'ideas' from the art of literary criticism; but not, in a foolish and impercipient reaction, to revive the impressionistic criticism which has sapped the English brain for a genera- tion past. The art of criticism is rigorous; impressions are merely its raw material; the life-blood of its activity is in the process of ordonnance of aesthetic impressions.[4]

The rejection of impressionism leads, if we think of Eliot, and of Murry himself, simply to a more rigorous formulation of the paradox of the impersonal artist. For Murry it meant comparing Christian and post- Shakespearean (especially romantic) ways of annihilating selfhood. Blake becomes even more crucial for such a formulation than Keats. G. W. Knight also joins this quest. Other rigorous escape routes, that lead through impres- sionism beyond it, make Shakespeare's language the main character of his plays, the everything and nothing. Empson's colloquial fracturing of Shakespeare's text, from *Seven Types* through *Complex Words*, as well as Leavis's emphasis on the "heuristico-creative quality of the diction" avoid, on the whole, totalizing structures. Rigor consists in having the local reading undo an established symmetry.

Another form of rigor, historical scholarship, can be outrageously specula- tive. (The trend was always there in the work of editors who unscrambled perplexing expressions or normalized daring ones.) One might escape the Shakespearean vortex by discovering a firm historical emplacement for the plays, by clarifying their occasion as well as the characters in them. The work of referring the plays back to sources mysteriously transformed by Shakespeare (minor Italian novellas, or poetics derived from Donatus and Terence, such as the "forward progress of the turmoils"[5]) gives way to an ambitious reconstruction of a particular, sponsoring event. The quest for the identity of W.H. or the Dark Lady or the exact festive occasion of *Twelfth Night* exerts a prosecutory charm that attests to the presence of character in the critic-investigator (that stubborn, scholarly sleuth) as well as in Shakespeare the historical personage. Consider what the ingenious Leslie Hotson does with the "jest nominal," or play on names. It is as intriguing as anything ventured by newfangled intertextualists.

Hotson claims in *The First Night of Twelfth Night* that the figure of Malvolio is a daring take-off of a high official in Elizabeth's court: Sir William Knollys, Earl of Banbury and Controller of her Majesty's household. This aging dignitary, we are told, had become infatuated with a young Maid of Honor at Court, Mall (Mary) Fitton. In the "allowed fooling" of Twelfth Night festivities, "old Beard Knollys," suggests Hotson, "is slaughtered in gross and detail." Here is his description of how it was done:

while exposing both the Controller's *ill-will* – towards hilarity and misrule – and his *amorousness* in the name *Mala-voglia* (Ill Will *or* Evil concupiscence) Shakespeare also deftly fetches up Knollys' ridiculous love-chase of Mistress Mall by a sly modulation of *Mala-Voglia* into *"Mal"-voglio* – which means "I want Mall," "I wish for Mall," "I will have Mall." It is a masterpiece of mockery heightened by merciless repetition, with the players ringing the changes of expression on *"Mal"-voglio* . . . it will bring down the house.[6]

The play becomes a *roman à clef*, and so delivers us from a verbal vertigo it exposes. Shakespeare's improvisational genius, moreover, his extreme wit and opportunism, may recall the methodical *bricolage* by which earlier mythmakers, according to Lévi-Strauss, sustained their tale. Here it explicitly pleases or shames the ears of a court-centered audience. Yet this shaming or delighting is not necessarily in the service of good sense or the *status quo*, for it can subvert as well as mock and purge. The one thing it does, as in the case of the Controller, is to acknowledge the law of gender – of generation and succession – which, as Erasmus saw, compels us to play the fool. Such allowed slander, whether or not reinforced by Elizabethan festivities, by periods of compulsory license, also penetrates Shakespearean tragedy:

> Even he, the father of gods and king of men, who shakes all heaven by a nod, is obliged to lay aside his three-pronged thunder and that Titanic aspect by which, when he pleases, he scares all the gods, and assume another character in the slavish manner of an actor, if he wishes to do what he never refrains from doing, that is to say, to beget children. . . . He will certainly lay by his gravity, smooth his brow, renounce his rock-bound principles, and for a few minutes toy and talk nonsense. . . . Venus herself would not deny that without the addition of my presence her strength would be enfeebled and ineffectual. So it is that from this brisk and silly little game of mine come forth the haughty philosophers.[7]

2

Generation and Succession are so fundamental to almost all classes and types of humanity that to reduce them to their verbal effects might seem trivializing. Yet, as Erasmus's Folly hints, the very category of the trivial is overturned by these forces. The "striving to please every day," which is the fate of the player, is equally that of lover and courtier. It quickens even as it exhausts our wit. It points to a relentless need for devices – words, stratagems. More is required than a "tiny little wit" to sustain what every day demands.[8]

There exist eloquent characterizations of Shakespeare's understanding of the common nature of mankind. As Bakhtin remarks of another great writer, Rabelais, there are crownings and uncrownings at every level.[9] No one is exempt, at any time, from that rise and fall, whether it is brought on by actual political events or social and sexual rivalry, or internalized pressures leading to self-destructive illusions and acts. The vicissitudes of Folly and Fortuna go hand in hand. Yet no conclusions are drawn; and it does not matter what class of person is involved – a Falstaff, a Harry, a King Henry; a clown, a count, a lady; a usurper, a porter. What happens happens across the board, and can therefore settle expressively in a language with a character of its own – apart from the decorum that fits it to the character of the person represented. The pun or quibble, Shakespeare's "fatal Cleopatra," is a quaint and powerful sign of that deceiving variety of life. Hazlitt, following Charles Lamb, remarks that Elizabethan "distinctions of dress, the badges of different professions, the very signs of the shops" were a sort of visible language for the imagination. "The surface of society was embossed with hieroglyphs."[10] Yet the showiest and most self-betraying thing in Shakespeare is the flow of language itself, which carries traces of an eruption from some incandescent and molten core, even when hard as basalt, that is, patently rhetorical.

Structurally too, the repetitions by which we discover an intent – a purposiveness – do not resolve themselves into a unity, a "one" free of sexual, hierarchical or personal differentiation. Feste's "one" is an Empsonian complex word, which seeks to distract us, by its very iteration, into a sense of closure. Yet there is never an objective correlative that sops up the action or organizes all the excrescent motives and verbal implications. Feste's phrase is found, for example, in the mouth of another clown figure, Fluellen, in a scene one could characterize as "Porn at Monmouth" (*Henry V*, IV. vii). The scene, through the solecisms and mispronunciations of Fluellen, his butchery of English, makes us aware of what is involved in the larger world of combat, to which he is marginal. The catachresis of "Kill the Poyes and the luggage!" expresses the cut-throat speed with which matters are moving toward indiscriminate slaughter. An end penetrates the middle of the drama; the grimace (if only linguistic) of death begins to show through.

Yet even here, as the action hits a dangerous juncture, as decisions become hasty and bloody, this verbally excessive interlude slows things down to a moment of humorous discrimination. Fluellen draws a comparison between Harry of Monmouth and "Alexander the Pig" of Macedon (*Henry V*, IV. vii). That "big" should issue as "pig" is a fertile and leveling pun, which the macabre turn of this near-graveyard scene could have exploited even more; but the uncrowning of Alexander in Fluellen's mouth leads to a series of images (mouth, fingers, figures) that suggest a "body" less mortal than its parts. Harry's transformation into King Henry, and Fluellen's comparison in his favor – that Harry's bloodthirsty anger is more justified than Alexander's – appear like a jesting in the throat of death, a vain distinction already undone by the battlefield context that levels all things, as by an earthy vernacular, or quasi-vernacular, that can slander all things in perfect good humor.

It seems impossible, then, to describe the poetical character of Shakespeare without raising certain questions. One concerns the character of the critic (choices to be made in reading so strong and productive a writer); another what happens to language as it nurtures a vernacular ideal that still dominates English literature. A third, related question is whether what that language does to character and to us can be summed up or unified by methodical inquiry. Does an "intellectual tradition" exist, as Richards thought, to guide us in reading that plentiful "Elizabethan" mixture? "The hierarchy of these modes is elaborate and variable," he writes about sixteenth- and seventeenth-century literature. To "read aright," Richards continues, "we need to shift with an at present indescribable adroitness and celerity from one mode to another."[11]

By "modes" Richards means different types of indirect statement, which he also characterizes as "metaphorical, allegorical, symbolical," yet does not define further. In some way they are all nonliteral; at least not directly literal. Like Coleridge, whom he quotes, Richards is impressed by the role that "wit" plays in Shakespeare's time, although he does not discuss the complicit or antagonistic and always showy relation between wit and will. He simply accepts Coleridge's thesis on wit and Shakespeare's time:

> when the English Court was still foster-mother of the State and the Muses; and when, in consequence, the courtiers and men of rank and fashion affected a display of wit, point, and sententious observation, that would be deemed intolerable at present – but in which a hundred years of controversy, involving every great political, and every dear domestic interest, had trained all but the lowest classes to participate. Add to this the very style of the sermons of the time, and the eagerness of the Protestants to distinguish themselves by long and frequent preaching, and it will be found that, from the reign of Henry VIII to the abdication of James II, no country ever received such a national education as England.[12]

Yet Coleridge's notion of "national education" may be too idealistic – Arnoldian before the letter. It downplays the subverting character of Shakespeare's wit, one that is not put so easily in the service of the nation-state and its movement toward a common language. The "prosperity of a pun," as M. M. Mahood calls it, in what is still the most sensitive exploration of the subject,[13] offended rather than pleased most refiners of English up to modern times. "Prosperity" may itself covertly play on "propriety," which is precisely what a pun questions. The speed and stenography, in any case, of Shakespeare's wordplay in the comic scenes undoes the hegemony of any single order of discourse, and compels us to realize the radically social and mobile nature of the language exchange. And, unlike the novel (which allows Bakhtin his most persuasive theorizing), these scenes display less a narrative or a pseudonarrative than *oral graffiti*. Verbally Shakespeare is a graffiti artist, using bold, often licentious strokes, that make sense because of the living context of stereotypes, the *commedia dell'arte*, and other vernacular or popular traditions.

Is it possible, then, to see Shakespeare *sub specie unitatis*, as the younger Murry thought? "There never has been and never will be a human mind which can resist such an inquiry if it is pursued with sufficient perseverance and understanding."[14] Yet in this very sentence "human mind" is fleetingly equivocal: does it refer only to the object of inquiry, Shakespeare's mind, or also to the interpreter's intellect, tempted by the riddle of Shakespeare? The later Murry too does not give up; but now the unity, the "all that's one," is frightening as well, and associated with *omnia abeunt in mysterium*: all things exit into mystery.[15]

It seems to me there is no mystery, no *Abgrund*, except language itself, whose revelatory revels are being staged, as if character were a function of language, rather than vice versa. More precisely, as if the locus of the dramatic action were the effect of language on character. *Twelfth Night* will allow us to examine how this language test is applied. If we admire, however ambivalently, the way Iago works on Othello by "damnable iteration" (cf. *Falstaff*: "O, thou hast damnable iteration, and art indeed able to corrupt a saint" (*1 Henry IV*, I. ii. 90), or the way Falstaff shamelessly converts abuse into flattery, we are already caught up in a rhetoric whose subversive motility, moment to moment, can bless or curse, praise or blame, corrupt words or (like Aristotle's eulogist) substitute collateral terms that "lean toward the best."[16] It is this instant possibility of moving either way, or simultaneously both ways, which defines the Shakespearean dramatic and poetical character. In *Twelfth Night*, with Feste a self-pronounced "corrupter of words" (III. i. 37), and Malvolio's censorious presence, the verbal action challenges all parties to find "comic remedies," or to extract sweets from weeds and poisons.[17]

3

"Excellent," says Sir Toby Belch, "I smell a device." "I have't in my nose too," Sir Andrew Aguecheek echoes him (II. iii. 162). Toby is referring to the plan concocted by Maria, Olivia's maid, of how to get even with the strutting and carping Malvolio, steward of the household. The device is a letter to be written by Maria in her lady's hand, which will entice Malvolio into believing Olivia is consumed with a secret passion for him, his yellow stockings, cross-garters and smile. The device (not the only one in the play – Bertrand Evans has counted seven persons who are active practisers operating six devices)[18] succeeds; and Malvolio, smiling hard, and wearing the colors he thinks are the sign commanded by his lady, but which she happens to detest, is taken for mad and put away.

The very words "I smell a device" contain a device. Toby, mostly drunk, knows how to choose his metaphors; and Andrew, not much of a wit ("I am a great eater of beef, and I believe that does harm to my wit"), merely echoes him, which makes the metaphor more literal and so more absurd. A device is also a figure, or flower of speech; both meanings may be present here, since the content of the device is literary, that is, a deceivingly flowery letter. Flowers smell, good or bad as the occasion may be. "Lillies that fester smell far worse than weeds" (Sonnet 94). Sometimes figures or metaphors fly by so thick and fast that we all are as perplexed as Sir Andrew:

> *Andrew:* Bless you, fair shrew.
> *Maria:* And you too, sir.
> *Toby:* Accost, Sir Andrew, accost. (. . .)
> *Andrew:* Good Mistress Accost, I desire better acquaintance.
> *Maria:* My name is Mary, sir.
> *Andrew:* Good Mistress Mary Accost —
> *Toby:* You mistake, knight. "Accost" is front her, board her, woo her, assail her.
> *Andrew:* By my troth, I would not undertake her in this company. Is that the meaning of "accost"?
> *Maria:* Fare you well, gentlemen.
> *Toby:* And thou let part so, Sir Andrew, would thou might'st never draw sword again!
> *Andrew:* And you part so, mistress, I would I might never draw sword again. Fair lady, do you think you have fools in hand?
> *Maria:* Sir, I have not you by th' hand.
> *Andrew:* Marry, but you shall have, and here's my hand.
> *Maria:* Now, sir, thought is free. I pray you bring your hand to th' buttery bar and let it drink.
> *Andrew:* Wherefore, sweetheart? What's your metaphor?
> *Maria:* It's dry, sir.

(I. iii. 46–72)

Awkward Andrew starts with a mild oxymoron and compounds the error of his address to Mary by a further innocent mistake – the transposition of a common verb into a proper noun, which not only unsettles parts of speech but creates a parallel euphemism to "fair shrew" through the idea of "good Accost." The entire scene is constructed out of such pleasant errors – failed connections or directions that hint at larger, decisive acts (accosting, undertaking, marrying). At line 62 the verbal plot becomes even more intricate, as Andrew strives to "address" Mary a second time. "Marry" (66) is an oath, a corruption of the Virgin's name; but here, in addition to echoing "Mary," it may be the common verb, as Andrew tries to be witty or gallant by saying in a slurred way (hey, I too can fling metaphors around!), "If you marry you'll have me by the hand, and here it is." (He forgets that that would make him a fool, like all married men.) Maria bests him, though, suggesting a freer kind of handling, with a new metaphor that – I think – may be licentious. What is that "buttery bar"? Probably, in function, a bar as today, for serving drinks; but could it be her breasts or . . . butt? That same "bar," by a further twist or trope, echoes in Maria's "marry, now I let go your hand, I am barren" (77). No wonder Andrew, out of his range, stutters, "Wherefore, sweetheart? What's your metaphor?"

Somewhere there is always a device, or a "hand" that could fool just about anyone. Nobody is spared, nobody escapes witting. Yet it remains harmless because all, except Malvolio, play along. There is rhetoric and repartee, puns and paranomasia, metaphor upon metaphor, as if these characters were signifying monkeys: the play expects every person to pass the test of wit, to stand at that bar of language. Yet "wherefore?" we ask, like simple Andrew.

That question returns us to the poetical character. It "is not itself," Keats wrote, "it has no self – it is every thing and nothing – It has no character." He says other things, too, which make it clear he is thinking mainly of Shakespeare. "It lives in gusto, be it foul or fair, high or low, rich or poor, mean or elevated – It has as much delight in conceiving an Iago as an Imogen. What shocks the virtuous philosopher [a Malvolio in this respect] delights the chameleon Poet. It does no harm from its relish of the dark side of things any more than for its taste for the bright one; because they both end in speculation" (letter to Richard Woodhouse, October 27, 1818).

Much depends on that word "speculation" in Keats; a "widening speculation," he also writes, eases the burden of life's mystery, takes away the heat and fever (letter to J. H. Reynolds, May 3, 1818). You have to have something to speculate with or on; some luxury, like a delicious voice, whose first impact you remember. Speculation is making the thing count again, as with money, yet *without fearing its loss*.[19] The Shakespearean language of wit is like that. Though penetrated by knowledge of loss, aware that the most loved or fancied thing can fall "into abatement and low price, / Even in a minute!" (I.i.13–14), it still spends itself in an incredibly generous manner, as if the treasury of words were always full. However strange it may seem, while everything in this play is, emotionally, up or down – each twin, for example, thinks the other dead; Olivia, in constant mourning and rejecting Orsino, is smitten by Viola / Cesario in the space of one interview – while everything vacillates, the language itself coins its metaphors and fertile exchanges beyond any calculus of loss and gain. When I hear the word "fool" repeated so many times, I also hear the word "full" emptied out or into it; so "Marry" and "Mary" and "madam" ("mad-dame") and "madman" collapse distinctions of character (personality) in favor of some prodigious receptacle that "receiveth as the sea" (I.i.11). No wonder modern critics have felt a Dionysian drift in the play, a doubling and effacing of persons as well as a riot of metaphors working against distinctions, until, to quote the ballad at the end, "that's all one."

4

I think, therefore I am. What does one do about "I act" or "I write"? What identity for that "I"? For the poet who shows himself in the inventive wit of all these personae? *Twelfth Night* gives an extraordinary amount of theatrical time to Sir Toby Belch and Sir Andrew Aguecheek, and to clowning generally. These scenes threaten to erupt into the main plot, which is absurd enough, where love is sudden and gratuitous, as in Orsino's infatuation for Olivia (two O's) or Viola's for Orsino, or Olivia's for Cesario. Everything goes o–a in this play, as if a character's destiny depended on voweling. "M.O.A.I. doth sway my life" (II.v.109). Whose *hand* directs this comic tumult of mistaken identities, disguises, devices, and names, that even when they are not Rabelaisian or musical scrabble (Olivia: Viola) or transparent like Malvolio (the evil eye, or evil wish) are silly attempts at self-assertion? So it doesn't really help when Sebastian in II.i.14–18 identifies himself. "You must know of me then, Antonio, my name is Sebastian, which I called Roderigo; my father was that Sebastian of Messaline whom I know you have heard of." We have two Sebastians, and one Sebastian is Roderigo. In addition, as we know by this point in the drama, Sebastian and Viola (that is, Cesario) are identical twins, born in the same hour, both saved from the "breach" a second time when they escape shipwreck and find themselves in a land with the suggestive name of Illyria – compounded, to the sensitive ear, out of Ill and liar/lyre. So also Viola enters the play punning, or off-rhyming. "And what should I do in Illyria? / My brother he is in Elysium" (I.ii.3–4).

The question, then, relates to identity and destiny, or who has what in hand; it is also related to the question of questioning itself, that kind of speech-act, so close to trial and testing, and the legalese or academic lingo in a play perhaps performed at an inn-of-court. In late medieval times, from the twelfth century on, there was a shift in "pedagogical technique (and corresponding literary forms) from the *lectio* to the *disputatio* and *questio* . . . from primary concern for the exegesis of authoritative texts and the laying of doctrinal foundations toward the resolution of particular (and sometimes minor) difficulties and even the questioning of matters no longer seriously doubted, for the sake of exploring the implications of a doctrine, revealing the limits of necessity and contingency, or demonstrating one's dialectical skills."[20] Another authority writes that "Even the points accepted by everybody and set forth in the most certain of terms were brought under scrutiny and subjected, by deliberate artifice, to the now usual processes of research. In brief, they were, literally speaking, 'called into question,' no longer because there was any real doubt about their truth, but because a deeper understanding of them was sought after."[21] From contemporary reports of the "Acts" at Oxford when Elizabeth visited, we know that these questions and *quodlibets* maintained themselves at least ceremonially.[22] Is *Twelfth Night*'s subtitle, "What You Will," a jocular translation of *quodlibet*? What significance may there be in the fact that in I. iii. 86–96 Toby passes from "No question" to "*Pourquoi*" to "Past question?" My own question is: *Pourquoi* these "kikshawses" ("quelques choses")? Wherefore, Shakespeare? What's your metaphor for?

Testing and questing seem connected immemorially: it is hard to think of the one without the other, especially in the realm of "Acts" which assert authority or identity by playful display. Even the Academy participates that much in the realm of romance. But my comments are meant to lead somewhat deeper into a drama that relishes the night-side of things with such good humor. If there are low-class mistakes, as when Andrew thinks Toby's "Accost" refers to Mary's name, there are also the high-class mistakes, Orsino's love, principally, that starts the play with a fine call for music in verses intimating that nothing can fill desire, fancy, love. Its appetite is like the sea, so capacious, so swallowing and changeable. "If music be the food of love, play on." *Play on* is what we do, as "Misprision in the highest degree" (I. v. 53) extends itself. Everything changes place or is mis-taken, so that Orsino believes himself in love with Olivia but settles "dexteriously," as the Clown might say, for Viola; while poor Malvolio is taken for mad and confined in a place as gloomy as his temperament. We tumble through the doubling, reversing, mistaking, clowning, even cloning; we never get away from the tumult of the words themselves, from the "gratillity" (another clown-word, that is, gratuitousness or greed for tips, tipsiness) of Feste's "gracious fooling," as when Andrew, probably tipsy himself, and stupidly good at mixing metaphors, mentions some of the clown's other coinages: "Pigrogromitus" and the "Vapians passing the equinoctial of Queubus" (II. iii. 23–4).

It is not that these funny, made-up words don't make sense: they make a kind of instant sense, as Shakespeare always does. Yet a sense that can't be proved, that remains to be guessed at and demands something from us. Does "equinoctial" hint at solstice or equinox festivals, if *Twelfth Night* was performed on the day the title suggests;[23] is "Queubus" mock Latin for the tail or male, or a corruption of "quibus," "a word of frequent occurrence in legal documents and so associated with verbal niceties or subtle distinctions" (C. T. Onions)? Did the audience know it was slang for fool in Dutch ("Kwibus")?

The text requires a certain tolerance or liberality of interpretation: yellow cross-garters in the realm of construing, "motley in the brain" (I. v. 55). To quote Andrew – and it should be inscribed on the doors of all literature departments: "I would I had bestowed that time in the tongues that I have in fencing, dancing, and bear-baiting. O, had I but followed the arts!" (I. iii. 90–3).

There exists a modern version of another "antic" song about the twelve days of Christmas (cf. II. iii. 85). If Twelfth Night, the climax of Christmastide rejoicing, asks that we fill up the daystar's ebb, then the emphasis falls on giving, on true-love giving. Twelfth Night, formally the feast of Epiphany, is when divinity appeared, when Christ was manifested to the Gentiles (the Magi or three kings). Presence rather than absence is the theme. *Twelfth Night* is not a religious play, and yet its "gracious fooling" may be full of grace. The great O of Shakespeare's stage draws into it the gift of tongues; and in addition to the legal or academic metaphors, the food and sexual metaphors, and other heterogeneous language strains, occasionally a religious pathos, impatient of all these indirections, maskings, devices, makes itself heard. "Wherefore are these things hid? Wherefore have these gifts a curtain before 'em?" (I. iii. 122–3) To the question, what filling (fulfilling) is in this fooling, the best reply might be that, in literature, everything aspires to the condition of language, to the gift of tongues; that the spirit – wanton as it may be – of language overrides such questions, including those of character and identity.

Does Orsino, the Duke, have an identity, or is he not a plaything of fancy; and is love not represented by him as both arbitrary in what it fixes on and as "full of shapes" and "fantastical" as the entire play? These people seem in love with words rather than with each other. More exactly, the embassy of words and the play of rhetoric are essential tests for both lover and object of love. When Curio tries to distract the Duke from his musical and effete reflections by "Will you go hunt, my lord?" (I. i. 16), Orsino answers, startled, "What, Curio?" meaning "What d'you say?", which is misunderstood when Curio replies, "The hart," after which the Duke can't restrain himself from an old quibble equating hart, the animal, and heart, the seat of love:

> Why, so I do [hunt], the noblest that I have.
> O, when mine eyes did see Olivia first,
> Methought she purg'd the air of pestilence;
> That instant was I turn'd into a hart,
> And my desires, like fell and cruel hounds,
> E'er since pursue me.
>
> (I. i. 18–23)

The hunter becomes the hunted; but it is also suggested (though we may not be convinced) that the Duke finds a heart in himself – a sensitivity where previously there was nothing but a sense of privilege.

We see how thorough this full fooling is. In Shakespeare the poetry – the prose too – is larger than the characters, enlarging them but also making their identities or egos devices in an overwhelming revel. The revels of language are never ended. This does not mean that language is discontinuous with the search for identity or a "heart." Orsino's first speech already introduces the gracious theme of giving and receiving, of feeding, surfeiting, dying, reviving, playing on. Love and music are identified through the metaphor of the "dying fall" (I.i.4), also alluding, possibly, to the end of the year; and, ironically enough, the Duke's moody speech suggests *a desire to get beyond desire* – to have done with such perturbations, with wooing and risking rejection, and trying to win through by gifts and maneuvers. "Give me excess of it, that, surfeiting, / The appetite [for love, not just for music] may sicken, and so die" (I.i.2–3). At the very end of the play, with the Clown's final song, this melancholy desire to be beyond desire returns in the refrain "The rain it raineth every day," and the internal chiming of "that's all one, our play is done." Even in this generous and least cynical of Shakespeare's comedies, love is an appetite that wants to be routinized or exhausted, and so borders on tragic sentiments.

In drama, giving and receiving take the form of dialogic repartee. Shakespeare makes of dialogue a charged occasion, two masked affections testing each other, always on guard. Usually, then, there is a healthy fear or respect for the other; or there is a subversive sense that what goes on in human relations is not dialogue at all but seduction and domination. To have real giving and receiving – in terms of speech and understanding – may be so strenuous that the mind seeks other ways to achieve a simulacrum of harmony: maybe an "equinoctial of Queubus" brings us into equilibrium, or maybe festivals, like Christmas, when there is at-one-ment, through licensed license, through the principle of "what you will," of freely doing or not doing. (Twelve, after all, is the sign of the temporal clock turning over into One.) But the turn is felt primarily at the level of "gracious fooling" in this Christmas play. Hazlitt goes so far as to say "It is perhaps too good-natured for comedy. It has little satire and no spleen." And he continues with an even more significant remark, which I now want to explore: "In a word, the best turn is given to everything, instead of the worst."

5

The poetical genius of Shakespeare is inseparable from an ability to trope anything and turn dialogue, like a fluctuating battle, to the worst or best surmise. I see the dramatic and linguistic action of *Twelfth Night* as a turning away of the evil eye. It averts a malevolent interpretation of life, basically Malvolio's. Though Malvolio is unjustly – by a mere "device" – put into a dark place, this too is for the good, for he must learn how to plead. That is, by a quasilegal, heartfelt rhetoric, he must now turn the evidence, from bad to good. In IV. ii. 12ff. a masquerade is acted out which not only compels us to sympathize with Malvolio, making him a figure of pathos, but which repeats, as a play within the play, the action of the whole. Malvolio is gulled once more, baited like a bear – the sport he objected to. Yet the spirit of this comedy is not that of revenge, malice or ritual expulsion. All these motives may participate, yet what rouses our pity and fear is the way language enters and preordains the outcome. Shakespeare brings out the schizoid nature of discourse by juxtaposing soft or good words, ordinary euphemisms ("Jove bless thee, Master Parson," "*Bonos dies*, Sir Toby," "Peace in this prison") with abusive imprecations ("Out, hyperbolical fiend," "Fie, thou dishonest Satan," "Madman, thou errest"). Malvolio is subjected to a ridiculous legal or religious quizzing: a "trial" by "constant question." As in so many infamous state proceedings, he can get nowhere. He has to cast himself, against his temperament, on the mercy of the clown he condemned, though never actually harmed: "Fool, I say," "Good fool, as ever thou wilt deserve well at my hand," "Ay, good fool," "Fool, fool, fool, I say!", "Good fool, help me to some light and some paper: I tell thee I am as well in my wits as any man in Illyria" ("*Feste*: "Well-a-day that you were, sir!""), "By this hand, I am! Good fool, some ink, paper, and light."

Every word suddenly receives its full value. A man's life or freedom depends on it. It is not quibbled away. Yet words remain words; they have to be received; the imploration is all. "By this hand" is more than a tender of good faith, the visible sign of imploration. It is the handwriting that could save Malvolio, as that other "hand," Maria's letter-device, fooled and trapped him. Ink, paper, and light, as for Shakespeare himself perhaps, are the necessities. They must dispel or counter-fool whatever plot has been, is being, woven.

The spectator sits safely, like a judge, on the bench; yet the reversal which obliges Malvolio to plead with the fool reminds us what it means to be dependent on what we say and how (generously or meanly) it is received. To please every day, like a courtier, lover or actor, leads us into improvisations beyond the ordinary scope of wit. It puts us all in the fool's place. It is everyone, not Feste alone, who is involved, when after a sally of nonsense Maria challenges him with "Make that good" (I. v. 7). That is, give it meaning, in a world where "hanging" and "colours" (collars, cholers, flags, figures of speech, I. v. 1–6) are realities. But also, to return to Hazlitt's insight, give what you've said the best turn, justify the metaphor at whatever bar (legal) or buttery (the milk of mercy) is the least "dry" (I. iii. 72). "The rain it raineth every day."

Bakhtin's view, inspired by the development of literary vernaculars in the Renaissance, that each national language is composed of many kinds of discourse, dialogic even when not formally so, and polyphonic in effect, can be extended to the question of Shakespeare's poetical character. There is no one heart or one will ("Will"). Andrew's querulous "What's your metaphor?" or Maria's testing "Make it good" or the Clown's patter ("'That that is, is'; so I, being Master Parson, am Master Parson; for what is 'that' but 'that'? and 'is' but 'is'?" (IV. ii. 15–17)) impinge also on the spectator/reader. Yet in this world of figures, catches, errors, reversals, songs, devices, plays within plays, where motley distinguishes more than the jester, and even Malvolio is gulled into a species of it, moments arise that suggest a more than formal resolution – more than the fatigue or resignation of "that's all one" or the proverbial "all's well that ends well." So when Viola, as the Duke's go-between, asks Olivia, "Good madam, let me see your face" (where the "good," as in all such appeals, is more than an adjective, approaching the status of an absolute construction: "Good, madam," similar in force to Maria's "Make it good"), there is the hint of a possible revelatory moment, of *clarification*. The challenge, moreover, is met by a facing up to it. Yet the metaphor of expositing a text, which had preceded, is continued, so that we remain in the text even when we are out of it.

Olivia: Now, sir, what is your text?
Viola: Most sweet lady –
Olivia: A comfortable doctrine, and much may be said of it. Where lies your text?
Viola: In Orsino's bosom.
Olivia: In his bosom? In what chapter of his bosom?
Viola: To answer by the method, in the first of his heart.
Olivia: O, I have read it: it is heresy. Have you no more to say?
Viola: Good madam, let me see your face.
Olivia: Have you any commission from your lord to negotiate with my face? You are now out of your text: but we will draw the curtain and show you the picture. [*Unveiling*] Look you, sir, such a one I was this present. Is't not well done?
Viola: Excellently done, if God did all.

(I. v. 223–39)

I was, not I am; by pretending she is a painting, just unveiled, the original I is no longer there, or only as this picture which points to a present in the way names or texts point to a meaning. The text, however, keeps turning. There is no "present": no absolute gift, or moment of pure being. Yet a sense of epiphany, however fleeting, is felt; a sense of mortality too and of artifice, as the text is sustained by the force of Olivia's wit. "Is't not well done?" Olivia, like Feste, must "make it good." The mocking elaboration of her own metaphor allows speech rather than embarrassed or astonished silence at this point. The play (including Olivia's "interlude") continues. There is always more to say.

Notes

1. All quotations from *Twelfth Night* are taken from the Arden Shakespeare edition, ed. J. M. Lothian and T. W. Craik (London and New York, 1975).
2. "Feste the jester", in *A Miscellany* (London, 1929), 217.
3. John Middleton Murry, *Shakespeare* (London, 1936), 17–19. At the end of his book Murry appends a short imaginary dialogue with Shakespeare, more fanciful than Bradley's surmise.
4. "Shakespeare criticism", in *Aspects of Literature* (New York, 1920), 200. Eliot's epigraph to *The Sacred Wood* (1921) from Rémy de Gourmont ("Eriger ses impressions en lois . . .") discloses the common problem of going beyond impressionism without becoming unduly scientific (i.e. following the Taine–Brunetière tradition).
5. Consult, for example, J. V. Cunningham, *Woe or Wonder: The Emotional Effect of Shakespearean Tragedy* (1951), especially "The Donatan tradition"; and Ruth Nevo, *Comic Transformations in Shakespeare* (London and New York, 1980).
6. Leslie Hotson, *The First Night of Twelfth Night* (New York, 1955), ch. 5, "Malvolio."
7. Desiderius Erasmus, *The Praise of Folly*, tr. from the Latin, with an essay and commentary, by Hoyt Hopewell Hudson, (Princeton, 1941), 14–15.
8. Consider, in this light, the vogue of courtesy books in the sixteenth century, of which the most famous, Baldassare Castiglione's *The Book of the Courtier*, was done into English by Sir Thomas Hoby in 1561, and reprinted 1577, 1588 and 1603. Book 2 of *The Courtier* treats exhaustively the decorum of jesting.
9. Mikhail Bakhtin, *Rabelais and His World*, tr. Helene Iswolsky (Cambridge, Mass., 1968). See especially ch. 3, "Popular-festive forms." Bakhtin mentions the feast of Epiphany, and claims that the common element of both official and unofficial carnivals was that "they are all related to time, which is the true hero of every feast, uncrowning the old and crowning the new." A significant footnote adds that, actually, "every feast day crowns and uncrowns." See also Bakhtin's second chapter on "The language of the marketplace in Rabelais." (For some amusing remarks on Shakespeare and Rabelais, cf. Hotson, op. cit., 155ff.) C. L. Barber in *Shakespeare's Festive Comedy: A Study of Dramatic Form and its Relation to Social Custom* (1959) explores the same area.
10. William Hazlitt, *Lectures on the Literature of the Age of Elizabeth* (1820), ch. 1.
11. I. A. Richards, *Coleridge on Imagination* (London, 1968), 193.
12. As quoted by Richards, op. cit., 193.
13. M. M. Mahood, *Shakespeare's Wordplay* (London, 1957).
14. Murry, *Aspects*, 199.
15. Murry, *Shakespeare*, 17–18.
16. See Hudson, op. cit., xxiii. Also, on the related matter of "praise-abuse," Bakhtin, op. cit., 458: "The virginal words of the oral vernacular which entered literary language for the first time are close, in a certain sense, to proper nouns. They are individualized and still contain a strong element of praise-abuse, which makes them suitable to nicknames." On word-formation in Rabelais (often suggestive

for Feste's "gracious fooling"), see Leo Spitzer, *Linguistics and Literary History* (Princeton, 1948).

17. William Hazlitt, *"Twelfth Night,"* in *Characters of Shakespeare's Plays* (1817).

18. Bertrand Evans, *Shakespeare's Comedies* (Oxford, 1960), 118.

19. Just as in comedy, according to Donatan principles, turns of fortune should not include the danger of death (*sine periculo vitae*, cf. Cunningham, op. cit.). Since Leibniz defined music as a species of unconscious counting or arithmetic, and music enters so prominently into *Twelfth Night* (as *musica speculativa* as well as *musica practica* – see John Hollander, "Musica mundana and *Twelfth Night"* (*English Institute Essays: Sound and Poetry*, ed. Northrop Frye (New York, 1957)), an interesting analogy begins to form between comedy, music, and the Shakespearean language of wit. In this respect, the issues of gender difference and succession return, for the action of *Twelfth Night* is simply the release of Orsino and Olivia from their single state, which cannot occur without the separating out of Viola/Cesario and Viola/Sebastian ("One face, one voice, one habit, and two persons! / A natural perspective, that is, and is not!" (V.i. 214–15)). That "one" is redeemed from both singleness and duplicity: the confounding in singleness, as Sonnet 8, with its explicit music metaphor, suggests, should turn into a harmony of "parts that thou shouldst bear," a concord of "all in one." Cf. however Marilyn French's surprising conclusion in *Shakespeare's Division of Experience* (New York, 1981) that the one not in harmony, Malvolio, wins out in the end as the embodiment of society's repressive stewardship. "Constancy is required; love must lead to marriage; and marriage must lead to procreation" (123).

20. David C. Lindberg, *Theories of Vision from Al-Kindi to Kepler* (Chicago and London, 1976), 145.

21. M.-D. Chenu, OP, *Understanding St Thomas*, as quoted by Lindberg, op. cit., 145.

22. See "The Grand Reception and Entertainment of Queen Elizabeth at Oxford in 1592," from a MS Account by Philip Stringer, printed in *Elizabethan Oxford*, ed. Charles Plummer (Oxford, 1877). Cf., on the quodlibets, the same collection of tracts, 18, and the unflattering description of such exercises as they still prevailed into the later eighteenth century, by Vicesimus Knox: *Reminiscences by Oxford Men, 1559–1850*, ed. Lilian M. Quiller Couch (Oxford, 1892), 160–7. According to J. Huizinga, *Homo Ludens* (1944), ch. 9, the "whole functioning of the medieval university was profoundly agonistic and ludic." The word "Act" was formally applied to the degree exercises which conferred the Bachelor and Master of Arts. The use of "act" in Shakespeare (as in *Hamlet* V.ii. 346 and *Winter's Tale* V.ii. 86ff.) includes that sense of the presence of a conferring authority.

23. Cf. T. H. Gaster, *Thespis: Ritual, Myth and Drama in the Ancient Near East* (New York, 1950). Chapter 2, especially, discerns in ritual dramas a uniform pattern of *kenosis*, or emptying, and *plerosis*, or filling. The twelve nights after which Shakespeare's play is named could reflect the *agon* or combat of those two tendencies: a combat to determine the character of such days, whether they are fasts or feasts, lenten (under the aegis of Malvolio) or copious. The twelve days between December 25 and January 6 have, moreover, a special relation to calendar time: they may be epagomenal or intercalary (Gaster, op. cit., 10, and cf. 369) and as such linked to an "occlusion of personality." Yet is not all fictional time intercalary? "Twelfth Night" in Shakespeare may stand for every such day or night which requires a *release* of that "lease" on life which has to be annually renewed, yet which here is a human and ever-present rather than ritually determined necessity.

4

PATRICIA PARKER

Shakespeare and rhetoric: "dilation" and "delation" in *Othello*

I

Let us begin with a textual crux. At the threshold of the great temptation scene which is often described as the hinge of the entire play, Iago begins to set Othello "on the rack" through those pauses, single words and pregnant phrases which seem to suggest something secret or withheld, a withholding which fills the Moor with the desire to hear more:

> I heard thee say even now, thou lik'st not that,
> When Cassio left my wife. What didst not like?
> And when I told thee he was of my counsel
> In my whole course of wooing, thou criedst, "Indeed!"
> And didst contract and purse thy brow together,
> As if thou then hadst shut up in thy brain
> Some horrible conceit. If thou dost love me,
> Show me thy thought.
>
> (III. iii. 109–16)

In the lines that follow in this scene, what Kenneth Burke has called Iago's rhetorical technique of "Say the Word" is, in the Folio version, referred to as "close dilations, working from the heart, / That passion cannot rule" (123–4). The fact of the appearance of these "close dilations" in F, and in all the authoritative texts of the play but one, might justify our pausing for a moment over this enigmatic phrase, if only because of the length and puzzlement of the commentary it has occasioned.[1]

In the course of editorial glosses from Warburton onwards, several meanings for "dilation" have been adduced. Steevens observes that "dilatic anciently signified delays," as in the phrase "dilacyon of vengeance" from the *Golden Legend*, while Malone cites Minsheu's famous Dictionary of 1617 to the effect that "to delate" (a variant spelling of "to dilate") meant simply, in English Renaissance usage, "to speak at large of anything." There is, however, one eccentric voice in this tradition of commentary: that of Samuel Johnson, who reads the Folio's "close dilations" as if it were "close delations," or "occult and secret accusations." Dr Johnson's reading, though clearly fascinating to subsequent editors, is frequently rejected on the grounds that, as Arden editor M. R. Ridley puts it, "there is no evidence of the use of the word in this, its Latin, sense" in Shakespeare's day. Ridley himself, puzzling over the Folio phrase and remarking that, since "it can hardly have been due to a mere blunder," whoever put it there must have "meant something by it," finally confesses that he has "very little idea what that was" and chooses the single other possible text ("close denotements") on the grounds (like Malone) that to this more neutral phrase at least, "no reasonable objection can be made."[2]

It may, however, be worth delving further into these enigmatic "close dilations," if only because the term "dilate" itself appears in two other highly significant contexts in *Othello*, both as "to speak at large" and as a form of dilatoriness or delay. The former sense – the rhetorical tradition of the dilation of discourse[3] which Shakespeare had already explicitly evoked when Egeon in *The Comedy of Errors* is asked to "dilate at full" (I. i. 122) the story of his life – figures prominently in the scene in which Othello appears accused of "witchcraft" before the Senate in Act I and tells of Desdemona's similar entreaty ("That I would all my pilgrimage dilate, / Whereof by parcels she had something heard," I. iii. 153–4). The latter – postponement or delay – appears when Iago, confronted with the need to slow down an impatient Roderigo in order to effect his plot, reminds him that "we work by wit, and not by witchcraft, / And wit depends on dilatory time" (II. iii. 372–3).

"Dilation," then, would seem to have in other important parts of the play a resonance which includes at least two of the meanings adduced by editors for the Folio's puzzling phrase. But there is even yet more reason for dwelling upon, and for the moment within, this textual crux. Though Dr Johnson's suggestion of "dilations" as "delations" or "accusations" is frequently rejected on the grounds that there is no evidence of its use in this sense in Shakespeare's time, in fact such instances abound. And the link between judicial "delation" and rhetorical amplification or "dilation" – a linking of judicial and rhetorical as old as Cicero and Quintilian – is one exploited by none other than Shakespeare himself. *Delatare* in Latin can mean "to bring before a judge, indict, accuse"; and in the variations of Renaissance English spelling, "dilate" as well as "delate" could be used both for "to amplify, or narrate" and for "to accuse," as in the (for *Othello* highly suggestive) example "dilatit of adultry" (1536) cited by the *OED*. In other words, "close dilations" would not necessarily need to be amended to "close delations," as Johnson supposed, to be capable of suggesting both meanings – amplification and accusation – in one. Indeed, at least one Renaissance text (Bishop Hall's "Away, then, ye cruel torturers of opinions, dilaters of errors, delators of your brethren") makes it clear that, even in the most serious of contexts, the two were related closely enough to be readily available for wordplay, or even pun. And in this particular instance, the very "dilaters of error" are also thereby "delators" or accusers, in a way which might be highly suggestive for that Iago who, as one critic puts it, is "virtually an archetype of the informer," or delator, in *Othello*.[4]

The textual crux and enigmatic phrase with which we began, then, might lead us not to mere puzzlement or to the necessity – and frequent editorial practice – of choosing one meaning *over* another, a process of elimination which so often presupposes a singularity of either definitive text or authoritative meaning, but rather to the possibility of reading *Othello* itself as if a phrase such as the Folio's "close dilations" might be a kind of semantic crossroads or freighted term suggestive of all three of those resonances – amplification, accusation, delay – which are so much a part of the unfolding of this particular tragedy. For "dilation" and "delation" in all of these related senses may be shown to be crucial not just at the level of single words and phrases which have been notoriously puzzling to commentators, but also at the more general level of this play's much-debated issues – from the criticisms of its passages of seemingly gratuitous amplification, "purple" rhetoric, or mere wordy filler, to its status as the most domestic of Shakespeare's tragedies, founded, as Rymer famously complained, upon a "trifle," to the classical problem of its apparent "double time" scheme.

Let us look, for example, at the resonance of a particular word. We have already observed that "dilation" and "delation" can summon up the sense both of accusation and of the provision of a narrative in response to interrogation. But what is even more important for the crossing of judicial and rhetorical in *Othello* is the fact that both depend on the provision of what were known as "circumstances" – a tradition which still survives in what we refer to as "circumstantial evidence" as well as in the basic principles of composition – and that Shakespeare himself founded a number of scenes on precisely this overlapping, or identity. "The circumstances are these," writes John Hoskins in his influential *Direccions for Speech and Style* (1599), reciting a list which, with minor variations, was repeated in countless Renaissance rhetorical handbooks: "the persons who and to whom, the matter, the intent, the time, the place, the manner, the consequences, and many more," and in echoing Bacon's oft-repeated dictum that "a way to amplify anything is . . . to examine it according to several circumstances," notes that such amplification "is more properly called *dilation*." But this detailing of "circumstances" was also the standard form of a legal indictment, as Shakespeare shows he knows only too well in Armado's dilated or wordy accusation of Costard in *Love's Labour's Lost* ("The time When? About the sixth hour . . . the ground Which? . . . the place Where? . . . ?" (I.i.231–48)) or in Autolycus's questioning of the frightened rustics in a passage which might have come straight out of descriptions of the "circumstances" most "commonly requisite in presentments before Justices of peace": "Your affairs there? what? with whom? the condition of that farthel? the place of your dwelling? your names? your ages? of what having? breeding? and any thing that is fitting to be known – discover" (*The Winter's Tale*, IV.iv.717–20).[5]

"Circumstances" dilate, then; but they may also indict. Both have to do with a discovery, uncovering, or bringing to light – the providing of information which could also enable the laying of one – and both frequently come as a response to interrogation or questioning, to someone's hunger, or demand, for narrative, as when Cymbeline, his curiosity aroused by the partial disclosure or "fierce abridgement" he has heard, demands to hear the whole story through, with all the "circumstantial branches, which / Distinction should be rich in," in order to satisfy his own "long interrogatories" (V.v.382–92), in a recognition scene which has to do with a mystery finally brought to light. The provision of such circumstances serves not only to amplify a narrative but to prove a case before a judge, including that judge who is the jealous husband of a woman "dilatit of adultry": Iago's promise to Othello soon after the "close dilations" of the temptation scene ("If imputation and strong circumstances / Which lead directly to the door of truth / Will give you satisfaction, you might have't" (III.iii.406–8)) might thus be placed beside Leontes' conviction, in the scene of Hermione's indictment, that his conjecture "lack'd sight only," since "all other circumstances / Made up to th' deed" (II.i.176–9), or beside Iachimo's urging of Posthumus to believe his wife's infidelity from the all-but-ocular proof he will provide ("my circumstances, / Being so near the truth as I will make them, / Must first induce you to believe" (*Cymbeline*, II.iv.61–3)).

Dilation, and delation, by "circumstance," however, not only links amplification and accusation in ways highly suggestive for *Othello*, but is intimately related to the other sense of "dilation" – as "delay." Minsheu gives under "circumstance" not only "a qualitie that accompanieth a thing, as time, place, person, etc." but also "circuit of words, compasses, or going about the bush," a sense which Shakespeare exploits both elsewhere and in the opening lines of the play itself, when Iago complains of the putting off of his "suit" (I.i.9) by the wordy evasion of Othello's "bumbast circumstance, / Horribly stuff'd with epithites of war" (13–14).[6] And this fuller resonance of "circumstance" – as the means, variously, of dilation, delation and delay – pervades a number of passages in *Othello*, from the Moor's curiously inflated "purple passage" of farewell to the "Pride, pomp, and circumstance of glorious war" (III.iii.

354) in a speech which dilates upon these very "circumstances" ("the plumed troops," "the neighing steed," "the spirit-stirring drum") to Iago's promise to make Othello a witness to Cassio's confession ("For I will make him tell the tale anew: / Where, how, how oft, how long ago, and when / He hath, and is again to cope your wife" (IV.i. 84–6)), to Cassio's fear of the interposition of delay in the pressing of his own "suit" ("Or breed itself so out of circumstances . . ." (III.iii. 13–18)), to Emilia's challenge to whatever "busy and insinuating rogue" has slandered Desdemona to prove his accusation ("Why should he call her whore? Who keeps her company? What place? what time? what form? what likelihood?" (IV.ii. 137–8)), to those lines at the end of Act III which have puzzled commentators but which – given that Cassio is engaged in attending on the "general" rather than (as in a favorite Shakespearean pun) on the circumstantial or particular, as well as submitting an impatient Bianca to further evasion and delay – also appear to pull its "circumstanc'd" within this orbit of association:

> *Bianca:* Leave you? Wherefore?
> *Cassio:* I do attend here on the general,
> And think it no addition, nor my wish,
> To have him see me woman'd. . . .
> 'Tis but a little way that I can bring you,
> For I attend here; but I'll see you soon.
> *Bianca:* 'Tis very good; I must be circumstanc'd.
> (III.iv. 192–201)

This same Bianca will later be summoned by Iago either to acquit herself or to stand accused ("Come, mistress, you must tell's another tale" (V.i. 125)) or, in other words, to be "circumstanc'd" in another sense as well. But the "circumstancing" of Bianca here, at the end of Act III, makes her by implication an adjunct or "addition" not just to Cassio but to the "general," a function which both catches the movement of the play from great things to small, general to particular, and also, as feminist critics of the play have seen, ultimately attaches to that Desdemona who, even as she is portrayed as the general's "general" (II.iii. 315), becomes increasingly an "adjunct," whose minute particulars increasingly preoccupy the "general" himself.[7]

2

Let us proceed from this preamble, then, to a reading of the play. It has often been remarked what an extraordinary emphasis is given in *Othello* to narrative and the demand for narrative, to the relating of a story or report. But what has still to be perceived is the relation of this demand to the crossing of rhetorical, judicial and temporal within the structure of "dilation" which the play itself so insistently exploits. The demand for narrative as the demand to know, as a response to an inquiry or interrogation, frequently calls attention both to the provision of "circumstances" and to the ferreting out of something enigmatic, hid or closed – a fact which gives to the play's oft-repeated "What is the matter?" the sense, as often elsewhere in Shakespeare, of a *materia* to be both enlarged upon and disclosed. Othello's suspicion of the "close dilations" of Iago in the temptation scene comes first from the way the Ensign seems to "contract and purse" his brow, as if he had "shut up" some "monster" in his "thought," too "hideous to be shown" (III. iii. 106–8). And the Moor's consequent demand to hear the whole – his suspicion that "This honest creature, doubtless, / See and knows more, much more, than he unfolds" (242–3) – recalls the conventionally familiar description of dilation or amplification as an "unfolding" of something at first hermetically "wrapt up" or closed.[8] But the play itself opens with a reference to something secret and, to the curious audience at least, unknown, as well as to a "purse," whose opening Shakespeare elsewhere links directly with the dilating or disclosing of a "matter" (*The Two Gentlemen of Verona*, I. i. 130, "Open your purse, that the money and the matter may be both at once deliver'd," or *Hamlet* on the wordy dilations of Osric: "His purse is empty already: all's golden words are spent" (V. ii. 131)); and it ends both with Iago's refusal to open that particular orifice again ("Demand me nothing; what you know, you know: / From this time forth I never will speak word" (V. ii. 303–4)) and with the promise of a further report (Lodovico's "Myself will straight aboard, and to the state / This heavy act with heavy heart relate" (370–1)).

The single most striking instance of the demand for narrative in Act I, however, both explicitly evokes the rhetorical tradition of the "dilation" of discourse and places that dilation within the context of a "delation" or accusation – Othello, accused by Brabantio before the judicial setting of the Venetian senate, and offering his story when the Duke observes that the circumstances of Brabantio's accusation are too "thin."[9] Othello's narrative is both a response to the senate's interrogations and a recall of Brabantio's own earlier desire to hear all through ("Her father lov'd me, oft invited me; / Still question'd me the story of my life . . . I ran it through, even from my boyish days / To th' very moment that he bade me tell it" (I. iii. 127–33)):

> It was my hint to speak – such was my process –
> And of the Cannibals that each other eat,
> The Anthropophagi, and men whose heads
> Do grow beneath their shoulders. These things to hear
> Would Desdemona seriously incline;
> But still the house affairs would draw her thence,
> Which ever as she could with haste dispatch,
> She'ld come again, and with a greedy ear
> Devour up my discourse. Which I observing,

Took once a pliant hour, and found good means
To draw from her a prayer of earnest heart
That I would all my pilgrimage dilate,
Whereof by parcels she had something heard,
But not intentively [F₂, "distinctively"]

(I. iii. 142–55)

The Second Folio's controversial "distinctively" would only strengthen the rhetorical resonance of "dilation" here, as in Cymbeline's demand to hear all the "circumstantial branches, which / Distinction should be rich in" (V. v. 382–3). The lines, as has often been remarked, summon up the figure not just of a demand for narrative but of a "greedy ear" which, juxtaposed with "Cannibals," suggests a hunger which will become more ominous when Iago begins to "abuse" Othello's increasingly insatiable "ear," just as their echo of Aeneas's "travellours tale" (F₁, 139) to Dido summons up a memory of a hunger for narrative potentially disastrous in its consequences. Character-based criticism would typically move from the description of Desdemona's "greedy ear" – as from those passages of Othello's seemingly uncharacteristic inflated rhetoric – to suggest what it reveals about some kind of flaw within the character concerned. But the chief import of such an image, in a scene whose "dilate" is to be echoed in Act III, might be not to reveal depths in Desdemona which would enable a psychologizing of what finally happens to her, but rather to introduce early on a reminder of the more ominous effect of such narrative dilation from an important Shakespearean intertext, and to anticipate the "witching" effect of Iago's larger unfolding of what his "close dilations" have only in "parcels," or in part, revealed.[10]

Othello's rhetorical "dilation" in this scene is rendered apparently innocent by its outcome: dilation by "circumstances" in the judicial and accusatory setting of Act I leads to acquittal, as part of that Act's oft-remarked comic structure. But the dilation which here takes place in the context of wooing, winning, and acquittal from the law becomes, after the "close dilations" of the great temptation scene, a witching of the ear by "circumstances" which prove an accusation or "delation" rather than dismissing it, and in which the accuser father becomes that instrument of "Justice" (V. ii. 17) who is Othello himself.

Othello's dilation of his narrative, however, also involves the interposing of a pause or delay, as Rymer's complaint against its tedious amplification suggests, or as the scene itself repeatedly emphasizes in its surrounding reminders of the "haste-post-haste" matter (I. ii. 37) of the war against the Turks.[11] And it is precisely such a slowing down which not only gives to so many of the play's speeches the sensation of having lasted longer than they have, but which also emerges in the next scene in which dilation is explicitly invoked, in lines crucial to the tension between delay and dispatch within the play as a whole:

Roderigo: I do follow here in the chase, not like a hound that hunts, but
one that fills up the cry. My money is almost spent, I have been
to-night exceedingly well cudgell'd; and I think the issue will
be, I shall have so much experience for my pains; and so, with
no money at all and a little more wit, return again to Venice.

Iago: How poor are they that have not patience!
What wound did ever heal but by degrees?
Thou know'st we work by wit, and not by witchcraft,
And wit depends on dilatory time. . . .
Nay, get thee gone. (*Exit Roderigo.*) Two things are to be done:
My wife must move for Cassio to her mistress –
I'll set her on –
Myself a while to draw the Moor apart,
And bring him jump when he may Cassio find
Soliciting his wife. Ay, that's the way;
Dull not device by coldness and delay.

(II. iii. 363–88)

Iago's emphasis on "patience" and slow working by "degrees" directly
echoes the advice given earlier to Brabantio by the Duke, whose dilated or
wordy *sententiae* are offered as a "grise or step" (I. iii. 200), while Roderigo's
image of a hunt – both of its goal and of simply filling up the space between –
recalls that of the earlier scene in Act II ("If this poor trash of Venice, whom I
trace / For his quick hunting, stand the putting on" (II. i. 303–4)), in lines
where Iago also proceeds with the gradual invention of his own end or
objective, step by step ("'Tis here; but yet confus'd" (311)).[12] Iago's stage-
managing of Roderigo (a feature not in Cinthio, but in *Othello* a reflection of
his manipulation of the Moor and of the larger plot as well) depends on
alternately delaying and inciting him, on both promising and putting off the
completion of his "suit" – a combination suggested in the juxtaposition
within these single lines of an invocation of "dilatory time" and a determination not to "dull . . . device by coldness and delay." "Thou know'st we work
by wit, and not by witchcraft" links this reminder of dilation as delay to that
verbal dilation which Othello earlier protests is the only "witchcraft" (I. iii.
169) he had used. And the entire passage is a crucial transition between
Othello's delaying narrative in Act I and the "close dilations" of Act III, when
it is Othello's own impatient demand for "satisfaction" which must be
met, and where Iago counsels his master both to delay the completion of
Cassio's suit ("hold him off awhile" (III. iii. 248)) and to "keep time in all"
(IV. i. 92).

"Dilation," then, both in the scene in Act I where the "post-post-haste"
dispatch of the business of the state (iii. 46) must pause while Othello tells his
tale, and in Iago's reminder of "dilatory time" in Act II, has to do with some
form of postponement or putting off. And this link between verbal dilation

and temporal delay itself may provide a perspective on other scenes as well. At the end of the Act which includes both Othello's dilation and Desdemona's plea to be allowed to "unfold" her own story (I.iii.243–4), Iago argues Roderigo out of the precipitate conclusion of suicide ("I will incontinently drown myself" (I.iii.305)) by reminding him that Desdemona's marriage is not necessarily an ending ("There are many events in the womb of time which will be deliver'd" (I.iii.369–70)), just as Desdemona will later counter Othello's wish for end, perfection, or conclusion ("If it were now to die, / 'Twere now to be most happy" (II.i.189–90)) with a reminder of process, dilation, or "increase" ("The heavens forbid / But that our loves and comforts should increase / Even as our days do grow" (II.i.193–5)), in a part of the play which repeatedly calls attention to a consummation both imminent and postponed. Between these two points, Act II itself opens with a scene whose delayed climax – Othello's arrival at shore in Cyprus – involves a lengthy exchange between Desdemona and Iago which critics have frequently felt to be unnecessarily wordy bombast, padding, or filler, like the scenes of "interlarding" put in by other playwrights simply to eke out the time of the play itself.[13] The scene, however, goes out of its way to call attention both to the space of "expectancy" (41) and to its own wordiness in ways which suggest that, in a play which is elsewhere so preoccupied with words, with verbal dilation, and with waiting or delay, this might be a piece not of dramatic miscalculation but of design, part of the play's larger emphasis on what Desdemona, when the consummation of her marriage is put off, calls a "heavy interim" (I.iii.258). For the space of delay or waiting here will, once the tragedy proper begins, become that even heavier interim or tormenting middle state before Othello's demand for certainty and conclusion can be satisfied, a link imagistically suggested when Othello himself, having murdered Desdemona in the very bed whose "wedding sheets" (IV.ii.105) recall that earlier consummation, proclaims: "Here is my journey's end, here is my butt, / And very sea-mark of my utmost sail" (V.ii.267–8).

The scene, in fact, even calls attention to a particular form of amplification or dilation by "circumstances" which can come only to the "door" of truth (III.iii.407) – that of the *blazon*:

> Montano: But, good lieutenant, is your general wiv'd?
> Cassio: Most fortunately: he hath achiev'd a maid
> That paragons description and wild fame:
> One that excels the quirks of blazoning pens,
> And in th' essential vesture of creation
> Does tire the ingener.
>
> (II.i.60–5)

The Folio's "ingeniuer" or inventor highlights both the activity and the potential insufficiency of "invention" even before Iago's own ominous figure for his *inventio* ("my invention / Comes from my pate as birdlime does from frieze" (125–6)), in lines which recall his earlier invocation (I. iii. 369–70) of dilation or unfolding as a bringing to birth ("my Muse labors, / And thus she is deliver'd" (II. i. 127–8)). The wordy paradoxes (138) which he proceeds to deliver again echo those "sentences" which in rhetoric serve to amplify, but which Brabantio observes are only "words" ("words are words; I never yet did hear / That the bruis'd heart was pierced through the ear" (I. iii. 216–19)). And Cassio's reminder of the insufficiency of that form of verbal amplification known as the *blazon* is followed precisely by Iago's extended rhetorical description of women in this scene of waiting or delay, a description whose climax – after a set piece amplified over several lines – is proclaimed by Desdemona herself to be a "most lame and impotent conclusion" (161). What is here, however, ominously termed the very "vouch" or testimony of "malice itself" (146) anticipates Iago's later "dilations" in the temptation scene, a description or merely verbal report of this same Desdemona in which nothing but words alone will lead Othello into a swoon, in lines which reaffirm the insufficiency of words just at the moment of their greatest power over him, and which end in a kind of ironic *blazon* ("It is not words that shakes me thus. Pish! Noses, ears and lips . . . [he falls down]" (IV. i. 41–3)).[14]

3

The scene of Othello's dilated narrative before the senate in Act I unfolds, as we have said, in an ultimately comic context where the provision of "circumstances" provides the means of acquittal. But Act I itself also provides instances of a more sinister or dubious reporting of events not present to the eye, or happening off-stage, from the rousing of Brabantio through mere description to the conflicting reports of the Turkish fleet in Scene iii. And even before the "close dilations" of the temptation scene, *Othello* keeps our attention not only on the provision of narrative but also on the demand for "circumstances" in response to an interrogation in the scene of the night brawl in Act II, where it is now Othello rather than Brabantio who demands repeatedly to know "What is the matter?" (II. iii. 164, 176, 192) and to have an "answer" (196) to his interrogations ("What . . . How . . . who . . . ?" (164–70)), to ferret out the circumstances of an action he has not been able to see with his own eyes.

It is, of course, the accusation and judgment of Cassio in this scene which leads directly to those "close dilations" which as amplifications only partial, "close," or incomplete have as their immediate effect the catching of Othello's own "greedy ear," just as the story heard only in "parcels" had earlier filled Desdemona with the desire that he would "all" his narrative "dilate." So insistent is the resonance of rhetorical dilation or "unfolding" as the temptation scene proceeds – as it is, indeed, throughout the play as a ıole – that we might begin to speculate on why this might be so in this Shakespearean tragedy in particular. Rhetorical dilation or *copia* is a principle of both invention and "increase," just as signs are notorious minims, capable of suggesting so much more beyond themselves. But as *Othello* frequently reminds us, jealousy is also founded on a principle of enlargement ("Trifles light as air / Are to the jealous confirmations strong / As proofs of holy writ" (III.iii. 322–4)). And the Ensign Iago's "dilations" open up a sense of something much larger than can be unfolded or shown, a disproportion finally figured in the "trifle" of the handkerchief (*Desdemona:* "What's the matter?" / *Othello:* "That handkerchief" (V.ii. 47–8)), a matter or *materia* both enlarged and itself the visual evidence of Desdemona's crime, a showing forth or exposure to the eye of something which cannot in itself be seen. Iago's "close dilations" neither completely hide nor completely reveal – like, indeed, a *jalousie* – and this sense of movement from a partial tantalizing glimpse to a fuller disclosure is part of one of the most influential descriptions of rhetorical dilation itself: that it is, as Erasmus remarks in the *De Copia*, "just like displaying some object for sale first of all through a lattice or inside a wrapping, and then unwrapping it and opening it out and displaying it more fully to the *gaze*" ("ac totam *oculis* exponat").[15]

The plot of jealousy in *Othello*, moreover, is one which not only repeatedly invokes the language of rhetorical amplification or dilation, but also one which substitutes such unfolding for more direct seeing or "ocular proof" ("Villain, be sure thou prove my love a whore; / Be sure of it. Give me the ocular proof" (III.iii. 359–60)). And the sense of dilation by "circumstances" as a transforming of the ear into a substitute *oculus* or eye, of providing that form of vivid description which in Latin is *evidentia* but which Puttenham translates more ominously into English as "Counterfeit Representation," runs through the entire rhetorical tradition.[16] It is significant, then, that when Othello makes his demand for "satisfaction" – "Make me to see't; or (at the least) so prove it / That the probation bear no hinge, nor loop, / To hang a doubt on" (III.iii. 364–6) – Iago graphically represents to him the impossibility of a more direct gazing ("Would you, the supervisor, grossly gape on? / Behold her topp'd?" (395–6)), just as he had roused Brabantio with nothing more substantial than that vivid description of "an old black ram" tupping his "white ewe" (I.i. 88–9), and offers instead precisely that form of "evidence" which is *evidentia*, those "strong circumstances / Which lead directly to the door of truth" (III.iii. 406–7). Dilation as an unfolding or showing forth of what was secret, closed or hid involves in so many of its charged descriptions an almost prurient sense of discovery, disclosure, or exposing to the eye. Erasmus's "unwrapping it and opening it out and displaying it more fully to the gaze" is joined by Peacham's description of dilation as "an apt and ready forme of speech to open the bosome of nature and to shew her branches, to that end they may be viewed and looked upon, discerned and knowen."[17] And both are only too suggestive beside the language of *Othello* as it moves forward from the insinuations of Iago in this scene – a showing forth of the private or "behind doors" suggested in the *double entendres* which surround the handkerchief itself, that "thing" which Emilia offers to her husband (III. iii. 301–2).

Such "ocular demonstration" or vivid description also, however, elides the distinction between false report and true, since it is capable of depicting fictional – or purely invented – events as if they were actually present before the eye. It is crucial to remember that such dilation by description, or counterfeit representation, is for this reason the master trope and illusion of drama itself, just as it is – as so often in *Othello* as it proceeds – the rhetorical instrument of messengers in tragedy, of the bearers of reports of what cannot be directly seen or shown. Iago is not only the "delator" or accuser of Desdemona but, as has been so often remarked, the dramatist within the play itself, not just in his manipulation of haste and "dilatory time," but also in his provision of such vivid details and reports – to Brabantio, to Roderigo, and ultimately to Othello himself. And this dilation by circumstances will be as well the delation of Desdemona which will enable Iago, like that mysterious "Signior Angelo" – the messenger of another off-stage event in Act I – to put his hearer in "false *gaze*" (I. iii. 19).[18]

This link between that aspect of dilation which is the provision of vivid details and the ability – like jealousy itself – to create "much" out of "little" (*ex paucis sententiis plures factae, ex paucis membris numerosiora*)[19] might lead us, finally, to suggest a relation between this play's insistent reminders of rhetorical dilation and the famous problem of its apparent "double time" scheme, the fact that there is simply no time for Desdemona to have had the "stol'n hours of lust" of which Othello suspects her (III. iii. 338), or to be guilty of his accusation that "she with Cassio hath the act of shame / A thousand times committed" (V. ii. 211–12). *Othello* observes the dramatic unities of time and place to an extent unusual in Shakespeare, and part of the sheer space given to narrative "unfolding" or report results from the fact that, in this contracted space, so much less can be directly seen on stage and must therefore be represented in words. Rymer complained of the tedious length of Othello's own narrative dilation – his vivid description of off-stage and hence unseen events – in Act I. But it may be that, far from committing the lapse of which Rymer accuses him, Shakespeare may instead very early on in *Othello* be calling attention to the difference between narrative time, or dilation, and the more compressed dramatic time in which there may not be time, or space, for the whole story to be revealed.

Cymbeline's desire to hear all of a story's "circumstantial branches," like Desdemona's hunger to hear Othello "dilate" all of a narrative she has heard only in part, comes as a result of the tantalizing "fierce abridgement" he has heard, and his frustration is that the "time" and "place" will not be large enough for such enlargement. In its dramatic context, this sounds very much like the problem of abridgement, of contracted time and place, which is the mode of drama itself – a space in which the "circumstances" or multiple details can only be suggested. The rhetorical handbooks repeatedly speak of dilation or amplification by circumstances as a means of suggesting a multitude of details behind or within a single brief sentence or phrase – as when a contracted general statement (such as "the city was taken by storm") is "opened up" to reveal that crowd of vivid details ("flames pouring through houses and temples, the crash of falling buildings") which so effectively move the passions of a judge.[20] In *Othello*, where Iago's "close dilations" function to suggest that so much more lies behind what has been seen or shown, the effect of that disproportion which we call "double time" might be not just the combination in the play of a sense of haste and a contrasting sense of waiting or delay, but also the creation of that rhetorical technique which, like jealousy itself, is capable of suggesting precisely such multiplicity. Francis Bacon, ever conscious of the potentially specious and even dangerous effect of such "dilation," notes the darker side of its ability to generate much out of little: "It often carries the minde away, yea, it deceyveth the sence," leaving "a suspition, as if more might be sayde then is expressed," a description of the power of "circumstances" to "deceive" which might well be set beside the inferences and insinuations of Iago in this play.[21] *Othello* may be not only the most domestic, or "trifling," of all of Shakespeare's tragedies, but the single most powerful Renaissance instance of the tragic potential of this technique.

4

The effect of Iago's only partial or "close dilations" is to put Othello in that tormenting middle state or "heavy interim" of uncertainty and doubt ("I swear 'tis better to be much abus'd / Than but to know't a little" (III.iii.336–7)) – a state of partial knowledge or half-glimpses which leads to his demand for certainty and proof ("I'll have some proof . . . / I'll not endure it. Would I were satisfied!" (III.iii.385–90)). As the temptation scene progresses, what is there termed a "foregone conclusion" (428) increasingly takes the form of a jumping to conclusion, of a proleptic or already accomplished closure in which the loss of Desdemona herself slips from future to past tense ("She's gone. I am abus'd, and my relief / Must be to loathe her" (III.iii.267–8); "Now do I see 'tis true. Look here, Iago, / All my fond love thus do I blow to heaven . . . / 'Tis gone" (444–6)); in which the imagery is increasingly of an impatient and even compulsive rushing to end or conclusion ("Like to the Pontic Sea . . . " (453–60)), or of those extremes of black and white, heaven and hell, which ironically echo Brabantio's earlier demand to be "satisfied"; and in which the sense of a closed system, or collapse of the space between a question and its answer, is echoed by the seemingly gratuitous scene of

wordplay which immediately follows this scene (*Desdemona*
inquire him out, and be edified by report?" *Clown:* "I will catechi:
for him, that is, make questions, and *by them* answer" (III.iv. 14–

A virtual replaying-in-little of the demand for narrative, in an
accusation or "delation," and as a means of ferreting out the ___, is
provided in the course of the play's final Acts – both in Emilia's demand for
the "circumstances" that would prove Desdemona's guilt (IV.ii. 137–8) and
in Iago's promise to Othello that he shall overhear Cassio's confession in
detail ("Where, how, how oft, how long ago, and when / He hath, and is again
to cope your wife" (IV.i. 84–6)), in a scene which repeatedly calls attention to
the unfolding of a tale ("I will make him tell the tale anew . . . Now he
importunes him / To tell it o'er . . . now he begins the story"). Desdemona's
desire to have Othello dilate his narrative was fanned by her hearing only
"parcels" of a conversation she could not hear, at first, in full; but in contrast
to Desdemona, what Othello gets is only those partial or "close dilations" on
which he constructs the whole assumption of her guilt, rather than that fuller
disclosure which, as the scene of her death reminds us, Cassio is never
summoned to provide ("his mouth is stopp'd" (V.ii. 71)). In the temptation
scene itself, when Iago says that, though he cannot provide direct or "ocular
proof," if "imputation and strong circumstances / Which lead directly to the
door of truth / Will give you satisfaction, you might ha't" (III.iii. 406–8),
more than one reader has surmised that Othello in this image is led in
imagination to stand outside the closed bedroom door.[22] After the scene of
Cassio's supposed confession, and hence of the demanded proof ("be sure
thou prove my love a whore" (III.iii. 359)), Othello goes beyond the "door"
to which "circumstances" alone could lead him, in that scene in Desdemona's
chamber in which she has indeed changed places with the Bianca of which
Cassio had earlier spoken, and in which Othello now treats her as that
"subtile whore" (IV.ii. 21) who keeps her "chamber" secret.

There is, finally, as the tragedy moves towards its ending, an increasing
sense of the need to keep "dilation" itself under control, both to prevent
further amplification or unfolding and to bring an end to delay. Othello's
demand for "proof" and "satisfaction" not only foreshortens time in its rush
to conclusion (his "Within these three days let me hear thee say / That Cassio's
not alive," answered by Iago's "My friend *is dead*; 'tis *done* at your request"
(III.iii. 472–4)); but in the scenes leading up to Desdemona's death, the
terrible sense of being "on the rack" of uncertainty or doubt is joined by a
determination not to allow time for further discourse ("Get me some poison,
Iago, this night. I'll not expostulate with her, lest her body and beauty
unprovide my mind again" (IV.i. 204–6)). The final scenes multiply the sense
of both a waiting or delay and of impatience with it – from Cassio's desire
"not [to] be delay'd" in the satisfaction of his "suit" (III.iv. 110–14) and
Desdemona's counsel of "patience" immediately following the temptation

scene, to Bianca's complaint of the "tedious" waiting upon Cassio in the scene in which she "must be circumstanc'd" (III. iv. 201), to Roderigo's frustration with Iago's continuing delay ("thou doffest me with some device" (IV. ii. 175)) and his final determination to "no longer endure it" (178).

Iago's plot, then, depends not only on "dilatory time" and on those "close dilations" which lead Othello to suspect that he knows more than he "unfolds," but finally also on keeping dilation – in both senses – under strict control, on moving quickly enough both to prevent Roderigo from making himself "known" directly to Desdemona (IV. ii. 197) and to forestall any further "unfolding" ("the Moor / May unfold me to him" (V. i. 21)). This sense of the need to limit "dilation" as the play moves towards its tragic ending includes the invocation of the misogynist topos of stopping the mouths of women and their proverbial *copia verborum* – a topos significantly evoked much earlier, in that scene of verbal dilation and delay on shore at Cyprus (II. i. 100–12), and kept in mind through Desdemona's pledge to Cassio to "talk" her husband "out of patience" in his cause (III. iii. 22–6): it extends, as *Othello* moves towards that end, from the call to keep Bianca from "railing" in the street, to Iago's command to Emilia to "speak within door" and "charm" her "tongue," to the violent and literal stopping of the mouth of Desdemona in her death.[23] It also involves the invocation of yet another form of controlling the extent of dilation, a recapitulation of the sense of strict linear movement from beginning to end, cause to consequence, which pervades the language of the play as a whole, from the punning "sentences" of Act I which are a form not just of verbal amplification but also of "doom," a syntax of movement toward what the play will term its own "bloody period" (V. ii. 358); to Iago's repeated manipulation of the model of sequence or succession, of movement from a premise or "position" to a conclusion; to the simultaneously logical, discursive and judicial resonance of the "cause" ("It is the cause, it is the cause, my soul" (V. ii. 1)) from which Othello finally proceeds to that "period."[24] Dilation in the handbooks is a principle of fertility, *copia*, and increase: but the prescriptions for it – including the forms of its marshalling in the service of a cause, accusation or proof – repeatedly caution towards its ordering or disposition as at least in part a means of keeping that potential fertility, or expansion, within bounds. And the controlled linearity of the movement from cause to consequence, beginning to end, is part of the tragic momentum of *Othello*'s own culminating scenes, a momentum which distinguishes it, as tragedy, from a romance like *The Winter's Tale*, which shares with it the motif of jealousy and its jumping to conclusions, but then provides a dilated interval or second chance, an extension or enlargement which ultimately averts that tragic consequence.

Iago's plot as a whole, then, involves what we might call – in that term suggested by the Folio's controversial text – a technique of "close dilations," an unfolding just far enough to suggest much more than can be shown, and then, in the final Acts, a countermovement to dilation, the prevention both of further discourse and of delay. The tragedy's final scene both brings the movement from cause to consequence to its final tragic end and provides to Othello's ear, only when it is too late, the details of a larger unfolding, as Roderigo's "letters" are found and Emilia refuses, finally, to "hold [her] peace" (218–22). The only respite or delay of doom and "justice" offered to Desdemona in this scene is for the purpose of confession (V.ii.54–7), a confession in which Othello himself assumes the role of that power whose judgment is traditionally put off for such a purpose.[25] And the play's ending virtually heaps up its instances of discourse withheld or demanded and discourse as only temporarily putting off – in Iago's definitive refusal to speak (V.ii.303–4), in the reiteration of the judicial power of the state to force that narrative from him ("Torments will ope your lips" (305)), and finally in that speech in which Othello himself, as in the dilation of his story in Act I, momentarily enacts a pause ("Soft you; a word or two" (338)) before the "bloody period" (358) of his suicide.

The controlling or repressing of dilation as the play moves to its own ending has what might almost be seen as its logical conclusion in Iago's "Demand me nothing; what you know, you know" (303) – a withholding of further discourse which has caught the hungry ear of critics determined to ferret out the secret of the Ensign's apparently motiveless malignity; while the play's concluding line – its promise of still more relation or report – places the emphasis yet once again on the telling, or repetition, of a tale, to listeners not present at the events themselves. "Dilation" and its controlling is, much more centrally than has been recognized, a feature of that self-reflexiveness which Calderwood has called Shakespearean "metadrama," not just a strategy of the plays themselves but a partial index to those differences we call distinctions of "genre." In comedy – such as *The Comedy of Errors*, which Othello's narrative dilation in this play's comic opening Act recalls – it is frequently a principle of respite and reprieve from law and judgment, however marshaled towards closure in a final recognition scene. In *Othello*, the coincidence of dilation with delation – of amplification with accusation – comes something closer to what Derrida calls the demand for narrative as the power of the police, that form of disclosure or bringing to light which Shakespeare elsewhere links with comic representatives of the law, but which here becomes something much more powerful, and sinister, in its effect.[26]

Approaching the language of Shakespeare's plays is often a matter of exercising the critic's own native wit or word-wariness, often inspired guess. More historical investigations of its immersion in the language of rhetoric have all too often, at least until recently (and in work inspired in part by the return to rhetoric in modern theory), been restricted to refuting the charge of Shakespeare's small Latin and less Greek, or simply to listing a multitude of tropes and devices, without exploring the larger implications of their presence within specific plays. Rhetoric in the Renaissance is inextricably embedded in other discourses – of logic and politics, of theology and the ideology of sexual difference:[27] when it speaks not only of dilation, or of fertile *copia,* but of *ordo* and "distribution," it needs to be heard on all of these levels, for it is a language which Shakespeare knew intimately enough both to manipulate and, frequently, to undermine. For the critic, familiarity with it, and investigations such as the present one, are only the beginning.

Notes

1. The text for all quotations from Shakespeare is *The Riverside Shakespeare* (Boston, 1974), unless otherwise noted. Kenneth Burke's "*Othello*: an essay to illustrate a method" (*Hudson Review*, 4, 2 (Summer 1951), 165–203) is, among other things, a pioneering investigation of rhetoric in relation to this play.

2. *The Plays of William Shakespeare* (London, 1813), vol. 19, is a useful source of early editorial glosses on the Folio's "close dilations." See also M. R. Ridley's extended note in the Arden edition of *Othello*, III. iii. 127. "Close denotements" is the text of the earliest Quarto.

3. I have explored this tradition and its relevance to structure and wordplay in *The Comedy of Errors, A Midsummer Night's Dream,* and *All's Well That Ends Well* in "Anagogic metaphor: breaking down the wall of partition," in E. Cook *et al.* (eds), *Centre and Labyrinth: Essays in Honour of Northrop Frye* (Toronto, 1983), 38–58; and "Dilation and delay: Renaissance matrices" (*Poetics Today*, 5, 3 (1984), 519–35). See also the discussion of "dilation," "partition," and "division" in T. W. Baldwin, *William Shakspere's Small Latine & Lesse Greeke,* 2 vols (Urbana, 1944), esp. II, 109–14 and 315–21, and Sister Miriam Joseph, *Shakespeare's Use of the Arts of Language* (New York, 1947), esp. 111–16.

4. Robert B. Heilman, *Magic in the Web* (Lexington, 1956), 63. See, for "dilators of error," Bishop Joseph Hall's *Christian Moderation* (1640) ed. Ward, 38/1. Steevens cites "without delacion" (i.e. delay) from *Candlemas Day* as well as the variant "dilacyon." The *OED* cites under "delate" three Renaissance uses of the term as "to accuse, bring a charge against, impeach, to inform against," including "dilatit of adultry"; under the meaning of "to report, inform of (an offence, crime, fault)," Ben Jonson's *Volpone* II. vi ("They may delate / My slacknesse to my patron"), and under "delation," "delatory," and "delator" ("an informer, a secret or professional accuser") a good number of Renaissance examples. For the variant spelling "delate" for "dilate," as "to speak at large" or amplify, see, for example, the 1581 edition of Thomas Howell's *Devises* ("Some . . . with delayes the matter will delate") in the Clarendon Press edition (Oxford, 1906), 53, or Nashe's *Piers Penilesse* (London, 1592 edn), 11, "Experience reproves me for a foole, for delating on so manifest a case."

5. See Abraham Fraunce, *The Lawiers Logike* (1588), 44; John Hoskins, *Directions for Speech and Style*, ed. Hoyt H. Hudson (Princeton, 1935), 22; Thomas Wilson's *Arte of Rhetoric* (1553), fol. 72–3; and Henry Peacham's *Garden of Eloquence* (1593 edn), 164–7.

6. John Minsheu, *A Guide into the Tongues* (1617). For examples of Shakespeare's use of "circumstance" in various senses, see the simultaneously judicial rhetoric

and tedious dilation of Polonius (*Hamlet*, II. ii. 127–8: "As they fell out by time, by means, and place, / All given to mine ear"; and 157–9, "If circumstances lead me, I will find / Where truth is hid, though it were hid indeed within the centre"); *Troilus and Cressida*, III. iii. 112–14 ("I do not strain at the position – / It is familiar – but at the author's drift, / Who in his circumstance expressly proves . . ."); the recognition scene in *Twelfth Night* ("Do not embrace me till each circumstance / Of place, time, fortune, do cohere and jump / That I am Viola" (V. i. 251–3)); *The Two Gentlemen of Verona*, I. i. 36–7; *Much Ado*'s "circumstances short'ned (for she has been too long a-talking of), the lady is disloyal" (III. ii. 102–4); *The Merchant of Venice*, I. i. 153–4 ("You . . . herein spend but time / To wind about my love with circumstance"); and the play on the "Lie Circumstantial and the Lie Direct" in *As You Like It* (V. iv. 81). "Circumstances" could either acquit the accused or find him guilty, as Thomas Wilson reminds us in *The Arte of Rhetorique*, fol. 62 – a dual possibility Shakespeare exploits in the intricate rhetorical parallelism of *Richard III*, I. i. 75–80.

7. For circumstance, epithet or "addition," and various forms of description all understood within the division between subjects and adjuncts, see Joseph, op. cit., 119–30, 318–22. Shakespeare's pervasive play on "general" and "particular," in *Troilus and Cressida* and elsewhere, is specifically associated with the rhetorical tradition of amplifying a general statement by detailing its attendant circumstances in Bottom's confusion of the two in *A Midsummer Night's Dream*, I. ii. 1–3 (a passage whose recall of a popular handbook example of dilation I have described in "Anagogic metaphor," 47). This language is echoed, I would suggest, in Iago's advice to Cassio on how to "recover the general again" (II. iii. 272), and in his assertion of the reversal of position between Othello and Desdemona ("Our general's wife is now the general – I may say so in this respect, for that he hath devoted and given up himself to the contemplation, mark and denotement of her parts and graces" (314–18)).

8. See, for example, George Puttenham's *Arte of English Poesie* (1589), 230–1, and Desdemona's plea for an "ear" to her "unfolding" in I. iii. 244. A quick glance at the Concordance entry for "unfold" will indicate Shakespeare's familiarity with the close link between this word and the rhetorical tradition of the dilation of discourse. For a powerful discussion of the demand for narrative in *Othello*, see Stephen Greenblatt, *Renaissance Self-Fashioning* (Chicago, 1980), 232–54.

9. "To vouch this is no proof, / Without more wider and more overt test / Than these thin habits and poor likelihoods" (I. iii. 106–8), a figure repeated in Iago's "this may help to thicken other proofs / That do demonstrate thinly" (III. iii. 430–1) in the temptation scene. The figure of "circumstances" as not the essence or substance but its clothing was conventional (see *OED*, "circumstance," meaning 8) and was exploited by Shakespeare with reference to amplification by division and to vivid description, in *Much Ado* (V. i. 225) and *Henry V* (IV. ii. 53–4). See Joseph, op. cit., 318–19, and 2 *Henry VI* ("He that loves himself / Hath not essentially, but by circumstance / The name of valor" (V. ii. 39–40)). The figure emerges in *Othello* in its punning on "suits," and in the suggestion of a gap between descriptive or subordinate "circumstance" and substance or essence, as in II. i. 62–4 and IV. i. 16–18, with reference to the "handkerchief."

10. The "witching" effect of narrative in the *Aeneid* appears in *Titus Andronicus*, V. iii. 80–7 (in a play where the Moor is in II. iii. 22 compared to Aeneas) and in 2 *Henry VI* ("To sit and witch me, as Ascanius did / When he to madding Dido would unfold / His father's acts commenc'd in burning Troy! / Am I not witch'd like her?" (III. ii. 116–19)). Desdemona in V. iii sings the willow song, and the

willow is associated with the abandoned Dido, as in *The Merchant of Venice*, V.i.10.

11. Thomas Rymer, *A Short View of Tragedy* (London, 1693), in C. A. Zimansky (ed.), *The Critical Works of Thomas Rymer* (New Haven, 1956), 138–9. Rymer's bludgeon frequently hits on an important aspect of the play, however perversely judged; as, for example, when he echoes the language of rhetorical dilation in his remark that Othello's rhetoric suggests a style of "spinning out" more appropriate to "some Affidavit-office" than to a soldier (145).

12. The *Riverside* edition glosses "trace" as meaning possibly to "check to make more eager," the sense of Steevens's widely accepted emendation "trash," which means to hang weights on a hound to prevent his hunting too fast. M. R. Ridley's complaint (p. 66 of the Arden edition) that it is unnecessary for Shakespeare to include both "trash" (or slowing down) and "putting on" or inciting ignores the possibility that the point might be precisely the juxtaposition of terms whose opposition runs through the entire play.

13. This sense of parallel functions between Desdemona and Iago may be further suggested by the curious later reference to Desdemona's "plenteous wit and invention" (IV.i.190). For criticism of the scene, including Rymer's charge of "interlarding," see the Arden edition, 54, and Rymer, op. cit., 145.

14. On the *blazon* as a form of dilation by description, see, *inter alia*, Puttenham, op. cit., 231.

15. See the opening of Desiderius Erasmus, *De Copia*, II, "Abundance of subject matter." The link in French (as in several languages) between jealousy and "jalousie" or lattice, exploited in Robbe-Grillet, may indeed be part of the subtle link, in *Othello*, between the emphasis on the eye, or on what Lacan calls the invidious desire to see, in the jealousy plot of the play and its exploitation of the language of "close dilations" as only partial glimpses. Florio's *Worlde of Wordes* (1598) gives for the Italian "gelosia" its double meaning of "iealousie, suspect, suspition, mistrust" and "a letteise window," and Spenser may have had some such underground link in mind in his picture of the gazing spectator Malbecco finally become "Gealosie" itself in *The Faerie Queene*, III.x, though the *OED* does not cite an English pun on the two until 1824: "We have jalousies not only to our windows, but to our breasts" (*Blackwood's Magazine*, XV, 462).

16. See, for example, Peacham, op. cit., 134. See also the report of off-stage events in *The Winter's Tale* ("Most true, if ever truth were pregnant by circumstance. That which you *hear* you'll swear you *see*, there is such unity in the proofs" (V.ii. 30–2, emphasis mine)), and Puttenham, op. cit., 245, a passage whose emphasis on the greater art required when what is reported is not "veritable" might be juxtaposed with Iago's report of events which, logically, could not have happened in the time available. For the ear become an *oculus* or eye, see the *Ad Herennium*, IV.lv; Cicero, *De Oratore*, III.liii.202; Quintilian, *Institutio Oratoria*, VIII.iii. 61–2 and IX.ii.40; and Peacham, op. cit., 121, on the power of "amplification" to bind the hearer to the speaker's will.

17. Peacham, op. cit., 123–4. See also Hamlet's punning play on "show" (III.ii. 144–6).

18. See Joseph, op. cit., 125, 129, 321, with Erasmus, op. cit., II, method 5; Terence Cave, *The Cornucopian Text* (Oxford, 1979), 30–1; and Marion Trousdale, *Shakespeare and the Rhetoricians* (Chapel Hill, 1982), 166. Though the name of "Signior Angelo" as the bearer of a false report which cannot withstand the "assay of reason" (I.iii.16–19) has frequently puzzled commentators, "angelo" literally means "messenger," and Iago later likens himself (II.iii.350–3) to that

devil who counterfeits an "angel of light" (2 Corinthians 11:14), a biblical figure
alluded to in the punning "angels" of *The Comedy of Errors*, in *Measure for
Measure*'s Angelo, and in *Love's Labour's Lost* (IV. iii. 253).

19. Joannes Sturmius, *De imitatione oratoria libri tres* (Strasbourg, 1574), 3L3.

20. This example, from Quintilian, op. cit., VIII. iii. 67ff., was repeated in Erasmus,
op. cit., II, method 5; Peacham, op. cit., 139–40, and numerous other descriptions of the way to "open up those things which were included in a single word"
(Erasmus), or to move from the "general" to the "particular."

21. Francis Bacon, "Of the Coulers of good and evill, a fragment," 21, published with
his *Essayes* in 1597.

22. See, for example, M. R. Ridley's gloss in the Arden edition, 118.

23. See IV. i. 162 ("She'll rail in the streets else"); Iago's injunction to Emilia to
"Speak within door" (IV. ii. 144), to "charm" her "tongue" (V. ii. 183) and hold
her "peace" (219), with her final declaration of the right to be "liberal" in her
speech (219–22). Smothering or literally stopping the mouth of Desdemona is
Shakespeare's invention: in Cinthio, the Moor's wife is killed by blows. Her
continuing to talk even after she is stifled (an element of the final scene on which
so much critical ink has been spilled) is, interestingly, itself attributed to the
proverbial talkativeness of women by Rymer, a ready source of this as of other
prejudices ("We may learn here, that a Woman never loses her Tongue, even tho'
after she is stifl'd" (161)). The violence of this misogynist topos in the Renaissance is suggested by the fact that *Garrulitas* is imaged, in emblem books such
as Alciati's influential *Emblemata* and Whitney's *Choice of Emblemes*, by
Procne / Philomel, who literally had her tongue cut out to prevent a speaking
dangerous to her violator. Shakespeare's exploitation of the tradition of women's
excessive *copia verborum* needs more investigation in relation to the dilative
copia of the plays themselves, and its final bringing to closure or ending. See
Suzanne W. Hull, *Chaste, Silent & Obedient* (San Marino, 1982).

24. See, for example, Iago's "It was a violent commencement in her, and thou shalt
see an answerable sequestration" (I. iii. 344–5), a "sequestration" which Dr
Johnson, Steevens, and others read as "sequel" as well as its other meanings;
Iago's textual figure for the movement from "an index and obscure prologue" to
an "incorporate conclusion" (II. i. 257–63) in the scene where he first commands
Roderigo's silence ("Lay thy finger thus" (221)) and then invokes the logical
model of sequence and consequence, "position" and what follows from it; and
his ironic warning that if Othello should take his "close dilations" further, his
"speech should fall into such vild success [Warburton, Johnson, "succession,"
"consequence"] / Which my thoughts aim'd not" (III. iii. 222–3). *Causa* or
"cause, because of which" is one of the several "circumstances" of both a
narrative and an indictment, as well as a word with more general judicial
overtones, as in *Measure for Measure*, II. i. 136–7. See also the play on the
crossing of *causa* and *locus* in the "ground which" and "ground where" of
Armado's delation of Costard in *Love's Labour's Lost*, with Baldwin, op. cit., II,
312. This pervasive motif of jumping to conclusion in *Othello*, from the rousing
of Brabantio in Act I, may be the reason for Iago's opening description of Cassio
as "A fellow almost damn'd in a fair wife" (I. i. 21) – rather than any suggestion of
the mysterious "wife" of Cassio (or of a lapse on Shakespeare's part) on which
such critical energy has been spent – since it echoes a conclusion so quickly
reached that it was proverbial. Ridley (Arden edition, 4) cites the Italian proverb
"l'hai tolta bella? tuo danno"; and Thomas Blundeville, in *The Arte of Logike*
(1599; London, 1619 edn), 102–3, in his discussion "Of Probable Accidents,

Coniectures, Presumptions, Signes, and Circumstances," cites as his prime example of an argument by "consequence" the sophistical "it follows that" of the sentence "Shee is a faire woman: Ergo, shee is unchaste." For Shakespeare's own playing with the interrelation of a logical and a narrative "it follows that," see *Hamlet*, II. ii. 413–20.

25. "Dilation" as rhetorical amplification easily combines in Shakespeare with "dilation" as the technical term for the deferral of apocalypse or judgment, for the purpose of repentance. See my "Dilation and delay," 524–5, and "Anagogic metaphor," 42–5.

26. See James L. Calderwood, *Shakespearean Metadrama* (Minneapolis, 1971) and *To Be and Not to Be: Negation and Metadrama in "Hamlet"* (New York, 1983); Jacques Derrida, "Living on: border lines," in Harold Bloom *et al.* (eds), *Deconstruction and Criticism* (New York, 1979), esp. 104–5; and, for a comic Shakespearean example of the law, the Constable Dogberry in *Much Ado*, V. i.

27. Such further study might begin, for example, with the emphasis on proper sequential order – as in "God, then man," "man, then woman" – in descriptions of the crucial ordering of rhetorical amplification and "variety" in Richard Sherry's *Treatise of Schemes & Tropes* (1550), 22, Peacham, op. cit., 118, and other handbooks of rhetoric and logic, as well as with an exploration of the crossing of rhetorical, political and economic within the notion of *distributio*.

II
The woman's part

5

ELAINE SHOWALTER

Representing Ophelia: women, madness, and the responsibilities of feminist criticism

"As a sort of a come-on, I announced that I would speak today about that piece of bait named Ophelia, and I'll be as good as my word." These are the words which begin the psychoanalytic seminar on *Hamlet* presented in Paris in 1959 by Jacques Lacan. But despite his promising come-on, Lacan was *not* as good as his word. He goes on for some 41 pages to speak about Hamlet, and when he does mention Ophelia, she is merely what Lacan calls "the object Ophelia" – that is, the object of Hamlet's male desire. The etymology of Ophelia, Lacan asserts, is "O-phallus," and her role in the drama can only be to function as the exteriorized figuration of what Lacan predictably and, in view of his own early work with psychotic women, disappointingly suggests is the phallus as transcendental signifier.[1] To play such a part obviously makes Ophelia "essential," as Lacan admits; but only because, in his words, "she is linked forever, for centuries, to the figure of Hamlet."

The bait-and-switch game that Lacan plays with Ophelia is a cynical but not unusual instance of her deployment in psychiatric and critical texts. For most critics of Shakespeare, Ophelia has been an insignificant minor character in the play, touching in her weakness and madness but chiefly interesting, of course, in what she tells us about Hamlet. And while female readers of Shakespeare have often attempted to champion Ophelia, even feminist critics have done so with a certain embarrassment. As Annette Kolodny ruefully admits: "it is after all, an imposition of high order to ask the viewer to attend to Ophelia's sufferings in a scene where, before, he's always so comfortably kept his eye fixed on Hamlet."[2]

Yet when feminist criticism allows Ophelia to upstage Hamlet, it also brings to the foreground the issues in an ongoing theoretical debate about the cultural links between femininity, female sexuality, insanity, and representation. Though she is neglected in criticism, Ophelia is probably the most frequently illustrated and cited of Shakespeare's heroines. Her visibility as a subject in literature, popular culture, and painting, from Redon who paints her drowning, to Bob Dylan, who places her on Desolation Row, to Cannon Mills, which has named a flowery sheet pattern after her, is in inverse relation to her invisibility in Shakespearean critical texts. Why has she been such a potent and obsessive figure in our cultural mythology? Insofar as Hamlet names Ophelia as "woman" and "frailty," substituting an ideological view of femininity for a personal one, is she indeed representative of Woman, and does her madness stand for the oppression of women in society as well as in tragedy? Furthermore, since Laertes calles Ophelia a "document in madness," does she represent the textual archetype of woman *as* madness or madness *as* woman? And finally, how should feminist criticism represent Ophelia in its own discourse? What is our responsibility towards her as character and as woman?

Feminist critics have offered a variety of responses to these questions. Some have maintained that we should represent Ophelia as a lawyer represents a client, that we should become her Horatia, in this harsh world reporting her and her cause aright to the unsatisfied. Carol Neely, for example, describes advocacy – speaking *for* Ophelia – as our proper role: "As a feminist critic," she writes, "I must 'tell' Ophelia's story."[3] But what can we mean by Ophelia's story? The story of her life? The story of her betrayal at the hands of her father, brother, lover, court, society? The story of her rejection and marginalization by male critics of Shakespeare? Shakespeare gives us very little information from which to imagine a past for Ophelia. She appears in only five of the play's twenty scenes; the pre-play course of her love story with Hamlet is known only by a few ambiguous flashbacks. Her tragedy is subordinated in the play; unlike Hamlet, she does not struggle with moral choices or alternatives. Thus another feminist critic, Lee Edwards, concludes that it is impossible to reconstruct Ophelia's biography from the text: "We can imagine Hamlet's story without Ophelia, but Ophelia literally has no story without Hamlet."[4]

If we turn from American to French feminist theory, Ophelia might confirm the impossibility of representing the feminine in patriarchal discourse as other than madness, incoherence, fluidity, or silence. In French theoretical criticism, the feminine or "Woman" is that which escapes representation in patriarchal language and symbolism; it remains on the side of negativity, absence, and lack. In comparison to Hamlet, Ophelia is certainly a creature of lack. "I think nothing, my lord," she tells him in the Mousetrap scene, and he cruelly twists her words:

Hamlet: That's a fair thought to lie between maids' legs.
Ophelia: What is, my lord?
Hamlet: Nothing.

(III. ii. 117–19)

In Elizabethan slang, "nothing" was a term for the female genitalia, as in *Much Ado About Nothing*. To Hamlet, then, "nothing" is what lies between maids' legs, for, in the male visual system of representation and desire, women's sexual organs, in the words of the French psychoanalyst Luce Irigaray, "represent the horror of having nothing to see."[5] When Ophelia is mad, Gertrude says that "Her speech is nothing," mere "unshaped use." Ophelia's speech thus represents the horror of having nothing to say in the public terms defined by the court. Deprived of thought, sexuality, language, Ophelia's story becomes the Story of O – the zero, the empty circle or mystery of feminine difference, the cipher of female sexuality to be deciphered by feminist interpretation.[6]

A third approach would be to read Ophelia's story as the female subtext of the tragedy, the repressed story of Hamlet. In this reading, Ophelia represents the strong emotions that the Elizabethans as well as the Freudians thought womanish and unmanly. When Laertes weeps for his dead sister he says of his tears that "When these are gone, / The woman will be out" – that is to say, that the feminine and shameful part of his nature will be purged. According to David Leverenz, in an important essay called "The Woman in *Hamlet*," Hamlet's disgust at the feminine passivity in himself is translated into violent revulsion against women, and into his brutal behavior towards Ophelia. Ophelia's suicide, Leverenz argues, then becomes "a microcosm of the male world's banishment of the female, because 'woman' represents everything denied by reasonable men."[7]

It is perhaps because Hamlet's emotional vulnerability can so readily be conceptualized as feminine that this is the only heroic male role in Shakespeare which has been regularly acted by women, in a tradition from Sarah Bernhardt to, most recently, Diane Venora, in a production directed by Joseph Papp. Leopold Bloom speculates on this tradition in *Ulysses*, musing on the Hamlet of the actress Mrs Bandman Palmer: "Male impersonator. Perhaps he was a woman? Why Ophelia committed suicide?"[8]

While all of these approaches have much to recommend them, each also presents critical problems. To liberate Ophelia from the text, or to make her its tragic center, is to re-appropriate her for our own ends; to dissolve her into a female symbolism of absence is to endorse our own marginality; to make her Hamlet's anima is to reduce her to a metaphor of male experience. I would like to propose instead that Ophelia *does* have a story of her own that feminist criticism can tell; it is neither her life story, nor her love story, nor Lacan's story, but rather the *history* of her representation. This essay tries to bring together some of the categories of French feminist thought about the

79

"feminine" with the empirical energies of American historical and critical research: to yoke French theory and Yankee knowhow.

Tracing the iconography of Ophelia in English and French painting, photography, psychiatry, and literature, as well as in theatrical production, I will be showing first of all the representational bonds between female insanity and female sexuality. Secondly, I want to demonstrate the two-way transaction between psychiatric theory and cultural representation. As one medical historian has observed, we could provide a manual of female insanity by chronicling the illustrations of Ophelia; this is so because the illustrations of Ophelia have played a major role in the theoretical construction of female insanity.[9] Finally, I want to suggest that the feminist revision of Ophelia comes as much from the actress's freedom as from the critic's interpretation.[10] When Shakespeare's heroines began to be played by women instead of boys, the presence of the female body and female voice, quite apart from details of interpretation, created new meanings and subversive tensions in these roles, and perhaps most importantly with Ophelia. Looking at Ophelia's history on and off the stage, I will point out the contest between male and female representations of Ophelia, cycles of critical repression and feminist reclamation of which contemporary feminist criticism is only the most recent phase. By beginning with these data from cultural history, instead of moving from the grid of literary theory, I hope to conclude with a fuller sense of the responsibilities of feminist criticism, as well as a new perspective on Ophelia.

*

"Of all the characters in *Hamlet*," Bridget Lyons has pointed out, "Ophelia is most persistently presented in terms of symbolic meanings."[11] Her behavior, her appearance, her gestures, her costume, her props, are freighted with emblematic significance, and for many generations of Shakespearean critics her part in the play has seemed to be primarily iconographic. Ophelia's symbolic meanings, moreover, are specifically feminine. Whereas for Hamlet madness is metaphysical, linked with culture, for Ophelia it is a product of the female body and female nature, perhaps that nature's purest form. On the Elizabethan stage, the conventions of female insanity were sharply defined. Ophelia dresses in white, decks herself with "fantastical garlands" of wild flowers, and enters, according to the stage directions of the "Bad" Quarto, "distracted" playing on a lute with her "hair down singing." Her speeches are marked by extravagant metaphors, lyrical free associations, and "explosive sexual imagery."[12] She sings wistful and bawdy ballads, and ends her life by drowning.

All of these conventions carry specific messages about femininity and sexuality. Ophelia's virginal and vacant white is contrasted with Hamlet's scholar's garb, his "suits of solemn black." Her flowers suggest the discordant double images of female sexuality as both innocent blossoming and whorish contamination; she is the "green girl" of pastoral, the virginal "Rose of May" and the sexually explicit madwoman who, in giving away her wild flowers and herbs, is symbolically deflowering herself. The "weedy trophies" and phallic "long purples" which she wears to her death intimate an improper and discordant sexuality that Gertrude's lovely elegy cannot quite obscure.[13] In Elizabethan and Jacobean drama, the stage direction that a woman enters with dishevelled hair indicates that she might either be mad or the victim of a rape; the disordered hair, her offense against decorum, suggests sensuality in each case.[14] The mad Ophelia's bawdy songs and verbal license, while they give her access to "an entirely different range of experience" from what she is allowed as the dutiful daughter, seem to be her one sanctioned form of self-assertion as a woman, quickly followed, as if in retribution, by her death.[15]

Drowning too was associated with the feminine, with female fluidity as opposed to masculine aridity. In his discussion of the "Ophelia complex," the phenomenologist Gaston Bachelard traces the symbolic connections between women, water, and death. Drowning, he suggests, becomes the truly feminine death in the dramas of literature and life, one which is a beautiful immersion and submersion in the female element. Water is the profound and organic symbol of the liquid woman whose eyes are so easily drowned in tears, as her body is the repository of blood, amniotic fluid, and milk. A man contemplating this feminine suicide understands it by reaching for what is feminine in himself, like Laertes, by a temporary surrender to his own fluidity – that is, his tears; and he becomes a man again in becoming once more dry – when his tears are stopped.[16]

Clinically speaking, Ophelia's behavior and appearance are characteristic of the malady the Elizabethans would have diagnosed as female love-melancholy, or erotomania. From about 1580, melancholy had become a fashionable disease among young men, especially in London, and Hamlet himself is a prototype of the melancholy hero. Yet the epidemic of melancholy associated with intellectual and imaginative genius "curiously bypassed women." Women's melancholy was seen instead as biological, and emotional in origins.[17]

On the stage, Ophelia's madness was presented as the predictable outcome of erotomania. From 1660, when women first appeared on the public stage, to the beginnings of the eighteenth century, the most celebrated of the actresses who played Ophelia were those whom rumor credited with disappointments in love. The greatest triumph was reserved for Susan Mountfort, a former actress at Lincoln's Inn Fields who had gone mad after her lover's betrayal. One night in 1720 she escaped from her keeper, rushed to the theater, and just as the Ophelia of the evening was to enter for her mad scene,

Figure 1 *"Sarah Siddons as Ophelia," courtesy of the Folger Shakespeare Library,*
Washington, D.C.

"sprang forward in her place . . . with wild eyes and wavering motion."[18] As a contemporary reported, "she was in truth *Ophelia herself*, to the amazement of the performers as well as of the audience – nature having made this last effort, her vital powers failed her and she died soon after."[19] These theatrical legends reinforced the belief of the age that female madness was a part of female nature, less to be imitated by an actress than demonstrated by a deranged woman in a performance of her emotions.

The subversive or violent possibilities of the mad scene were nearly eliminated, however, on the eighteenth-century stage. Late Augustan stereotypes of female love-melancholy were sentimentalized versions which minimized the force of female sexuality, and made female insanity a pretty stimulant to male sensibility. Actresses such as Mrs Lessingham in 1772, and Mary Bolton in 1811, played Ophelia in this decorous style, relying on the familiar images of the white dress, loose hair, and wild flowers to convey a polite feminine distraction, highly suitable for pictorial reproduction, and appropriate for Samuel Johnson's description of Ophelia as young, beautiful, harmless, and pious. Even Mrs Siddons in 1785 played the mad scene with stately and classical dignity. (See Figure 1.) For much of the period, in fact, Augustan objections to the levity and indecency of Ophelia's language and behavior led to censorship of the part. Her lines were frequently cut, and the role was often assigned to a singer instead of an actress, making the mode of representation musical rather than visual or verbal.

But whereas the Augustan response to madness was a denial, the romantic response was an embrace.[20] The figure of the madwoman permeates romantic literature, from the gothic novelists to Wordsworth and Scott in such texts as "The Thorn" and *The Heart of Midlothian*, where she stands for sexual victimization, bereavement, and thrilling emotional extremity. Romantic artists such as Thomas Barker and George Shepheard painted pathetically abandoned Crazy Kates and Crazy Anns, while Henry Fuseli's "Mad Kate" is almost demonically possessed, an orphan of the romantic storm.

In the Shakespearean theater, Ophelia's romantic revival began in France rather than England. When Charles Kemble made his Paris debut as Hamlet with an English troupe in 1827, his Ophelia was a young Irish ingénue named Harriet Smithson. Smithson used "her extensive command of mime to depict in precise gesture the state of Ophelia's confused mind."[21] In the mad scene, she entered in a long black veil, suggesting the standard imagery of female sexual mystery in the gothic novel, with scattered bedlamish wisps of straw in her hair. (See Figure 2.) Spreading the veil on the ground as she sang, she spread flowers upon it in the shape of a cross, as if to make her father's grave, and mimed a burial, a piece of stage business which remained in vogue for the rest of the century.

The French audiences were stunned. Dumas recalled that "it was the first time I saw in the theatre real passions, giving life to men and women of flesh and blood."[22] The 23-year-old Hector Berlioz, who was in the audience on the first night, fell madly in love, and eventually married Harriet Smithson despite his family's frantic opposition. Her image as the mad Ophelia was represented in popular lithographs and exhibited in bookshop and printshop windows. Her costume was imitated by the fashionable, and a coiffure "à la folle," consisting of a "black veil with wisps of straw tastefully interwoven" in the hair, was widely copied by the Parisian beau monde, always on the lookout for something new.[23]

Although Smithson never acted Ophelia on the English stage, her intensely visual performance quickly influenced English productions as well; and indeed the romantic Ophelia – a young girl passionately and visibly driven to picturesque madness – became the dominant international acting style for the next 150 years, from Helena Modjeska in Poland in 1871, to the 18-year-old Jean Simmons in the Laurence Olivier film of 1948.

Whereas the romantic Hamlet, in Coleridge's famous dictum, thinks too much, has an "overbalance of the contemplative faculty" and an overactive intellect, the romantic Ophelia is a girl who *feels* too much, who drowns in feeling. The romantic critics seem to have felt that the less said about Ophelia the better; the point was to *look* at her. Hazlitt, for one, is speechless before

Figure 2 *"Harriet Smithson as Ophelia," courtesy of the Folger Shakespeare Library, Washington, D.C.*

her, calling her "a character almost too exquisitely touching to be dwelt upon."[24] While the Augustans represent Ophelia as music, the romantics transform her into an *objet d'art*, as if to take literally Claudius's lament, "poor Ophelia / Divided from herself and her fair judgment, / Without the which we are pictures."

Smithson's performance is best recaptured in a series of pictures done by Delacroix from 1830 to 1850, which show a strong romantic interest in the relation of female sexuality and insanity.[25] The most innovative and influential of Delacroix's lithographs is *La Mort d'Ophélie* of 1843, the first of three studies. Its sensual languor, with Ophelia half-suspended in the stream as her dress slips from her body, anticipated the fascination with the erotic trance of the hysteric as it would be studied by Jean-Martin Charcot and his students, including Janet and Freud. Delacroix's interest in the drowning Ophelia is also reproduced to the point of obsession in later nineteenth-century painting. The English Pre-Raphaelites painted her again and again, choosing the drowning which is only described in the play, and where no actress's image had preceded them or interfered with their imaginative supremacy.

In the Royal Academy show of 1852, Arthur Hughes's entry shows a tiny waif-like creature – a sort of Tinker Bell Ophelia – in a filmy white gown, perched on a tree trunk by the stream. The overall effect is softened, sexless, and hazy, although the straw in her hair resembles a crown of thorns. Hughes's juxtaposition of childlike femininity and Christian martyrdom was overpowered, however, by John Everett Millais's great painting of Ophelia in the same show. (See Figure 3.) While Millais's Ophelia is sensuous siren as well as victim, the artist rather than the subject dominates the scene. The division of space between Ophelia and the natural details Millais had so painstakingly pursued reduces her to one more visual object; and the painting has such a hard surface, strangely flattened perspective, and brilliant light that it seems cruelly indifferent to the woman's death.

*

These Pre-Raphaelite images were part of a new and intricate traffic between images of women and madness in late nineteenth-century literature, psychiatry, drama, and art. First of all, superintendents of Victorian lunatic asylums were also enthusiasts of Shakespeare, who turned to his dramas for models of mental aberration that could be applied to their clinical practice. The case study of Ophelia was one that seemed particularly useful as an account of hysteria or mental breakdown in adolescence, a period of sexual instability which the Victorians regarded as risky for women's mental health. As Dr John Charles Bucknill, president of the Medico-Psychological Association,

Figure 3 John Everett Millais, "Ophelia," courtesy of the Folger Shakespeare Library, Washington, D.C.

remarked in 1859, "Ophelia is the very type of a class of cases by no means uncommon. Every mental physician of moderately extensive experience must have seen many Ophelias. It is a copy from nature, after the fashion of the Pre-Raphaelite school."[26] Dr John Conolly, the celebrated superintendent of the Hanwell Asylum, and founder of the committee to make Stratford a national trust, concurred. In his *Study of Hamlet* in 1863 he noted that even casual visitors to mental institutions could recognize an Ophelia in the wards: "the same young years, the same faded beauty, the same fantastic dress and interrupted song."[27] Medical textbooks illustrated their discussions of female patients with sketches of Ophelia-like maidens.

But Conolly also pointed out that the graceful Ophelias who dominated the Victorian stage were quite unlike the women who had become the majority of the inmate population in Victorian public asylums. "It seems to be supposed," he protested, "that it is an easy task to play the part of a crazy girl, and that it is chiefly composed of singing and prettiness. The habitual courtesy, the partial rudeness of mental disorder, are things to be witnessed. . . . An actress, ambitious of something beyond cold imitation, might find the contemplation of such cases a not unprofitable study."[28]

Yet when Ellen Terry took up Conolly's challenge, and went to an asylum to observe real madwomen, she found them "too *theatrical*" to teach her anything.[29] This was because the iconography of the romantic Ophelia had begun to infiltrate reality, to define a style for mad young women seeking to express and communicate their distress. And where the women themselves did not willingly throw themselves into Ophelia-like postures, asylum superintendents, armed with the new technology of photography, imposed the costume, gesture, props, and expression of Ophelia upon them. In England, the camera was introduced to asylum work in the 1850s by Dr Hugh Welch Diamond, who photographed his female patients at the Surrey Asylum and at Bethlem. Diamond was heavily influenced by literary and visual models in his posing of the female subjects. His pictures of madwomen, posed in prayer, or decked with Ophelia-like garlands, were copied for Victorian consumption as touched-up lithographs in professional journals.[30] (See Figure 4.)

Reality, psychiatry, and representational convention were even more confused in the photographic records of hysteria produced in the 1870s by Jean-Martin Charcot. Charcot was the first clinician to install a fully-equipped photographic atelier in his Paris hospital, La Salpêtrière, to record the performances of his hysterical stars. Charcot's clinic became, as he said, a "living theatre" of female pathology; his women patients were coached in their performances for the camera, and, under hypnosis, were sometimes instructed to play heroines from Shakespeare. Among them, a 15-year-old girl named Augustine was featured in the published volumes called *Iconographies* in every posture of *la grande hystérie*. With her white hospital gown and flowing locks, Augustine frequently resembles the reproductions

*Figure 4   Hugh W. Diamond, photograph of a Victorian madwoman at Surrey
Asylum, by permission of the Royal Society of Medicine, London*

of Ophelia as icon and actress which had been in wide circulation.[31] (See
Figure 5.)

But if the Victorian madwoman looks mutely out from men's pictures, and
acts a part men had staged and directed, she is very differently represented in
the feminist revision of Ophelia initiated by newly powerful and respectable
Victorian actresses, and by women critics of Shakespeare. In their efforts to
defend Ophelia, they invent a story for her drawn from their own experiences,
grievances, and desires.

*

Probably the most famous of the Victorian feminist revisions of the Ophelia
story was Mary Cowden Clarke's *The Girlhood of Shakespeare's Heroines*,
published in 1852. Unlike other Victorian moralizing and didactic studies of
the female characters of Shakespeare's plays, Clarke's was specifically
addressed to the wrongs of women, and especially to the sexual double
standard. In a chapter on Ophelia called "The rose of Elsinore," Clarke tells
how the child Ophelia was left behind in the care of a peasant couple when
Polonius was called to the court at Paris, and raised in a cottage with a

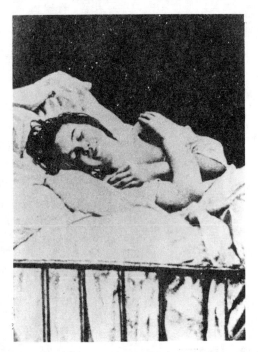

Figure 5   R. Regnard, photograph of "Augustine," "Iconographie photographique
de la Salpêtrière," 1878, Princeton University Library

foster-sister and brother, Jutha and Ulf. Jutha is seduced and betrayed by a
deceitful knight, and Ophelia discovers the bodies of Jutha and her still-born
child, lying "white, rigid, and still" in the deserted parlor of the cottage in the
middle of the night. Ulf, a "hairy loutish boy," likes to torture flies, to eat
songbirds, and to rip the petals off roses, and he is also very eager to give little
Ophelia what he calls a bear-hug. Both repelled and masochistically attracted
by Ulf, Ophelia is repeatedly cornered by him as she grows up; once she
escapes the hug by hitting him with a branch of wild roses; another time, he
sneaks into her bedroom "in his brutish pertinacity to obtain the hug he had
promised himself," but just as he bends over her trembling body, Ophelia is
saved by the reappearance of her real mother.

A few years later, back at the court, she discovers the hanged body of
another friend, who has killed herself after being "victimized and deserted by
the same evil seducer." Not surprisingly, Ophelia breaks down with brain
fever – a staple mental illness of Victorian fiction – and has prophetic
hallucinations of a brook beneath willow trees where something bad will
happen to her. The warnings of Polonius and Laertes have little to add to this
history of female sexual trauma.[32]

On the Victorian stage, it was Ellen Terry, daring and unconventional in her own life, who led the way in acting Ophelia in feminist terms as a consistent psychological study in sexual intimidation, a girl terrified of her father, of her lover, and of life itself. Terry's debut as Ophelia in Henry Irving's production in 1878 was a landmark. According to one reviewer, her Ophelia was "the terrible spectacle of a normal girl becoming hopelessly imbecile as the result of overwhelming mental agony. Hers was an insanity without wrath or rage, without exaltation or paroxysms."[33] Her "poetic and intellectual performance" also inspired other actresses to rebel against the conventions of invisibility and negation associated with the part.

Terry was the first to challenge the tradition of Ophelia's dressing in emblematic white. For the French poets, such as Rimbaud, Hugo, Musset, Mallarmé and Laforgue, whiteness was part of Ophelia's essential feminine symbolism; they call her "blanche Ophélia" and compare her to a lily, a cloud, or snow. Yet whiteness also made her a transparency, an absence that took on the colors of Hamlet's moods, and that, for the symbolists like Mallarmé, made her a blank page to be written over or on by the male imagination. Although Irving was able to prevent Terry from wearing black in the mad scene, exclaiming "My God, Madam, there must be only *one* black figure in this play, and that's Hamlet!" (Irving, of course, was playing Hamlet), nonetheless actresses such as Gertrude Eliot, Helen Maude, Nora de Silva, and in Russia Vera Komisarjevskaya, gradually won the right to intensify Ophelia's presence by clothing her in Hamlet's black.[34]

By the turn of the century, there was both a male and a female discourse on Ophelia. A. C. Bradley spoke for the Victorian male tradition when he noted in *Shakespearean Tragedy* (1906) that "a large number of readers feel a kind of personal irritation against Ophelia; they seem unable to forgive her for not having been a heroine."[35] The feminist counterview was represented by actresses in such works as Helena Faucit's study of Shakespeare's female characters, and *The True Ophelia*, written by an anonymous actress in 1914, which protested against the "insipid little creature" of criticism, and advocated a strong and intelligent woman destroyed by the heartlessness of men.[36] In women's paintings of the *fin de siècle* as well, Ophelia is depicted as an inspiring, even sanctified emblem of righteousness.[37]

While the widely read and influential essays of Mary Cowden Clarke are now mocked as the epitome of naive criticism, these Victorian studies of the girlhood of Shakespeare's heroines are of course alive and well as psychoanalytic criticism, which has imagined its own prehistories of oedipal conflict and neurotic fixation; and I say this not to mock psychoanalytic criticism, but to suggest that Clarke's musings on Ophelia are a pre-Freudian speculation on the traumatic sources of a female sexual identity. The Freudian interpretation of *Hamlet* concentrated on the hero, but also had much to do with the re-sexualization of Ophelia. As early as 1900, Freud had traced Hamlet's irresolution to an Oedipus complex, and Ernest Jones, his leading British disciple, developed this view, influencing the performances of John Gielgud and Alec Guinness in the 1930s. In his final version of the study, *Hamlet and Oedipus*, published in 1949, Jones argued that "Ophelia should be unmistakably sensual, as she seldom is on stage. She may be 'innocent' and docile, but she is very aware of her body."[38]

In the theater and in criticism, this Freudian edict has produced such extreme readings as that Shakespeare intends us to see Ophelia as a loose woman, and that she has been sleeping with Hamlet. Rebecca West has argued that Ophelia was not "a correct and timid virgin of exquisite sensibilities," a view she attributes to the popularity of the Millais painting; but rather "a disreputable young woman."[39] In his delightful autobiography, Laurence Olivier, who made a special pilgrimage to Ernest Jones when he was preparing his *Hamlet* in the 1930s, recalls that one of his predecessors as actor-manager had said in response to the earnest question, "Did Hamlet sleep with Ophelia?" – "In my company, always."[40]

The most extreme Freudian interpretation reads *Hamlet* as two parallel male and female psychodramas, the counterpointed stories of the incestuous attachments of Hamlet and Ophelia. As Theodor Lidz presents this view, while Hamlet is neurotically attached to his mother, Ophelia has an unresolved oedipal attachment to her father. She has fantasies of a lover who will abduct her from or even kill her father, and when this actually happens, her reason is destroyed by guilt as well as by lingering incestuous feelings. According to Lidz, Ophelia breaks down because she fails in the female developmental task of shifting her sexual attachment from her father "to a man who can bring her fulfillment as a woman."[41] We see the effects of this Freudian Ophelia on stage productions since the 1950s, where directors have hinted at an incestuous link between Ophelia and her father, or more recently, because this staging conflicts with the usual ironic treatment of Polonius, between Ophelia and Laertes. Trevor Nunn's production with Helen Mirren in 1970, for example, made Ophelia and Laertes flirtatious doubles, almost twins in their matching fur-trimmed doublets, playing duets on the lute with Polonius looking on, like Peter, Paul, and Mary. In other productions of the same period, Marianne Faithfull was a haggard Ophelia equally attracted to Hamlet and Laertes, and, in one of the few performances directed by a woman, Yvonne Nicholson sat on Laertes' lap in the advice scene, and played the part with "rough sexual bravado."[42]

Since the 1960s, the Freudian representation of Ophelia has been supplemented by an antipsychiatry that represents Ophelia's madness in more contemporary terms. In contrast to the psychoanalytic representation of Ophelia's sexual unconscious that connected her essential femininity to Freud's essays on female sexuality and hysteria, her madness is now seen in medical and biochemical terms, as schizophrenia. This is so in part because the schizophrenic woman has become the cultural icon of dualistic femininity in the mid-twentieth century as the erotomaniac was in the seventeenth and the hysteric in the nineteenth. It might also be traced to the work of R. D. Laing on female schizophrenia in the 1960s. Laing argued that schizophrenia was an intelligible response to the experience of invalidation within the family network, especially to the conflicting emotional messages and mystifying double binds experienced by daughters. Ophelia, he noted in *The Divided Self*, is an empty space. "In her madness there is no one there. . . . There is no integral selfhood expressed through her actions or utterances. Incomprehensible statements are said by nothing. She has already died. There is now only a vacuum where there was once a person."[43]

Despite his sympathy for Ophelia, Laing's readings silence her, equate her with "nothing," more completely than any since the Augustans; and they have been translated into performances which only make Ophelia a graphic study of mental pathology. The sickest Ophelias on the contemporary stage have been those in the productions of the pathologist-director Jonathan Miller. In 1974 at the Greenwich Theatre his Ophelia sucked her thumb; by 1981, at the Warehouse in London, she was played by an actress much taller and heavier than the Hamlet (perhaps punningly cast as the young actor Anton Lesser). She began the play with a set of nervous tics and tuggings of hair which by the mad scene had become a full set of schizophrenic routines – head banging, twitching, wincing, grimacing, and drooling.[44]

But since the 1970s too we have had a feminist discourse which has offered a new perspective on Ophelia's madness as protest and rebellion. For many feminist theorists, the madwoman is a heroine, a powerful figure who rebels against the family and the social order; and the hysteric who refuses to speak the language of the patriarchal order, who speaks otherwise, is a sister.[45] In terms of effect on the theater, the most radical application of these ideas was probably realized in Melissa Murray's agitprop play *Ophelia*, written in 1979 for the English women's theater group "Hormone Imbalance." In this blank verse retelling of the Hamlet story, Ophelia becomes a lesbian and runs off with a woman servant to join a guerrilla commune.[46]

While I've always regretted that I missed this production, I can't proclaim that this defiant ideological gesture, however effective politically or theatrically, is all that feminist criticism desires, or all to which it should aspire. When feminist criticism chooses to deal with representation, rather than with women's writing, it must aim for a maximum interdisciplinary contextualism, in which the complexity of attitudes towards the feminine can be analyzed in their fullest cultural and historical frame. The alternation of strong and weak Ophelias on the stage, virginal and seductive Ophelias in art, inadequate or oppressed Ophelias in criticism, tells us how these representations have overflowed the text, and how they have reflected the ideological character of their times, erupting as debates between dominant and feminist views in periods of gender crisis and redefinition. The representation of

Ophelia changes independently of theories of the meaning of the play or the Prince, for it depends on attitudes towards women and madness. The decorous and pious Ophelia of the Augustan age and the postmodern schizophrenic heroine who might have stepped from the pages of Laing can be derived from the same figure; they are both contradictory and complementary images of female sexuality in which madness seems to act as the "switching-point, the concept which allows the co-existence of both sides of the representation."[47] There is no "true" Ophelia for whom feminist criticism must unambiguously speak, but perhaps only a Cubist Ophelia of multiple perspectives, more than the sum of all her parts.

But in exposing the ideology of representation, feminist critics have also the responsibility to acknowledge and to examine the boundaries of our own ideological positions as products of our gender and our time. A degree of humility in an age of critical hubris can be our greatest strength, for it is by occupying this position of historical self-consciousness in both feminism and criticism that we maintain our credibility in representing Ophelia, and that, unlike Lacan, when we promise to speak about her, we make good our word.

Notes

1. Jacques Lacan, "Desire and the interpretation of desire in *Hamlet*," in *Literature and Psychoanalysis: The Question of Reading: Otherwise*, ed. Shoshana Felman (Baltimore, 1982), 11, 20, 23. Lacan is also wrong about the etymology of Ophelia, which probably derives from the Greek for "help" or "succour." Charlotte M. Yonge suggested a derivation from "ophis," "serpent." See her *History of Christian Names* (1884, republished Chicago, 1966), 346–7. I am indebted to Walter Jackson Bate for this reference.
2. Annette Kolodny, "Dancing through the minefield: some observations on the theory, practice, and politics of feminist literary criticism" (*Feminist Studies*, 6 (1980)), 7.
3. Carol Neely, "Feminist modes of Shakespearean criticism" (*Women's Studies*, 9 (1981)), 11.
4. Lee Edwards, "The labors of Psyche" (*Critical Inquiry*, 6 (1979)), 36.
5. Luce Irigaray: see *New French Feminisms*, ed. Elaine Marks and Isabelle de Courtivron (New York, 1982), 101. The quotation above, from III.ii, is taken from the Arden Shakespeare, *Hamlet*, ed. Harold Jenkins (London and New York, 1982), 295. All quotations from *Hamlet* are from this text.
6. On images of negation and feminine enclosure, see David Wilbern, "Shakespeare's 'nothing'," in *Representing Shakespeare: New Psychoanalytic Essays*, ed. Murray M. Schwartz and Coppélia Kahn (Baltimore, 1981).
7. David Leverenz, "The woman in *Hamlet*: an interpersonal view" (*Signs*, 4 (1978)), 303.
8. James Joyce, *Ulysses* (New York, 1961), 76.
9. Sander L. Gilman, *Seeing the Insane* (New York, 1981), 126.

10. See Michael Goldman, *The Actor's Freedom: Toward a Theory of Drama* (New York, 1975), for a stimulating discussion of the interpretative interaction between actor and audience.

11. Bridget Lyons, "The iconography of Ophelia" (*English Literary History*, 44 (1977), 61.

12. See Maurice and Hanna Charney, "The language of Shakespeare's madwomen" (*Signs*, 3 (1977)), 451, 457; and Carroll Camden, "On Ophelia's madness" (*Shakespeare Quarterly* (1964)), 254.

13. See Margery Garber, *Coming of Age in Shakespeare* (London, 1981), 155–7; and Lyons, op. cit., 65, 70–2.

14. On dishevelled hair as a signifier of madness or rape, see Charney and Charney, op. cit., 452–3, 457; and Allan Dessen, *Elizabethan Stage Conventions and Modern Interpreters* (Cambridge, 1984), 36–8. Thanks to Allan Dessen for letting me see advance proofs of his book.

15. Charney and Charney, op. cit., 456.

16. Gaston Bachelard, *L'Eau et les rêves* (Paris, 1942), 109–25. See also Brigitte Peucker, "Dröste-Hulshof's Ophelia and the recovery of voice" (*The Journal of English and Germanic Philology* (1983)), 374–91.

17. Vieda Skultans, *English Madness: Ideas on Insanity 1580–1890* (London, 1977), 79–81. On historical cases of love-melancholy, see Michael MacDonald, *Mystical Bedlam* (Cambridge, 1982).

18. C. E. L. Wingate, *Shakespeare's Heroines on the Stage* (New York, 1895), 283–4, 288–9.

19. Charles Hiatt, *Ellen Terry* (London, 1898), 11.

20. Max Byrd, *Visits to Bedlam: Madness and Literature in the Eighteenth Century* (Columbia, 1974), xiv.

21. Peter Raby, *Fair Ophelia: Harriet Smithson Berlioz* (Cambridge, 1982), 63.

22. Ibid., 68.

23. Ibid., 72, 75.

24. Quoted in Camden, op. cit., 247.

25. Raby, op. cit., 182.

26. J. C. Bucknill, *The Psychology of Shakespeare* (London, 1859, reprinted New York, 1970), 110. For more extensive discussions of Victorian psychiatry and Ophelia figures, see Elaine Showalter, *The Female Malady: Women, Madness and English Culture* (New York, forthcoming 1985).

27. John Conolly, *Study of Hamlet* (London, 1863), 177.

28. Ibid., 177–8, 180.

29. Ellen Terry, *The Story of My Life* (London, 1908), 154.

30. Diamond's photographs are reproduced in Sander L. Gilman, *The Face of Madness: Hugh W. Diamond and the Origin of Psychiatric Photography* (New York, 1976).

31. See Georges Didi-Huberman, *L'Invention de l'hystérie* (Paris, 1982), and Stephen Heath, *The Sexual Fix* (London, 1983), 36.

32. Mary Cowden Clarke, *The Girlhood of Shakespeare's Heroines* (London, 1852). See also George C. Gross, "Mary Cowden Clarke, *The Girlhood of Shakespeare's Heroines*, and the sex education of Victorian women" (*Victorian Studies*, 16 (1972)), 37–58, and Nina Auerbach, *Woman and the Demon* (Cambridge, Mass., 1983), 210–15.

33. Hiatt, op. cit., 114. See also Wingate, op. cit., 304–5.

34. Terry, op. cit., 155–6.

35. Andrew C. Bradley, *Shakespearean Tragedy* (London, 1906), 160.

36. Helena Faucit Martin, *On Some of Shakespeare's Female Characters* (Edinburgh and London, 1891), 4, 18; and *The True Ophelia* (New York, 1914), 15.
37. Among these paintings are the Ophelias of Henrietta Rae and Mrs F. Littler. Sarah Bernhardt sculpted a bas relief of Ophelia for the Women's Pavilion at the Chicago World's Fair in 1893.
38. Ernest Jones, *Hamlet and Oedipus* (New York, 1949), 139.
39. Rebecca West, *The Court and the Castle* (New Haven, 1958), 18.
40. Laurence Olivier, *Confessions of an Actor* (Harmondsworth, 1982), 102, 152.
41. Theodor Lidz, *Hamlet's Enemy: Madness and Myth in Hamlet* (New York, 1975), 88, 113.
42. Richard David, *Shakespeare in the Theatre* (Cambridge, 1978), 75. This was the production directed by Buzz Goodbody, a brilliant young feminist radical who killed herself that year. See Colin Chambers, *Other Spaces: New Theatre and the RSC* (London, 1980), especially 63–7.
43. R. D. Laing, *The Divided Self* (Harmondsworth, 1965), 195n.
44. David, op. cit., 82–3; thanks to Marianne DeKoven, Rutgers University, for the description of the 1981 Warehouse production.
45. See, for example, Hélène Cixous and Catherine Clément, *La Jeune Née* (Paris, 1975).
46. For an account of this production, see Micheline Wandor, *Understudies: Theatre and Sexual Politics* (London, 1981), 47.
47. I am indebted for this formulation to a critique of my earlier draft of this paper by Carl Friedman, at the Wesleyan Center for the Humanities, April 1984.

6

NANCY VICKERS

"The blazon of sweet beauty's best": Shakespeare's *Lucrece*

When, in Sonnet 106, Shakespeare's speaker alludes to "the blazon of sweet beauty's best" (5) he identifies "blazon" with "descriptions of the fairest wights" (2), with poetic portraits "in praise of ladies dead and lovely knights" (4).[1] He then goes on to qualify "blazon," to suggest that it is an outdated poetic mode standing in contrast to a present, paradoxically silent, one: "For we which now behold these present days / Have eyes to wonder, but lack tongues to praise" (13–14). The term "blazon" derives both from the French *blasonner* and from the English "to blaze" ("to proclaim as with a trumpet, to publish, and, by extension, to defame or celebrate").[2] Its usage was firmly rooted in two specific descriptive traditions, the one heraldic and the other poetic. A blazon was, first, a conventional heraldic description of a shield, and, second, a conventional poetic description of an object praised or blamed by a rhetorician-poet. The most celebrated examples of French poetic blazon were the *Blasons anatomiques du corps femenin* (1543), a collective work in which each poem praised a separate part of the female body, each poet literally spoke either "of hand, of foot, of lip, of eye," or "of brow" (6). Within the English tradition, poetic blazon typically consisted of a catalogue listing each of these particular beauties, their sum constituting an exquisite, if none the less troubling, totality; their rhetoric inscribing them in a Petrarchan world of "ideal types, beautiful monsters composed of every individual perfection."[3] Shakespeare's speaker implies that blazon's inventory of fragmented and reified parts – a strategy in some senses inherent to any descriptive project but, in its exaggerated form, characteristic of Petrarch and the

95

Petrarchans – falls short of re-presenting present beauty: "I see their antique pen *would have* express'd / Even such a beauty as you master now" (7–8, my italics): "They had not skill enough your worth to sing" (12).[4] Before a new manifestation of "sweet beauty's best," either a new language of descriptive praise must be invented or a new awareness of the celebratory power of silence acknowledged.

This essay looks not to what that new descriptive language might be, but rather centers on reading the old language of blazon, on examining the limits – indeed the dangers – of that inherited, insufficient, descriptive rhetoric. It centers therefore on a narrative, *Lucrece* (1594), that is set in motion by a descriptive occasion, by a competition between husbands each blazoning his wife. By situating blazon within a story, Shakespeare's narrative provides a locus for reading this specific mode of description not as isolated icon, but rather as motivated discourse positioned within a specific context that produces and consumes it. *Lucrece* thus reveals the rhetorical strategies that descriptive occasions generate, and underlines the potential consequences of being female matter for male oratory. The canonical legacy of description in praise of beauty is, after all, a legacy shaped predominantly by the male imagination for the male imagination; it is, in large part, the product of men talking to men about women. In *Lucrece*, occasion, rhetoric, and result are all informed by, and thus inscribe, a battle between men that is first figuratively and then literally fought on the fields of woman's "celebrated" body. Here, metaphors commonly read as signs of a battle between the sexes emerge rather from a homosocial struggle, in this case a male rivalry, which positions a third (female) term in a median space from which it is initially used and finally eliminated.[5] The plotting of such a "libidinal and cultural – hence political, typically masculine – economy" of description then permits speculation as to how descriptive rhetoric, to cite Hélène Cixous, has "more than confiscated" woman's body, has turned her into "the uncanny stranger on display."[6]

"To display" – from the Latin *displicare* (to scatter and, later, to unfold as in unfolding a banner to view) – is "to spread something out, to exhibit it to be seen, and, by extension, to exhibit it ostentatiously." In the "display of heraldry" it signifies "to lay or place a human or animal form with the limbs extended"; in the "display of rhetoric," "to set forth in representation, to depict, to describe." Description, then, is a gesture of display, a separating off and a signaling of particulars destined to make visible that which is described. Its object or matter is thus submitted to a double power-relation inherent in the gesture itself: on the one hand, the describer controls, possesses, and uses that matter to his own ends; and, on the other, his reader / listener is extended the privilege or pleasure of "seeing." In Sonnet 102, Shakespeare's speaker initially argues that he loves "not less" though he may "less the show appear" (2) and then elaborates: "That love is merchandiz'd whose rich esteeming /

The owner's tongue doth publish everywhere" (3–4). The speaker, in contrast, resists the ornaments of hyperbolic praise so as not to "dull" (both "to bore" and "to diminish") his beloved with fashionable, common verse. By rejecting the mode of blazon, the display of "the fairest wights" through the itemization of their ideal parts and the equation of those parts to "all things rare" (Sonnet 21, l. 7), he would avoid the trap of "proud compare" (Sonnet 21, l. 5); he would resist the temptation to confer divine properties on mortal flesh, to convert "heaven itself" into a rhetorical "ornament" (Sonnet 21, l. 3). Sonnet 130, in enumerating examples of what it calls "false compare" (14), once more refuses each element of the descriptive code rejected in Sonnet 21; and it too reserves a privileged status for a misguided simile of the heavenly category: "My mistress eyes are nothing like the sun" (1). Shakespeare's speaker, who, "true in love," would "truly write" (Sonnet 21, l. 9), thus challenges typically Petrarchan description on at least two related levels: first, he argues, its hyperbolic display implies a boast; and second, the extravagance of that boast implies a lie. Were one to take Petrarch and his followers at their word, the motives of their rhetoric would at the very least seem questionable: "I will not praise," writes the poet-critic, "that purpose not to sell" (Sonnet 21, l. 14).

By introducing the concept of merchandizing into the economy of description, Shakespeare's speaker, moreover, transforms the direct line one would expect to unite lover and beloved into a triangle. Here a lyric "I" does not privately speak to a lyric "you" but rather, by "publishing" his love, interjects a third term: "I" speaks "you" to an audience that, it is hoped, will in turn purchase "you." The relationship so constructed involves an active buyer, an active seller, and a passive object for sale. Within this context it is only logical that canonical descriptions of "you," descriptions characterized as embedded in the hyperbolic language of salesmanship, would be wholly inappropriate to one who "truly loves" either an anti-Petrarchan "dark lady" or an anti-Petrarchan "master mistress." For, on the one hand, unless "I" intends to give or to sell "you," which he does not, any indulgence in false or proud comparison in the presence of a third person dangerously flirts with theft; it is a foolish miscalculation. And, on the other, any "seller's praise" does violence to "you" in that it converts "you" into an object, albeit precious, of exchange. The violent nature of such an appropriation, moreover, is all the more effectively unmasked when a male "I" celebrates a male "you," for the male beloved is thus incongruously placed in a "normalized" female position, that of a commodity in the traffic between men.[7]

It is not surprising, then, that in his figuration of an "other" voice, a voice not actively engaged in buying or selling, the speaker would turn to the silenced voice of the "Other," to Philomela: "Therefore like her, I sometime hold my tongue, / Because I would not dull you with my song" (Sonnet 102, ll. 13–14). Although referring to a Philomela already metamorphosed into a nightingale, into a bird that sings in the spring but not in the summer night when the "wild music" of other birds "burthens every bough" (11), the speaker none the less acknowledges the pathos of her preceding story: her songs are "mournful hymns" (10). For Philomela, a raped and mutilated woman, has no tongue to hold; it was cut out by her rapist so that she could not speak in blame. The "speech" of Philomela, then, as Patricia Joplin has brilliantly argued, is a speech lost to the violence inherent in the traffic in women, a speech to be painfully reconstituted through the "voice of the shuttle."[8] It is not without irony, then, that here a male speaker appropriates that voice in a maneuver that is, at least at some level, a strategy of winning favor within the world of men. It is through his humble silence, his modest rhetoric, that he would set himself apart from other male speakers, that he would triumph over the flock of Petrarchan versifiers. Anxiously confronting the impoverished language of praise and its troubling implications, the speaker who would be different confronts the threat of his own inarticulate-ness by espousing the female figure of silencing, the violated voice of the raped woman.

*

Lucrece opens as Tarquin, the son of a usurper king, leaves the Roman military encampment outside of the city of Ardea. His hasty departure was inspired, the narrator hypothesizes, by Collatine's laudatory description of his wife, Lucrece. A relative, friend, and fellow soldier of Collatine, Tarquin has determined that he must possess his comrade's chaste and beautiful wife. When he arrives at Collatium, Lucrece welcomes him and provides him with lodging. During the night he rapes her and leaves. Lucrece's grief takes the form of a series of laments and a lengthy meditation on a "skilful painting" (1387) of the fall of Troy in which she seeks an image sufficient to mirror her suffering. She sends for Collatine, and, when he and his men arrive, she tells them about the rape, swears them to revenge, names the rapist, and commits suicide. Brutus seizes the moment to call for the banishment of Tarquin, and, inspired by the display of Lucrece's body, the Romans consent. Indeed, Roman history recounts their reaction as a revolt: they overthrow the government of Tarquin's father, and replace a monarchy with a republic. Collatine and Brutus, notably, are its first consuls. Shakespeare's poem is clearly divided by the rape: in the first half, the motives and meditations of the rapist dominate; in the second, the lamentations of the victim. Both place lengthy descriptions in the foreground; but the first, where the extensive blazons of Lucrece appear, constitutes the textual ground of this study.

The initiating event in Lucrece is a contest. The poem's opening focus is on "lust-breathed Tarquin" (3) as he speeds away from the Roman camp; but within the space of one stanza that focus shifts to present a flashback revealing the origins of his uncontrollable desire:

> Haply that name of "chaste" unhapp'ly set
> This bateless edge on his keen appetite,
> When Collatine unwisely did not let
> To praise the clear unmatched red and white
> Which triumph'd in that sky of his delight;
>   Where mortal stars as bright as heaven's beauties,
>   With pure aspects did him peculiar duties.
>
> For he the night before, in Tarquin's tent
> Unlock'd the treasure of his happy state:
> What priceless wealth the heavens had him lent,
> In the possession of his beauteous mate;
> Reck'ning his fortune at such high proud rate
>   That kings might be espoused to more fame,
>   But king nor peer to such a peerless dame. . . .
>
> Perchance his boast of Lucrece' sov'reignty
> Suggested this proud issue of a king;
> For by our ears our hearts oft tainted be.
> Perchance that envy of so rich a thing,
> Braving compare, disdainfully did sting
>   His high-pitch'd thoughts, that meaner men should vaunt
>   That golden hap which their superiors want.
>
> (8–21; 36–42)

Shakespeare locates the ultimate cause of Tarquin's crime, and Lucrece's subsequent suicide, in an evening's entertainment. The prose "Argument" that precedes the poem adds further clarification: "In their discourses after supper everyone commended the virtues of his own wife; among whom Collatinus extolled the incomparable chastity of his wife Lucretia."[9] The prose next narrates an event that Shakespeare significantly writes out of the poetry: the competitors ride from Ardea to Rome to test their wives and, with the exception of Lucrece, all are "found dancing and revelling, or in several disports." It is for this reason that "the noblemen yielded Collatinus the victory, and his wife the fame." The "Argument," in contrast to the poem, then, remains faithful to Shakespeare's two principal sources, Ovid and Livy.

> Young Tarquin entertained his comrades with feast and wine: . . . Each praised his wife: in their eagerness dispute ran high, and every tongue and heart grew hot with deep draughts of wine. Then up and spake the man who from Collatia took his famous name: No need of words! Trust deeds!
>
> (Ovid, *Fasti*, II, 725–6; 731–4)[10]

The young princes for their part passed their idle hours together at dinners and drinking bouts. It chanced, as they were drinking . . . that the subject of wives came up. Every man fell to praising his own wife with enthusiasm, and, as their rivalry grew hot, Collatinus said that there was no need to talk about it, for it was in their power to know . . . how far the rest were excelled by his own Lucretia.

(Livy, *From the Founding of the City*, I, lvii, 5–7)[11]

Rereading Shakespeare's classical models reveals the radical way in which he transforms them.[12] The descriptive occasion remains the same – the light-hearted boasting contest – but the all-important test, ironically proposed by Collatine in both Ovid and Livy, has been eliminated. In *Lucrece* Collatine becomes a foolish orator, not an enemy of words but their champion. He who stops the descriptive speeches is now blamed for not knowing when to stop: "When Collatine unwisely did not let / To praise . . ." (10–11). Moreover, in both Latin sources the sight of Lucrece inflames Tarquin's passion; in *Lucrece* he sets off for Collatium without having seen her. The result, then, of this rewriting is a heightened insistence on the power of description, on the dangers inherent in descriptive occasions. Here, Collatine's rhetoric, not Lucrece's behavior, wins over his companions; Collatine's rhetoric, not Lucrece's beauty, prompts Tarquin's departure.

What transpires in Tarquin's tent, then, is an after-dinner conversation during which, in a "pleasant humour" ("Argument"), his warrior guests divert each other through a contest of epideictic oratory, oratory intended to persuade, in this case, through hyperbolic praise of its female subject.[13] Shakespeare's soldiers present "discourses" ("Argument"), and his narrator characterizes them as orators (30). Collatine is labeled a "publisher" of his possession (33), his descriptive speech is called a "boast" (36), and his rhetoric is thus specifically in the mode of competitive "blazon." A similar context, the one that sets in motion the plot of narrowly averted rape in *Cymbeline*, provides, I think, clues to reading the rhetoric of the initiating event of *Lucrece*:

It was much like an argument that fell out last night, where each of us fell in praise of our country mistresses; this gentleman at that time vouching (and upon warrant of bloody affirmation) his to be more fair, virtuous, wise, chaste, constant, qualified and less attemptable than any the rarest of our ladies in France.

(*Cymbeline*, I.v. 53–9)

This recollection of two previous boasting contests predictably prompts still another, and from that final one evolves the wager that sends Iachimo to test the honor of Imogen. At the end of the play, when a repentant Iachimo reflects back on the evening of feasting and oratory that led him astray, he recalls how

Posthumus was drawn into the competition by hearing other guests "praise [their] loves of Italy / For beauty, that made barren the swell'd boast / Of him that best could speak" (V.v.161–3). It was then that Posthumus picked up the oratorical challenge and began "His mistress' picture, which, by his tongue, being made" (V.v.175), proved the others "unspeaking sots" (V.v. 178). Iachimo confesses that he "made scruple" of Posthumus's praise, and for that reason "wager'd with him" (V.v.182).

Returning to *Cymbeline*, I.v, Iachimo's making "scruple" of Posthumus's praise takes the form of a debate about the colors of rhetorical ornamentation, about the terms of acceptable versus "proud compare." Iachimo elaborates:

> If she went before others I have seen, as that diamond of yours outlustres many I have beheld, I could not but believe she excelled many: but I have not seen the most precious diamond that is, nor you the lady.
>
> (*Cymbeline*, I.v.69–73)

Posthumus's justification of his use of the superlative ("I prais'd her as I rated her: so do I my stone" (I.v.74)) underlines an emerging reification of Imogen, a reification implicating one of the most conventional Petrarchan conceits – beautiful eyes framed by blond hair are diamonds set in gold. Imogen's position becomes that of a splendid jewel placed between buyer and seller. Shakespeare's scene, after all, is a gentlemanly transposition of what is an after-dinner conversation among merchants in the *Decameron*; it is, at some level, a descent into shop talk. Although Posthumus rejects the vocabulary of merchandizing ("the one may be sold or given. . . . The other is not a thing for sale, and only the gift of the gods" (I.v.79–82)), he none the less unwisely engages in it through his own prideful rhetoric.[14] When Iachimo responds that the very notion of a perfect woman, like that of a perfect jewel, invites theft, he challenges the judgment of the describer, he questions the wisdom of describing. The narrator of *Lucrece* explicitly poses that same question:

> Beauty itself doth of itself persuade
> The eyes of men without an orator;
> What needeth then apologies be made,
> To set forth that which is so singular?
> Or why is Collatine the publisher
>   Of that rich jewel he should keep unknown
>   From thievish ears, because it is his own?
>
> (29–35)

Collatine, of course, is not content to enjoy his "treasure" (16), his "priceless wealth" (17), his "fortune" (19) in silence since, within the economy of a competition, wealth is not wealth unless flaunted, unless inspiring envy, unless affirming superiority. Collatine's descriptive gesture, then, entails a risk inherent in the gesture itself: he generates description, he opens Lucrece up for display, *in order to* inspire jealousy; and jealousy, once inspired, may be carried to its logical conclusion – theft. Indeed Shakespeare's narrator specifically casts Tarquin's desire for Lucrece as desire for lucre:[15]

> Those that much covet are with gain so fond
> That what they have not, that which they possess
> They scatter and unloose it from their bond;
> And so by hoping more they have but less,
> Of gaining more, the profit of excess
>   Is but to surfeit, and such griefs sustain,
>   That they prove bankrout in this poor rich gain.
>
> (134–40)

Before the rape Tarquin wonders "What win I if I gain the thing I seek?" (211); after, Lucrece declares herself, and thus Collatine, "robb'd and ransack'd by injurious theft" (838). The cause of the rape ("the act of taking anything by force, violent seizure (of goods), robbery, and, after 1481, violation of a woman") is precisely that Collatine's self-serving oratory has fallen on "thievish" rather than passive, but none the less envious, ears. As Catherine Stimpson points out, "men rape what other men possess."[16] Tarquin's family has recently assumed power and is thus "espoused to more fame" (20), but it is Collatine who claims the "peerless dame" (21). In that Lucrece is "peerless," is "so rich a thing, / Braving compare" (39–40), she would seem destined for royal possession: "Her peerless feature, joined with her birth, / Approves her fit for none but for a king" (*1 Henry VI*, V.v.68–9). In the play of power between Tarquin and Collatine, at least for the privileged duration of this after-dinner sport, Collatine has carried the day – or, rather, the evening – by usurping royal prerogative. Description within a like context clearly serves the describer and not the described; extravagant praise of Lucrece is more precisely praise of Collatine, be it as proud possessor or as proud rhetorician. The rapist is indeed the villain of the piece, but the instigation of this particular villainy is more correctly located along the fine line walked by the boaster. Rape is the price Lucrece pays for having been described.

The matter for Collatine's rhetoric, the argument suggests, is Lucrece's chastity; the poem, however, progressively shifts its reader's perspective. Although virtue is always at issue, it soon competes with beauty for the distinction of being Lucrece's most appreciable quality. By the time of the rape Tarquin considers only "beauty" to be his "prize" (279); he tells Lucrece, "Thy beauty hath ensnar'd thee to this night" (485). Beauty, we know, does not need the embellishments of an orator: "Beauty itself doth of itself persuade" (29). It "excels the quirks of blazoning pens," and is sufficiently persuasive "in the essential vesture of creation" (*Othello*, II.i.

63–4). And still in Tarquin's tent it seems that Collatine called upon all the conceits of descriptive convention to outdo his comrades at arms:

> When Collatine unwisely did not let
> To praise the clear unmatched red and white
> Which triumph'd in that sky of his delight;
>> Where mortal stars as bright as heaven's beauties,
>> With pure aspects did him peculiar duties.
>
>> (10–14)

The body Collatine praised, the narrator tells us, is a partial body, a face; its distinctive features are the conventional colors of its flesh and the brightness of its eyes. Collatine's description depends, moreover, on a well-worn Petrarchan conceit: the lady's face is a clear sky; her eyes, its stars. It should be noted that this specific conceit dominates the discarded descriptive mode of Sonnet 21, where the speaker rejects the use of "heav'n itself for ornament" (3). The problem, thus, seems to reside in the unacceptable boast, the coupling of what is mortal to what is heavenly, that determines the line: "Where mortal stars *as* bright *as* heaven's beauties" (13, my italics). By the time the reader, like Tarquin, first "sees" Lucrece, the stage has been set for a repeat performance of a now familiar rhetorical portrait:

> When at Collatium this false lord [Tarquin] arrived,
> Well was he welcom'd by the Roman dame [Lucrece],
> Within whose face beauty and virtue strived
> Which of them both should underprop her fame.
> When virtue bragg'd, beauty would blush for shame;
>> When beauty boasted blushes, in despite
>> Virtue would stain that o'er with silver white.
>
> But beauty in that white entituled
> From Venus' doves, doth challenge that fair field;
> Then virtue claims from beauty beauty's red,
> Which virtue gave the golden age to gild
> Their silver cheeks, and call'd it then their shield;
>> Teaching them thus to use it in the fight,
>> When shame assail'd, the red should fence the white.
>
> This heraldry in Lucrece' face was seen,
> Argu'd by beauty's red and virtue's white;
> Of either's colour was the other queen,
> Proving from world's minority their right.
> Yet their ambition makes them still to fight;
>> The sov'reignty of either being so great,
>> That oft they interchange each other's seat. . . .

103

Now thinks he that her husband's shallow tongue, –
The niggard prodigal that prais'd her so, –
In that high task hath done her beauty wrong,
Which far exceeds his barren skill to show.
Therefore that praise which Collatine doth owe
   Enchanted Tarquin answers with surmise,
   In silent wonder of still-gazing eyes.

(50–70; 78–84)

In the presence of the "silent war of lilies and of roses" (71) in Lucrece's "fair face's field" (72), Tarquin stands awestruck, frozen. And yet his mind is filled with Collatine's evening oratory; before a real, as opposed to a rhetorical, beauty his thoughts tellingly return to an assessment of the paradoxes inherent in Collatine's speech. Tarquin mentally characterizes the previous blazon of Lucrece as an expression of both a prideful need to possess and a foolish propensity to squander. For Collatine, an orator whose skill is barren, had lavished "poor rich" praise through a catalogue of overblown clichés, rich in exaggeration but poor before the splendor of their subject; Tarquin, at least momentarily, has "eyes to wonder" but lacks a tongue "to praise" (Sonnet 106, l. 14).

More important, however, when the reader "sees" what Tarquin sees, that spectacle proves to be little more than a heraldic amplification of one element of Collatine's description, an amplification operated through the introduction of a conceit that literalizes the rivalry already prefigured in the narrator's synopsis (her "unmatched red and white . . . triumph'd" (11–12)). Lucrece's face becomes an animated shield colored in alternating red and white. Collatine's original praise was "unwise" to dilate or expand upon that coloration, and yet here her milky complexion and rosy blush fill four stanzas. Shakespeare's narrator, it appears, would outdo Collatine in rhetorical *copia*. His strategy, of course, is not a new one: the original *blasonneurs*, each outdoing the others by displaying *his* part of woman's body, repeatedly employed the body/shield metaphor. In Sidney's *Astrophil and Stella*, 13, Astrophil praised Stella by inventing a competition among male gods as to "whose armes the fairest were" (2): Cupid won, "for on his crest there lies / *Stella's* faire haire, her face he makes his sheild" (10).[17] The narrator of *Lucrece*, claiming his own poetic status through a dazzling blazon, paints his subject in the colors of heraldic terminology. Lucrece's face becomes a red and white ground or field (its "colours") bearing stars (its "charges") on the surface. The imagistic network thus set in motion figures Lucrece's beauty throughout the poem.

In Tudor England, coats of arms held "an immense and imposing place in everyday life."[18] The term "armes," John Guillim advised, had to be understood "in a metaphoricall sense" since heraldic "arms" assumed that name "by way of a figure called *Metonymia subiecti*" from "martiall instruments."[19] With the introduction of gunpowder, shields were less and less the practical gear of the warrior. They remained his emblem, however, and figured in nostalgically chivalric court entertainments; in pageants, tilts, and tourneys; and in a variety of decorative contexts, where they displayed the symbolic marks of gentlemanly pedigree. Guillim notes their double function: on the one hand, "they doe delight the beholder, and greatly grace and beautifie" the people and places they adorn; and, on the other, they signify personal status by identifying the owner's property and ancestry.[20] Coats of arms displayed the "precious gem" of honor by marking the distinction between the "gentle" and the "ungentle," the "difference twixt the Lord and Page."[21] Their complex system of charges and colors served also to make further distinctions: only monarchs, for example, could display the sun on their coat; only knights ennobled by monarchs could display precious stones. To confuse the correspondence of symbol to social status was forbidden, "for that it [was] a thing unfitting, either to handle a meane argument in a loftie stile, or a stately argument in a meane."[22] Family arms, name and property – in many senses coextensive – were bound within a patriarchal system of entitlement: "It was the male line whose ancestry was traced so diligently by the genealogists and heralds, and in almost all cases via the male line that titles were inherited."[23] The "name of the house" could not be preserved by a woman since, once married, she took her "denomination" and her "colors" from her husband. Lucrece's face, then, is not her shield, but rather her husband's: "Collatine," she says, "thine honour lay in me" (834).[24]

Read as a martial image, Lucrece's body as shield stands between Tarquin and Collatine to deflect blows, to prevent direct hits; read as a heraldic image, that same body is the medium assuring the passage of Collatium from father to as yet unborn son. Once raped, a polluted medium threatens the family with "nameless bastardy" (522).[25] Tarquin's crime, in essence the wearing of another man's coat of arms, was, according to Gerard Leigh, not only punishable by death in the England of the 1590s but also by attaintment. The marking or scarring of a shield for behavior so scandalous as to contaminate the honor of an entire family, attaintment was prescribed for a variety of crimes, not only for the defiling of a "maid, wife, or widow" but also for "too much boasting" of oneself in "manhood and martial acts."[26] Clearly, "Honour and beauty in the owner's arms, / Are weakly fortress'd from a world of harms" (27–8), when those arms are "unwisely" displayed, are made vulnerable to usurpation. The form the narrator's description of Lucrece assumes, moreover, makes plain the implications of the metaphor upon which it depends: here metaphor re-enacts the descriptive scene which narrative has just recounted. What we read in Lucrece's face is the story of a competition that, although between allegorical queens, is entirely cast in the vocabulary of gentlemanly combat: first, beauty and virtue strive for pre-dominance ("virtue bragg'd" (54) and "beauty boasted" (55)); then, moving to territorially figured counter-claims for the right to display the other's colors, they shift ground to a field where the "red should fence the white" (63); and finally skirmish becomes serious as two ambitious warriors con-front each other, "The sov'reignty of either being so great, / That oft they interchange each other's seat" (69–70). Indeed, Tarquin advances toward Lucrece "like a foul usurper" who plots "from this fair throne to heave the owner out" (412–13). The embattled tale inscribed in Lucrece's face is, then, the tale of *Lucrece*: it proceeds from a boasting match (as in Tarquin's tent), to a claim for the opponent's "field" and "colors" (as we will see in the rape), to an exchange of sovereignty (as will follow the action of the poem).

Lucrece is fully blazoned only when Tarquin approaches her bed.[27] He draws back the curtain, and his eyes begin "to wink, being blinded with a greater light" (375): the beauty of Lucrece "dazzleth" (377) her spectator into a state of suspended contemplation. The narrator describes Lucrece's body part by part, through a series of rhetorically highlighted "couplements" (flesh *like* an April daisy, hair *like* golden threads, and so on). Although his description introduces new colors, it opens and closes with variations of Collatine's "red and white": "Her lily hand her rosy cheek lies under" (386); "Her coral lips, her snow-white dimpled chin" (420).[28] Tarquin's initial assault, in the form of a touch, awakens Lucrece, and he tellingly explains his presence by evoking not what he has just seen with his eyes (her hands, her hair, her breasts), but rather what he had previously "seen" with his ears:

> First like a trumpet doth his tongue begin
> To sound a parley to his heartless foe, ...
>
> But she with vehement prayers urgeth still
> Under what colour he commits this ill.
>
> Thus he replies: "The colour in thy face,
> That even for anger makes the lily pale
> And the red rose blush at her own disgrace,
> Shall plead for me and tell my loving tale.
> Under that colour am I come to scale
> Thy never-conquer'd fort: the fault is thine,
> For those thine eyes betray thee unto mine.
>
> (470–1; 475–83)

Tarquin would persuade Lucrece with flattery. Indeed, taken out of the context of a rape, his language is that conventional to "loving tales": he celebrates her complexion; he represents her as a virtuously unassailable fortress; he praises the irresistible beauty of her eyes.

Tarquin goes on to define two moments in which Lucrece's beauty has acted upon him: first the moment in which her described beauty destined her to be raped; and second the moment, after his period of self-questioning, in which her perceived beauty reinforced his conviction. It is clear, however, that the determining moment is the first: in *Lucrece* vision is shaped by description. The rapist returns obsessively to the narrator's five-line synopsis of Collatine's winning blazon; he locates motive in that initial fragmentary portrait; he speaks to his victim only of the bright eyes that "charge" and of the red and white that "colour" her shield. Although Tarquin assigns responsibility to Lucrece ("the fault is thine" (482)), his rhetoric of praise reveals its agonistic subtext. Indeed, his descriptive strategies literally repeat those of Collatine: he moves from Lucrece's complexion to her eyes; his final line ("For those thine eyes betray thee unto mine" (483)) usurps the "peculiar duties" (14) of Collatine's conclusion.

In addition, Tarquin's pun on the word "colour" – a word that appears more often in *Lucrece* than in any other Shakespearean text – signals the rhetorical origins of the crime. Lucrece asks under what "colour" (pretext) he commits "this ill" (476), and he responds that the color in her face will serve as orator to justify his action, that under that color he rapes her. This wordplay is not new to Tarquin; he has already used it in his self-vindicating soliloquy:

> O how her fear did make her colour rise!
>   First red as roses that on lawn we lay,
>   Then white as lawn, the roses took away. . . .
>
> Why hunt I then for colour or excuses?
> All orators are dumb when beauty pleadeth.
>   (257–9; 267–8)

Semantic play here depends upon the sixteenth-century possibilities of the term "colour": the "colours" of Lucrece's flesh (the red and white of her face) are indistinguishable from the "colours" of heraldry (the symbolic colors on the shield that is her face) which, in turn, are indistinguishable from the "colors" of Collatine's rhetoric (the embellishing figures that fatally represent that face). Here body, shield, and rhetoric become one.

After the rape, the "heraldry in Lucrece' face" is transformed: she perceives herself as marked or tainted;[29] her face wears "sorrow's livery" (1222). Her maid wonders but dares not ask, "Why her two suns were cloud-eclipsed so, / Nor why her fair cheeks over-wash'd with woe" (1224–5). When Collatine arrives, he stares "amazedly" at "her sad face" (1591), at "her lively colour kill'd with deadly cares" (1593), and asks, tellingly, "what spite hath [her] fair colour spent" (1600). The double implication of the verb "to spend," meaning also "to speak," points to the irony of Collatine's question; for in spending (speaking) her "fair colour" he has also spent (wasted or consumed) it. At the sight of Lucrece's suicide, Collatine and his men stand "stone-still, astonish'd with this deadly deed" (1730). As the color pours out of her body, her father and her husband compete for possession of the corpse: "Then one doth call her his, the other his, / Yet neither may possess the claim they lay" (1793-4).[30] Her father laments the loss of that "fair fresh mirror" that revealed in its complexion (its red and white) the blush of his youth: "O from thy cheeks my image thou hast torn" (1762). Her husband, "the hopeless merchant of this loss" (1660), "bathes the pale fear in his face" (white) (1775) in Lucrece's "bleeding stream" (red, now tainted with black) (1774) and then, significantly, fails to make rhetoric of his experience:

> The deep vexation of his inward soul
> Hath serv'd a dumb arrest upon his tongue;
> Who, mad that sorrow should his use control
> Or keep him from heart-easing words so long,
> Begins to talk; but through his lips do throng
>   Weak words, so thick come in his poor heart's aid
>   That no man could distinguish what he said.
>
> (1779-85)

Shakespeare's poem closes as it opened, as men rhetorically compete with each other over Lucrece's body. Now that the victorious orator has been rendered incomprehensible, another takes over with a call to revenge. The events that begin in a playful rhetoric of praise end in a serious rhetoric of blame. *Lucrece*, then, is clearly "about the rhetoric of display, about the motives of eloquence,"[31] but what is "displayed" at each privileged moment is the woman's body raped at the narrative's center. When the warriors move "To show her bleeding body thorough Rome, / And so to publish Tarquin's foul offence" (1851-2), display of Lucrece in death parallels display of Lucrece in life: the bloodiness and pallor of her corpse stand as a sign of Tarquin's dishonor, just as her "unmatched red and white" stood as a sign of Collatine's honor.

Lucrece is rare among Shakespeare's texts in that it is dedicated: "*Lucrece*: To the Right Honourable Henry Wriothesley, Earl of Southampton and Baron of Titchfield." Its dedicatory epistle predictably expresses devotion to a young dedicatee suggestively identified, by some, as the young "master mistress" of the Sonnets. The epistle suggests that the poet's "untutored lines" are hardly worthy of their noble patron, and yet Shakespeare's lines are anything but "untutored." Indeed, *Lucrece* is a masterpiece, that is, a piece "made by an artist to prove he is a master."[32] The closing of the London theaters in the early 1590s compelled young playwrights to impose themselves as masters of alternative genres; patrons, like Southampton, had to be courted and rival poets, like those evoked in the Sonnets, conquered. The glossy rhetorical surface of *Lucrece* – the insistent foregrounding of "display pieces" that has prompted so much critical praise and blame[33] – serves above all to demonstrate the prowess of the poet. And it is in this sense that Shakespeare moves in two directions at once: he dramatically calls into question descriptive fashion while amply demonstrating that he controls it.[34] Entered like Collatine in a contest of skill, Shakespeare's encomium of Lucrece – his publication of *Lucrece* – stands as a shield, as an artfully constructed sign of identity, as a proof of excellence.

*

When, in his *Accedence of Armorie*, Gerard Leigh enumerates the nine "sundry fashions" of shields, he begins with the "firste, and ancients of all others."[35] The source for this postulation of origin, we are told, is to be found in "the Poets" who tell of the transformation of an exquisitely beautiful woman, Medusa, into an "ouglie, monstrous shape."[36] Medusa figures in two contexts as a face on a shield: first, Perseus uses a shield to reflect her image and thus to enable him to decapitate her either by avoiding the need to look at her directly or by stupefying her with the sight of her own reflection; and second, when the battles of Perseus are done and Medusa's head is no longer needed to petrify male rivals, he gives it to Athena, who bears it on her shield, a shield in turn copied by later warriors. It is the latter shield, the Gorgon-bearing shield of Athena, "godesse of Herehaughts [heralds],"[37] that Leigh goes on to describe as follows:

> this targe of the celestial goddes sheweth thincestious life and filthy act committed by Medusa daughter to King Phorcius, who spared not a publique place for holy rites. Ye the sacred Temple of Minerva to practise her filthy lust, with that same godde Neptune, wherof as she openly fled the discipline of womanly shamfastnes, she was by the godes decree for hir so foule a fault, bereft of all dame Bewties shape, with every comely ornament of Natures decking. The glyding eye framed to fancies amorous lust, turned was to wan and deadlie beholding. And for those golden and crisped lockes, rose fowle and hideous serpents . . . Thus everie seemelie gifte transformed into loathsome annoiance, of a beautiful Queene, is made a beastlie monster, horrible to mankinde, a mirror for Venus minions.[38]

Leigh, writing during the reign of a "most gorgious and bewtifull" virgin queen,[39] reports the story of Medusa as a moral tale, as a lesson about the dangers of straying from "womanly shamfastnes" and, by implication, of frequenting women who do. Gifted with every "comely ornament" of conventional Petrarchan beauty – bright eyes, curly golden hair – Medusa's fair face's field is metamorphosed in the name of punishment for a sin Leigh elsewhere refers to as an "adulterie."[40] The Gorgon's face, then, stands as the reverse of Lucrece's face, and the act defining that difference, in Leigh's rendition, would seem to be any unlawful expression of female sexuality.

The report Leigh makes of Medusa is, of course, precisely the report Lucrece most fears for herself: her suicide is specifically motivated by a desire not to be matter for epideictic orators who might speak in blame or for "feast-finding minstrels" who might win profit by "tuning [her] defame" (815–19). Her dramatic refusal to live is, in part, a refusal to encourage wantonness in women. And yet what is strikingly coincident in the narratives of both Medusa and Lucrece is the determining presence of a rape. For, at least in Ovid's most familiar account, Medusa too is not only a paragon of beauty but also a victim of violation:

> she both in comly port
> And beautie, every other wight surmounted in such sort,
> That many suters unto hir did earnestly resort.
> And though that whole from top to toe most bewtifull she were,
> In all hir bodie was no part more goodly than hir heare.
> I know some parties yet alive, that say they did her see.
> It is reported how she should abusde by Neptune bee
> In Pallas Church.[41]

Rape, according to Ovid, is the price Medusa pays for being "beauty's best"; monstrousness, the price for having been raped. But the line separating idealization from denigration, beauty from the beast, is marked here by a male, not a female, gesture of violation.

"Medusa," wrote the Italian humanist Coluccio Salutati, "is artful eloquence."[42] Salutati explained his suggestive identification of a beautiful/ monstrous woman's face with artful speech by elaborating a false etymology, one that depends upon reading the name of Medusa's father, Forcus, as derived from the Latin *for* ("to speak"). And yet the pairing of Medusa with eloquence appears not only in the work of Salutati, but also in a privileged classical source. During still another lighthearted male contest of both drinking and oratory, the *Symposium*, a flattering Socrates tells Agathon, the speaker who immediately precedes him, that he was held spellbound by the dazzling display of Agathon's speech. He compares Agathon to the master rhetorician Gorgias, and then permits himself a witty play on words: "I was afraid that when Agathon got near the end he would arm his speech against mine with the Gorgon's head of Gorgias' eloquence, and strike me as dumb as a stone" (198c).[43] As the woman's face that one carries into battle, that reduces eloquent rivals to silent stone, the apotropaic power of the "Gorgon's head of Gorgias' eloquence" resides in its ability to stupefy a male opponent: "Whatever the horror the Medusa represents to the male imagination," writes John Freccero, "it is in some sense a female horror. In mythology, the Medusa is said to be powerless against women, for it was her feminine beauty that constituted the mortal threat to her admirers."[44] And that threat is a threat of forgetting: "By Medusa he [Fulgentius] wants to signify oblivion (which is without doubt to signify rhetorically); by changing the states of mind of men, she makes them forget previous thoughts."[45]

Shakespeare returns repeatedly to the dangers of falling victim to the manipulation of descriptive rhetoric about women: one need only think of Othello's vulnerability to Iago, or Posthumus's to Iachimo. More specifically, at the end of *I Henry VI*, the Earl of Suffolk outmaneuvers his king by displaying a Gorgon's head of gorgeous eloquence that makes his young monarch forget all former engagements: "Your wondrous rare description, noble Earl, / Of beauteous Margaret hath *astonish'd* me" (V.v. 1–2, my italics). Suffolk protests that his praise has been but superficial:

> The chief perfections of that lovely dame,
> Had I sufficient skill to utter them,
> Would make a volume of enticing lines,
> Able to ravish any dull conceit;
> (*I Henry VI*, V.v. 12–15)

The play's concluding lines point to the disastrous consequences of both Suffolk's ample rhetorical skill and Henry's defenselessness before the "force of [his] report" (V.v. 79). Suffolk momentarily prevails, and thus advances his plot to rule not only Margaret but, more importantly, "the King, and realm" (V.v. 108). Similarly, in the single stanza between the narrator's report of Collatine's descriptive blazon and the vision of Lucrece's face as shield, an astonished Tarquin speeds to Collatium, "His honour, his affairs, his friends, his state, / Neglected all" (45–6). Suffolk's consciously motivated description, like Collatine's carelessly miscalculated boast, clearly stupefied the opposition; it functioned as did perfect shields "in such glorious and glittering manner, that they dazzled the eyes of the beholders."[46] Here rhetorical display and heraldic display seem of a like purpose; and here both turn upon a male figuration of a woman's face.

When in the final poem of the *Rime Sparse*, Petrarch's speaker turns toward the Virgin, that "solid shield of afflicted people" (366, 17), he simultaneously turns away from a Laura now recognized to be a Medusa: "Medusa and my error have made me a stone" (366, 111).[47] That same Laura had, of course, constituted the obsessive fixation of an entire "volume of enticing lines" informed by a specifically descriptive project: "Love, who first set free my tongue, wishes me to depict and show her to whoever did not see her, and therefore a thousand times he was vainly put to work wit, time, pens, papers, inks" (*Rime Sparse*, 309, 5–8). The poet's labor is vain only in the sense that verse will never successfully represent her; and yet each failure provokes another attempt; each fragmentary portrait, because fragmentary, generates another. It is his mastery of what George Puttenham would later label "The Gorgious" that makes of Petrarch a poet's poet, that wins him the laurel crown. "The Gorgious" designates for Puttenham "the last and principall figure of our poeticall Ornament": it is the figure by which we "polish our speech and as it were attire it with copious and pleasant amplifications and much varietie of sentences, all running upon one point and one intent."[48] Petrarch's dazzling descriptive display, all running upon the figuration of Laura's beauty, functions – to continue Puttenham's analogy – as does the placing of "gorgious apparell" on a naked body, or the polishing of "marble or porphorite . . . so smoth and cleere, as ye may see your face in it."[49] It is indeed that fixity of vision, Petrarch would suggest, that turns him to *petra* ("stone"); but it is also that self-glorifying fixity that makes of him Petrarca: "Medusa is, like the lady of stone, no historic character at all, but the poet's own creation. Its threat is the threat of idolatry. In terms of mythological *exempla*, petrification by the Medusa is the real consequence of Pygmalion's folly."[50]

One might then wonder, following Mary Jacobus, if there is a woman in this text explicitly dedicated to the celebration of a woman.[51] Or, rather, does the shield of Laura/lauro but stand as a glossy surface positioned both to reflect Petrarch's own image of himself and to dazzle a world of rival poets stupefied by its display? For it is, in some senses, the fascination with that "feminized" median surface of one's own creation that must be conquered: if it threatens petrification, one must first petrify it. Thus Petrarch's characteristic descriptive moves – fragmentation and reification – are, like the moves of Perseus, designed not only to neutralize but also to appropriate the threat. By first decapitating Medusa and then converting her severed head into an object of use in his own defense, Perseus conquers the fear of that which both repels and fascinates, the fear cast from a Freudian, male perspective as fear of the female (the mother's) body. And yet, as recent critics have shown, the sexual threat figured as the face of the Medusa serves in turn to figure other threats – "male hysteria under political pressure," for example, or male anxiety before the limits of representation.[52] The male rhetorician, both politician and artist, thus places the shield of eloquence between himself and the "world of harms" that surrounds him. That shield, of course, is artfully painted on both faces; it speaks both in praise and in blame. The turn of the shield, like the flip of a Lucrece/Medusa coin, is a gesture subject only to his potentially capricious will. And, as Shakespeare demonstrates, even when that gesture problematizes its own status, it none the less remains embedded in the descriptive rhetoric it undercuts. The merging of the heraldic and the rhetorical, central to the very notion of a "blazon of sweet beauty's best," then, emblematizes the trap which description has traditionally constructed for "woman"; it remains, it would seem, to women to write their way out of it.[53]

Notes

Many colleagues and friends have contributed their expertise to the preparation of this essay. My gratitude is extended to all, although I mention only a few: Kevin Brownlee and David Kastan for patient and critical reading; Albert Ascoli, Rachel Jacoff, and Christian Wolff each for a singular insight or reference. Portions of this essay have appeared in *Poetics Today*, 6 (1985), 171–84, a special issue entitled *The Female Body in Western Culture: Semiotic Perspectives*, ed. Susan R. Suleiman; that issue will be published in an expanded version by Harvard University Press (1986).

1. Quotations from Shakespeare's Sonnets are from *The Riverside Shakespeare*, ed. G. Blakemore Evans (Boston, 1974). All other Shakespeare quotations are from the relevant Arden edition. Text and line references are indicated in parentheses following each quotation.

2. The verb "to blazon" ("to inscribe with arms . . . in some ornamental way, to describe fitly, to publish vauntingly or boastfully, to proclaim") first appears in English in the sixteenth century. All references in this essay to sixteenth-century definitions of terms are adapted from the *Oxford English Dictionary*. The rhetoric of "blazon" is, of course, part of the broader category of epideictic rhetoric, rhetoric in praise or blame. For a recent discussion of epideixis and Shakespeare's Sonnets, with bibliography, see Joel Fineman, "Shakespeare's 'Perjur'd Eye'" (*Representations*, 7 (1984)), 82–3, n. 8.

3. Elizabeth Cropper, "On beautiful women, Parmigianino, *Petrarchismo*, and the vernacular style" (*Art Bulletin*, 58 (1976)), 376.

4. The use of "skill" here represents an emendation of the 1609 text which shows "still." Here I follow Stephen Booth's edition of Shakespeare's *Sonnets* (New Haven and London, 1977), 341–2, n. 12. Booth gives a brief history of this emendation which he judges "generally accepted since the eighteenth century."

5. My theoretical framework clearly suggests the triangulated construct of mimetic desire outlined by René Girard, but as recast in the work of a number of feminist critics attentive to the role played by gender in the positioning of individuals upon that triangle. My formulation specifically echoes Mary Jacobus, "Is there a woman in this text?" (*New Literary History*, 14 (1982)), 119. For discussions of Girard in this context, see Jacobus, op. cit., 130–7; Patricia Klindienst Joplin, "The voice of the shuttle is ours" (*Stanford Literature Review*, 1 (1984), 35–6); and Eve Kosofsky Sedgwick, "Homophobia, misogyny, and capital: the example of *Our Mutual Friend*" (*Raritan*, 2, 3 (1983), 130–1). Coppélia Kahn characterizes *Lucrece* as a drama of male rivalry in "The Rape in Shakespeare's *Lucrece*" (*Shakespeare Studies*, 9 (1976), 53–4). Our interpretations differ in that she reads the "rhetorical display-pieces" as a "happy escape from the poem's insistent concern with the relationship between sex and power" (45), and I read them as inscribed within that relationship. I take the adjective "homosocial" from Sedgwick's work on "male homosocial (*including* homosexual) bonds" in the cited essay, as well as in "Sexualism and the citizen of the world: Wycherley, Sterne, and male homosocial desire" (*Critical Inquiry*, 11 (1984), 226–45).

6. Hélène Cixous, "The laugh of the Medusa," tr. Keith Cohen and Paula Cohen, in Elaine Marks and Isabelle de Courtivron (eds), *New French Feminisms* (Amherst, 1980), 249–50.

7. The classic essay on this subject is Gayle Rubin's "The traffic in women: notes on the 'political economy' of sex," in Rayna R. Reiter (ed.), *Toward an Anthropology of Women* (New York and London, 1975), 157–210. See also Joplin, op. cit., 31–43; and Sedgwick, "Homophobia, misogyny, and capital," 126–7.

8. On the problem of the appropriation of Philomela by male artists, see Joplin, op. cit., 43–53; and Jane Marcus, "Liberty, sorority, misogyny," in Edward Said (ed.), *Literature and Society: Selected Papers from the English Institute* (Baltimore, 1980), 61–2.

9. It should be noted that the authorship of the "Argument" has been questioned. Michael Platt usefully compares the frame provided by the "Argument" to "an action whose beginning is 'kings' and whose end is 'consuls,'" in "*The Rape of Lucrece* and the republic for which it stands" (*Centennial Review*, 19 (1975)), 64. The criticism on *Lucrece* is too abundant to be outlined here, but four discussions of the poem have particularly influenced this study: Clark Hulse on the iconic nature of *Lucrece*, in "'A piece of skilful painting' in Shakespeare's 'Lucrece'" (*Shakespeare Survey*, 31 (1978)), 13–22; Richard Lanham on the centrality of rhetoric as motive, *The Motives of Eloquence: Literary Rhetoric in the Renaissance* (New Haven and London, 1976); Coppélia Kahn's excellent essay on the politics of patriarchy; and Catherine R. Stimpson, "Shakespeare and the soil of rape," in Carolyn R. S. Lenz, Gayle Greene, and Carol T. Neely (eds), *The Woman's Part: Feminist Criticism of Shakespeare* (Urbana, Chicago and London, 1980), 56–64.

10. Ovid, *Fasti*, tr. James G. Frazer (London, 1931).

11. Livy, *From the Founding of the City*, tr. B. O. Foster (London, 1939).

12. Numerous critics have noted not only the folly of Collatine's boast, but also the discrepancy between the "Argument" (in line with the sources) and the poem. For a particularly persuasive description, followed by an interpretation very different from my own, see Roy W. Battenhouse, *Shakespearean Tragedy: Its Art and Its Christian Premises* (Bloomington, 1969), 7–8. See also Geoffrey Bullough (ed.), *Narrative and Dramatic Sources of Shakespeare*, I (London, 1957), 180; and Lanham, op. cit., 96.

13. Many sixteenth-century texts evoke similar descriptive occasions. Frederico Luigini's *Il Libro della Bella Donna* (Venice, 1554), for example, concludes a day of hunting and a hearty meal with an after-dinner game in which each hunter forms in words an ideal woman.

14. On the "shallow self-assertiveness" of Posthumus, see David S. Kastan, *Shakespeare and the Shapes of Time* (London and Basingstoke, 1982), 149.

15. On Lucrece as money or wealth, see Kahn, op. cit., 53–6.

16. Stimpson, op. cit., 58. See also Kahn, op. cit., 71, n. 19.

17. William A. Ringler, Jr (ed.), *The Poems of Sir Philip Sidney* (Oxford, 1962).

18. Guy C. Rothery, *The Heraldry of Shakespeare: A Commentary with Annotations* (London, 1930), 10.

19. John Guillim, *A Display of Heraldrie* (London, 1611), 2.

20. Ibid., 2.

21. In the verse epistles of Thomas Guillim and John St George, preceding Guillim, n. pag.

22. Guillim, op. cit., 7.

23. Lawrence Stone, *The Crisis of the Aristocracy 1558–1641* (Oxford, 1965), 591. Cited by Kahn, op. cit., 46.

24. My reading here is clearly at variance with that of Hulse, op. cit., 14.

25. See Kahn, op. cit., 47–8, 60–1.

26. Rothery, op. cit., 37.

27. This scene is recalled, and indeed alluded to, in Iachimo's approach to Imogen's bed (*Cymbeline*, II.ii); on the way in which Shakespeare's narrator implicates himself with a gaze "hardly less lewd than the rapist Tarquin's," see Joplin, op. cit., 33–4, n. 16.

28. For an analysis of the metaphors here comparing Lucrece's body to a city or country about to be attacked, see Kahn, op. cit., 56–7.

29. Ibid., 46–7.

30. Ibid., 55–6.

31. Lanham, op. cit., 82.

32. Ibid., 82.

33. See Muriel C. Bradbrook, *Shakespeare and Elizabethan Poetry: A Study of His Earlier Work in Relation to the Poetry of the Time* (New York, 1952), 115.

34. On "the dual role of the author" who "can move in both directions at the same time" (again in a context where human beings have become an exchange value), see René Girard, " 'To entrap the wisest': a reading of *The Merchant of Venice*," in Said (ed.), *Literature and Society*, 110.

35. Gerard Leigh, *Accedence of Armorie* (London, 1591), 16.

36. Ibid., p. 16^v.

37. Ibid., 16^v.

38. Ibid., 118^v–19^r.

39. George Puttenham, *The Arte of English Poesie*, ed. Edward Arber (London, 1869), 255.

40. Leigh, op. cit., 16.

41. W. H. D. Rouse (ed.), *Shakespeare's Ovid Being Arthur Golding's Translation of the Metamorphoses* (London, 1904), 101.

42. Coluccio Salutati, *De Laboribus Herculis*, ed. B. L. Ullman (Zurich, 1951), 418. My translation.

43. Plato, *Symposium*, tr. Michael Joyce, in Edith Hamilton and Huntington Cairns (eds), *The Collected Dialogues of Plato* (Princeton, 1961), 550.

44. John Freccero, "Medusa: the letter and the spirit" (*Yearbook of Italian Studies* (1972)), 7.

45. Salutati, op. cit., 417. My translation.

46. Guillim, *A Display of Heraldrie*, 4th edn (London, 1660), 6.

47. Petrarch, *Rime Sparse*, tr. Robert Durling, in *Petrarch's Lyric Poems* (Cambridge, Mass., 1976). All further references to Petrarch are to this edition and translation of the *Rime Sparse*, and will appear in parentheses in the text.

48. Puttenham, op. cit., 254.

49. Ibid., 254.

50. Freccero, op. cit., 13.

51. Jacobus, op. cit.

52. See Neil Hertz, "Medusa's head: male hysteria under political pressure" (*Representations*, 4 (1983), 27–54); and Louis Marin, *Détruire la peinture* (Paris, 1977).

53. "If Medusa has become a central figure for the woman artist to struggle with," writes Joplin, "it is because, herself a silenced woman, she has been used to silence other women" (op. cit., 50). See also Cixous, op. cit.

7

JONATHAN GOLDBERG

Shakespearean inscriptions: the voicing of power

> The penis is what men have and women do not; the phallus is the attribute of power which neither men nor women have.
> (Jane Gallop, *The Daughter's Seduction*)

> Les masles et femelles sont jettez en mesme moule.
> (Montaigne, *Sur des vers de Virgile*)

I want to open this essay with some guiding presuppositions; these will not be the matter of my argument, although without them I could not make it. I depend upon the work of a number of literary historians who have investigated the nature of genre in Renaissance theory and practice. From them, I derive the principle implicit in Rosalie Colie's title, *The Resources of Kind*,[1] that generic categories in the period are liberating, rather than confining, and that the identification of specific limitations within any hypothetical generic type does not match the actuality of the uses of the kinds. Pure forms are a Renaissance anomaly; hybrids are the rule. And, to turn to the subject of this essay, when Shakespeare makes use of the kinds of drama, there is, as Stephen Orgel argues, a sense of genre as a matrix of refiguration, genre allowing for the redistribution of materials; or, as Louise George Clubb demonstrates, a play like *Hamlet* is an anthology of generic principles, playing prescriptions against each other, an investigation into the limits of genre and an extension beyond those limits.[2] At the end, Hamlet commands Horatio "to tell my story" and to Fortinbras he sends his "dying voice" (V.ii.360, 367).[3] Representation continues and multiplies.

I begin by invoking the work of Colie, Orgel, and Clubb, because recently there has arisen a body of criticism that ignores such complexities of genre, and that seems intent upon straitlacing the Shakespearean text into rigidities of form and meaning. Thus, to take a recent example, Linda Bamber, in *Comic Women, Tragic Men: A Study of Gender and Genre in Shakespeare*,[4] sets out to argue what her title implies, a division of genre and gender in Shakespeare that allows for little traffic between the kinds, and that denies the play and energy that the critics I began with might argue characterize the multiplicity of the Shakespearean text. In such feminist criticism, Shakespeare is seen as inevitably expressing the positions of a patriarchal culture and replicating them in depictions of men who are capable of tragedy and of women who have power only in the less exacting world of comedy; for Bamber, Shakespeare can only see men from the inside, and his women remain other, incapable of change and often little more than the projections of male fantasy, since it is impossible for a male author to inhabit a woman's mind or body.

My argument is not with feminism, however, but with the particular kinds of blindness that seem implicit in an account like Bamber's. For, surely, the rigidity that she brings to the Shakespearean text is her own; her categories do not correspond to the historical specificity of the Shakespearean text. Bamber employs a strategy analogous to a mode of historical criticism that used to find in Shakespeare support for the so-called Elizabethan world picture and commonplaces about law and order. Yet Shakespeare's inhabitation of the conceptual apparatus of his time is far more problematic than that; replication of one ideological strain is not his position. Again, I cannot possibly do more here than point to Stephen Greenblatt's masterful account of the improvisatory relationship of Shakespeare to his culture for a persuasive counterstatement.[5] When we add the recognition that the norms of the period (let us return to genre as our example) are themselves always in play, we must acknowledge the falsity of a scheme that rigidly locates the Shakespearean text. To this, it must be emphasized that Bamber assumes a male/female opposition and a notion of character that lacks historical support.[6] In this, she is not so much like the historical critics just mentioned; rather, like many another Shakespearean critic, she has assumed that an informed common sense will lead her to correct perceptions about this most universal of geniuses.

I pause unconscionably long over Bamber's work because it is in danger of being hailed as the forefront of a new approach to Shakespeare. Carolyn Heilbrun, reviewing three feminist readings of Shakespeare which preceded Bamber's, compliments them for revealing "Shakespeare's essential conservatism and phallocentrism"; she continues:

> the facts are clear enough: Shakespeare, who encompassed all the world, was himself a victim of its essential restrictions upon experience for women, even as he recognized the dangers of these feminine restrictions

upon men. Shakespeare did not conceal male weakness or villainy, but he did fail to recognize the possibility of female autonomy and growth.[7]

Although I would not for a moment deny that "the world" inevitably represents a limit upon perception and experience, "the world" is nonetheless a larger and more complex item than Heilbrun imagines. And, in Shakespeare's time, it excludes most of the conceptual categories (e.g. autonomy and growth) that she projects from her modern, liberal vantage point upon his world. To say, at once, that it is larger and yet more exclusive than Heilbrun imagines is my attempt to register two facts at once; that the categories of the period are not our own, but that our divisions of genre and gender (to return to the theme of this essay) are not Shakespeare's either.

These are large claims, I realize, and to substantiate them properly would take more than an essay. Nonetheless, something can be done here. To think oneself into the multiple forms of Shakespearean experience and beyond the divisions of genre and gender requires a radical readjustment of approach and vocabulary: to give up, for instance, notions of character as self-same, owned, capable of autonomy and change; to give up, for instance, the notion that biological difference is an *a priori* fact, and to return to Simone de Beauvoir's essential insight in *The Second Sex* that woman is a cultural construct and category, and therefore not the same then as now. The leap I imagine is one that has been attempted by feminists trying to escape the deadlock of either/or and the same, a deadlock usually called masculine logic. For, ironically, feminists like Bamber reimpose the prescriptions they mean to erase by restating the oppressive categories that must be seen through and must be read beyond for a genuine feminist discourse to arise. My argument here is that such a discourse can be made available even in the Shakespearean text if only because it does not (re)inscribe the differences Bamber enunciates.

I propose here to look at the field of men and women talking within the Shakespearean text. My concern is genre, gender, and power. If it is (among other things) the position in language that points to the powers and limits which situate the sexes, then we might ask of Shakespeare the question Roland Barthes asked so often: "who is speaking?" This question directs us to a number of issues. Who (or what) speaks in the voice that articulates (it)self? Who, especially, speaks when I do? (I have tried to open this essay in the mouths of others to affirm one essential position for us, since we are in discourse invariably.) The radical shiftiness of the "I" may blur the proprietariness of gender, obscure the differences. In making arguments about the patriarchalism of Shakespeare's culture, critics forget that boys and girls in the Renaissance wear female clothes in their early years; femininity is there the undifferentiated sex from which maleness comes. On Shakespeare's stage, there are only men; the image of the culture is reversed. Both images – that there is but one sex – are the culture's. Both images – there is not one sex – are the culture's.

Who is in question. Speaking is in question. Do I speak or does something speak in me, something no smaller than the entire culture with all its multiple capacities? In arguments of the sort that I am calling into question, it is said that women in Shakespeare lack the autonomy of a voice, and are barred from discourse or limited and placed by male discourse. Cordelia – to whom I shall return towards the end of this paper – might be an example of this. But my point here is that no one – neither men nor women in Shakespeare – has such autonomy or such power. As an immediate complication in the claim that it is only women who lack voice, we might recall Coriolanus, home from the wars, greeting his wife as his "gracious silence" (II.i.192), but we must remember, too, that Coriolanus will not lend his lips to gain the people's voice, and that he seals his doom when, after his mother has spoken for more than 50 uninterrupted lines, *he holds her by the hand, silent* (V.iii.182), as the eloquent stage direction describes the moment that determines his fate.

Authority in the Shakespearean text is a matter not of having a voice but of voicing. This is the field of history, a stage of power. "Hear him but reason ... ; Hear him debate ... ; List his discourse ...," begins Canterbury's rapt account in the opening scene of *Henry V*, describing the transformed Prince Hal, now on the throne and securing his power. Power is voicing here, just as in the *Henry IV* plays it is always a matter of representation, the imposition of stories and the insistence on their truth. Canterbury describes the essential shape of a power play around the issue of voice. Henry's is the voicing of a world of discourse passing through him, vocalized powerfully. And if Henry's domain – "the world" of Heilbrun's review – comprises theology, statecraft, martial discourses and *raison d'état*, his placement in speech also functions to make others voiceless, or to point up the inadequacies of their vocalizations. Here, in part, is Canterbury's account:

> Hear him but reason in divinity,
> And, all-admiring, with an inward wish
> You would desire the King were made a prelate;
> Hear him debate of commonwealth affairs,
> You would say it hath been all in all his study;
> List his discourse of war, and you shall hear
> A fearful battle rend'red you in music;
> Turn him to any cause of policy,
> The Gordian knot of it he will unloose,
> Familiar as his garter; that, when he speaks,
> The air, a charter'd libertine, is still,
> And the mute wonder lurketh in men's ears
> To steal his sweet and honey'd sentences.
>
> (I.i.38–50)

As radical as Bottom's wish in *A Midsummer Night's Dream*, that he might play all the parts, is Henry's accomplishment, conquering the territories of discourse as if he perfectly possessed them and not they him. The effect of the voice in Henry is the provocation of desire, the elicitation of wishes and dreams, the inscription of a life story at odds with the facts, a scene of bodily familiarity as ordinary as the choice of clothes; yet here clothes make the man. On the other side of this vocalization is silence; the inscrutability of Henry within this discursive field, the still air and mute wonder in which the audience is suspended, the bees of the commonwealth swarming around the honeyed eloquence that the king manufactures. The effect of speech is to release a Henry apt for anyone's thought, and a release and constraint upon thought so that it takes the shape of the air itself, a "charter'd libertine," licensed and constrained, vocalized and silenced at once. Henry's entrance into discourse involves a suppression of another story (his own) and of others' stories, a play upon the air: voice is breath, atmosphere. It is the field of power. To be in history, Henry must assume this vocalic situation; it is the mirror of the position the monarchs of Shakespeare's time affirmed. Both Elizabeth and James declared that the king was one set upon a stage.[8]

The play of history (and the history play, that mixed genre) provides the discursive field against which I would read comedy and tragedy, and the situation of men and women voicing power. In tragedy and comedy, I pursue and am no doubt caught within the traces of a complicity that Gayatri Chakravorty Spivak enunciates as the field of special concern to the critic who is both a deconstructionist and a feminist (if we must use labels). She writes that the aspect of deconstructive practice that interests her most is "the recognition, within deconstructive practice, of provisional and intractable starting points in any investigative effort; its disclosure of complicities where a will to knowledge would create oppositions; its insistence that in disclosing complicities the critic-as-subject is herself complicit with the object of her critique; its emphasis upon 'history' and the ethico-political as the 'trace' of that complicity – the proof that we do not inhabit a clearly defined critical space free of such traces; and, finally, the acknowledgement that its own discourse can never be adequate to its example."[9]

*

First: to examine the law of the patriarch and to find within its power the slippages that undermine authority and permit vocalization. My example is Portia, my main concern her court appearance. My argument, in brief, is that the play fully problematizes the notion of the law and that Portia has a voice *within* the law; not that it constricts and denies her, not that she must submit to the father, but that she *becomes* the father precisely because the law is not the father's and not exclusively a male territory.[10] The law Portia enacts knows no kind; it is the law of genre.[11]

In the fourth act of *The Merchant of Venice*, Portia arrives in the court of law to function in place of the learned Bellario in offering an opinion on the legality of Shylock's proceeding against Antonio. Portia comes "furnished" (IV. i. 157) with Bellario's opinion and clothed as Balthazar, bearing the name of the servant she dispatched with a letter to the learned lawyer when she sought his advice (in III. iv). The letter completes its circuit, returning; before Portia appears in the court of law, a letter from Bellario serves as her credentials. In it, Portia is presented not merely as furnished with his opinion, but as one whose outer appearance belies an inner state. For, having "turned o'er many books together" (IV. i. 156–7), Bellario can report that although Portia bears a young body she has an old head. "I beseech you, let his lack of years be no impediment to let him lack a reverend estimation; for I never knew so young a body with so old a head" (161–4). Portia herself had commented, upon dispatching her letter to Bellario, that a certain "lack" would be furnished in her Venetian appearance, telling Nerissa that she will arrive in the court "in such a habit / That they shall think we are accomplished / With that we lack" (III. iv. 60–2).

The pattern here is clear, apparently. In order to assume the authority of Bellario, Portia must arrive clothed inwardly and outwardly as a man. Her mind has been made mature through perusal of the law books and by having been "furnished" with Bellario's knowledge; her outer form bears testament to this inner state, for the lack she suffers as a female is compensated for in her male accoutrements. Yet Bellario's letter asks for externality to be discounted. The form of the supposed boy is not to serve as an impediment to the receipt of the graver wisdom of his mature mind. So, the pattern is not in fact as clear as it seems to be. On the one hand, the words that Portia says upon sending the letter, and the words that the letter contain, echo: lack against lack, habit against furnishing. Yet, on the other, although the echoing texts offer a principle of simple repetition, of mere superimposition, the letter as it returns would seem to deny the principle of echo itself. It invites a cleavage between inner and outer equipage. The letter as it returns cleaves the letter itself; in the circuit of the letter something more (and less) than the circulation of the self-same seems to be in question.

The letter equivocates, offering itself as a credential which cannot stand the credence of the audience that knows that Portia and Bellario have communicated solely by letter, and that the conference reported in the letter is as much a fabrication as the name that Portia has taken or the disguise she wears. Even when Portia imagined the power she would have in disguise, it was to tell "quaint lies" (III. iv. 69) about the power of men (her power as a man), to slay women by denying them love, to offer repentance when it is too late. In short, she says, "I have within my mind / A thousand raw tricks of these bragging

Jacks, / Which I will practise" (III. iv. 76–8). In the certifying letter, however, her mind is furnished with the tricks of the law, and they become her practice. Nerissa's response to Portia's project – which she calls a device – is instructive: "Why, shall we turn to men?" (78) she asks, and Portia hears the equivocation in her words: shall we become men? shall we lend ourselves to male purposes? "Fie, what a question's that, / If thou wert near a lewd interpreter!" (79–80). Is the assumption of male power the submission to male domination? Does the accomplishment of the lack only serve to reinforce it? What is the circuit from the letter to the ring?

The "turn" that Portia takes calls into question the differences upon which the play rests, male and female, Jew and Christian, letter and spirit, for the lewdness of the play that she initiates – sending the letter and donning the disguise (the device) – rests upon equivocations within the letter, differences within the self-same. Portia's "whole device" (III. iv. 81) involves filling a place – the place of Bellario, the place of the law – through an act of replacement that calls into question the possibility of duplication (the repeatability and self-sameness upon which the law rests). Portia "comes . . . to fill up your Grace's request in my stead" (IV. i. 159–61). She appears as the equivocation of an *instead*, furnished with a voice that carries the letter and the body as the meeting point of within and without. The lies she will speak, the lewdness of her play, are carried on an equivocal vocal reed. She tells Nerissa that she will "wear my dagger with the braver grace, / And speak between the change of man and boy / With a reed voice, and turn two mincing steps / Into a manly stride" (III. iv. 65–8). The lack is supplied doubly, with a dagger and a voice, a reed. The reed is the instrument that conveys the turn, the change, a state between inside and outside, man and boy (the undifferentiated), man and mincer. To be the reed: poet's instrument. Pan and Syrinx. "Shall we turn to men?" (III. iv. 78). "We turned o'er many books together" (IV. i. 156–7). The circuit of the letter.

Portia begins the play under the bind of the law, deprived her will because of her father's will, inscribed in the living force of his dead letter, locked in a leaden casket. "So is the will of a living daughter curb'd by the will of a dead father" (I. ii. 25–6). The equivocal form she assumes in Act IV conveys the law of the father. Although she is (within the father's will) inert and inexpressive, a dead letter to be penetrated, she is also the meaning of the letter, the life which can be released. "Who chooses his meaning chooses you," Nerissa comments (I. ii. 33–4); Bassanio views the leaden casket and comments, "Thy paleness moves me more than eloquence" (III. ii. 106). Silent Portia, sacrificed for her father's word; Bassanio chooses, and words – in "excess" – are released, the "shadow" within the casket "confirm'd, sign'd, ratified" by Portia (III. ii. 112, 128, 149). The former contract is apparently re-inscribed, the rings the tokens, when Portia submits to Bassanio as to "her lord, her governor, her king" (167); but Bassanio reports himself as speechless now as Portia, and similarly awed, like a subject hearing "some oration fairly spoke / By a beloved prince" (180–1). The experience is so excessive that it surpasses the differences upon which meaning rests: "Every something, being blent together, / Turns to a wild of nothing, save of joy / Express'd and not express'd" (183–5). These turns, relays of power, express the circuit of the letter, the equivocations of voice articulated "between the change," "Express'd and not express'd." In the blending together in which the law (the contract – the bond) is ratified, the signature – the kiss – renders difference problematic.

In the lawcourt, Portia replays her contract with Bassanio, that marriage of her father's will and her own; she replays it with another father deprived of his daughter and his ducats (see II. viii), crying for justice to repair what he lacks, to exact his loss upon another, to make the word flesh ("my own flesh and blood to rebel" (III. i. 37), Shylock laments when Jessica has fled). It is a grim scene, and it should not be sentimentalized. Shylock may have a legitimate complaint against the society that has treated him like a scapegoat and carried off his daughter in a masquerade not unlike the one Portia plays with him in this scene, but that does not exonerate his murderousness. Portia explicates mercy but offers justice; justice is what Shylock desires. There is no going outside of the law, for its excess lies within, in the return of the letter, in the closing of the circuit: "A Daniel come to judgment! yea, a Daniel!"; "A second Daniel! a Daniel, Jew!" (IV. i. 223, 333). Nothing is the same the second time.

The travesty of the law, the transvestitism of the law, is *already inscribed* in the father's will, in the circuit of the letter, in the return in which doubling discovers the difference *already* within the same. Two wills are satisfied at once. "There is no power in Venice / Can alter a decree established" (IV. i. 218–19), the Duke declares; "There is no power in the tongue of man / To alter me," Shylock swears (241–2). The power is in "the very words" (254). "A Daniel, still say I, a second Daniel! / I thank, thee, Jew, for teaching me that word" (340–1). Within the word Portia pauses, to find "something else" (305): "This bond doth give thee here no jot of blood; / The words expressly are 'a pound of flesh'" (306–7). The limit represents an exclusion, releases a superfluity: no more or less means nothing at all. This was Portia's condition under the law, the "good sentences, and well pronounc'd" (I. ii. 11) that Nerissa read in her state, bound to a father's will and deprived her own. Portia comes to ratify the law and to reveal its bankruptcy in the very superfluity of her "sentence" (IV. i. 304). The word cuts two ways, and she is the lewd interpreter of the turn upon itself that the letter represents. "The Jew shall have all justice. Soft, no haste. / He shall have nothing but the penalty" (321–2). Having all he has nothing, Bassanio's condition when Portia submitted entirely to his dominion, putting herself in bonds with him, ringing him round. Her signature was the kiss. And Shylock's? All but ratified, he vocalizes his "content" (394), that will-less middle ground that is no place (no more, no less). His final word promises the signature that will deliver him, signed, sealed and bound – and forever silent: "I pray you give me leave to go from hence. / I am not well. Send the deed after me, / And I will sign it" (395–7). The circuit of the letter, completing one loop (the rings lie ahead), turns upon itself. "Your Grace shall understand that at the receipt of your letter I am very sick" (150–1), so Bellario/Portia begins; then, the letter can become the ring, the circular bond returning upon itself, making two wills one, binding father and daughter, male and female, inner and outer: turning to men. "Pardon me, Bassanio; / For, by this ring, the doctor lay with me" (V.i.258–9). Lewd interpretation of the letter.

*

Or, to put it more succinctly, listen to the lesson Theseus preaches to Hermia in the opening scene of *A Midsummer Night's Dream*:

> To you your father should be as a god,
> One that compos'd your beauties, yea, and one
> To whom you are but as a form in wax
> By him imprinted, and within his power
> To leave the figure or disfigure it.
>
> (I.i.47–51)

At the end of the play, Theseus overrules Egeus, imposes his will, inscribing both father and daughter within his power and law, and Hermia responds, "Methinks I see these things with parted eye, / When every thing seems double" (IV.i.193–4); a moment later she agrees to follow the Duke. "Yea," she says, "and my father" (199). It is her last word. Figured and disfigured; doubly stamped by the authorizing powers: testaments to the inscription of the letter, the circuit of desire turning back upon itself, encompassing *both* father and daughter, male and female, within its course.

*

Portia's career in *The Merchant of Venice* takes place between the will of her father and Shylock's suspended signature, the imprimatur that would authorize her position. His voice is silenced. The voice that Portia assumes, however, is not a man's voice, nor does she merely affirm the coincidence of her will with her father's, or the coincidence of the legalism she displays with Shylock's demand that only the letter of the law be observed. Portia's equivocal place in the text, her voice "between," her ratification, plays on the "turns" taken by the circuit of the text. Through the letter she passes. Rather than reading her career as her inscription in the patriarchal order, let us read it otherwise. Not that she has found some realm of feminine discourse. Rather, she moves through the text, affirming the meeting of, the suspension of, difference. Almost as Luce Irigaray would have it, Portia's voice plays on the unconscious of the text, reveals what is repressed when the law acts as if it were univocal, when the father acts as if his impress would turn the blank page of the daughter into his character. The return of the letter doubles back upon itself, revealing the duplicity in the text, revealing, in Irigaray's terms, the sex that is not one.

> In her statements . . . woman retouches herself constantly. . . . One must listen to her differently in order to hear an *"other meaning" which is constantly in the process of weaving itself, at the same time ceaselessly embracing words and yet casting them off to avoid becoming fixed, immobilized.* For when "she" says something, it is already no longer identical to anything.[12]

Such is the circuit of the letter.

*

Such, too, is the law of genre, if I may borrow Derrida's title[13] and recapitulate his argument merely through the act of (re)citation. Derrida argues that, although the law of genre insists on demarcation and difference, genre is self-invaginated, cast, as Montaigne would have it, in the same mould. The very law that establishes genre – the will, contract and rings in *The Merchant of Venice*, for example – is no law outside of textual play, but implicated in the play: Portia in her father's place; Portia as the law. Genre represents an arbitrary limit upon the generativity of language; it provides the end which otherwise would not be reached.

If we have seen that Portia's acquisition of voice and Shylock's silencing cannot merely be described as the ratification of the patriarchal order, we can best explore the question of the loss of voice – as the fate of both men and women – and the coincidence of this loss with the law of genre, in the final moments of *Measure for Measure*, a play, as I take it, intent upon representing itself (as the figure of the Duke suggests) – representing itself as representation.[14] The drama of substitution and replacement which I have argued for in *The Merchant of Venice* hardly needs to be argued in the later play. From the initial replacement of the Duke with his deputy, Angelo, to the plot to substitute Mariana for Isabella, the question of replacement is in the foreground, in the disposition of character and in the arguments they make, for what the Duke plots for Isabella is also her argument with Angelo, that he should put himself in another's place and think of Claudio's crime as his own. The Duke's substitution plot satisfies Isabella's argument.

Generation by substitution is the representational law of the play, its mode of government, a literalization and corporealization of the drama of representation. No one is above this law in the play. The Duke, who appears to initiate the chain of substitutions and to call it to a halt, has to endure Lucio's representations of him to the very end of the play – in part because he has engendered himself as a substitute in the guise of Friar Lodowick. Although the Duke may appear to be in control of or outside the situation of the play (may appear, that is, as the dramatist within the play), there is no outside of representation, and the play suggests this, too, by seeming to include King James in its designs. Within the play, resistance to representation is to be found not only in the Duke's protestations, but as the essence of the role of Barnardine. As the Duke attempts – not all that successfully – to juggle heads and find a substitute for the condemned Claudio, he lights upon Barnardine, named in a letter Angelo has sent to the prison (IV. ii. 119ff.). Barnardine's name, so casually introduced as a counterpart to Claudio's, is picked up by the Duke; the convict's history is told – a life spent in prison, more often drunk than sober, more often asleep than awake. Barnardine would seem to live solely to die; yet, when he is brought forth in the following scene, he will have none of the Duke's scheme or Angelo's; as far as he is concerned, their letters are no warrant and, refusing to consent to die, he returns to his straw and drink.

Yet, this is *represented* resistance. Barnardine's refusal to be Claudio's substitute only further identifies him with Claudio – for Claudio does not die. Yet he almost does, and the generation of Claudio through the last acts of *Measure for Measure* is through such substitutes as Barnardine. The Duke's abandonment of Claudio to death – "Be absolute for death" (III. i. 5ff.) is his counterpart to Isabella's more violent repudiation of her brother – is itself abandoned. From his images of life as death, inanition, decay – at best sleep – Barnardine emerges as the corporealization of those words, "a man that apprehends death no more dreadfully but as a drunken sleep" (IV. ii. 149– 50). If life and death are as indifferent and as much alike as the Duke's speech argues, Barnardine takes him (as it were) at his word. He refuses to die. And the Duke, in a rage like Isabella's at Claudio, sputters, "Unfit to live, or die" (IV. iii. 68), naming thereby the equivocal space of representation filled by Barnardine.

Not by him alone; from such equivocations, the end of the play is reached. Claudio, although saved, is silenced; after III. i, he barely says another word, and exists through his substitutes (Barnardine, the head of Ragozine the pirate) and through the substitutive plots of the Duke and Isabella. He is placed by the plot and replaced by it; the law of the play determines and limits his position. This explains the curious nature of Claudio's final appearance. Unlike Shylock, who disappears to be replaced and whose signature hovers over the play's end, Claudio's body needs to be displayed as the sign that justifies the substitutive play of the last acts of *Measure for Measure*. Yet within the economy of the play's conclusion, Claudio has been reduced to a cipher and there is no need for the character to speak, barely the need for him to be recognized. Thus, no one says a word to him at his final appearance, nor does he speak. The provost "unmuffles" him, identifying him as "another prisoner that I sav'd, / Who should have died when Claudio lost his head; / As like almost to Claudio as himself" (V.i.491–3).

Claudio appears in the company of Barnardine and in a nomination in which self-sameness is affirmed as an otherness, self-sameness only as proximate as the likeness of one self to oneself. At the end of the play, this is also Isabella's position, silenced, too, as the Duke enacts a justice that might better be called his voicing of the power of a text in which he, too, is inscribed. For, as much in the compulsion of genre as anyone, the Duke turns to Isabella – silent from the moment her represented brother stands before her – to invite her into a proper finale. His words echo against the provost's problematic identification of Claudio:

> If he be like your brother, for his sake
> Is he pardon'd; and for your lovely sake –
> Give me your hand, and say you will be mine –
> He is my brother too. But fitter time for that.
>
> (V.i.495–8)

Isabella is asked into a family of similitudes, the moving principle of replacement and representation in which she finds her end, like unto like, "his sake," "your . . . sake." The Duke asks for the hand that would ratify, the voice that would assent. Some lines later, he reiterates his proposal; repetition is the other side of the silence of Isabella and Claudio.

To remind us of the coincidence of the law of representation with the justice that the Duke enacts in the final scene – giving measure for measure in reductive and silencing replacements – we need only to notice Lucio's last words in the play. Condemned – like Angelo, like the Duke – to marry the woman he has wronged, he utters a final protest: "Marrying a punk, my lord, is pressing to death, whipping, and hanging" (V.i.528–9). Lucio treats his marriage as a punishment, and with "pressing to death" he summons up the grisly fate of one who rather than admit his guilt or plead his innocence suffered *peine forte et dure*, "being crushed slowly to death by weights on top of his body,"[15] the sole right of silence granted those who refused to accept the constructions of others and wished to preserve their own – their property, if not their lives (Shylock's case inverted).

Thus far, I have taken my examples from comedy. But the situation I am describing applies in tragedy too. Deprivation of voice does not signal the marginalization of women. Let us, for example, consider the silencing of Portia in *Julius Caesar*. In Act IV, Brutus reports her death to Cassius: "No man bears sorrow better. Portia is dead" (IV.iii.147), and proceeds to describe it in response to Cassius's question, "upon what sickness?":

> Impatient of my absence,
> And grief that young Octavius with Mark Antony
> Have made themselves so strong, – for with her death
> That tidings came, – with this she fell distract,
> And, her attendants absent, swallow'd fire.
>
> (IV. iii. 152–6)

Brutus's lines embed Portia's death in political action: his repeated preposition is *with*; the alliance of Antony with Caesar arrives in the letter bearing the news of Portia's death. Their proximity in report makes for Brutus's causal linking. It is "with this" alliance that Portia "fell distract"; her lord's "absence" doubled with "her attendants absent" led to self-slaughter. Portia suffocates herself, denying herself life and breath by swallowing fire. The mouth incapable of speaking now swallows its own silence.

Portia's suicide is a political act. In a play in which wounds speak, Portia's death reverses the flow of power that streams from Caesar's corpse. Antony articulates the connection of voice and power which marks the death of Portia – and ultimately of Brutus, too:

> Over thy wounds now do I prophesy,
> Which, like dumb mouths, do ope their ruby lips
> To beg the voice and utterance of my tongue: . . .
> And Caesar's spirit, ranging for revenge,
> With Ate by his side come hot from hell,
> Shall in these confines with a monarch's voice
> Cry "Havoc," and let slip the dogs of war,
> That this foul deed shall smell above the earth
> With carrion men, groaning for burial.
>
> (III. i. 259–61, 270–5)

The silencing of Portia shows her place in Antony's text, a script that the play unabashedly calls the sphere of power, politics, and history.

Yet Portia's silence is not the result of her exclusion from the world where men destroy themselves and each other. Rather, it marks her participation. Brutus, reading her death in the letter that marks his own fate, is not merely projecting or unconsciously amalgamating her death with his own. The division (from herself, her husband, her servants) and the multiplication (Octavius with Antony, "with her death . . . with this") point to the constitutive alienation of her participation in the plot. Literally. Early in the play, Portia has a voice, demanding from Brutus that he acknowledge the equality of their partnership by revealing to her the distraction that so palpably divides him from himself. She recounts her repeated questionings, her urgings, her insistence, her voice – and Brutus's refusal to speak. "It will not let you eat, nor talk, nor sleep" (II. i. 252), she concludes, and were what is consuming him to surface, Brutus would be effaced, unknowable. It is with this "it" that Portia begs acquaintance (256). Brutus at first insists that it is a sickness – though, if it is, it is the sickness which kills Portia – but Portia discounts this reading, driving towards "some sick offense within your mind" (268). Portia would be *with* Brutus, and within him. She takes literally their incorporation (273), asks Brutus to take the mantle off, to unmuffle himself, to speak out. For, she assures him, once she has received the words, she will not reveal them. The power lies in that promise, just as it is intimated in the thigh wound to which she points as a sign of her constancy. Yet this is not merely a scene of wifely submission, for it is how she becomes again her husband's equal. Portia kneels, but Brutus will not have her on her knees; Portia complains of being exiled to "the suburbs" of his heart (285–6), and Brutus affirms her right to occupy the secret, to penetrate the mask, to break the silence, to participate in what is within. He offers her the "ruddy drops" of his heart (289), promising an off-stage revelation that has occurred when Portia next is seen on stage. Here is the promise:

> Thy bosom shall partake
> The secrets of my heart.
> All my engagements I will construe to thee,
> All the charactery of my sad brows.
>
> (II. i. 305–8)

The revelation of the plot is like the dagger offered to her thigh or the one that will plunge into Brutus's breast. Portia has insisted that Brutus read to her what lies within the text that is his body, what lies charactered on his forehead. The opening of the body, the revelation of the equivocal life-in-death of the text, will place Portia within the economy that leads to her silencing.

After this scene, Portia can only speak with two voices. Tormented, self-divided, she sends word to her husband that she is merry when she is anything but; desirous of imparting the disease that now eats at her, she cannot speak. Swallowing fire is the counterpart to the voice that has been divided against itself, condemned to the equivocations in which self-sameness is lost forever. One with Brutus, she is two. And the testimony of this inheres not only in the suicide that she becomes – that assault on her throat, the suffocation of her breath and spirit in token of the raging, burning spirit of Caesar – it lies in Brutus's response to her death. For, as we know, there are two responses to it. One we have seen, with its poised marks of alienation and participation, of absence and presence cohering in the destructivity of the plot, in the effacing of his character, razing the tablet. But then, as if to mark further that erasure, Brutus responds again. "Had you your letters from your wife, my lord," Messala asks (IV.iii.181), just after Brutus and Cassius have recemented their friendship, grieving over Portia. Brutus denies the letter, denies all knowledge, coaxing Messala to reveal the brutal truth: "she is dead" (189). "Why, farewell, Portia," Brutus responds. A politic suppression, a bid for power, Brutus almost swallows fire himself, dividing himself from himself in this answer. Both he and his dead wife bear a single character, share a voice of power and alienation that divides the self from the self, that marries the self to its otherness.

*

The generation of character from text, the effacement of voice, or the submission of voice (silence *or* speech) to serve the generic design that limits text – this, then, is the argument of this essay. Portia returns to Belmont, completing the circuit of her career, carrier of the letter, enacting its course. When Bassanio first mentions her as the "lady richly left" (I.i.161), she is rightly named: "Sometimes from her eyes / I did receive fair speechless messages. / Her name is Portia, nothing undervalu'd / To Cato's daughter, Brutus' Portia" (163–6). She and Portia in *Julius Caesar* are counter-examples, their careers inverse and complementary mirrors of the condition of having a voice. At the end, when Portia returns, she is heard first ... as a voice: "That is the voice, / Or I am much deceiv'd, of Portia" (V.i.110–11).

*

Entrance into voice, then, although it may mean arrival on the scene of power, always bears its equivocations. When speech occurs, when the voice sounds, there is always another in the voice, an otherness that accompanies the utterer. In the examples we have considered thus far, that voice may be called the text, if by text we mean not something that is self-same on the page, not the inertness of an implacable letter, but rather those slippages and multiplications which determine and fix only to unmoor again, making all places provisional, all sites relational, all identity a matter of differences scarcely perceivable because forever changing. The situation of being in the text is one that governs men and women in Shakespeare; becoming voiceless, effacement, is the end of all characters traced on his mystic writing pad. Acquiring voice, characters sustain the play and are caught within the play. It is not necessarily a sign of power to have a voice, not necessarily a sign of subjection to lose it. The economy of the text, generic disposition, determines the distribution of parts and provides the arbitrary limit on texts that would never end otherwise (as the characters at ends of plays so often suggest, directing us beyond the end with promises of revelations or recoveries not evident on a stage filled with corpses or married couples). True, the Renaissance has more than its share of the fear of giving women power, or allowing them to have a voice, but that is not invariably the situation within the plays, and, when it is, the fear is not limited to one sex.[16] No one escapes bearing the trace of an otherness which shows the equivocation of the letter. Or, as Lacan would say (for he has been behind this text throughout and perhaps should be named now, allowed the flourish of his signature), when I speak it is always from and to an Other, my voice passes through and attempts to return to that unacknowledged, unreachable goal. The entrance into the symbolic stage – the entrance into language – is marked by the alienation of voice that raises Roland Barthes's question: Who is speaking?

That question pervades *Othello*; all relationships in that play are carried on the voice, and the play represents a struggle to discover if anyone can be said to have or own a voice.[17] At the end, paradoxically, the answer to this question finds power in inarticulation. The perils of speech are marked from the start, in Othello's "witchcraft," when he seduces Desdemona by rehearsing "the story of my life" (I. iii. 129). It is because she displays "a greedy ear" to "devour up my discourse" (149–50) that Othello reads in her rapt and silent attention a desire to hear his words and to take them in. Desdemona's desire is for his voice. This becomes a fear, but even as he first reports it, Desdemona's desire is itself accompanied by a resistance: "She wish'd she had not heard it; yet she wish'd / That Heaven had made her such a man" (162–3) – wished she were a man, wished such a man had been made *for* her. Othello's story overcomes Desdemona's resistance; retelling it to the Venetians, he overcomes theirs to his marriage to her. When Desdemona appears before them, her voice is heroic; she requires from the senators a "prosperous ear," asking them to give "voice" to her desires; Othello reiterates her words: "Let her have your voice" (245, 246, 261).

And Iago is nothing if not a voice, his device, to "abuse Othello's ear" (I. iii. 401); a full range of mimicry and the assumption of voices is his province. "I'll pour this pestilence into his ear" (II. iii. 362), Iago affirms, yet the situation is more complex than that, for it repeats the wooing and commingling of Othello and Desdemona. The voice that he offers Othello is so much a version of his own, so complete an echo, that Othello loses all ability to identify himself or his wife. "What dost thou think? / Think, my lord? / Think, my lord? By heaven, he echoes me" (III. iii. 105–6). Iago stages his silence as more significant than his speech; Othello draws from him those words which he desires and wishes not to hear. The scene recasts the wooing of Desdemona; here, too, a reading of hints delivers the voice of an ambivalent desire. To want another's story is to want a part in it. To recognize one's desire in another's story is to affirm that one's desire is not one's own but for and of another. In *Othello*, everyone is caught within the desire that catches Othello; even Cassio was his go-between, carrying words to Desdemona.

so can imagine that his wife has done in bed what Cassio has done in words; here is, perhaps, no difference.

In *Othello*, speech and desire are the same thing, and the murder of Desdemona, denying her breath and speech, is a sexual assault; mouth and throat are the visible zones of sexuality in the play. "Will you think so? Think so, Iago: What, / To kiss in private? An unauthoriz'd kiss" (IV.i.1–2). Two voices as one, echoing; conversation in the middle, sustained on a vocality that goes beyond the utterer; the unauthorized kiss the counterpart of speech without author, speech against authority, breaking down the resistances of desire, the structures of law and order. To speak, to kiss, to die: a conjunction that provokes stifling; to assail the voice because the voice is itself an assault. To launch speech but not to be *in* speech, to sustain silence in speech, would be, in this play, the nature of genuine power. It is manifest at the end.

Desdemona dies, kissed and stifled; dead, she speaks nonetheless, identifying "Nobody" with "I myself" (V.ii.124). Emilia bursts forth despite Iago's attempt to "charm" her tongue: "I will not charm my tongue; I am bound to speak" (V.ii.183–4), bound as in an Elizabethan court of law where witnesses had no right to silence, even if speaking was self-incriminating.[18] Emilia pays for speech with her life. And Iago, *agent provocateur* throughout so much of the play, ventriloquizer of the voices of others and supplier of an excess to his own voice so that we can never be sure we have him – Iago, at the end, embraces silence: "Demand me nothing; what you know, you know. / From this time forth I never will speak word" (V.ii.303–4). The assertion of inscrutability, the refusal to be accountable or to recount, represents a seizure, a taking hold through the voice, of the situation others arrive at at the ends of plays, rendered silent by the plot, mastered by an otherness, stifled, self-mastered. All these solutions are appropriated by Iago's final assertion in which the condition of character at the end of the play becomes something he takes control over by relinquishing – by withholding – his voice.

*

The god of eloquence – Hermes – has his finger on his lips.[19]

*

What we cannot hear may be a sign of depletion, or of a reserve that is impenetrable. Full speech always carries with it, as its other side, an emptiness; recall Henry V: not only does he render others silent, but the very mastery of discourse that he displays leaves obscure who he is, where he is in his discourse. Voice masters and dissolves the limits of the self; character is a function of voice. The silence of Iago is his power. It is Cordelia's power, too, as is suggested at the end of *King Lear*, when Lear looks to Cordelia's lips as if from them words and breath yet might come. Cordelia begins the play wedded to silence, and she ends there, implacable. Her claims to an interiority and an integrity are as potent as Iago's slippages, his maintenance of a fort of silence about a self that exists only by not being articulated, his refusal to breach definitively the inside and outside through an owned vocalization. Cordelia refuses to enter the sphere of speech because to speak is always a kind of betrayal, a violation of interiority, an emptying of value that exists when it stays inside. She refuses her father's plot of exchanges. The structure here is not unlike the opening of *Othello* or of *The Merchant of Venice*. Here, too, the articulation of love is the problematic zone.[20] Cordelia's power in the play lies in her refusal of construction – the demand that her silence represents, a resistance to the end of the megalomaniac acquisitiveness marked in Lear's attempt to appropriate everything, even her death. Her silence resists his speech, making his initial rages appear to be childish tantrums. His final negations are more finely tuned to her silence, a submission at last to the limits of utterance, a facing of the unutterable disowning displayed by a universe seemingly without respect for human values and constructions. The shriveled sphere of human survival lies in the divestment that Edgar represents; what remains is not a man's sphere necessarily but the impulse to stage power, to save voice – or the illusion of one's own voice – perhaps by withholding, perhaps by disowned expenditure. Cleopatra lurks in the wings.

"The rest," as Hamlet says, "is silence" (V.ii.369). This is the universal fate. But, as Hamlet adds, those who survive do so to tell the story again. Representation is the only truth, one that in fact has no end despite the arbitrariness of the ending of any particular performance. This, too, is the point about the epilogue of *The Tempest*, the extension of the play into the hands of the audience, attributing to us the breath and life necessary to send Prospero to Naples, his sails filled with the air we can move, by our applause, or prayers, or hisses. This turn to the audience represents Prospero's last attempt to appropriate responses, a desire shown up throughout the play – in Act IV, for instance, when Prospero commands silence before the performance of the masque, only to be interrupted by Ferdinand (at 118) and distracted from the play that goes on while Ceres and Juno whisper behind his back. Unheard vocalization is the manifestation of their life, a sign of the limits of authority and authorship, of a slippage in control as readily apparent at the end of *The Tempest* when Antonio, seemingly chastened, stonily silent, says just enough to make it clear that the experience of Prospero's play has meant nothing to him. So much for the power men have over others, the power fathers have to shape the world to their desires, so much even for the playwright's fantasy that he can claim the words in his text as his own. There are laws beyond that law too.

One last case: in the final act of *A Midsummer Night's Dream*, Hermia and

Helena, vocal throughout the play, are silent. They say nothing after their marriages (reported in IV. ii). After the forest, they return to Athens as bodies, married, barred from discourse. The text marks, but does not necessarily condone, their place in patriarchal culture. And in the last act, Hippolyta, also married, is hardly silent, and the fullness, range, complexity, and diversity of her vocality must be read in counterpoint to the silence of Hermia and Helena. Both these are images of women. And for the men? Hippolyta urges Theseus not to hear the play and he responds that he must hear it, claiming *noblesse oblige*, his capacity to make something out of nothing. The ironies are deep – for, of course, the men comment upon the play without a trace of self-recognition (and Hermia and Helena's may be a knowing silence). But here is a final irony: this play, performed before Queen Elizabeth, pays homage to her voice, too. Theseus's claim, however ironic when taken to refer to him, is perfectly straight elsewhere – we need simply to recall how often Elizabeth interrupted performances put on before her, how graciously she supplied whatever the performers lacked.[21]

In her coronation procession through the streets of London, Elizabeth paused repeatedly before the various shows staged for her benefit. She paused and spoke, demanded silence so that the actors could be heard, answered them, delivered speeches of her own with all the spontaneity of a good actor. This is one way of staging power in the voice, one way that monarchs on the throne are like those on stage. Here is the other: James repeated Elizabeth's performance, trod the same streets, stopped at the same scaffolds, attended to their plays. And he never said a word. Power lay in the withholding of utterance, the staging of the self as a spectacle unfathomable because inaccessible.[22]

But is Elizabeth in her voice? James in his silence? Their performances are invitations to decipherment, parts of the design that placed them on those prescribed streets, following those routes. The theatricalization of power is not confined to theaters, but extends into the streets. Perhaps – just perhaps – the reason we cannot find Shakespeare reflecting his culture's supposed patriarchalism and sexism[23] is that the culture represented on stage *is* the culture off-stage. Saying that does not mean denying the real, material, legal, social, and educational differences between men and women in Shakespeare's time. Thus, no woman, as Roman law declared, could actually have the power invested in a lawyer's voice; as Constance Jordan has pointed out to me, having a voice – as a legal right – must be distinguished from voicing. Portia's performance, in that regard, is a fantasy that blurs the distinction. But the point is that the fantasy is *also* part of the culture. It is inconceivable that Shakespeare was the only person to have it; his words found a responsive audience. Numerous anti-feminine tracts deplored women's voices; unauthorized, they were nonetheless clearly powerful enough to be heard. Elizabeth's rule (and Mary's before her), especially in her insistence both on her femininity *and* her male sovereignty (she called herself a prince), represents a serious complication in the alignment of power with sexual difference. Her verbal skills (or James's silences) *realize* aspects of the culture that challenge modern readings of patriarchy as a simple dualistic hierarchy of the sexes operating with an all-embracing, hegemonic power. Power entails a disturbing heterogeneity, owned by no one voice – a voicing, as Luce Irigaray might say, that is not one.

Notes

1. Rosalie Colie, *The Resources of Kind: Genre Theory in the Renaissance* (Berkeley and Los Angeles, 1973).
2. Stephen Orgel, "Shakespeare and the kinds of drama" (*Critical Inquiry*, 6 (1979), 107–23); Louise George Clubb, "The arts of genre: *Torrismondo* and *Hamlet*" (*ELH*, 47 (1980), 657–69).
3. All citations from *The New Cambridge Shakespeare* (Cambridge, Mass., 1942).
4. Linda Bamber, *Comic Women, Tragic Men: A Study of Gender and Genre in Shakespeare* (Stanford, 1982).
5. Stephen Greenblatt, *Renaissance Self-Fashioning: From More to Shakespeare* (Chicago, 1980).
6. For further arguments along these lines, see Ann Rosalind Jones, "Writing the body: toward an understanding of *l'écriture feminine*" (*Feminist Studies*, 7 (1981), 247–63), esp. 253–5, where Jones argues for the historic specificity of the terms male/female.
7. Carolyn Heilbrun, in *Signs*, 8 (1982), 182–6. For a somewhat more sophisticated argument along these lines, see Coppélia Kahn, *Man's Estate: Masculine Identity in Shakespeare* (Berkeley and Los Angeles, 1981); Kahn at least sees that patriarchy is problematized in Shakespeare.
8. For documentation and discussion of these remarks see Stephen Greenblatt, "Invisible bullets: Renaissance authority and its subversion" (*Glyph, 8: Johns Hopkins Textual Studies* (Baltimore, 1981), 40–61), and Jonathan Goldberg, *James I and the Politics of Literature* (Baltimore, 1983), ch. 3.
9. "Foreword" to Gayatri Chakravorty Spivak's translation of "Draupadi" by Mahasveta Devi (*Critical Inquiry*, 8 (1981), 382–3).
10. Legally, it is true, women in Renaissance England were bound and powerless except in very special circumstances (they were not denied the right to speak in court, however). Yet Renaissance legal theory is full of holes, and attempts to place women in the law ran into all sorts of difficulties. These are briefly and suggestively traced in Ian Maclean's *The Renaissance Notion of Women* (Cambridge, 1980), 69–81, where Maclean notes that feminist arguments enter legal writing as early as Agrippa (1529). More broadly, Maclean's book shows that, within the most conservative discourses of the Renaissance, contradictions are rampant, and 1580–1630 seems to be the period in which the elaborate synthesis, which marked and limited the place of women, began to crack because of its own internal contradictions, as well as the pressures of history and alternative discourses.
11. René Girard has argued for the doubling of Antonio/Shylock and of Shylock/Portia and the problematics of difference in "'To entrap the wisest': a reading of

The Merchant of Venice," in *Literature and Society,* ed. Edward W. Said (Baltimore, 1980); see also Leonard Tennenhouse, "The counterfeit order of *The Merchant of Venice,*" in *Representing Shakespeare,* ed. Murray M. Schwartz and Coppélia Kahn (Baltimore, 1980), which points to recalcitrances in the text, including the ways in which Portia replaces Shylock as the troubler of Antonio's relation to Bassanio (63, 66). For a suggestion about the ideological yoking in the trial scene, see Walter Cohen, "*The Merchant of Venice* and the possibilities of historical criticism' (*ELH,* 49 (1982)), 776.

12. *New French Feminisms,* ed. Elaine Marks and Isabelle de Courtivron (New York, 1981), 103.

13. "La loi du genre / The law of genre" (*Glyph 7: Johns Hopkins Textual Studies* (Baltimore, 1980), 176–232).

14. For a further elaboration of my argument, see my *James I and the Politics of Literature,* 230–9. I also depend upon the suggestive remarks of Stephen Orgel (op. cit.), 122–3. The best study of substitution in *Measure for Measure* is by Nancy S. Leonard, "Substitution in Shakespeare's problem comedies" (*English Literary Renaissance,* 9 (1979), 281–301).

15. Penry Williams, *The Tudor Regime* (Oxford, 1979), 234. On the development of *peine forte et dure* as a response to the notion that no one should be judged solely on the basis of others' testimony, see W. S. Holdsworth, *A History of English Law* (London, 1926), IX, 179.

16. Summing up hundreds of commonplace books, Keith Thomas notes, "her chief ornament was silence, and her sole duty obedience," in "Women and the Civil War sects" (*Past and Present,* 13 (1958)), 43. Yet it is precisely the work of Thomas, or of Natalie Zemon Davis in *Society and Culture in Early Modern France* (Stanford, 1975), to show the space between theory and practice. This is also the argument of Maclean (op. cit.), and some of the equivocations with regard to the virtue of silence are discussed on pp. 15, 20–1, 23, 66. More generally, Maclean notes the contradictions between notions of sexual difference and virtues versus social differences. These matters are also debated in Book 3 of Castiglione's *The Courtier,* where the prime and distinguishing virtue of the court lady is (in Hoby's translation) "a certain sweetnesse of language" (Everyman edn, 190). On the literature of female gentility, Ruth Kelso comments in *Doctrine for the Lady of the Renaissance* (Urbana, 1956), "The purposes of these writers are too disparate and the elements too antithetic to each other; they have no central figure in common as the writers on the gentleman have" (3). Modern historians and critics, in short, must be wary of reifying Renaissance commonplaces.

17. My discussion depends throughout on Stephen Greenblatt's (op. cit.).

18. "Right down to the middle of the seventeenth century, the examination of the accused is the central feature of the criminal procedure of the common law. Nor do we read anywhere that a witness could refuse to answer on the ground that his answer might incriminate him" (Holdsworth, op. cit., IX, 199).

19. For the emblem, see Edgar Wind, *Pagan Mysteries in the Renaissance* (New York, 1968), 12n., 196, fig. 23.

20. Cf. Stanley Cavell, "The avoidance of love," in his *Must We Mean What We Say?* (New York, 1969).

21. See, for example, descriptions of Elizabeth's behavior on progresses, in J. E. Neale, *Queen Elizabeth I* (London, 1934), 207–10. As Maureen Quilligan notes in *Milton's Spenser: The Politics of Reading* (Ithaca, 1983), 215–16, Theseus's display of *noblesse oblige* "recalls a famous episode of Elizabeth's early career when she managed a fearful schoolmaster by telling him before he began: 'Be not

afrayde' . . . and complimenting him afterward: 'It is the best that ever I heard'"
(John Nichols, *The Progresses and Public Processions of Queen Elizabeth*
(London, 1823), II, 155–9).

22. For further discussion, see my *James I and the Politics of Literature*, 28–35.

23. In a provocative essay, "'Shaping fantasies': figurations of gender and power in
Elizabethan culture" (*Representations*, 1 (1983), 61–94), Louis Adrian Mont-
rose argues for the manifold ways in which *A Midsummer Night's Dream* is
shaped by – and shapes – cultural fantasies; he argues that its patriarchal designs
conflict with and yet crosscut the designs of the Virgin Queen. At one point,
however, he admits that "in its intermittent ironies, dissonances, and contradictions . . . the text of *A Midsummer Night's Dream* discloses – perhaps, in a sense
despite itself – that patriarchal norms are compensatory for the vulnerability of
men to the powers of women" (75). It has been my argument here that a pursuit of
such slippages within the Shakespearean text undermines apparent hegemonic
discourses, that what is "despite itself" marks the limits of textual control and
leads to the principal mode in which texts are cultural inscriptions.

Since this essay was written, manuscripts by Stephen Greenblatt and Thomas
Laqueur, currently in circulation, have begun the historical work of the recovery
of Renaissance discourses of sexual difference. To these might be added Lisa
Jardine, *Still Harping on Daughters: Women and Drama in the Age of
Shakespeare* (Brighton, 1983), which offers some vigorous arguments against the
ahistorical tendencies in feminist criticism explored in this essay.

8

JOEL FINEMAN

The turn of the shrew

> *Hortensio:* Now go thy ways, thou hast tam'd a curst shrow.
> *Lucentio:* 'Tis a wonder, by your leave, she will be tam'd so.
>
> (V. ii. 188–9)

In ways which are so traditional that they might be called proverbial, Shakespeare's *Taming of the Shrew* assumes – it turns out to make no difference whether it does so ironically – that the language of woman is at odds with the order and authority of man. At the same time, again in ways which are nothing but traditional, the play self-consciously associates this thematically subversive discourse of woman with its own literariness and theatricality. The result, however, is a play that speaks neither for the language of woman nor against the authority of man. Quite the contrary: at the end of the play things are pretty much the same – which is to say, patriarchally inflected – as they were at or before its beginning, the only difference being that now, because there are more shrews than ever, they are more so. It cannot be surprising that a major and perennially popular play by Shakespeare, which is part of a corpus that, at least in an English literary tradition, is synonymous with what is understood to be canonical, begins and ends as something orthodox. Nevertheless, there is reason to wonder – as my epigraph, the last lines of the play, suggests – how it happens that a discourse of subversion, explicitly presented as such, manages to resecure, equally explicitly, the very order to which it seems, at both first and second sight, to be opposed. This question, raised by the play in a thematic register, and posed practically by the play by virtue of the play's historical success, leads to another: is it possible to voice a language, whether of man or of woman, that does not speak, sooner or later, self-consciously or unconsciously, for the order and authority of man?

Formulated at considerably greater levels of generality, such questions have been advanced by much recent literary, and not only literary, theory, much of which finds it very difficult to sustain in any intelligible fashion an effective critical and adversary distance or difference between itself and any of a variety of master points of view, each of which claims special access to a global, universalizing truth. It is, however, in the debates and polemics growing out of and centering upon the imperial claims of psychoanalysis that such questions have been raised in the very same terms and at precisely the level of generality proposed by *The Taming of the Shrew* – the level of generality measured by the specificity of rubrics as massive and as allegorically suggestive as Man, Woman, and Language – for it is psychoanalysis, especially the psychoanalysis associated with the name of Jacques Lacan, that has most coherently developed an account of human subjectivity which is based upon the fact that human beings speak. Very much taking this speech to heart, psychoanalysis has organized, in much the same ways as does *The Taming of the Shrew*, the relationship of generic Man to generic Woman by reference to the apparently inescapable patriarchalism occasioned by the structuring effects of language – of Language, that is to say, which is also understood in broad genericizing terms. In turn, the most forceful criticisms of psychoanalysis, responding to the psychoanalytic provocation with a proverbial response, have all been obliged, again repeating the thematics of *The Taming of the Shrew*, to speak against this Language for which the psychoanalytic speaks.

Thus it is not surprising, to take the most important and sophisticated example of this debate, that Jacques Derrida's (by comparison) very general critique of logocentric metaphysics, his deconstructive readings of what he calls the ontotheological ideology of presence in the history of the west, turns more specifically into a critique of phallogocentric erotics in the course of a series of rather pointed (and, for Derrida, unusually vociferous) attacks on Lacanian psychoanalysis. Lacan serves Derrida as a kind of limit case of such western "presence," to the extent that Lacan, centering the psychology of the human subject on a lack disclosed by language, deriving human desire out of a linguistic want, is prepared to make a presence even out of absence, and, therefore, as Derrida objects, a God out of a gap. As is well known, Derrida opposes to the determinate and determining logic of the language of Lacan – though with a dialectic that is of course more complicated than that of any simply polar opposition – an alternative logic of *différance* and writing, associating this a-logical logic with a "question of style" whose status as an irreducible question keeps alive, by foreclosing any univocal answer, the deconstructive power of a corresponding "question of woman." Here again, however, it is possible to identify the formulaic ways in which this Derridean alternative to a psychoanalytic logos recapitulates, because it predicates itself as something Supplementary and Other, the general thematics of *The Taming of the Shrew*. And this recapitulation has remained remarkably consistent, we might add, in the more explicitly feminist extensions of the deconstructive line traced out by Derrida, all of which, for all the differences between them, attempt to speak up for, and even to speak, a different kind of language than that of psychoanalytic man (e.g. the preverbal, presymbolic "semiotic" of Julia Kristeva, the *écriture féminine* of Hélène Cixous, the intentionally duplicitous or bilabial eroticism of Luce Irigaray, the Nietzschean narcissism of Sarah Kofman).[1]

This theoretical debate between psychoanalysis and the deconstructive feminisms that can be called, loosely speaking, its most significant other is in principle interminable to the extent that psychoanalysis can see in such resistance to its Language, as Freud did with Dora, a symptomatic confirmation of all psychoanalytic thought. In the context of this debate, *The Taming of the Shrew* initially possesses the interest of an exceptionally apt literary example, one to which the different claims of different theories – about language, desire, gender – might be fruitfully applied. On the other hand, to the extent that this debate appears itself to re-enact the action that is staged within *The Taming of the Shrew*, there exists the more than merely formal possibility that the play itself defines the context in which such debate about the play will necessarily take place. Understood in this way, the theoretical quarrel that might take place about *The Taming of the Shrew* would then emerge as nothing more than an unwitting reproduction of the thematic quarrel – between Man and Woman or between two different kinds of language – that already finds itself in motion in *The Taming of the Shrew*. If this were the case – and it remains to determine with what kind of language one might even say that this is the case – then the self-conscious literariness of *The Taming of the Shrew*, the reflexively recursive metatheatricality with which the play presents itself as an example of what it represents, would acquire its own explanatory, but not exactly theoretical, value. Glossing its own literariness, the play becomes the story of why it is the way it is, and this in turn becomes a performative account or self-example of the way a theoretical debate centered around the topoi of sexuality, gender, and language appears to do no more than once again repeat, to no apparent end, an old and still ongoing story.

That the story is in fact an old one is initially suggested by the ancient history attaching to the three stories joined within *The Taming of the Shrew*: the Christopher Sly framing plot, where a lord tricks a peasant into thinking himself a lord, which goes back at least as far as a fable in *The Arabian Nights*; the story of Lucentio's wooing of Bianca, which can be traced back, through Gascoigne and Ariosto, to Plautus or Menander; and the taming story proper, Petruchio's domestication of the shrewish Kate, which is built up out of innumerable literary and folklore analogues, all of which can claim an antique provenance. Correlated with each other by means of verbal, thematic, and structural cross-references, these three independent stories become in *The Taming of the Shrew* a single narrative of a kind whose twists and turns would seem familiar even on first hearing. Indeed, the only thing that is really novel about the plotting of *The Taming of the Shrew* is the way the play concatenates these three quite different stories so as to make it seem as though each one of them depends upon and is a necessary version of the other two.

Moreover, the play itself insists upon the fact that it retells a master plot of western literary history. By alluding to previous dramatic, literary, and biblical texts, by quoting and misquoting familiar tags and phrases, by parodically citing or miming more serious literary modes (e.g. Ovidian narrative and Petrarchan lyric), the play situates itself within a literary tradition to which even its mockery remains both faithful and respectful. This is especially the case with regard to the taming subplot that gives the play its name. Soon after he enters, for example, Petruchio cites proverbial precursors for the cursing Kate, in one brief passage linking her not only to the alter ego of the Wife of Bath but also to the Cumaean Sibyl and Socrates' Xantippe (I. ii. 69–71) (these references later to be counterbalanced by Kate's translation to "a second Grissel, and Roman Lucrece" (II. i. 295–6)).[2] Such women are all touchstones of misogynistic gynecology. The commonplace way in which Petruchio evokes them here, drawing from a thesaurus of women whose voices will systematically contradict the dictates of male diction, is characteristic of the way, from beginning to end, the play works to give archetypal resonance and mythological significance to Kate's specifically female speech, locating it in the context of a perennial iconography for which the language of woman – prophetic and erotic, enigmatic and scolding, excessive and incessant – stands as continually nagging interference with, or as seductive and violent interruption of, or, finally, as loyally complicitous opposition to, the language of man.

What kind of language is it, therefore, that woman speaks, and in what way does it differ, always and forever, from the language of man? The first answer given by *The Taming of the Shrew* is that it is the kind of language Petruchio speaks when he sets out to teach to Kate the folly of her ways. "He is more shrew than she" (IV. i. 85) summarizes the homeopathic logic of the taming strategy in accord with which Petruchio, assimilating to himself the attributes of Kate, will hold his own lunatic self up as mirror of Kate's unnatural nature. As perfect instance and reproving object lesson of his wife's excess, Petruchio thus finds "a way to kill a wife with kindness" (IV. i. 208). As an example which is simultaneously a counter-example, "He kills her in her own humour" (IV. i. 180). All Petruchio's odd behavior – his paradoxical and contradictory assertions, his peremptory capriciousness, his "lunacy," to use a word and image that is central to *The Taming of the Shrew* – presupposes this systematic and admonitory program of an eye for an eye, or, as the play defines the principle: "being mad herself, she's madly mated. / I warrant him, Petruchio is Kated" (III. ii. 244–5; "mated" here meaning "amazed" as well as "matched"). Moreover, all this madness bespeaks the language of woman, for Petruchio's lunatic behavior, even when it is itself nonverbal, is understood to be a corollary function, a derivative example, of the shrewish voice of Kate, as when Petruchio's horrific marriage costume, a demonstrative insult to appropriate decorum – "A monster, a very monster in apparel" (III. ii. 69 –70) – is taken as a statement filled with a didactic sense: "He hath some meaning in his mad attire" (III. ii. 124).

In Act I, Scene ii, which is the first scene of the taming subplot, Grumio, Petruchio's servant, explains the meaning as well as the method of Petruchio's madness. At the same time, he suggests how this is to be related to all the action, especially the verbal action, of the play:

> A' my word, and she knew him as well as I do, she would think scolding would do little good upon him. She may perhaps call him half a score knaves or so. Why, that's nothing; and he begin once, he'll rail in his rope-tricks. I'll tell you what, sir, and she stand him but a little, he will throw a figure in her face, and so disfigure her with it that she shall have no more eyes to see withal than a cat.
>
> (I. ii. 108–15)

This is an obscure passage, perhaps intentionally so, but "the general sense," as the editor of the Oxford edition says, "must be that Petruchio's railing will be more violent than Katherine's."[3] Even so, it is the manner of the passage, more than its somewhat bewildering matter, that best conveys "the general sense" of Petruchio's project, a point brought out by the apparently unanswerable puzzle posed by "rope-tricks." On "rope-tricks" the Oxford editor says: "If emendation is thought necessary, 'rhetricks' is the best yet offered; but 'rope-tricks' may well be correct and may mean tricks that can be punished adequately only by hanging." The *Riverside* edition offers a similar answer to the "rope-tricks" question, but does so with even more uncertainty, as evidenced by the parenthetical question-marks that interrupt the gloss: "*rope-tricks*: blunder for *rhetoric* (an interpretation supported by *figure* in line 114(?) or tricks that deserve hanging(?)."

On the face of it, neither of these edgily tentative editorial comments is especially helpful in determining, one way or the other, whether Petruchio, when he "rails in his rope-tricks," will be doing something with language or, instead, performing tricks for which he should be hanged. The "interpretation," as the *Riverside* edition calls it, remains indeterminate. But such determination is of course not the point. The editors recognize – and so too, presumably, does an audience – that it is for what he does with language that Petruchio runs any risk with (bawdy) rope. Hence the special suitability of "rope-tricks" as a term to describe the way in which Petruchio will respond to Kate in verbal kind. Playing on "rhetoric" and on "rope," but being neither, "rope-tricks" simultaneously advances, one way *and* the other, both the crime (rape) and the punishment (rope) attaching to the extraordinary speech the play associates with Kate (rhetoric). "Rope-tricks," moreover, is a uniquely performative word for rhetoric, since "rope-tricks" *is* rhetoric precisely because it is not "rhetoric," and thus discloses, by pointing to itself, a kind of necessary disjunction between itself as a verbal signifier and what, as a signifier, it means to signify. In this way, as a kind of self-remarking case of rhetoric in action, "rope-tricks" becomes the general name not only for all the figurative language in the play but, also, for all the action in the play which seems literally to mean one thing but in fact means another: for prime example, the way in which Petruchio will speak the language of woman in order to silence Kate.

The point to notice about this is that, as far as the play is concerned, the "interpretation" of "rope-tricks," its meaning, is not altogether indeterminate or, rather, if it is indeterminate, this indeterminacy is itself very strictly determined. "Rope-tricks" is a word that univocally insists upon its own equivocation, and this definitive indeterminacy is what defines its "general sense." In a way that is not at all paradoxical, and in terms which are in no sense uncertain, the question posed by "rope-tricks" has as its answer the question of rhetoric, and the play uses this circularity – the circularity that makes the rhetoricity of a rhetorical question itself the answer to the question that it poses – as a paradigmatic model for the way in which, throughout the play, Petruchio will obsessively answer Kate with hysterical tit for hysterical tat.

Understood in this way, as "rope-tricks," we can say that the words and actions of *The Taming of the Shrew* rehearse a familiar antagonism, not simply the battle between the sexes but, more specifically, though still rather generally, the battle between the determinate, literal language traditionally spoken by man and the figurative, indeterminate language traditionally spoken by woman. But by saying this we are only returned, once again, to the question with which we began, for if such indeterminacy is what rhetoric always means to say, if this is the literal significance of its "general sense," why is it that this indeterminacy seems in *The Taming of the Shrew* so definitively to entail the domestication of Kate? Petruchio is never so patriarchal as when he speaks the language of woman – "He is more shrew than she" – just as Kate's capitulation occurs at the moment when she obediently takes her husband at his lunatic, female, figurative word. This happens first when Petruchio forces Kate to call the sun the moon, and then when Petruchio forces Kate to address a reverend father as "young budding virgin," a purely verbal mix-up of the sexes that leads an onlooker to remark: "A will make the man mad, to make a woman of him" (IV.v.35–6). In accord with what asymmetrical *quid pro quo* does Petruchio propose to silence Kate by speaking the language she speaks, and why does the play assume that the orthodox order of the sexes for which it is the spokesman is reconfirmed when, madly translating a man into a mad woman, it gives explicit voice to such erotic paradox? Why, we can ask, do things not happen the other way around?

These are questions that bear on current theory. The editorial question-marks that punctuate the gloss on "rope-tricks" mark the same site of rhetorico-sexual indeterminacy on which Derrida, for example, will hinge his correlation of "the question of style" with "the question of woman" (this is the same disruptive question-mark, we can note, that Dora dreams of when she dreams about her father's death).[4] But again, such questions are fore-grounded *as* questions in *The Taming of the Shrew*, and in a far from naive manner. We learn, for example, in the very first lines of the play performed for Christopher Sly that Lucentio has come "to see fair Padua, the nursery of arts" (I.i.2), having left his father's "Pisa, renowned for grave citizens" (I.i.10). Lucentio's purpose, he says, is to "study / Virtue and that part of philosophy / . . . that treats of happiness" (I.i.17–19). This purpose stated, and the crazy psychogeography of Padua thus established by its opposition to sober Pisa, Tranio, Lucentio's servant, then rushes to caution his master against too single-minded a "resolve / To suck the sweets of sweet philoso-phy" (27–8): "Let's be no Stoics nor no stocks," says Tranio, "Or so devote to Aristotle's checks / As Ovid be an outcast quite abjur'd" (31–2). Instead, Tranio advises his master to pursue his studies with a certain moderation. On the one hand, says Tranio, Lucentio should "Balk logic with acquaintance that you have," but, on the other, he should also "practice rhetoric in your common talk" (34–5). This is the initial distinction to which all the subse-quent action of the play consistently and quite explicitly refers, a distinction that starts out as the difference between logic and rhetoric, or between philosophy and poetry, or between Aristotle and Ovid, but which then becomes, through the rhetorical question raised by "rope-tricks," the gener-alized and – for this is the point – quite *obviously* problematic difference between literal and figurative language on which the sexual difference between man and woman is seen to depend.

Tranio's pun on "Stoics"/"stocks," a pun which is a tired commonplace in Elizabethan comic literature, suggests both the nature of the problem and the way in which the play thematically exploits it. The pun puts the verbal difference between its two terms into question, into specifically rhetorical question, and so it happens that each term is sounded as the mimic simulation of the other. If language can do this to the difference between "Stoics" and "stocks," what can it do to the difference between "man" and "woman"? Is the one the mimic simulation of the other? This is a practical, as well as a rhetorical, question raised by the play, because the play gives countless demonstrations of the way in which the operation of stressedly rhetorical language puts into question the possibility of distinguishing between itself and the literal language it tropes. Petruchio, for example, when we first meet him, even before he hears of Kate, tells Grumio, his servant, to "knock me at the gate" (I.ii. 11). The predictable misunderstanding that thereupon ensues is then compounded further when a helpful intermediary offers to "compound this quarrel" (27). These are trivial puns, the play on "knock" and the play on "compound," but their very triviality suggests the troubling way in which the problematic question raised by one word may eventually spread to, and be raised by, all. "Knock at the gate," asks Grumio, "O heavens! Spake you not these words plain?" (39–40).

Given the apparently unavoidable ambiguity of language or, at least, the everpresent possibility of such ambiguity, it is precisely the question, the rhetorical question, of speaking plainly that Grumio raises, as though one cannot help but "practice rhetoric" in one's "common talk." Moreover, as the play develops it, this argument between the master and his servant, an argument spawned by the rhetoricity of language, is made to seem the explanation of Kate's ongoing quarrel with the men who are her master. For example, the same kind of "knocking" violence that leads Petruchio and Grumio to act out the rhetorical question that divides them is what later leads Kate to break her lute upon her music-master's head: "I did but tell her she mistook her frets ... And with that word she strook me on the head" (II.i. 149–53).

Such "fretful" verbal confusions occur very frequently in the play, and every instance of them points up the way in which any given statement, however intended, can always mean something other than what its speaker means to say. For this reason, it is significant that, in almost the first lines of the play, Christopher Sly, after being threatened with "a pair of stocks" (Ind.i. 2), explains not only why this is possibly the case but, really, why this is necessarily the case, formulating, in a "rope-trick" way, a general principle that accounts for the inevitability of such linguistic indeterminacy. "*Paucas pallabris*," says Christopher Sly, "let the world slide" (Ind.i. 5). The bad Spanish here is a misquotation from *The Spanish Tragedy*, Hieronimo's famous call for silence. An Elizabethan audience would have heard Sly's "*paucas pallabris*" as the comic application of an otherwise serious cliché, i.e. as an amusing deformation of a formulaic tag (analogous to Holofernes' "*pauca verba*" in *Love's Labour's Lost* (IV.ii. 165)), whose "disfiguring" corresponds to the troping way in which Sly mistakenly recalls Hieronimo by swearing by "Saint Jeronimy" (Ind.i. 9). So too with Sly's "let the world slide," which is equally proverbial, and which is here invoked as something comically and ostentatiously familiar, as something novel just *because* it sounds passé, being half of a proverb whose other half Sly pronounces at the end of the frame, in the last line of the Induction, which serves as introduction to the play within the play: "Come madam wife, sit by my side, and let the world slip, we shall ne'er be younger" (Ind. ii. 142–3).

Taken together, and recognizing the register of self-parody on which, without Sly's knowing it, they seem to insist, the two phrases make a point about language that can serve as a motto for the rest of the play. There are always fewer words than there are meanings, because a multiplicity of meanings not only can but always will attach to any single utterance. Every word bears the burden of its hermeneutic history – the extended scope of its past, present, and future meanings – and for this reason every word carries with it a kind of surplus semiotic baggage, an excess of significance, whose looming, even if unspoken, presence cannot be kept quiet. Through inadvertent cognate homophonies, through uncontrollable etymological resonance, through unconscious allusions and citations, through unanticipatable effects of translation (*translatio* being the technical term for metaphor), through syntactic slips of the tongue, through unpredictable contextual transformations – in short, through the operation of "rope-tricks," the Word (for example, Sly's "world") will "slide" over a plurality of significances, to no single one of which can it be unambiguously tied down. Sly's self-belying cry for silence is itself an instance of a speech which is confounded by its excess meaning, of literal speech which is beggared, despite its literal intention, by an embarrassment of unintended semiotic riches. But the play performed before Sly – with its many malapropisms, its comic language lesson, its mangled Latin and Italian, its dramatic vivifications of figurative play, as when Petruchio bandies puns with Kate – demonstrates repeatedly and almost heavy-handedly that the rhetorical question raised by Grumio is always in the polysemic air: "Spake you not these words plain?"

It would be easy enough to relate the principle of "*paucas pallabris*" to Derrida's many characterizations of the way the everpresent possibility of self-citation – not necessarily parodic citation – codes every utterance with an irreducible indeterminacy, leaving every utterance undecidably suspended, at least in principle, between its literal and figurative senses. Even more specifically, it would be possible to relate the many proverbial ways in which the "wor(l)d" "slides" in The Taming of the Shrew – " 'He that is giddy thinks the world goes round' " (V. ii. 26), a proverb that can lead, as Kate remarks, to "A very mean meaning" (31) – to Lacan's various discussions of the not so freely floating signifier.[5] But, even if it is granted, on just these theoretical grounds, that the rhetoricity of language enforces this kind of general question about the possibility of a speaker's ever really being able to mean exactly what he means to say, and even if it is further granted that the "practice" of "rhetoric" in "common talk" is a self-conscious issue in The Taming of the Shrew, still, several other, perhaps more pressing, questions still remain. Why, for example, does the indeterminate question of rhetoric call forth the very determinate patriarchal narrative enacted in The Taming of the Shrew? Putting the same question in a theoretical register, we can ask why the question of rhetoric evokes from psychoanalysis the patriarchalism for which Lacan appears to be the most explicit mouthpiece, just as the same question provokes, instead, the antipatriarchal gender deconstructions – the chiasmically invaginated differences, the differentiated differences, between male and female – for which we might take Derrida to be the most outspoken spokesman.

To begin to think about these questions, it is necessary first to recognize that *The Taming of the Shrew* is somewhat more specific in its account of female language than I have so far been suggesting. For there is of course another woman in the play whose voice is strictly counterposed to the "scolding tongue" (I. i. 252) of Kate, and if Kate, as shrew, is shown to speak a misanthropic, "fretful" language, her sister, the ideal Bianca of the wooing story, quite clearly speaks, and sometimes even sings, another and, at least at first, a more inviting tune. There are, that is to say, at least two kinds of language that the play associates with women – one good, one bad – and the play invents two antithetical stereotypes of woman – again, one good, one bad – to be the voice of these two different kinds of female speech.

This is a distinction or an opposition whose specific content is often overlooked, perhaps because Bianca's voice, since it is initially identified with silence, seems to speak a language about which there is not that much to say. Nevertheless, this silence of Bianca has its own substantial nature, and it points up what is wrong with what, in contrast, is Kate's vocal or vociferating speech. In the first scene of the play within the play, which is where we first meet these two women, Lucentio is made to be a witness to the shrewish voice of Kate – "That wench is stark mad or wonderful froward" (I. i. 69) – and this loquacity of Kate is placed in pointed contrast to Bianca's virgin muteness: "But in the other's silence do I see / Maid's mild behavior and sobriety" (70–1). This opposition, speech versus silence, is important, but even more important is the fact that it is developed in the play through the more inclusive opposition here suggested by the metaphorical way in which Lucentio "sees" Bianca's "silence." For Bianca does in fact speak quite often in the play – she is not literally mute – but the play describes this speech, as it does Bianca, with a set of images and motifs, figures of speech, that give both to Bianca and to her speaking a specific phenomenality which is understood to be *equivalent* to silence. This quality, almost a physical materiality, can be generally summarized – indeed, generically summarized – in terms of an essential visibility: that is to say, Bianca and her language both are silent because the two of them are something to be *seen*.

One way to illustrate this is to recall how the first scene repeatedly emphasizes the fact that Lucentio falls in love with Bianca at first sight: "let me be a slave, t'achieve that maid / Whose sudden sight hath thrall'd my wounded eye" (I. i. 219–20). A good deal of Petrarchan imagery underlies the visuality of Lucentio's erotic vision: "But see, while idly I stood looking on, / I found the effect of love in idleness" (I.i. 150–1). More specifically, however, this modality of vision, this generic specularity, is made to seem the central point of difference between two different kinds of female language whose different natures then elicit in response two different kinds of male desire. There is, that is to say, a polar contrast, erotically inflected, between, on the one hand, the admirably dumb visual language of Bianca and, on the other, the objectionably noisy "tongue" (I.i. 89) of Kate:

> *Tranio:*   Master, you look'd so longly on the maid . . .
> *Lucentio:* O yes, I saw sweet beauty in her face . . .
> *Tranio:*   Saw you no more? Mark'd you not how her sister
>   Began to scold, and raise up such a storm
>   That mortal ears might hardly endure the din?
> *Lucentio:* Tranio, I saw her mortal lips to move,
>   And with her breath she did perfume the air.
>   Sacred and sweet was all I saw in her.
>
> (I.i. 165–76)

In *The Taming of the Shrew* this opposition between vision and language – rather, between a language which is visual, of the eye, and therefore silent, and language which is vocal, of the tongue, and therefore heard – is very strong. Moreover, as the play develops it, this is a dynamic and a violent, not a static, opposition, for it is just such vision that the vocal or linguistic language of Kate is shown repeatedly to speak against. In the first scene this happens quite explicitly, when Kate says of Bianca, in what are almost the first words out of Kate's mouth, "A pretty peat! It is best / Put a finger in the eye, and she knew why" (I.i. 78–9). But this opposition runs throughout the play, governing its largest dramatic as well as its thematic movements. To take an example which is especially significant in the light of what has so far been said, we can recall that the "rope-tricks" passage concludes when it prophetically imagines Kate's ultimate capitulation in terms of a blinding cognate with the name of Kate: "She shall have no more eyes to see withal than a cat." Again, it is in terms of just such (figurative) blindness that Kate will later act out her ultimate subjection, not only to man but to the language of man: "Pardon old father, my mistaking eyes, / That have been so bedazzled with the sun . . . Now I perceive thou art a reverent father. / Pardon, I pray thee, for my mad mistaking" (IV.v. 45–9).

I have argued elsewhere that this conflict between visionary and verbal language is not only a very traditional one but one to which Shakespeare in his Sonnets gives a new subjective twist when he assimilates it to the psychology, and not only to the erotic psychology, of his first-person lyric voice.[6] In addition, I have also argued that Shakespeare's different manipulations of this vision / language opposition produce generically different characterological or subjectivity effects in Shakespearean comedy, tragedy, and romance. It is far from the case, however, that Shakespeare invents this conflict between visual and verbal speech, for it is also possible to demonstrate that the terms of this opposition very much inform the metaphorical language through which language is imagined and described in the philosophico-literary tradition that begins in antiquity and extends at least up through the Renaissance, if not farther. While it is not possible to develop in a brief essay such as this the detailed and coherent ways in which this visual/verbal conflict operates in traditionary texts, it is possible to indicate, very schematically, the general logic of this perennial opposition by looking at the two rather well-known illustrations reproduced on pages 150 and 152. These pictures are by Robert Fludd, the seventeenth-century hermeticist, and they employ a thoroughly conventional iconography.[7] A brief review of the two pictures will be worthwhile, for this will allow us to understand how it happens that a traditional question about rhetoric amounts to an answer to an equally traditional question about gender. This in turn will allow us to return not only to *The Taming of the Shrew* but also to the larger theoretical question with which we began, namely, whether it is possible to speak a Language, whether of Man or of Woman, that does not speak for the Language of Man.

The first picture, Figure 6, is Fludd's illustration of the seventh verse of Psalm 63 (misnumbered in the picture as verse 8). "*In alarum tuarum umbra canam,*" says or sings King David, and the picture shows precisely this. King David kneels in prayer beneath an eyeball sun, while from out of his mouth, in line with the rays of theophanic light which stream down on him, a verse of psalm ascends up to a brightness which is supported, shaded, and revealed by its extended wings. Because King David is the master psalmist, and because the picture employs perennial motifs, it would be fair to say that Fludd's picture is an illustration of psalmic speech *per se*. In the picture we see traditional figurations of the way a special kind of anagogic language does homage to an elevated referent. This referent, moreover, represented as an eye which is both seeing and seen, is itself a figure of a special kind of speech, as is indicated by the Hebrew letters inscribed upon its iris. These letters – *yod, he, vau, he* – spell out the name of God, "*Jehova,*" which is the "Name" in which, according to the fourth verse of the psalm, King David lifts up his hands: "Thus wil I magnifie thee all my life, and lift up mine hands in the Name."[8] However, though these letters spell out this holy name, nevertheless, in principle they do not sound it out, for these are letters whose literality, when combined in this famous Tetragrammaton, must never be pronounced. Instead, in accord with both orthodox and heterodox mystical prohibitions, this written name of god, which is the only proper name of God, will be properly articulated only through attributive periphrasis, with the letters vocalized either as *Adonai*, "the Lord," or as *Ha Shem*, "the Name" or even "the Word."

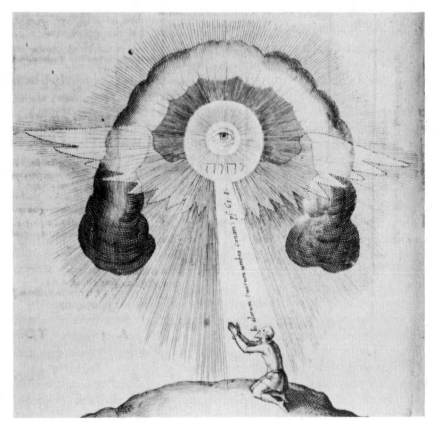

Figure 6   Fludd's illustration of the seventh verse of Psalm 63

In Fludd's picture, where the verse of psalm and *"Jehova"* lie at oblique angles to each other, it is clearly the case that King David does not literally voice the name of God. It is possible, however, reading either up or down, to take inscribed *"Jehova"* as an unspoken part of David's praising speech, either as its apostrophized addressee or as the direct object of its *"canam."* This syntactic, but still silent, link between the Latin and the Hebrew is significant, for unspeakable *"Jehova"* thus becomes the predicated precondition through which or across which what the psalmist says is translated into what the psalmist sees. The picture is concerned to illustrate the effect of this translation, showing David's verse to be the medium of his immediate vision of the sun, drawing David's verse as though it were itself a beam of holy light. In this way, because the verse is pictured as the very brightness that it promises to sing or speak about, Fludd's picture manages to motivate its portrait of a genuinely visionary speech. In the psalm, the reason why the psalmist praises is the very substance of his praise: "For thy loving kindnes is better then life: therefore my lippes shal praise thee." The same thing happens in the picture, where we see the future tense of "*canam*" rendered present, and where the promise of praise amounts to the fulfillment of the promise. But again, all this visionary predication depends upon the odd graphesis of unspeakable "*Jehova*," which is the signifier of all signifiers that even King David cannot bring himself to utter, just as it is the writing on his iris that even Jehova cannot read.

In an elementary etymological sense – remembering that "ideal" comes from Greek "*idein*," "to see" – Fludd's picture is a portrait of ideal language, of language that is at once ideal and idealizing. As the picture shows it, King David speaks a visual speech, a language *of* vision that promotes a vision *of* language, a language which is of the mouth only in so far as it is for the eye. This visual and visionary logos is nothing but familiar. Psalmic speech in particular and the language of praise in general (and it should be recalled that up through the Renaissance *all* poetry is understood to be a poetry of praise) are regularly imagined through such visual imagery, just as the referential object of such reverential praise is regularly conceived of as both agent and patient of sight. (Dante's vision of *luce etterna* at the end of the *Paradiso* would be a good example, though here again the height of vision is figured through a transcendental darkness, when power fails the poet's "*alta fanta-sia*," and the poet's "will and desire" then "turn" ("*volgeva*") with "the love that moves the sun and the other stars.")

In the second picture, Figure 7, which is by no means a strictly Elizabethan world picture (since its details go back at least to Macrobius and, therefore, through Plotinus, to Plato) we see the idealist aesthetics, metaphysics, and cosmology traditionally unpacked from and attaching to this visual idealism or visual idealization of the Word. As the title indicates, all arts are images of the specularity of integrated nature because both art and nature reciprocally will simulate the *eidola* or likenesses of beatific light. This commonplace eidetic reduction, which, by commutation, enables representation iconically to replicate whatever it presents, is what makes both art and nature into psalmic panegyric. Art becomes an art of nature just as nature is itself a kind of art, because they both reflect, but do not speak, the holy name which is the signifier and the signified of art and nature both. From this phenomenologi-cally mutual admiration, which makes of art and nature each other's *special* (from *specere*, "to look at") likeness, it is easy to derive the ontotheological imperatives that inform all visionary art, for example, the poetics of *ut pictura poesis* and "speaking picture." Suspended from the hand of God, the great chain of mimetic being (which Macrobius describes as a series of successive and declensive mirrors) reaches down to nature, and through her to man, the ape of nature, whose artful calibration of a represented little world produces a demiurgic *mise en abyme* that in no way disturbs – indeed, one whose

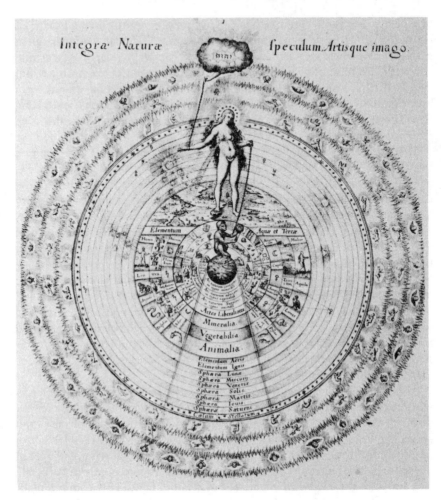

Figure 7   Fludd's encyclopedic picture of the hierarchic cosmos

recursive reflections do nothing but confirm – the stability of the material world on which the ape of nature squats.

Not surprisingly, Fludd's encyclopedic picture of the hierarchic cosmos also includes a representation of a corresponding gender hierarchy. We can see this by looking at the circle of animals where, on the left, the picture illustrates generic man or *Homo* with his arms unfolded towards the sun, in complementary contrast to the way that woman or *Mulier*, at the right of the circle of animals, looks instead up to the moon which is the pale reflection of the sun that shines above it. It is fair to say that this opposition, which makes woman the mimetic simulacrum of man, sketches out the horizontal gender opposition on which the vertical, metaphysical hierarchy of the cosmos perpendicularly depends. For this reason, however, it is important to notice that, as the picture shows it, this is not a simple or a simply polar contrast. Man is figured by the sun which is always the same as itself, whereas woman is figured by a waxing-waning-changing moon which is always other than itself, because its mimic light of likeness is what illuminates its difference from the sameness of the sun. Perhaps this constitutes a paradox, this lunar light which folds up likeness into difference. But if so, it is a paradox that stands in service of an orthodox erotics for which woman is the other to man, the hetero- to *Homo*, precisely because her essence is *to be* this lunatic difference between sameness and difference. In the same conventional way (conventional, certainly, at least up through Milton) that the difference between the sun and the moon *is* the moon, so too, and equally traditionally, the difference between man and woman is woman herself.[9] This is a piety, moreover, that we see fleshed out in the ornaments of nature, who sports, with all decorum, a sun on one breast, a moon on the other, and, as the castrated and castrating difference between them, a second fetishistic moon upon her beatific crotch. Such is the erotics that is called for by traditional metaphysics. The word whose solar brightness is revealed by that which clouds it bespeaks a female darkness which is veiled by lunar brightness. The sickle-crescent moon of nature, which is cut and cutting both at once, indicates a mystery beyond it which is complementary to the way the odd graphesis of "*Jehova*" is constitutively eccentric to the centered wholeness of the world.

I have put this point in this way so as to point up the fact that there is really only one way to read Fludd's picture, and this precisely because there are two ways to read it. As with "rope-tricks," indeterminacy here again determines a specific story. On the one hand, given a set of assumptions about mimesis that go back at least to Plato, woman is the subordinate sub-version of originary man, in the same way that the moon is nothing more than an inferior reflection of the sun. In this sense, woman is nothing other than the likeness of a likeness. On the other hand, woman is equally the radical subversion of man, an insubordinate sub-version, because this system of mimesis inexorably calls forth a principle of difference which, as difference, is intrinsically excessive to such hierarchic likeness. In this sense, as the embodiment of difference – as, specifically, the difference *of* likeness – woman is nothing other than the other itself. The point to recognize, however, is not simply that these two hands go happily together – the logic of sub-version logically entailing its own subversion, the "Mirror of Nature" already displaying what Luce Irigaray will call the *speculum de l'autre femme* – but, more important, that the necessity of this double reading is no esoteric piece of wisdom. Quite the contrary; what we see in Fludd's picture is that this is a profoundly orthodox paradox, one whose formal heterogeneity, whose essential duplicity, is regularly figured and expressed by commonplace placeholders of the difference between sameness and difference, as, for example, unspeakable

"*Jehova*," whose circumlocutory logos tangentially straddles the inside and the outside of the universal wholeness, or the titillating hole between the legs of nature whose absent presence is highlighted by discretionary light.

What Fludd's picture shows us, therefore, is that traditional iconography regularly assumes, as though it goes necessarily without saying, that there cannot be a picture of visionary language which is not at the same time an emblem of the limits of vision. This limit, however, as a limit, is built into Fludd's Wittgensteinian picture theory of language, within it as precisely that which such a theory is without. "*Jehova*," for example, is a part of *because* it is apart from the ideal specularity of the praising integrated world, and so too with the secret private parts of nature, whose hole we here see integrated into the deep recesses of nature's integrated whole. Out of this internal contradiction, figured through such motivating motifs, there derives, therefore, a very traditional story about the way the language of ideal desire is correlated with a desire for an ideal language. We see this story outlined in the circle of minerals, where man is associated with *Plumbum*, lead, and where woman is associated with *Cuprum*, named for the copper mines in Cyprus, birthplace of Venus, the goddess of love. Here we are to assume an alchemical reaction whereby Venus, the "Cyprian Queen," at once the object and the motive of desire, as a kind of catalytic converter, translates lead into gold, thereby supernaturally changing sub-nature into super-nature. And we can put this point more strongly by asserting that what Fludd's picture depicts is the thoroughly conventional way in which a universe of logical sameness is built up *on* its logical contra-diction (or, as it is sometimes written nowadays, as though this were a feminist gesture, its "cuntra-diction," i.e. the language of woman) because it is the very lunacy of discourse that returns both man and woman to the golden, solar order of the patriarchal Word.

At this level of allegorical generality, we can very quickly turn back to *The Taming of the Shrew* and understand how it happens that Petruchio re-establishes the difference between the sexes by speaking the lunatic language of woman. The language of woman *is* the difference between the sexes, a difference Petruchio becomes when, speaking "rope-tricks," he is "Kated." And this translation is dramatically persuasive because the play fleshes it out by invoking the sub-versive, subversive terms and logic of traditional iconography. In the taming story, the first moment of Kate's capitulation occurs when Petruchio, changing his mind, forces Kate first to call the sun the moon and then again the sun: "Then God be blest, it is the blessed sun, / But sun it is not, when you say it is not; / And the moon changes even as your mind. / What you will have it nam'd, even that it is, / And so it shall be so for Katherine" (IV.v.18–22). We can call Kate's articulation of "change" the naming of the shrew which is the instrument of her taming, for it is this transcendentalizing, heliotropic, ontotheological paradox of "change" – "Then God be blest" – that leads Kate then to beg a patriarchal pardon for her blind confusion of the sexes: "Pardon, old father, my mistaking eyes, / That have been so be-dazzled with the sun." And the same thing happens at the climax of the wooing story, when Lucentio, until then disguised as Cambio, kneels down before his father and reveals his proper self. "Cambio is chang'd into Lucentio" (V.i. 123) is the line with which this revelation is theatrically announced. This formula serves to return the father and his son, along with the master and his servant, back to their proper order. But it also offers us an economical example of the way in which the very operation of rhetorical translation serves to change "change" into light.

To say that this paradox is orthodox is not to say that it describes a complete logical circle. Quite the contrary, as is indicated by the aporetic structure of Fludd's pictures, it is *as* a logical problem for logic, as an everpresent, irreducible, and ongoing question raised by self-reflection, that the paradox acquires its effective power. This is the question consistently raised by the insistent question of rhetoric, which is why, when Kate is tamed and order restored, the heretofore silent and good women of the play immediately turn into shrews. The subversive language of woman with which the play begins, and in resistance to which the movement of the play is predicated, reappears at the end of the play so that its very sounding predicts the future as a repetition of the same old story. This is the final moral of *The Taming of the Shrew*: that it is not possible to close the story of closure, for the very idea and idealization of closure, like the wholeness of Fludd's comprehensive cosmos, is thought through a logic and a logos whose internal disruption forever defers, even as this deferment elicits a desire for, a summary conclusion.

Hence, we can add, the function of the larger frame. Speaking very generally – and recalling, on the one hand, the Petrarchan idealism of the wooing story and, on the other, the parodic Petrarchanism, the Petruchioism, of the taming story – we can say that the two subplots of *The Taming of the Shrew* together present what in the western literary tradition is the master plot of the relation between language and desire. Sly, however, to whom this story is presented, wishes that his entertainment soon were over, for only when the play is over will Sly get to go to bed with new-found wife. "Would 'twere done!" (I.i. 254), says Sly (these being the last words we hear from him), of a play which, as far as Sly is concerned, is nothing but foreplay. The joke here is surely on Sly, for the audience knows full well that the consummation Sly so devoutly desires will never be achieved; if ever it happens that Sly sleeps with his wife, he will soon enough discover that she is a he in drag disguise. This defines, perhaps, the ultimate perversity of the kinky lord who "long[s] to hear" his pageboy "call the drunkard husband" (Ind. i. 133), and who arranges for Sly to be subjected in this tantalizing way to what for Sly is nothing but the tedious unfolding of the play within the play. But it is not only Sly's desire that is thus seductively frustrated; and this suggests the presence, behind the play, of an even kinkier lord. I refer here to the ongoing editorial question regarding the absence of a final frame; for this response to the play's apparent omission of a formal conclusion to the Sly story is evidence enough that the audience for the entirety of the play is left at its conclusion with a desire for closure that the play calls forth *in order* to postpone. To say that this is a desire that leaves something to be desired – a desire, therefore, that will go on and on forever – goes a good way towards explaining the abiding popularity of *The Taming of the Shrew*.[10]

Perhaps this also explains why, at first glance, it looks as though the current theoretical controversy to which I have referred presents us with a lovers' quarrel in which psychoanalysis plays Petruchio to its critics' Kate. It is tempting to see in the debate between Lacan and Derrida, for example, a domestic and domesticating quarrel that re-enacts in an increasingly more sophisticated but, for this reason, an increasingly more hapless fashion a proverbial literary predicament. However, this is not the conclusion that I would like to draw from the fact that current theoretical polemic so faithfully shapes itself to traditional literary contours and so voraciously stuffs itself with traditional literary topoi. Again it would be possible to relate the logic of sub-versive subversion, as it appears in Fludd and Shakespeare, to Derrida's gnostic, a-logical logic of the copulating supplement. And again, and again even more specifically, it would be possible to relate all this to Lacan's account of "The function and field of speech and language in psychoanalysis." Lacan's characterization of the relation of the imaginary to the symbolic very straightforwardly repeats the motifs of a traditional verbal/visual conflict, and it does so in a way that fully incorporates into itself its equally traditional intrinsic deconstruction, e.g. when Lacan says that the real is that which cannot be represented. When Lacan says, to take just a few examples, that the being of the woman is that she does not exist, or that the function of the universal quantifier, by means of which man becomes the all, is thought through its negation in woman's not-all, when he says that there is no sexual relation, or when he says that castration, the $-\phi$, is what allows us to count from o to 1, he is not only evoking the elementary paradox displayed in Fludd's picture – the class of all classes that do not classify themselves – he is also ornamenting this familiar paradox with its traditional figurative clothing.[11] Thus it is that Lacan, like Derrida, is a master of the commonplace, as when he says that there is no such thing as metalanguage, or that "*La femme n'ex-siste pas,*" or that "*Si j'ai dit que le langage est ce comme quoi l'inconscient est structuré, c'est bien parce que le langage, d'abord, ça n'existe pas. Le langage est ce qu'on essaye de savoir concernant la fonction de lalangue.*"[12]

To recognize the fact that all of this is commonplace is to see that the argument between Lacan and Derrida, between psychoanalysis and its other (an argument that already takes place within Lacan and within psychoanalysis), repeats, not only in its structure but also in its thematic and illustrative details, a master plot of literature. To see this is also to recognize that coarse generic terms of a magnitude corresponding to that of man, woman, language historically carry with them an internal narrative logic which works to motivate a story in which every rubric gets to play and to explain its integrated role. At this level of generality it goes without saying that the language of woman inexorably speaks for the language of man, and it is therefore not surprising that a feminist critique of psychoanalysis which is conducted at this level of generality will necessarily recathect the story that is fleshed out in *The Taming of the Shrew*. If "Cambio is chang'd into Lucentio," so too, for example, is "Cambio" changed into Luce Irigaray.

It is, however, the great and exemplary value of both Lacan and Derrida that in their quarrel with each other they do more than scrupulously restrict their readings of the central topoi of western self-reflexive language to the level of generality appropriate to the register of allegorical abstraction called for by such massive metaphoremes and motifs. In addition, they recognize this level of generality for what it is: the logic of the literary word in the west. Doing so, they open up the possibility of an extraliterary reading of literature. In a specifically literary context, Shakespeare is interesting because in Shakespeare's texts (from Freud's reading of which, we should recall, psychoanalysis originally derives) we see how, at a certain point in literary history, allegorical abstractions such as man, woman, language – formerly related to each other in accord with the psychomachian dynamics which are sketched out in Fludd's pictures – are introduced into a psychologistic literature, thereby initiating a recognizably modern literature of individuated, motivated character. But the relation to literature is not itself a literary relation, and there is no compelling reason, therefore, especially with the examples of Lacan and Derrida before them, why readers or critics of master literary texts should in their theory or their practice act out what they read.

Notes

1. Derrida's most explicit criticisms of Lacan can be found in "The purveyor of truth" (*Yale French Studies*, 52 (1975)); and in *Positions*, tr. Alan Bass (Chicago, 1981). See also *Spurs: Nietzsche's Styles*, tr. Barbara Harlow (Chicago, 1979); *La Carte postale* (Paris, 1980), which republishes and expands upon "The purveyor of truth"; Julia Kristeva, *Desire in Language: A Semiotic Approach to Literature and Art* (New York, 1980); Hélène Cixous, *La Jeune Née* (with Catherine Clément) (Paris, 1975); "The laugh of the Medusa," tr. K. Cohen and P. Cohen (*Signs*, 1 (Summer 1976), 875–99); Luce Irigaray, *Speculum de l'autre femme* (Paris, 1974); *Ce sexe qui n'est pas un* (Paris, 1977); Sarah Kofman, "The narcissistic woman: Freud and Girard" (*Diacritics* (Fall 1980), 36–45); *Nietzsche et la scène philosophique* (Paris, 1979).

2. All Shakespeare references are to *The Riverside Shakespeare*, ed. G. B. Evans (Boston, 1974).
3. *The Taming of the Shrew*, ed. H. J. Oliver (Oxford, 1982), 124.
4. "It was at this point that the addendum of there having been a question-mark after the word 'like' occurred to Dora, and she then recognized these words as a quotation out of a letter from Frau K. which had contained the invitation to L_____, the place by the lake. In that letter there had been a question mark placed, in a most unusual fashion, in the very middle of a sentence, after the intercalated words 'if you would like to come'" (Sigmund Freud, *Dora: An Analysis of a Case of Hysteria* (1905), tr. J. Strachey (New York, 1963), 118). Dora dreams here, quite literally, of *écriture féminine*, but Frau K's peculiar question-mark, even if its interruption is taken as a signal of the lesbianism Freud insists on in the story, still marks the specifically Freudian question of female desire: "What does woman want?" This question – not simply "if you would like to come" but, instead, "if you would like to like to come," i.e. do you desire desire? – remains a question at the end of the Dora case; and it seems clear enough that this enigma not only stimulates Freud's counter-transference to Dora's transference (Freud introduces the concept of transference in the Dora case), but also accounts for Freud's failure to analyze, on the one hand, his patient's relation to him and, on the other, his relation to his patient. This double failure explains why the Dora case, like *The Taming of the Shrew*, concludes inconclusively. As Freud reports it, the analysis of Dora amounts to a battle between doctor and patient wherein, in response to Freud's demand that Dora admit her desire for Herr K – i.e. that she avow her Freudian desire – Dora refuses to say what she wants. This is a characteristic Freudian frustration. As in Freud's dream of Irma's injection, where Freud looks into Irma's mouth for evidence of a specifically psychoanalytic sexuality that would prove Freud's psychoanalytic theory true, so Freud wants Dora to speak her desire so as thereby to satisfy Freud's desire for a confirmation of his theory of desire. In the Irma dream, Freud receives as enigmatic answer to this question the uncanny image of "Trimethylamin" – not only a picture of a word, but a picture of the very word that formulates female sexuality – whereas in the Dora case the question is answered with the re-marked question-mark. In both cases, however, it is the question of female desire, staged as an essential and essentializing question, that leads Freud on in a seductive way. When Dora, manhandling Freud, breaks off her analysis, she leaves Freud with the question of woman, the answer to which Freud will pursue for the rest of his life, up through the late, again inconclusive, essays on gender, in all of which Freud argues for a determinate indeterminacy, a teleological interminability.
5. For example, "The function and field of speech and language in psychoanalysis," in Jacques Lacan, *Ecrits*, tr. Alan Sheridan (New York, 1977), 30–113.
6. Joel Fineman, *Shakespeare's Perjured Eye: The Invention of Poetic Subjectivity in the Sonnets* (Berkeley, 1985).
7. Figure 6 comes from Fludd's *Tomi Secundi Tractatus Secundus; De Præternaturali Utriusque Cosmi Majoris* ... (Oppenheim, 1621); Figure 7 comes from *Utriusque Cosmi Majoris* ... (Oppenheim, 1617). There is a convenient collection of Fludd's illustrations in Joscelyn Godwin's *Robert Fludd* (London, 1979).
8. All quotations from the psalm are from the Geneva translation.
9. See Milton, *Paradise Lost*, III, 722–32.
10. It is here that the affinities of *The Taming of the Shrew* with Henry James's *The Turn of the Screw*, to which I am of course alluding in my title, are most apparent. In both texts a specifically rhetorical "turning," "troping," "versing," under-

stood on the model of "rope-tricks," generates an interpretive mystery which is then correlated with a sexual tropism towards, or an apotropaic aversion from, an uncanny, true-false, *female* admixture of male and female. In *The Taming of the Shrew* Sly's framing desire for the pageboy disguised as a woman is a metatheatrical filter that puts into question any univocal understanding of the coupling of Petruchio and Kate. Hence the continuing critical question as to whether the Pauline patriarchalism of Kate's final speech should be understood ironically, i.e. whether she is most a shrew when she is most submissive. This hermeneutic question with regard to Kate corresponds to the traditional duplicity of woman: Sly's metatheatrical desire for the pageboy defines the essence of femininity as masquerade. So too with *The Turn of the Screw*, which shares with *The Taming of the Shrew* the same heavy-handed, play-within-play, *mise en abyme* structure, and which uses this reflexive literariness to invite and to excite a series of relevant but irresolvable, and therefore continuing, critical questions, for example, is the governess's story true or false? is the governess crazy or sane? In *The Turn of the Screw* such interpretive questions find their objectification, their objectification *as* questions, in "Peter Quint," a kind of verbal pageboy whose nominality evokes the primal scene – half-real, half-fantasy – that motivates the governess's hysterico-obsessive desire for Miles and Flora. Again the point to notice is the way in which rhetorical indeterminacy generates a determinate erotics. The name that couples male and female genitals, "Peter" and "Quint," produces a specifically *female* uncanny: the name is quaint – indeed, "cunt" – because both "Peter" and "Quint." So too, a master text such as *The Turn of the Screw* uses precisely this indeterminacy to resecure the place of the "Master" in relation to his servants.

11. See, especially, Jacques Lacan, *Encore* (Paris, 1975), 49–94.
12. For Lacan's remarks on "metalanguage," see, in *Ecrits*, "On a question preliminary to any possible treatment of psychosis." The concluding two quotations come, respectively, from *Télévision* (Paris, 1974), 60, and *Encore*, 126.

III
Politics, economy, history

9

STEPHEN GREENBLATT

Shakespeare and the exorcists

Between the spring of 1585 and the summer of 1586, a group of English Catholic priests led by the Jesuit William Weston, alias Father Edmunds, conducted a series of spectacular exorcisms, principally in the house of a recusant gentleman, Sir George Peckham of Denham, Buckinghamshire. The priests were outlaws – by an Act of 1585 the mere presence in England of a Jesuit or seminary priest constituted high treason – and those who sheltered them were guilty of a felony, punishable by death. Yet the exorcisms, though clandestine, drew large crowds, almost certainly in the hundreds, and must have been common knowledge to hundreds more. In 1603, long after the arrest and punishment of those involved, Samuel Harsnett, then chaplain to the Bishop of London, wrote a detailed account of the cases, based upon sworn statements taken from four of the demoniacs and one of the priests. It has been recognized since the eighteenth century that Shakespeare was reading Harsnett's book, *A Declaration of Egregious Popish Impostures*, as he was writing *King Lear*.[1]

My concern is with the relation between these two texts, and I want to suggest that our understanding of this relation is greatly enhanced by the theoretical ferment that has affected (some would say afflicted) literary studies during the past decade. This claim may arouse scepticism on several counts. Source study is, as we all know, the elephants' graveyard of literary history. My own work, moreover, has consistently failed to make the move that can redeem, on these occasions, such unpromising beginnings: the move from a local problem to a universal, encompassing, and abstract problematic within which the initial concerns are situated. For me the study of the literary is the study of contingent, particular, intended, and historically embedded works; if theory inevitably involves the desire to escape from contingency into a higher realm, a realm in which signs are purified of the slime of history, then this paper is written *against* theory.[2]

But I am not convinced that theory necessarily drives toward the abstract purity of autonomous signification, and, even when it does, its influence upon the study of literature may be quite distinct from its own designs. Indeed, I believe that the most important effect of contemporary theory upon the practice of literary criticism, and certainly upon *my* practice, is to subvert the tendency to think of aesthetic representation as ultimately autonomous, separable from its cultural context and hence divorced from the social, ideological, and material matrix in which all art is produced and consumed. This subversion is true not only of Marxist theory explicitly engaged in polemics against literary autonomy, but also of deconstructionist theory, even at its most hermetic and abstract. For the undecidability that deconstruction repeatedly discovers in literary signification also calls into question the boundaries between the literary and the nonliterary. The intention to produce a work of literature does not guarantee an autonomous text, since the signifiers always exceed and thus undermine intention. This constant exceeding (which is the paradoxical expression of an endless deferral of meaning) forces the collapse of all stable oppositions, or rather compels interpretation to acknowledge that one position is always infected with traces of its radical antithesis.[3] Insofar as the absolute disjunction of the literary and the nonliterary had been the root assumption of mainstream Anglo-American criticism in the mid-twentieth century, deconstruction emerged as a liberating challenge, a salutary return of the literary text to the condition of all other texts and a simultaneous assault on the positivist certitude of the nonliterary, the privileged realm of historical fact. History cannot be divorced from textuality, and all texts can be compelled to confront the crisis of undecidability revealed in the literary text. Hence history loses its epistemological innocence, while literature loses an isolation that had come to seem more a prison than a privilege.

The problem with this theoretical liberation, in my view, is that it is forced, by definition, to discount the specific, institutional interests served both by local episodes of undecidability and contradiction and by the powerful if conceptually imperfect differentiation between the literary and the nonliterary. Deconstruction is occasionally attacked as if it were a satanic doctrine, but I sometimes think that it is not satanic enough; as John Wesley wrote to his brother, "If I have any fear, it is not of falling into hell, but of falling into nothing."[4] Deconstructionist readings lead too readily and predictably to the void; in actual literary practice the perplexities into which one is led are not moments of pure, untrammeled *aporia* but localized strategies in particular historical encounters. Similarly, it is important to expose the theoretical untenability of the conventional boundaries between facts and artifacts, but the particular terms of this boundary at a specific time and place cannot simply be discarded. On the contrary, as I will try to demonstrate in some detail, these impure terms that mark the difference between the literary and the nonliterary are the currency in crucial institutional negotiations and exchange. This institutional economy is one of the central concerns of the critical method that I have called cultural poetics.

Let us return to Samuel Harsnett. The relation between *King Lear* and *A Declaration of Egregious Popish Impostures* has, as I have remarked, been known for centuries, but the knowledge has remained almost entirely inert, locked in the conventional pieties of source study. From Harsnett, we are told, Shakespeare borrowed the names of the foul fiends by whom Edgar, in his disguise as the Bedlam beggar Poor Tom, claims to be possessed. From Harsnett, too, the playwright derived some of the language of madness, several of the attributes of hell, and a substantial number of colorful adjectives. These and other possible borrowings have been carefully catalogued, but the question of their significance has been not only unanswered but unasked.[5] Until recently, the prevailing model for the study of literary sources, a model in effect parceled out between the old historicism and the new criticism, blocked such a question. As a freestanding, self-sufficient, disinterested art-work produced by a solitary genius, *King Lear* has only an accidental relation to its sources: they provide a glimpse of the "raw material" that the artist fashioned. In so far as this "material" is taken seriously at all, it is as part of the work's "historical background," a phrase that reduces history to a decorative setting or a convenient, well-lighted pigeonhole. But once the differentiations upon which this model is based begin to crumble, then source study is compelled to change its character: history cannot simply be set against literary texts as either stable antithesis or stable background, and the protective isolation of those texts gives way to a sense of their interaction with other texts and hence to the permeability of their boundaries. "When I play with my cat," writes Montaigne, "who knows if I am not a pastime to her more than she is to me?"[6] When Shakespeare borrows from Harsnett, who knows if Harsnett has not already, in a deep sense, borrowed from Shakespeare's theater what Shakespeare borrows back? Whose interests are served by the borrowing? And is there a larger cultural text produced by the exchange?

Such questions do not lead, for me at least, to the *O altitudo!* of radical indeterminacy. They lead rather to an exploration of the institutional strategies in which both *King Lear* and Harsnett's *Declaration* are embedded. These strategies, I suggest, are part of an intense and sustained struggle in late sixteenth- and early seventeenth-century England to redefine the central values of society. Such a redefinition entailed a transformation of the prevailing standards of judgment and action, a rethinking of the conceptual categories by which the ruling élites constructed their world, and which they attempted to impose upon the majority of the population. At the heart of this struggle, which had as its outcome a murderous civil war, was the definition of the sacred, a definition that directly involved secular as well as religious institutions, since the legitimacy of the state rested explicitly upon its claim to a measure of sacredness. What is the sacred? Who defines and polices its boundaries? How can society distinguish between legitimate and illegitimate claims to sacred authority? In early modern England, rivalry among elites competing for the major share of authority was characteristically expressed not only in parliamentary factions but in bitter struggles over religious doctrine and practice.

Harsnett's *Declaration* is a weapon in one such struggle, the attempt by the established and state-supported Church of England to eliminate competing religious authorities by wiping out pockets of rivalrous charisma. Charisma, in Edward Shils's phrase, is "awe-arousing centrality,"[7] the sense of breaking through the routine into the realm of the "extraordinary," and hence the sense of making direct contact with the ultimate, vital sources of legitimacy, authority, and sacredness. Exorcism was for centuries one of the supreme manifestations in Latin Christianity of this charisma; "in the healing of the possessed," Peter Brown writes, "the *præsentia* of the saints was held to be registered with unfailing accuracy, and their ideal power, their *potentia*, shown most fully and in the most reassuring manner."[8] Reassuring, that is, not only or even primarily to the demoniac, but to the community of believers who bore witness to the ritual and indeed, through their tears and prayers and thanksgiving, participated in it. For unlike sorcery, which occurred most frequently in the dark corners of the land, in remote rural hamlets and isolated cottages, demonic possession seems largely an urban phenomenon. The devil depended upon an audience, as did the charismatic healer: the great exorcisms of the late middle ages and early Renaissance took place at the heart of cities, in cathedrals packed with spectators. They were, as voluminous contemporary accounts declare, moving testimonials to the power of the true faith. But in Protestant England of the late sixteenth century, neither the *præsentia* nor the *potentia* of the exorcist was any longer reassuring to religious authorities, and the Anglican Church had no desire to treat the urban masses to a spectacle whose edifying value had been called into question. Even relatively small assemblies, gathered far from the cities in the obscurity of private houses, had come to represent a threat.

In the *Declaration*, Harsnett specifically attacks exorcism as practiced by Jesuits, but he had earlier leveled the same charges at the Puritan exorcist John Darrell.[9] And he does so not, as we might expect, to claim a monopoly on the practice for the Anglican Church, but to expose exorcism itself as a fraud. On behalf of established religious and secular authority, Harsnett wishes, in effect, to cap permanently the great rushing geysers of charisma released in rituals of exorcism. Spiritual *potentia* will henceforth be distributed with greater moderation and control through the whole of the Anglican hierarchy, a hierarchy at whose pinnacle is placed the sole legitimate possessor of absolute charismatic authority, the monarch, supreme head of the Church in England.

The arguments that Harsnett marshalls against exorcism have a rationalistic cast that may mislead us, for despite appearances v·e are not dealing with an Enlightenment attempt to construct a rational faith. Harsnett denies the presence of the demonic in those whom Father Edmunds claimed to exorcize, but finds it in the exorcists themselves:

> And who was the deuil, the brocher, herald, and perswader of these vnutterable treasons, but *Weston* [*alias* Edmunds] the Iesuit, the chief plotter, and . . . all the holy Couey of the twelue deuilish comedians in their seuerall turnes: for there was neither deuil, nor vrchin, nor Elfe, but themselues.[10]

Hence, writes Harsnett, the "Dialogue between *Edmunds*, & the deuil" was in reality a dialogue between "the deuil *Edmunds*, and *Edmunds* the deuil, for he played both parts himself".[11]

This strategy – the reinscription of evil onto the professed enemies of evil – is one of the characteristic operations of religious authority in the early modern period, and has its secular analogues in more recent history when famous revolutionaries are paraded forth to be tried as counter-revolutionaries. The paradigmatic Renaissance instance is the case of the *benandanti*, analyzed brilliantly by the historian Carlo Ginzburg.[12] The *benandanti* were members of a northern Italian folk cult who believed that their spirits went forth seasonally to battle with fennel stalks against their enemies, the witches. If the *benandanti* triumphed, their victory assured the peasants of good harvests; if they lost, the witches would be free to work their mischief. The Inquisition first became interested in the practice in the late sixteenth century; after conducting a series of lengthy inquiries, the Holy Office determined that the cult was demonic, and in subsequent interrogations attempted, with some success, to persuade the witch-fighting *benandanti* that they were themselves witches.

Harsnett does not hope to persuade exorcists that they are devils; he wishes to expose their fraudulence and relies upon the state to punish them. But he is not willing to abandon the demonic altogether, and it hovers in his work, half-accusation, half-metaphor, whenever he refers to Father Edmunds or the Pope. Satan served too important a function to be cast off lightly by the early seventeenth-century clerical establishment. The same state Church that sponsored the attacks on superstition in the *Declaration of Egregious Popish Impostures* continued to cooperate, if less enthusiastically than before, in the ferocious prosecutions of witches. These prosecutions significantly were handled by the secular judicial apparatus – witchcraft was a criminal offense like aggravated assault or murder – and hence reinforced rather than rivaled the bureaucratic control of authority. The eruption of the demonic into the human world was not denied altogether, but the problem was to be processed through the proper, secular channels. In cases of witchcraft, the devil was defeated in the courts through the simple expedient of hanging his human agents and not, as in cases of possession, compelled by a spectacular spiritual counterforce to speak out and depart.

Witchcraft, then, was distinct from possession, and though Harsnett himself is skeptical about accusations of witchcraft, his principal purpose is to expose a nexus of chicanery and delusion in the practice of exorcism.[13] By doing so he hopes to drive the practice out of society's central zone, to deprive it of its prestige and discredit its apparent efficacy. In late antiquity, as Peter Brown has demonstrated, exorcism was based upon the model of the Roman judicial system: the exorcist conducted a formal *quæstio* in which the demon, under torture, was forced to confess the truth.[14] Now, after more than a millennium, this power would once again be vested solely in the state.

Harsnett's efforts, backed by his powerful superiors, did seriously restrict the practice of exorcism. Canon 72 of the new Church Canons of 1604 ruled that henceforth no minister, unless he had the special permission of his bishop, was to attempt "upon any pretense whatsoever, whether of possession or obsession, by fasting and prayer, to cast out any devil or devils, under pain of the imputation of imposture or cozenage and deposition from the minstery."[15] Since special permission was rarely if ever granted, exorcism had, in effect, been officially halted. But it proved easier to drive exorcism from the center to the periphery than to strip it entirely of its power. Exorcism had been a process of reintegration as well as a manifestation of authority; as the ethnographer Shirokogorov observed of the shamans of Siberia, exorcists could "master" harmful spirits and restore "psychic equilibrium" to whole communities as well as to individuals.[16] The pronouncements of English bishops could not suddenly banish from the land inner demons who stood, as Peter Brown puts it, "for the intangible emotional undertones of ambiguous situations and for the uncertain motives of refractory individuals."[17] The possessed gave voice to the rage, anxiety, and sexual frustration that built up particularly easily in the authoritarian, patriarchal, impoverished, and plague-ridden world of early modern England. The Anglicans attempted to dismantle a corrupt and inadequate therapy without effecting a new and successful cure. In the absence of exorcism, Harsnett could only offer the possessed the very slender reed of Jacobean medicine; if the recently deciphered journal of the Buckinghamshire physician, Richard Napier, is at all representative, doctors in the period struggled to treat a substantial number of cases of possession.[18] But for Harsnett the problem does not really exist, for he argues that the great majority of cases of possession are either fraudulent or subtly called into existence by the ritual designed to treat them. Eliminate the cure and you eliminate the disease. He is forced to concede that at some distant time possession and exorcism were authentic, for, after all,

Jesus himself had driven a legion of unclean spirits out of a possessed man and into the Gadarene swine (Mark 5: 1–19); but the age of miracles has passed, and corporeal possession by demons is no longer possible. The spirit abroad is "the spirit of illusion."[19] Whether they profess to be Catholics or Calvinists does not matter; all modern exorcists practice the same time-honored trade: "the feate of iugling and deluding the people by counterfeyt miracles."[20] Exorcists sometimes contend, acknowledges Harsnett, that the casting out of devils is not a miracle but a wonder – "*mirandum & non miraculum*" – but "both tearmes spring from one roote of wonder or maruell: an effect which a thing strangely done doth procure in the minds of the beholders, as being aboue the reach of nature and reason."[21]

The significance of exorcism, then, lies not in any intrinsic quality of the ritual nor in the precise character of the marks of possession: it lies entirely in the impression made upon the spectators. It may appear that the exorcist and the possessed are utterly absorbed in their terrifying confrontation, but in the midst of the sound and fury – "crying, gnashing of teeth, wallowing, foaming, extraordinarie and supernaturall strength, and supernaturall knowledge"[22] – the real object of the performers' attention is the crowd of beholders.

To counter these effects, Harsnett needed an analytical tool that would enable him to demystify exorcism, to show his readers why the ritual could be so empty and yet so powerful, why beholders could be induced to believe that they were witnessing the ultimate confrontation of good and evil, why a few miserable shifts could produce the experience of horror and wonder. He finds that tool in *theater*.

In the most powerful artistic practice of his age, Harsnett claims to reveal the analytical key to disclosing the degradation of the ancient spiritual practice: exorcisms are stage plays fashioned by cunning clerical dramatists and performed by actors skilled in improvisation. Harsnett first used this theatrical analysis in his attack on Darrell, but it was not until three years later, in his polemic against the Jesuit exorcists, that he worked out its implications in detail.[23] In the account presented in the *Declaration of Egregious Popish Impostures*, some of the participants are self-conscious professionals, like Father Edmunds and his cohorts; others (mostly impressionable young serving women and unstable, down-at-heel young gentlemen) are amateurs cunningly drawn into the demonic stage business. Those selected to play the possessed are in effect taught their roles without realizing at first that they *are* roles.

The priests begin by talking conspicuously about the way successful exorcisms abroad had taken place, and describing in lurid detail the precise symptoms of the possessed. They then await occasions upon which to improvise: a serving man, "beeing pinched with penurie, & hunger, did lie but a night, or two, abroad in the fieldes, and beeing a melancholicke person, was scared with lightning, and thunder, that happened in the night, & loe, an euident signe, that the man was possessed";[24] a dissolute young gentleman "had a spice of the *Hysterica passio*" or, as it is popularly called, "the Moother,"[25] and that too is a sign of possession. An inflamed toe, a pain in the side, a fright taken from the sudden leaping of a cat, a fall in the kitchen, an intense depression following the loss of a beloved child – all are occasions for the priests to step forward and detect the awful presence of the demonic, whereupon the young "scholers," as Harsnett wryly terms the naive performers, "*frame* themselues iumpe and fit vnto the Priests humors, to mop, mow, iest, raile, raue, roare, commend & discommend, and as the priests would haue them, vpon fitting occasions (according to the differences of times, places, and commers in) in all things to play the deuils accordinglie."[26]

The theatricality of exorcism, to which the *Declaration* insistently calls attention, has been repeatedly noted by modern ethnographers who do not share Harsnett's reforming zeal or his sense of outrage. In an illuminating study of possession among the Ethiopians of Gondar, Michel Leiris notes that the healer carefully instructs the *zar*, or spirit, who has seized upon someone, how to behave: the types of cries appropriate to the occasion, the expected violent contortions, the "decorum," as Harsnett would put it, of the trance state.[27] The treatment is in effect an initiation into the performance of the symptoms, which are then cured precisely because they conform to the stereotype of the healing process. One must not conclude, writes Leiris, that there are no "real" – that is, sincerely experienced – cases of possession, for many of the patients (principally young women and slaves) seem genuinely ill, but at the same time there are no cases that are exempt from artifice.[28] Between authentic possession, spontaneous and involuntary, and inauthentic possession, simulated to provide a show or extract some material or moral benefit, there are so many subtle shadings that it is impossible to draw a firm boundary.[29] Possession in Gondar *is* theater, but theater that cannot confess its own theatrical nature, for this is not "theater played" (*théâtre joué*) but "theater lived" (*théâtre vécu*), lived not only by the spirit-haunted actor but by the audience. Those who witness a possession may at any moment be themselves possessed, and even if they are untouched by the *zar*, they remain participants rather than passive spectators. For the theatrical performance is not shielded from them by an impermeable membrane; possession is extraordinary but not marginal, a heightened but not separate state. In possession, writes Leiris, the collective life itself takes the form of theater.[30]

Precisely those qualities that fascinate and charm the ethnographer disgust the embattled Harsnett: where the former can write of "authentic" possession, in the unspoken assurance that none of his readers actually believes in the existence of "*zars*," the latter, granted no such assurance and culturally threatened by the alternative vision of reality, struggles to prove that possession is by definition inauthentic; where the former sees a complex ritual integrated into the social process, the latter sees "a *Stygian* comedy to make silly people afraid";[31] where the former sees the theatrical expression of collective life, the latter sees the theatrical promotion of specific and malevolent institutional interests. And where Leiris's central point is that possession is a theater that does not confess its own theatricality, Harsnett's concern is to enforce precisely such a confession: the last 102 pages of the *Declaration of Egregious Popish Impostures* reprint the "severall Examinations, and confessions of the parties pretended to be possessed, and dispossessed by *Weston* the Iesuit, and his adherents: set downe word for worde as they were taken vpon oath before her Maiesties Commissioners for causes Ecclesiasticall."[32] These transcripts prove, according to Harsnett, that the solemn ceremony of exorcism is a "play of sacred miracles," a "wonderful pageant," a "deuil Theater."[33]

The force of this confession, for Harsnett, is to demolish exorcism. Theater is not the disinterested expression of the popular spirit, but the indelible mark of falsity, tawdriness, and rhetorical manipulation. And these sinister qualities are rendered diabolical by that which so appeals to Leiris: exorcism's cunning concealment of its own theatricality. The spectators do not know that they are responding to a powerful if sleazy tragicomedy; hence their tears and joy, their transports of "commiseration and compassion,"[34] are rendered up, not to a troupe of acknowledged players, but to seditious Puritans or to the supremely dangerous Catholic Church. The theatrical seduction is not, for Harsnett, merely a Jesuitical strategy; it is the essence of the Church itself: Catholicism is a "Mimick superstition."[35]

Harsnett's response is to try to compel the Church to become the theater, just as Catholic clerical garments – the copes and albs and amices and stoles that were the glories of medieval textile crafts – were sold during the Reformation to the players. When an actor in a history play took the part of an English bishop, he could conceivably have worn the actual robes of the character he was representing. Far more is involved here than thrift: the transmigration of a single ecclesiastical cloak from the vestry to the wardrobe may stand as an emblem of the more complex and elusive institutional exchanges that are my subject: a sacred sign, designed to be displayed before a crowd of men and women, is emptied, made negotiable, traded from one institution to another. Such exchanges are rarely so tangible; they are not usually registered in inventories, not often sealed with a cash payment. Nonetheless they occur constantly, for it is precisely through the process of institutional negotiation and exchange that differentiated expressive systems, distinct cultural discourses, are fashioned. We may term such fashioning cultural poesis; the sale of clerical garments is an instance of the ideological labor that such poesis entails. What happens when the piece of cloth is passed from the church to the playhouse? A consecrated object is reclassified, assigned a cash value, transferred from a sacred to a profane setting, deemed suitable to be staged. The theater company is willing to pay for the object not because it contributes to naturalistic representation but because it still bears a symbolic value, however attenuated. On the bare Elizabethan stage, costumes were particularly important – companies were willing to pay more for a good costume than for a good play – and that importance in turn reflected culture's fetishistic obsession with clothes as a mark of status and degree. And if for the theater the acquisition of clerical garments was a significant appropriation of symbolic power, why would the Church part with that power? Because selling Catholic vestments to the players was a form of symbolic aggression: a vivid, wry reminder that Catholicism, as Harsnett puts it, is "the Pope's playhouse."[36]

This blend of appropriation and aggression is similarly at work in the transfer of possession and exorcism from sacred to profane representation. Hence the *Declaration* takes pains to identify exorcism not merely with "the theatrical" – a category that scarcely exists for Harsnett – but with the actual theater; at issue is not so much a metaphorical concept as a functioning institution. For if Harsnett can drive exorcism into the theater – if he can show that the stately houses in which the rituals were performed were playhouses, that the sacred garments were what he calls a "lousie holy wardrop,"[37] that the terrifying writhings were simulations, that the uncanny signs and wonders were contemptible stage tricks, that the devils were the "cassiered woodden-beaten" Vices from medieval drama,[38] and that the exorcists were "vagabond players, that coast from Towne to Towne"[39] – then the ceremony and everything for which it stands will, as far as he is concerned, be emptied out. And, with this emptying out, Harsnett will have driven exorcism from the center to the periphery – in the case of London, quite literally to the periphery, where increasingly stringent urban regulation had already driven the public playhouses.

It is in this symbolically charged zone of pollution, disease, and licentious entertainment that Harsnett seeks to situate the practice of exorcism.[40] What had once occurred in solemn glory at the very center of the city would now be staged alongside the culture's other vulgar spectacles and illusions. Indeed the sense of the theater's tawdriness, marginality, and emptiness – the sense that everything the players touch is thereby rendered hollow – underlies Harsnett's analysis not only of exorcism but of the entire Catholic Church. Demonic possession is a particularly attractive cornerstone for such an analysis, not only because of its histrionic intensity but because the theater itself is by its very nature bound up with possession. Harsnett did not have to believe that the cult of Dionysus out of which the Greek drama evolved was a cult of possession; even the ordinary and familiar theater of his own time depended upon the apparent transformation of the actor into the voice, the actions, and the face of another.

*

With his characteristic opportunism and artistic self-consciousness, Shakespeare in his first known play, *The Comedy of Errors* (1590), was already toying with the connection between theater, illusion, and spurious possession. Antipholus of Syracuse, accosted by his twin's mistress, imagines that he is encountering the devil: "Satan avoid I charge thee tempt me not" (IV. iii. 46). The Ephesian Antipholus's wife, Adriana, dismayed by the apparently mad behavior of her husband, imagines that the devil has possessed him, and she dutifully calls in an exorcist: "Good Doctor Pinch, you are a conjurer; / Establish him in his true sense again" (IV. iv. 45–6). Pinch begins the solemn ritual:

> I charge thee, Satan, hous'd within this man,
> To yield possession to my holy prayers,
> And to thy state of darkness hie thee straight;
> I conjure thee by all the saints in heaven.
> (IV. iv. 52–5)

only to be interrupted with a box on the ears from the outraged husband: "Peace, doting wizard, peace; I am not mad." For the exorcist, such denials only confirm the presence of an evil spirit: "the fiend is strong within him" (IV.iv.105). At the scene's end, Antipholus is dragged away to be "bound and laid in some dark room."

The false presumption of demonic possession in *The Comedy of Errors* is not the result of deception; it is an instance of what one of Shakespeare's sources calls a "suppose" – an attempt to make sense of a series of bizarre actions gleefully generated by the comedy's screwball coincidences. Exorcism is the kind of straw people clutch at when the world seems to have gone mad. In *Twelfth Night*, written some ten years later, Shakespeare's view of exorcism, though still comic, has darkened. Possession now is not a mistaken "suppose" but a fraud, a malicious practical joke played upon Malvolio. "Pray God he be not bewitched" (III. iv. 102), Maria piously intones at the sight of the cross-gartered, leering gull, and when he is out of earshot Fabian laughs, "If this were played upon a stage now, I could condemn it as an improbable fiction" (III.iv.128–9).[41] The theatrical self-consciousness is intensified when Feste the clown is brought in to conduct a mock-exorcism; "I would I were the first that ever dissembled in such a gown" (IV. ii. 5–6), he remarks sententiously as he disguises himself as Sir Topas the curate. If the gibe had a specific reference for the play's original audience, it would be to the Puritan Darrell who had only recently been convicted of dissembling in the exorcism of William Sommers of Nottingham. Now, the scene would suggest, the tables are being turned on the self-righteous fanatic. "Good Sir Topas," pleads Malvolio, "do not think I am mad. They have laid me here in hideous darkness." "Fie, thou dishonest Satan!" Feste replies. "I call thee by the most modest terms, for I am one of those gentle ones that will use the devil himself with courtesy" (IV. ii. 29–34).

By 1600 then Shakespeare had clearly marked out possession and exorcism as frauds, so much so that in *All's Well That Ends Well*, a few years later, he could casually use the term "exorcist" as a synonym for illusion-monger: "Is there no exorcist / Beguiles the truer office of mine eyes?" cries the King of France when Helena, whom he thought dead, appears before him: "Is't real that I see?" (V. iii. 298–300). When in 1603 Harsnett was whipping exorcism toward the theater, Shakespeare was already at the entrance to the Globe to welcome it.

Given Harsnett's frequent expressions of the "anti-theatrical prejudice," this welcome may seem strange, but in fact nothing in the *Declaration of Egregious Popish Impostures* necessarily implies hostility to the theater as a professional institution. It was Darrell, and not Harsnett, who represented an implacable threat to the theater, for where the Anglican polemicist saw the theatrical in the demonic the Puritan polemicist saw the demonic in the theatrical: "The Devil," wrote Stephen Gosson, "is the efficient cause of plays."[42] Harsnett's work attacks a form of theater that pretends that it is not entertainment but sober reality; hence his polemic virtually depends upon the existence of an officially designated commercial theater, marked off openly from all other forms and ceremonies of public life precisely by virtue of its freely acknowledged fictionality. Where there is no pretense to truth, there can be no *imposture*: it is this argument that permits so ontologically anxious a figure as Sir Philip Sidney to defend poetry – "Now for the poet, he nothing affirms, and therefore never lieth."[43]

In this spirit Puck playfully defends *A Midsummer Night's Dream*:

> If we shadows have offended,
> Think but this, and all is mended,
> That you have but slumber'd here
> While these visions did appear.
> And this weak and idle theme,
> No more yielding but a dream.
> (V. i. 409–14)

With a similarly frank admission of illusion Shakespeare can open the theater to Harsnett's polemic. Indeed, as if Harsnett's momentum carried *him* into the theater along with the fraud he hotly pursues, Shakespeare in *King Lear* stages not only exorcism, but Harsnett *on* exorcism:

Five fiends have been in poor Tom at once; as Oberdicut, of lust; Hober-didance, prince of dumbness; Mahu, of stealing; Modo, of murder; Flibbertigibbet, of mopping and mowing; who since possesses chamber-maids and waiting-women.[44]

(IV. i. 57–62)

Those in the audience who had read Harsnett's book or heard of the notorious Buckinghamshire exorcisms would recognize in Edgar's lines an odd, joking allusion to the chambermaids, Sara and Friswood Williams, and the waiting woman, Ann Smith, principal actors in Father Edmund's "Devil Theater." The humor of the anachronism here is akin to the Fool's earlier quip, "This prophecy Merlin shall make; for I live before his time" (III. ii. 95–6); both are bursts of a cheeky self-consciousness that dares deliberately to violate the historical setting in order to remind the audience of the play's conspicuous doubleness, its simultaneous distance and contemporaneity.

A *Declaration of Egregious Popish Impostures* supplies Shakespeare not only with an uncanny anachronism but with the model for Edgar's histrionic disguise. For it is not the *authenticity* of the demonology that the playwright finds in Harsnett – the usual reason for authorial recourse to a specialized source (as, for example, to a military or legal handbook) – but rather the inauthenticity of a theatrical role. Shakespeare appropriates for Edgar, then, a documented fraud, complete with an impressive collection of what the *Declaration* calls "uncouth non-significant names"[45] that have been made up to sound exotic and that carry with them a faint but ineradicable odor of spuriousness.

In Sidney's *Arcadia*, which provided the outline of the Gloucester subplot, the good son, having escaped his father's misguided attempt to kill him, becomes a soldier in another land and quickly distinguishes himself. Shakespeare insists not only on Edgar's perilous fall from his father's favor but upon his marginalization: Edgar becomes the possessed Poor Tom, the outcast with no possibility of working his way back in toward the center. "My neighbours," writes John Bunyan in the 1660s, "were amazed at this my great conversion from prodigious profaneness to something like a moral life; and truly so well they might for this my conversion was as great as for a Tom of Bethlem to become a sober man."[46] Of course, Edgar is only a pretend Tom o' Bedlam and hence can return to the community when it is safe to do so; but the force of Harsnett's argument is to make mimed possession even more marginal and desperate than the real thing.

Indeed, Edgar's desperation is bound up with the stress of "counterfeiting," a stress he has already noted in the presence of the mad and ruined Lear and now, in the lines I have just quoted, feels still more intensely in the presence of his blinded and ruined father. He is struggling with the urge to stop playing or, as he puts it, with the feeling that he "cannot daub it further" (IV. i. 51). Why he does not simply reveal himself to Gloucester at this point is entirely unclear. "And yet I must" is all he says of his continued disguise, as he recites the catalog of devils and leads his despairing father off to Dover Cliff.[47]

The subsequent episode – Gloucester's suicide attempt – deepens the play's brooding upon spurious exorcism. "It is a good *decorum* in a Comedie," writes Harsnett, "To giue us emptie names for things, and to tell us of strange Monsters within, where there be none";[48] so too the "Miracle-minter," Father Edmunds, and his fellow exorcists manipulate their impressionable gulls: "The priests doe report often in their patients hearing the dreadful formes, similitudes, and shapes, that the deuils vse to depart in out of those possessed bodies . . . : and this they tell with so graue a countenance, pathetical termes, and accomodate action, as it leaues a very deepe impression in the memory, and fancie of their actors."[49] Thus by the power of theatrical suggestion, the anxious subjects on whom the priests work their charms come to believe that they too have witnessed the devil depart in grotesque form from their own bodies, whereupon the priests turn their eyes heavenward and give thanks to the Blessed Virgin. In much the same manner Edgar persuades Gloucester that he stands on a high cliff, and then, after his credulous father has flung himself forward, Edgar switches roles and pretends that he is a bystander who has seen a demon depart from the old man:

> As I stood here below methought his eyes
> Were two full moons; he had a thousand noses,
> Horns whelk'd and wav'd like the enridged sea:
> It was some fiend; therefore, thou happy father,
> Think that the clearest Gods, who make them honours
> Of men's impossibilities, have preserved thee.
>
> (IV. vi. 69–74)

Edgar tries to create in Gloucester an experience of awe and wonder so intense that it can shatter his suicidal despair and restore his faith in the benevolence of the gods: "Thy life's a miracle," he tells his father.[50] For Shakespeare, as for Harsnett, this miracle-minting is the product of specifically histrionic manipulations; the scene at Dover is simultaneously a disenchanted analysis of religious and of theatrical illusions. Walking about on a perfectly flat stage, Edgar does to Gloucester what the theater usually does to the audience: he persuades his father to discount the evidence of his senses – "Methinks the ground is even" – and to accept a palpable fiction: "Horrible steep." But the audience at a play, of course, never absolutely accepts such fictions: we enjoy being brazenly lied to, we welcome for the sake of pleasure what we know to be untrue, but we withhold from the theater the simple assent that we grant to everyday reality. And we enact this withholding when, depending on the staging, either we refuse to believe that Gloucester is on a cliff above Dover beach or we realize that what we thought was a cliff (in the convention of theatrical representation) is in reality flat ground.

Hence, in the midst of Shakespeare's demonstration of the convergence of exorcism and theater, we return to the difference that enables *King Lear* to borrow comfortably from Harsnett: the theater elicits from us complicity rather than belief. Demonic possession is responsibly marked out for the audience as a theatrical fraud, designed to gull the unsuspecting: monsters such as the fiend with the thousand noses are illusions most easily imposed on the old, the blind, and the despairing; evil comes not from the mysterious otherworld of demons but from this world, the world of court and family intrigue. In *King Lear* there are no ghosts, as there are in *Richard III*, *Julius Caesar*, or *Hamlet*; no witches, as in *Macbeth*; no mysterious music of departing demons, as in *Antony and Cleopatra*.

King Lear is haunted by a sense of rituals and beliefs that are no longer efficacious, that have been *emptied out*. The characters appeal again and again to the pagan gods, but the gods remain utterly silent.[51] Nothing answers to human questions but human voices; nothing breeds about the heart but human desires; nothing inspires awe or terror but human suffering and human depravity. For all the invocation of the gods in *King Lear*, it is quite clear that there are no devils.

Edgar is no more possessed than the sanest of us, and we can see for ourselves that there was no demon standing by Gloucester's side. Likewise Lear's madness does not have a supernatural origin; it is linked, as in Harsnett, to *hysterica passio*, exposure to the elements, and extreme anguish, and its cure comes at the hands not of an exorcist but of a doctor. His prescription involves neither religious rituals (as in Catholicism) nor fasting and prayer (as in Puritanism), but tranquillized sleep:

> Our foster-nurse of nature is repose,
> The which he lacks; that to provoke in him,
> Are many simples operative, whose power
> Will close the eye of anguish.
>
> (IV. iv. 12–15)[52]

King Lear's relation to Harsnett's book, then, is essentially one of reiteration, a reiteration that signals a deeper and unexpressed institutional exchange. The official church dismantles and cedes to the players the powerful mechanisms of an unwanted and dangerous charisma; in return, the players confirm the charge that those mechanisms are theatrical and hence illusory. The material structure of Elizabethan and Jacobean public theaters heightened this confirmation, since, unlike medieval drama with its fuller integration into society, Shakespeare's drama took place in carefully demarcated playgrounds. *King Lear* offers then a double corroboration of Harsnett's arguments: within the play, Edgar's possession is clearly designated as a fiction, while the play itself is bounded by the institutional signs of fictionality: the wooden walls of the play space, payment for admission, known actors playing the parts, applause, the dances that followed the performance.

The theatrical confirmation of the official position is neither superficial nor unstable. And yet, I want now to suggest, Harsnett's arguments are alienated from themselves when they make their appearance on the Shakespearean stage. This alienation may be set in the context of a more general observation: the closer Shakespeare seems to a source, the more faithfully he reproduces it on stage, the more devastating and decisive his transformation of it. Let us take, for a small, initial instance, Shakespeare's borrowing from Harsnett of the unusual adjective "corky" – i.e. sapless, dry, withered. The word appears in the *Declaration* in the course of a sardonic explanation of why, despite the canonists' declaration that only old women are to be exorcized, Father Edmunds and his crew have a particular fondness for tying in a chair and exorcizing young women. Along with more graphic sexual innuendoes, Harsnett observes that the theatrical role of a demoniac requires "certain actions, motions, distortions, writhings, tumblings, and turbulent passions . . . not to be performed but by suppleness of sinewes. . . . It would (I feare mee) pose all the cunning Exorcists, that are this day to be found, to teach an old corkie woman to writhe, tumble, curvet, and fetch her morice gamboles."[53]

Now Shakespeare's eye was caught by the word "corkie," and he repro-duces it in a reference to old Gloucester. But what had been a flourish of Harsnett's typically bullying comic style becomes part of the horror of an almost unendurable scene, a scene of torture that begins when Cornwall orders his servant to take the captive Gloucester and "Bind fast his corky arms" (III. vii. 29) The note of bullying humor is still present in the word, but it is present in the character of the torturer.

This one-word instance of repetition as transvaluation may suggest in the tiniest compass what happens to Harsnett's work in the course of *Lear*. The *Declaration*'s arguments are loyally reiterated but in a curiously divided form. The voice of skepticism is assimilated to Cornwall, to Goneril, and above all to Edmund, whose "naturalism" is exposed as the argument of the younger and illegitimate son bent on displacing his legitimate older brother and eventually on destroying his father. The fraudulent possession and exorcism are given to the legitimate Edgar, who is forced to such shifts by the nightmarish persecution directed against him. Edgar adopts the role of Poor Tom not out of a corrupt will to deceive, but out of a commendable desire to survive. Modu, Mabu, and the rest are fakes, exactly as Harsnett said they were, but they are the venial sins of a will to endure. And even "venial sins" is too strong: they are the clever inventions that enable a decent and unjustly persecuted man to live. Similarly, there is no grotesque monster standing on the cliff with Gloucester – there isn't even any cliff – but Edgar, himself hunted down like an animal, is trying desperately to save his father from suicidal despair.

All of this has an odd and unsettling resemblance to the situation of the Jesuits in England, if viewed from an unofficial perspective. The resemblance does not necessarily resolve itself into an allegory in which Catholicism is revealed to be the persecuted, legitimate elder brother forced to defend himself by means of theatrical illusions against the cold persecution of his skeptical bastard brother Protestantism. But the possibility of such a radical undermining of the orthodox position exists, and not merely in the cool light of our own historical distance. In 1610 a company of traveling players in Yorkshire included *King Lear* and *Pericles* in a repertoire that included a "St Christopher Play" whose performance came to the attention of the Star Chamber. The plays were performed in the manor house of a recusant couple, Sir John and Lady Julyan Yorke, and the players themselves and their organizer, Sir Richard Cholmeley, were denounced for recusancy by their Puritan neighbor, Sir Posthumus Hoby.[54] It is difficult to resist the conclusion that someone in Stuart Yorkshire believed that, despite its apparent staging of a fraudulent possession, *King Lear* was not hostile, was strangely sympathetic even, to the situation of persecuted Catholics. At the very least, we may suggest, the current of sympathy is enough to undermine the intended effect of Harsnett's *Declaration*: an intensified adherence to the central system of official values. In Shakespeare, the realization that demonic possession is a theatrical imposture leads not to a clarification – the clear-eyed satisfaction of the man who refuses to be gulled – but to a deeper uncertainty, a loss of moorings, in the face of evil.

"Let them anatomize Regan," Lear raves, "see what breeds about her heart. Is there any cause in nature that makes these hard hearts?" (III. vi. 74–6). We know that there is no cause *beyond* nature; the voices of evil in the play – "Thou, Nature, art my goddess"; "What need one?"; "Bind fast his corky arms" – come from the unpossessed. Does it make it any better to know this? Is it a relief to understand that the evil was not visited upon the characters by demonic agents but released from the structure of the family and the state by Lear himself?

Edgar's pretended demonic possession, by ironic contrast, is of the homiletic variety; the devil compels him to acts of self-punishment, the desperate masochism of the very poor, but not to acts of viciousness. On the contrary, like the demoniacs in Harsnett's contemptuous account who praise the Mass and the Catholic Church, Poor Tom gives a highly moral performance:

Take heed o' th'foul fiend. Obey thy parents; keep thy word justly; swear not; commit not with man's sworn spouse; set not thy sweet heart on proud array. Tom's a-cold. (III. iv. 78–81)

Is it a relief to know that Edgar is only miming this little sermon?

All attempts by the characters to explain or relieve their sufferings through the invocation of transcendent forces are baffled. Gloucester's belief in the influence of "These late eclipses in the sun and moon" (I. ii. 100) is decisively dismissed, even if the spokesman for the dismissal is the villainous Edmund. Lear's almost constant appeals to the gods

> O Heavens,
> If you do love old men, if your sweet sway
> Allow obedience, if you yourselves are old,
> Make it your cause; send down and take my part!
>
> (II. iv. 187–90)

are constantly left unanswered. The storm in the play seems to several characters to be of more than natural intensity, and Lear above all tries desperately to make it *mean* something (a symbol of his daughters' ingratitude, a punishment for evil, a sign from the gods of the impending universal judgment); but the thunder refuses to speak. When Albany calls Goneril a "devil" and a "fiend" (IV. ii. 59, 66), we know that he is not identifying her as a supernatural being – it is impossible, in this play, to witness the eruption of the denizens of hell into the human world – just as we know that Albany's prayer for "visible spirits" to be sent down by the heavens "to tame these vilde offences" (IV. ii. 46–7) will be unanswered.

In *King Lear*, as Harsnett says of the Catholic Church, "neither God, Angel, nor devil can be gotten to speake."[55] For Harsnett this silence betokens a liberation from lies; we have learned, as the last sentence of his tract puts it, "to loath these despicable Impostures and returne vnto the truth."[56] But for Shakespeare the silence leads to the desolation of the play's close:

> Lend me a looking-glass;
> If that her breath will mist or stain the stone,
> Why, then she lives.
>
> (V. iii. 260–2)

The lines give voice to a hope by which the audience has been repeatedly tantalized: a hope that Cordelia will not die, that the play will build toward a revelation powerful enough to justify Lear's atrocious suffering, that we are in the midst of what the Italians called a *tragedia di fin lieto*, that is, a play where the villains absorb the tragic punishment while the good are wondrously restored.[57] Shakespeare in effect invokes the conventions of this genre, only to insist with appalling finality that Cordelia is "dead as earth."

In the wake of Lear's first attempt to see some sign of life in Cordelia, Kent asks, "Is this the promis'd end?" Edgar echoes the question, "Or image of that horror?" And Albany says, "Fall and cease." By itself Kent's question has an oddly literary quality, as if he were remarking on the end of the play, either wondering what kind of ending this is or implicitly objecting to the disastrous turn of events. Edgar's response suggests that the "end" is the end of the world, the Last Judgment, here experienced not as a "promise" – the punishment of the wicked, the reward of the good – but as a "horror." But, like Kent, Edgar is not certain about what he is seeing: his question suggests that he may be witnessing not the end itself but a possible "image" of it, while Albany's enigmatic "Fall and cease" empties even that image of significance. The theatrical means that might have produced a "counterfeit miracle" out of this moment are abjured; there will be no imposture, no histrionic revelation of the supernatural.

Lear repeats this miserable emptying out of the redemptive hope in his next lines:

> This feather stirs; she lives! if it be so,
> It is a chance which does redeem all sorrows
> That ever I have felt.
>
> (V. iii. 264–6)

Deeply moved by the sight of the mad king, a nameless gentleman had earlier remarked, "Thou hast one daughter, / who redeems nature from the general curse / Which twain have brought her to" (IV. vi. 202–4). Now, in Lear's words, this vision of universal redemption through Cordelia is glimpsed again, intensified by the king's own conscious investment in it. What would it mean to "redeem" Lear's sorrows? To buy them back from the chaos and brute meaninglessness they now seem to signify, to reward the king with a gift so great that it outweighs the sum of misery in his entire long life, to reinterpret his pain as the necessary preparation – the price to be paid – for a consummate bliss. In the theater such reinterpretation would be represented by a spectacular turn in the plot – a surprise unmasking, a sudden reversal of fortunes, a resurrection – and this dramatic redemption, however secularized, would almost invariably recall the consummation devoutly wished by centuries of Christian believers. This consummation had in fact been represented again and again in medieval resurrection plays which offered the spectators ocular proof that Christ had risen.[58] Despite the pre-Christian setting of Shakespeare's play, Lear's craving for just such proof – "This feather stirs; she lives!" – would seem to evoke precisely this theatrical and religious tradition, only in order to reveal itself, in C. L. Barber's acute phrase, as "post-Christian."[59] *If it be so*: Lear's sorrows are not redeemed; nothing can turn them into joy, but the forlorn hope of an impossible redemption persists, drained of its institutional and doctrinal significance, empty and vain, cut off even from a theatrical realization but, like the dream of exorcism, ineradicable.

The close of *King Lear* in effect acknowledges that it can never satisfy this dream, but the acknowledgment must not obscure the fact that the play itself has generated the craving for such satisfaction. That is, Shakespeare does not simply inherit and make use of an anthropological given; rather, at the moment when the official religious and secular institutions were, for their own reasons, abjuring the rituals they themselves had once fostered, Shakespeare's theater moves to appropriate this function. On stage the ritual is effectively contained in the ways we have examined, but Shakespeare intensifies as theatrical experience the need for exorcism, and his demystification of the practice is not identical in its interests to Harsnett's.

Harsnett's polemic is directed toward a bracing anger against the lying agents of the Catholic Church and a loyal adherence to the true, established Church of England. He writes as a representative of that true Church, and this institutional identity is reinforced by the secular institutional imprimatur on the confessions that are appended to the text. The joint religious and secular apparatus works to strip away imposture and discover the hidden reality which is, Harsnett says, the theater. Shakespeare's play dutifully reiterates this discovery: when Lear thinks he has found in Poor Tom "the thing itself," "unaccommodated man," he has in fact found a man playing a theatrical role. But if false religion is theater, and if the difference between true and false religion is the presence of theater, what happens when this difference is enacted in the theater?

What happens, as we have already begun to see, is that the official position is *emptied out*, even as it is loyally confirmed. This "emptying out" bears a certain resemblance to Brecht's "alienation effect," and still more to Althusser and Macherey's "internal distantiation." But the most fruitful terms for describing the felt difference between Shakespeare's art and the religious ideology to which it gives voice are to be found, I think, within the theological system to which Harsnett adhered. What is the status of the Law, asks Hooker, after the coming of Christ? Clearly the Saviour effected the "evacuation of the Law of Moses." But did that abolition mean "that the very name of Altar, of Priest, of Sacrifice itself, should be banished out of the world"? No, replies Hooker, even after evacuation, "the words which were do continue; the only difference is, that whereas before they had a literal, they now have a metaphorical use, and are as so many notes of remembrance unto us, that what they did signify in the letter is accomplished in the truth."[60] Both exorcism and Harsnett's own attack on exorcism undergo a comparable process of evacuation and transformed reiteration in *King Lear*. Whereas before they had a literal, they now have a literary use, and are as so many notes of remembrance unto us, that what they did signify in the letter is accomplished – with a drastic swerve from the sacred to the secular – in the theater.

Edgar's possession is a theatrical performance, exactly in Harsnett's terms, but there is no saving institution, purged of theater, against which it may be set, nor is there a demonic institution which the performance may be shown to serve. On the contrary, Edgar's miming is a response to a free-floating, contagious evil more terrible than anything Harsnett would allow. For Harsnett the wicked are corrupt individuals in the service of a corrupt

Church; in *King Lear* there are neither individuals nor institutions adequate to contain the released and enacted wickedness; the force of evil in the play is larger than any local habitation or name. In this sense, Shakespeare's tragedy reconstitutes as theater the demonic principle demystified by Harsnett. Edgar's fraudulent, histrionic performance is a response to this principle: evacuated rituals, drained of their original meaning, are preferable to no rituals at all.

Shakespeare does not counsel, in effect, that one accept as true the fraudulent institution for the sake of the dream of a cure – the argument of the Grand Inquisitor. He writes for the greater glory and profit of the theater, a fraudulent institution that never pretends to be anything but fraudulent, an institution that calls forth what is not, that signifies absence, that transforms the literal into the metaphorical, that evacuates everything it represents. By doing so the theater makes for itself the hollow round space within which it survives. The force of *King Lear* is to make us love the theater, to seek out its satisfactions, to serve its interests, to confer upon it a place of its own, to grant it life by permitting it to reproduce itself over generations. Shakespeare's theater has outlived the institutions to which it paid homage, has lived to pay homage to other, competing institutions which in turn it seems to represent and empty out. This complex, limited institutional independence, this marginal and impure autonomy, arises not out of an inherent, formal self-reflexiveness but out of the ideological matrix in which Shakespeare's theater is created and recreated.

There are, of course, further institutional strategies that lie beyond a love for the theater. In a move that Ben Jonson rather than Shakespeare seems to have anticipated, the theater itself comes to be emptied out in the interests of reading. In the argument made famous by Charles Lamb and Coleridge, and reiterated by Bradley, theatricality must be discarded to achieve absorption, and Shakespeare's imagination yields forth its sublime power not to a spectator but to one who, like Keats, sits down to reread *King Lear*. Where institutions like the King's Men had been thought to generate their texts, now texts like *King Lear* appear to generate their institutions. The commercial contingency of the theater gives way to the philosophical necessity of literature.

Why has our culture embraced *King Lear*'s massive display of mimed suffering and fraudulent exorcism? Because the judicial torture and expulsion of evil have for centuries been bound up with the display of power at the center of society. Because we no longer believe in the magical ceremonies through which devils were once made to speak and were driven out of the bodies of the possessed. Because the play recuperates and intensifies our need for these ceremonies, even though we do not believe in them, and performs them, carefully marked out for us as frauds, for our continued consumption. Because, with our full complicity, Shakespeare's company and scores of companies that followed have catered profitably to our desire for spectacular impostures.

And also, perhaps, because the Harsnetts of the world would free us from the oppression of false belief only in order to reclaim us more firmly for the official state Church, and the "solution" – confirmed by the rechristening, as it were, of the devil as the Pope – is hateful. Hence we embrace an alternative that seems to confirm the official line and thereby to take its place in the central system of values, yet that works at the same time to unsettle all official lines.[61] Shakespeare's theater empties out the center that it represents, and in its cruelty – Edmund, Goneril, Regan, Cornwall, Gloucester, Cordelia, Lear: all dead as earth – paradoxically creates in us the intimation of a fullness that we can only savor in the conviction of its irremediable loss:

> we that are young
> Shall never see so much, nor live so long.

Appendix

Hooker, *Laws of Ecclesiastical Polity*:

"They which honour the Law as an image of the wisdom of God himself, are notwithstanding to know that the same had an end in Christ. But what? Was the Law so abolished with Christ, that after his ascension the office of Priests became immediately wicked, and the very name hateful, as importing the exercise of an ungodly function? No, as long as the glory of the Temple continued, and till the time of that final desolation was accomplished, the very Christian Jews did continue with their sacrifices and other parts of legal service. That very Law therefore which our Saviour was to abolish, did not *so soon* become unlawful to be observed as some imagine; nor was it afterwards unlawful *so far*, that the very name of Altar, of Priest, of Sacrifice itself, should be banished out of the world. For though God do now hate sacrifice, whether it be heathenish or Jewish, so that we cannot have the same things which they had but with impiety; yet unless there be some greater let than the only evacuation of the Law of Moses, the names themselves may (I hope) be retained without sin, in respect of that proportion which things established by our Saviour have unto them which by him are abrogated. And so throughout all the writings of the ancient Fathers we see that the words which were do continue; the only difference is, that whereas before they had a literal, they now have a metaphorical use, and are as so many notes of remembrance unto us, that what they did signify in the letter is accomplished in the truth. And as no man can deprive the Church of this liberty, to use names whereunto the Law was accustomed, so neither are we generally forbidden the use of things which the Law hath; though it neither command us any particular rite, as it did the Jews a number, and the weightiest which it did command them are unto us in the Gospel prohibited." (IV. xi. 10)

Notes

1. Samuel Harsnett, *A Declaration of Egregious Popish Impostures* (London, 1603). Harsnett's influence is noted in Lewis Theobald's edition of Shakespeare, first published in 1733. On the clandestine exorcisms I am particularly indebted to D. P. Walker, *Unclean Spirits: Possession and Exorcism in France and England in the Late Sixteenth and Early Seventeenth Centuries* (Philadelphia, 1981). *King Lear* is quoted from the New Arden text, ed. Kenneth Muir (London, 1972). All other quotations from Shakespeare are taken from the Arden editions.

2. For extended arguments for and against theory, see Walter Michaels and Steven Knapp, "Against theory" (*Critical Inquiry*, 8 (1982), 723–42), and the ensuing controversy in *Critical Inquiry*, 9 (1983), 725–800.

3. I am indebted to an important critique of Marxist and deconstructive literary theory by D. A. Miller, "Discipline in different voices: bureaucracy, police, family and *Bleak House*" (*Representations*, 1 (1983), 59–89).

4. *John Wesley*, ed. Albert C. Outler (New York, 1964), 82.

5. A major exception, with conclusions different from my own, has just been published: John L. Murphy, *Darkness and Devils: Exorcism and "King Lear"* (Athens, Ohio, 1984). Murphy's fascinating study, which he kindly allowed me to read in galleys after hearing the present paper delivered as a lecture, argues that exorcism is an aspect of clandestine political and religious resistance to Queen Elizabeth's rule. See also, for interesting reflections, William Elton, *"King Lear" and the Gods* (San Marino, 1966). For useful accounts of Harsnett's relation to *Lear*, see Geoffrey Bullough (ed.), *Narrative and Dramatic Sources of Shakespeare* (London, 1975), 7, 299–302; Kenneth Muir, "Samuel Harsnett and King Lear" (*Review of English Studies*, 2 (1951), 11–21); Kenneth Muir (ed.), *King Lear* (London, 1972), 239–42.

6. Michel de Montaigne, "Apology for Raymond Sebond," in *Complete Essays*, tr. Donald Frame (Stanford, 1948), 331.

7. Edward Shils, *Center and Periphery: Essays in Macrosociology* (Chicago, 1975), 3. My account of institutional strategies is indebted to Shils.

8. Peter Brown, *The Cult of the Saints: Its Rise and Function in Latin Christianity* (Chicago, 1981), 107.

9. Samuel Harsnett, *A Discovery of the Fraudulent Practices of John Darrel* (London, 1599).

10. Harsnett, *Declaration*, 154–5.

11. Ibid., 86.

12. Carlo Ginzburg, *I benandanti: Recerche sulla stregoneria e sui culti agrari tra Cinquecento e Seicento* (Turin, 1966).

13. For Harsnett's comments on witchcraft, see *Declaration*, 135–6. The relation between demonic possession and witchcraft is extremely complex. John Darrell evidently had frequent recourse, in the midst of his exorcisms, to accusations of witchcraft whose evidence was precisely the demonic possessions; Harsnett remarks wryly that "Of all the partes of the tragicall Comedie acted between him and *Somers*, there was no one Scene in it, wherein M. *Darrell* did with more courage & boldnes acte his part, then in this of the discouerie of witches" (*Discovery*, 142). There is a helpful discussion of possession and witchcraft, along with an important account of Harsnett and Darrell, in Keith Thomas, *Religion and the Decline of Magic* (London, 1971).

14. Brown, op. cit., 109–11.

15. Thomas, op. cit., 485.

16. S. M. Shirokogorov, *The Psycho-Mental Complex of the Tungus* (Peking and London, 1935), 265.
17. Brown, op. cit., 110.
18. Michael MacDonald, *Mystical Bedlam* (Cambridge, 1981).
19. Harsnett, *Declaration*, A3^r.
20. Harsnett, *Discovery*, A2^r.
21. Ibid., A4^{r-v}.
22. Ibid., 29.
23. D. P. Walker suggests that the attack on the Jesuits is a screen for an attack on the more politically sensitive nonconformists; in early seventeenth-century England, when in doubt it was safer to attack a Catholic.
24. Harsnett, *Declaration*, 24.
25. Ibid., 25. See Edmund Jorden, *A Briefe Discourse of a Disease Called the Suffocation of the Mother* (London, 1603).
26. Harsnett, *Declaration*, 38.
27. Michel Leiris, *La Possession et ses aspects théâtraux chez les Ethiopiens de Gondar* (Paris, 1958).
28. Ibid., 27–8.
29. Ibid., 94–5.
30. Ibid., 96.
31. Harsnett, *Declaration*, 69.
32. Ibid., 172.
33. Ibid., 2, 106.
34. Ibid., 74.
35. Ibid., 20. This argument has the curious effect of identifying all exorcisms, including those conducted by nonconformist preachers, with the Pope. On attacks on the Catholic Church as a theater, see Jonas Barish, *The Antitheatrical Prejudice* (Berkeley, 1981), 66–131 *passim*.
36. Harsnett, *Discovery*, A3^r.
37. Ibid., 78.
38. Ibid., 114–15.
39. Ibid., 149.
40. Harsnett was not, of course, alone. See, for example, John Gee: "The Jesuits being or having Actors of such dexterity, I see no reason but that they should set up a company for themselves, which surely will put down The Fortune, Red-Bull, Cock-pit, and Globe" (*New Shreds of the Old Snare* (London, 1624)). I owe this reference, along with powerful reflections on the significance of the public theater's physical marginality, to Steven Mullaney.
41. This sentiment could serve as the epigraph to both of Harsnett's books on exorcism; it is the root perception from which most of Harsnett's rhetoric grows.
42. Stephen Gosson, *Plays Confuted in Five Actions* (London, *c.* 1582), cited in E. K. Chambers, *The Elizabethan Stage* (Oxford, 1923), 215.
43. Philip Sidney, *The Defense of Poesie* (1583), in *Literary Criticism: Plato to Dryden*, ed. Allan H. Gilbert (Detroit, 1962), 439.
44. These lines were included in the Quarto but omitted from the Folio. For the tangled textual history, see Michael J. Warren, "Quarto and Folio *King Lear*, and the interpretation of Albany and Edgar," in David Bevington and Jay L. Halio (eds), *Shakespeare: Pattern of Excelling Nature* (Newark, Del., 1978), 95–107; Steven Urkowitz, *Shakespeare's Revision of "King Lear"* (Princeton, 1980); and Gary Taylor, "The war in *King Lear*" (*Shakespeare Survey*, 33 (1980), 27–34).

Presumably, by the time the Folio appeared, the point of the allusion to Harsnett would have been lost, and the lines were dropped.

45. Harsnett, *Declaration*, 46.
46. John Bunyan, *Grace Abounding to the Chief of Sinners*, ed. Roger Sharrock (Oxford, 1966), 15.
47. Edgar's later explanation – that he feared for his father's ability to sustain the shock of an encounter – is, like so many explanations in *King Lear*, too little, too late. On this characteristic belatedness as an element of the play's greatness, see Stephen Booth, *"King Lear," "Macbeth," Indefinition, and Tragedy* (New Haven, 1983).
48. Harsnett, *Declaration*, 142.
49. Ibid., 142–3.
50. On the production of "counterfeit miracles" in order to arouse awe and wonder, see especially Harsnett, *Discovery*, "Epistle to the reader."
51. Words, signs, gestures that claim to be in touch with super-reality, with absolute goodness and absolute evil, are exposed as vacant – illusions manipulated by the clever and imposed upon the gullible.
52. This is, in effect, Edmund Jorden's prescription for cases such as Lear's.
53. Harsnett, *Declaration*, 23.
54. On the Yorkshire performance, see Murphy, op. cit., 93–118.
55. Harsnett, *Declaration*, 169.
56. Ibid., 171.
57. In willing this disenchantment against the evidence of our senses, we pay tribute to the theater. Harsnett has been twisted around to make this tribute possible.
58. O. B. Hardison, Jr, *Christian Rite and Christian Drama in the Middle Ages: Essays in the Origin and Early History of Modern Drama* (Baltimore, 1965), esp. 220–52.
59. C. L. Barber, "The family in Shakespeare's development: tragedy and sacredness," in *Representing Shakespeare: New Psychoanalytic Essays*, ed. Murray M. Schwartz and Coppélia Kahn (Baltimore, 1980), 196.
60. Hooker, *Laws of Ecclesiastical Polity*, IV. xi. 10. This truth, which is the triumph of the metaphorical over the literal, confers upon the Church the liberty to use certain names and rites, even though they have been abolished. For the entire passage from Hooker, see Appendix. I am indebted for the reference to Richard Hooker to John Coolidge.
61. Roland Barthes, *Mythologies*, tr. Annette Lavers (New York, 1972), 135.

10

RENÉ GIRARD

The politics of desire in
Troilus and Cressida

In Act IV, Scene ii, Troilus and Cressida are getting up after their first and only night together. More than ever, Cressida speaks the language of love. She has not changed, or, if she has, the change goes in the direction of more love, not less.

Troilus has definitely changed, but in the other direction. He no longer speaks like a man in love:

> *Troilus:* Dear, trouble not yourself; the morn is cold.
> *Cressida:* Then, sweet my lord, I'll call mine uncle down;
> He shall unbolt the gates.
> *Troilus:* Trouble him not;
> To bed, to bed! Sleep kill those pretty eyes,
> And give as soft attachment to thy senses
> As infants empty of all thought.
> *Cressida:* Good morrow, then.
> *Troilus:* I prithee now, to bed.
>
> (IV. ii. 1–7)[1]

This concern for Cressida's health is a transparent excuse. Troilus wants to leave. His only desire, at this point, is to send the girl back to bed . . . alone. He tries to hide his indifference but Cressida is not fooled: "Are you aweary of me?" (IV. ii. 7).

Listen to the highly artificial lyricism in Troilus's protestations of love. This is the language of the Shakespearean male, when he lies to a woman in love, unsuccessfully:

> O Cressida, but that the busy day,
> Wak'd by the lark, hath rous'd the ribald crows,
> And dreaming night will hide our joys no longer,
> I would not from thee.
>
> > (IV.ii. 8–11)

The rhetoric cannot be sincere. Cressida sighs:

> Night hath been too brief.
> > (IV.ii. 11)

Once again, Troilus tries to escape. He is in a great hurry:

> You will catch cold, and curse me.
> *Cressida:*   Prithee tarry.
> You men will never tarry.
> O foolish Cressid, I might have still held off,
> And then you would have tarried.
> > (IV.ii. 15–18)

"I might still have held off" takes us back to a prophetic monologue of Cressida at the end of I.ii. As long as Pandarus was around, loudly praising Troilus, Cressida had feigned she was not in love with the young man. As soon as she was alone, however, she acknowledged the truth and she explained why she did not want Troilus to know it:

> But more in Troilus thousand-fold I see
> Than in the glass of Pandar's praise may be;
> Yet hold I off. Women are angels, wooing:
> Things won are done; joy's soul lies in the doing.
> That she belov'd knows naught that knows not this:
> Men prize the thing ungain'd more than it is.
> That she was never yet that ever knew
> Love got so sweet as when desire did sue.
> Therefore this maxim out of love I teach:
> "Achievement is command; ungain'd beseech."
> Then though my heart's content firm love doth bear,
> Nothing of that shall from mine eyes appear.
> > (I.ii. 289–300)

There is nothing genuinely capricious about erotic caprice. A man loses interest in a woman who yields too easily to his desires. Desire, especially masculine desire, has its own implacable laws. Since they rarely fail, since they are constantly verified, these laws are easy to know. A woman who does not know them and does not act accordingly is inexcusable. If she is abandoned, she has only herself to blame.

Cressida's theory is better than her practice. She would have been well advised to abide by her resolution, but she did not have the courage. During her great love scene with Troilus, just before the two go to bed together, she abandoned herself to the dizziness of the moment. She did not "hold off." She confessed her sentiments too freely for her own good. She kept blaming herself for being too open, too trusting, and yet she went on and on. The temptation proved irresistible.

In Shakespeare, intersubjective strategy, rather than oedipal or social taboos, generates the forces of repression. In Cressida's case, these do not win. In one of the most erotic scenes that Shakespeare ever wrote, uninhibited desire triumphs.

Cressida cannot resist glamor. Like Emma Bovary, I believe, she succumbs to fascination even more than to her senses, but we sympathize with her incompetence as a hypocrite, with her inability to speak and behave in a manner that contradicts her emotions.

With such men as Troilus, women will always come to grief unless they systematically hide their true feelings. They must relentlessly follow the strategic course outlined in the monologue. When desire suggests abandonment they must "hold off." And now Cressida must condemn her one and only virtue. This is what Troilus has done to her, Troilus even more than Pandarus.

Things won are done; joy's soul lies in the doing. The intensity and durability of a man's desire for a woman will prove inversely proportional to her willingness to satisfy it. Cressida did not "hold off," and the result is as sad as it was predictable. Cressida is not about to be caught a second time.

The rest of the scene provides more clues to the callous indifference of Troilus. The next incident is the arrival of Pandarus. He makes some tasteless jokes at the expense of his niece. She tries to stop Pandarus, but she receives no help from her lover. Instead of rushing to her rescue, Troilus becomes the silent accomplice of the go-between.

Then comes a knock on the door. After inviting Pandarus to answer, Cressida asks Troilus to retire with her into her bedroom. At this time of day, she does not want to be seen with a young man in her apartment.

> *Cressida:* Who's that at door? Good uncle, go and see.
> My lord, come you again into my chamber.
> You smile and mock me, as if I meant naughtily.
> (IV. ii. 36–8)

Troilus interprets Cressida's fear for her reputation as an invitation to more amorous embraces. Not only does he fail to take offense at the bawdiness of Pandarus, but he is spurred into a sense of emulation. This is an interesting example of mimetic behavior. The sensitive spectator finds Troilus insufferable. Behind the naivety of the youth and the smooth polish of the aristocrat, a certain coarseness is revealed.

Shakespeare has carefully engineered all this for the enlightenment of at least the most perceptive part of his audience. The real enjoyment of the play lies in a shared complicity between author and spectator, a complicity of intentions made more valuable by the lightness of the touch, the discreet treatment of some crucial points, and the probability that, like Troilus himself, many in the audience will be too dull-witted, or too conventional, to understand what is really going on.

Traditionally, the critics of the play have shut their eyes to the behavior of Troilus on that early morning. They demanded a "positive" hero, and if none was there to be found they did not hesitate to make one up. They turned *Troilus and Cressida* into a romantic drama, alien not only to the spirit but to the letter of the Shakespearean play, just about fit for the opera Verdi never wrote but could have written.

Until a few years ago, the false exigencies of conventional morality dominated the academic establishment so much that the text was disregarded, even though it was worshipped in the abstract. In order to end up with a play that met their criteria of the permissible, with such a great writer as Shakespeare, these critics did not have to rewrite the play. They only had to read it selectively; they simply skipped the passages they regarded as unworthy of Shakespeare, such as the one we are now reading.

Most obligingly, Shakespeare facilitates their task to those who want to blunt the sharp edges of his message. He never had the burning missionary zeal of our *engagé* playwrights and critics. Unlike a Jean-Paul Sartre, a Bertolt Brecht, or a Hamlet, who ardently desire to "catch the conscience of the king" in the net of their dramas, for motives it may be better not to probe too deeply, Shakespeare wanted above all to please the largest possible audience. Part of that audience must have been highly sophisticated, endowed with a great sense of humor; the other part must have been stodgy and crude.

As a rule, Shakespeare manages the extraordinary feat of pleasing both groups simultaneously. When he most daringly contradicts the conventions and traditions to which one type of spectator is attached, he does it in a fashion discreet enough to be understood only by the other type. The conventional message is also featured in the play, more prominently than the subtler message but in such a ridiculous fashion that it will be discounted by the knowledgeable few.

The conventional message, here, finds its mouthpiece in Pandarus, who acts as a go-between not only with the people around him but with posterity. He has Troilus and Cressida swear a perfectly inane oath just before they go to bed together. He says to Troilus:

> ... Here I hold your hand, here my cousin's. If ever you prove false one to another, since I have taken such pains to bring you together, let all pitiful goers-between be called to the world's end after my name: call them all Pandars: let all constant men be Troiluses, all false women Cressids. . . . Say "Amen."
>
> Troilus: Amen.
> Cressida: Amen.
>
> (III. ii. 196–205)

According to a long tradition that a superficial reading of the Shakespearean play seems to confirm, Cressida has falseness and infidelity written all over her from the beginning. She alone behaves disgracefully, and Troilus never commits any sin against the faith the two lovers swore to each other.

Is it possible to interpret the indifference of Troilus as a minor lapse, a temporary effect of physical satiety? The fact that, a few minutes later, Troilus becomes fiercely jealous of Cressida looks like a powerful argument in favor of this view. Troilus's desire for Cressida quickly recovers an intensity that seems to give the lie to my nasty suspicion. Should we not conclude that, at some deep level in the young man's psyche, the desire for Cressida had retained its essential strength?

We should not. The later jealousy does not cancel the previous indifference. It is not continuous with this indifference. In the meantime something has happened that completely transforms once again the relationship between Troilus and Cressida.

We delude ourselves if we attribute the attitude of Troilus merely to the peace of his senses, following a long night of amorous pleasures. If we excuse this behavior on any grounds, if we find it compatible with a "deep and abiding love for Cressida," we moralize the play and, simultaneously, we mistake it for the "real life" that it is not. What could be the point of Shakespeare insisting slyly on the collapse of Troilus's desire if, at the same time, that collapse had to be discounted as irrelevant? What playwright would waste his time on such trivial nonsense?

All efforts to minimize Troilus's sin against "true love" are rooted not in the text of Shakespeare but in the moralistic attachment of many critics to the concept of the "positive" hero. At least one "positive" hero is traditionally regarded as the minimum requirement for "serious drama." The cardboard characters of "serious drama" are just about as un-Shakespearean as the bland heroes of Soviet-style neo-realism.

It is true, of course, that Troilus is never physically unfaithful to Cressida. This is a necessary component of the conventional message. From the standpoint of the subtler message, this fidelity of Troilus means nothing. Cressida did not give him the time to be unfaithful. By making him insanely jealous, she changed the whole course of the relationship. Shakespeare respects the letter of the conventional view but not the spirit.

We should not turn Cressida into a heroine. If we did, we would replace one myth with another and misunderstand Shakespeare, once again. But her intelligence as well as her inability to play the coquette make her more likable than Troilus and all the male heroes who do not even perceive the identity of their lechery and of their war.

Shakespeare makes allowance for the male chauvinism in his audience, just as he makes allowance for the prejudice against Shylock in *The Merchant of Venice*. In both instances, the traditional clichés are restated, to the satisfaction of the groundlings and many English departments in prestigious universities, but the subtler message invariably subverts and reverses the conventional message.

The indifference of Troilus should strike us as tragic because it results from the very cause Cressida revealed: the total gift of herself. She is no longer "the thing ungain'd" that men prize "more than it is." She has fallen in love so unreservedly that the possibility of her falling out of it cannot occur to someone like Troilus. His possession of the girl seems so well assured that he, in turn, feels possessed, a prisoner of love, and his only desire is to flee.

The conquest of a beautiful woman makes an inexperienced young man such as Troilus feel on top of the world. To be fully enjoyed, this great triumph needs witnesses. The woman herself is far from enough. Troilus needs the admiring look of other men, in very much the same sense that Achilles does in another part of the play. It always takes other men to make an erotic or a military conquest truly valuable in the eyes of the conqueror himself.

Like many Shakespearean men, like the unfortunate Collatine, the husband of Lucrece, imprudent enough to boast about the perfection of his wife in the presence of his own king, Troilus is ready for a little boasting with his 99 brothers and the entire Trojan army as well. That is the reason he is in such a hurry, and that is the reason he cannot fail to lose Cressida.

Only the Stephen Dedalus of *Ulysses*, in his misunderstood lecture at the Dublin National Library, understands the importance of the other men's looks in this kind of affair and in the whole work of Shakespeare. Troilus does not even realize what he is doing to Cressida. His masculine vanity and his naivety blind him to the possibilities inherent in the situation.

At the normal levels, desire does not understand its dependence on otherness. Troilus lacks intelligence, no doubt, but Shakespeare's main point does not lie with the purely individual factors in this equation of desire; it lies with the equation itself, with the particular configuration the scene illustrates: the extinction of desire as a result of undisturbed possession.

The phase during which the desire of Troilus simply collapses is rather brief, but it does not really end with the knock on the door, or even with the news that follows the knock. Troilus needs a few moments to assess the full significance of this news. He also needs a little prodding from Cressida.

The news at the door is that Cressida must leave Troy immediately. She must rejoin her father who is already in the Greek camp. She is being exchanged for Antenor, a Trojan warrior taken prisoner by the Greeks.

In all probability, the girl's departure will be fatal to her love affair with Troilus. Only Pandarus seems really affected. His concern at this point seems greater than either Cressida's or Troilus's. He feels shattered at the thought that all the loving care he has dispensed on the newly hatched liaison will have been for nought, or almost. As for Cressida, a veritable frenzy of grief overcomes her; but she herself describes it as a pleasurable experience. She insists that, whatever happens, she will not leave Troy.

Troilus takes the news most calmly, even philosophically. He resorts to reason. He preaches the wisdom of resignation. Cressida must go. Her father's wish has the backing of all the leaders in both camps and she cannot disobey. To visit her, Troilus promises, he will clandestinely cross the line of battle.

In these first moments, Troilus feels more serene than ever: the decision fulfills his secret wish. The impending transfer will put just the right distance between himself and a woman whose excessive devotion he finds flattering, natural, legitimate, but cumbersome. The line of battle seems the perfect barrier. Troilus will cross it with relative ease, but not Cressida. Troilus does not want to renounce his newly acquired mistress. Both for pleasure and for prestige, she is a highly decorative asset but, from now on, he will be able to visit her only when he so desires. Between each encounter, the interval will be as long as he, not she, chooses.

The solution is ideal, moreover, because it is a decision of the old leaders. Like everything else, including Cressida, it was handed to Troilus on a platter. The responsibility for the separation does not lie with him. No one can blame Troilus for the impending separation. He cannot even blame himself. More than ever, he feels on top of the world.

It is too late for Cressida to "hold off," but a woman in her position has a weapon of last resort against such a lover as Troilus. The possibility that his mistress, unleashed among thousands of Greek warriors, might prove disloyal cannot yet enter his mind. His self-confidence remains boundless. He probably feels that the girl could not bring herself to betray him even if she tried.

In her despondency, a woman can say many forgettable things, and Cressida does; but occasionally she can also come up with something unforgettable, something like the following line which Cressida seems to utter absentmindedly:

> A woeful Cressid 'mongst the merry Greeks:
> When shall we see again?
>
> (IV. iv. 55–6)

At the time of Shakespeare, "merry Greeks" was a proverbial expression for people addicted to the pleasures of the senses. Troilus immediately catches the phrase since his first reaction is already negative, but it will take him a little time, as usual, before the picture conveyed by "the merry Greeks" fully crystallizes in his mind:

> Hear me, my love: be thou but true of heart –
>
> (IV. iv. 57)

A new note of suspicion is struck, of which Cressida is perfectly aware; and she in turn reacts negatively:

> I, true? How now, what wicked deem is this?
>
> (IV. iv. 58)

Troilus replies:

> I speak not 'Be thou true,' as fearing thee –
> For I will throw my glove to Death himself
> That there's no maculation in thy heart –
> But 'Be thou true' say I to fashion in
> My sequent protestation: be thou true,
> And I will see thee.
> *Cressida:* O you shall be expos'd, my lord, to dangers
> As infinite as imminent! But I'll be true.
> *Troilus:* And I'll grow friend with danger: wear this sleeve.
> *Cressida:* And you this glove: when shall I see you?
> *Troilus:* I will corrupt the Grecian sentinels
> To give to thee nightly visitation.
> But yet be true. (IV. iv. 61–73)

As Troilus repeats his "be true, be true," just as before he kept repeating "you'll catch a cold," we can almost watch his progress in the absorption of the "merry Greeks." The disagreeable but still vague impression of a moment before gradually gives way to a clear picture of the dangerously seductive milieu which Cressida is about to enter. With each "be true, be true" Cressida becomes more impatient:

> O heavens – 'Be true' again?
> *Troilus:* Hear why I speak it, love.
> The Grecian youths are full of quality,
> Their loving well compos'd, with gifts of nature flowing,
> And swelling o'er with arts and exercise.

How novelty may move, and parts with person,
Alas, a kind of godly jealousy –
Which I beseech you call a virtuous sin –
Makes me afeard.

(IV. iv. 73–81)

Did Cressida clearly understand what she was doing when she mentioned the "merry Greeks," did she think of the implications? Whatever the answer, she can be satisfied with the results. With seven words only, she brought about a complete revolution in her relationship with Troilus.

The very thought of losing her to the "merry Greeks," has turned Cressida once again into the "thing ungain'd" that men prize "more than it is." Complacency has given way to panic fear. In Troilus's appraisal of Cressida, of himself, of the entire situation, nothing remains the same. Troilus, the god of love of an instant ago, is transformed into a clumsy peasant. The real gods are the Greeks.

Troilus suffers from two disadvantages. Not only do his Greek rivals have the marvelous qualities that he so temptingly, so imprudently enumerates to Cressida, but they will now have the direct and permanent access to the girl that he is about to lose. One minute ago, Cressida was an over-possessive mistress and the battleline was a welcome relief; now it is a diabolical obstacle, in the service of the superior rivals who interfere with "true love."

Just as she knew that possession kills desire, Cressida seems to know the one efficient method for reviving a dead desire: jealousy. To such a girl, at such a time, in such circumstances, the second strategy will prove easier to practice and more efficient than the first, the "hold off" strategy.

The ancient game of love and jealousy is the object of countless plays, poems, novels, etc. It is the daily bread of western literature. Many critics find it a little trivial. It does not excite their curiosity. They prefer loftier subjects of meditation. Jealousy intensifies desire! How interesting! What else is new?

And yet what else is there in *Troilus and Cressida*, including the political scenes, if not the twists and turns of human desire in the presence or absence of other competing desires? If we are not interested in this, how can we be interested in this bizarre but quintessentially Shakespearean play?

In *Deceit, Desire and the Novel*, I observed that the ordinary definition of jealousy conforms to the presuppositions and illusions of the jealous individual. Jealousy is supposed to occur when a second desire focuses on the object the jealous individual feels should be desired by no one but himself, because he was first on the stage, he was the first to desire that object. Any desire interfering with his desire, he regards as illegitimate. For each desirable object, ideally, there should be only one desiring subject, and the first one to show up should have precedence. The two desires compete for the same object, and the "jealous" desire bases his proprietary claim on his chronological priority.

Troilus is a textbook case for this illusion. His was undoubtedly the first desire. He certainly came before the Greeks. Hence his great indignation when Cressida becomes actually unfaithful. His self-righteousness is based on his prior occupation of the premises. He is convinced that he has a moral, if not a legal *right* to the undisturbed possession of the young woman.

From the standpoint of Cressida, of course, Troilus has forfeited whatever rights his night with her had given him at first.

Troilus did not perceive his own indifference, his vanity, his selfishness, his boorishness, on that early morning and, whatever he understood then, he certainly forgot with the arrival of Diomed. Like all idealists, he is totally "sincere." The critics too are sincere. Until doomsday, there will be those who see in Troilus what he sees in himself, the genuine article, the real incarnation of "true love." But Cressida understands and remembers.

Troilus is a remarkable example of bad faith. As soon as he becomes jealous, he feels like an innocent victim. He has pushed Cressida into the arms of Diomed, but he does not realize this any more than he realizes Cressida was first pushed into his arms by the other man who desires her, Pandarus. Like all of us, he remembers selectively. Among his sentiments and his actions, he remembers only those that consolidate his image of himself as a virtuous man, abominably wronged by others but never guilty himself. He does not remember the discontinuity in his love for Cressida.

Troilus, indeed, has the "facts" on his side. But these "facts" grossly distort the higher truth of the relationship. Not only did he betray Cressida too, but he betrayed her first and her own betrayal can be read, at least in part, as an act of retaliation, of vengeful escalation, and therefore as an *imitation* of what Troilus has done to her.

As I said before, Shakespeare himself, up to a point, fostered the misunderstanding. He made the eclipse in Troilus's desire so brief and inconclusive, so devoid of concrete consequences, that it could remain unseen by the spectators as well as erased from the text, first by the cuckolded hero from the text of his memory, and then by the traditional critics from the text of the printed play.

If the desire of Troilus is really extinguished, even for a brief moment, the subsequent jealousy is truly "godly" in its power. It does more than "intensify" an already existing desire. It resurrects a dead one or, better still, it creates an entirely new desire.

If we deny all continuity between the first and the second desire, we must not describe Troilus as *jealous* in the ordinary sense. The jealous desire is not a desire that preceded the arrival of the Greeks and existed independently. The order should be reversed. The Greeks were there first, if not in reality, at least in the mind of Troilus. Until the "merry Greeks" entered the picture the indifference of Troilus remained monolithic.

In one instant, a desire for Cressida was generated in Troilus that cannot be rooted in him, the subject, since one minute before he could not muster such a desire, neither can it be rooted in Cressida. She has not changed in the slightest and, until then, on that early morning, she has proved totally unexciting. Where else? There is only one more possibility, the "merry Greeks." They did not merely "intensify" an already existing desire, they triggered a new one.

The second desire duplicates the first and can only result from an imitation of it, a kind of copy. This is what I call imitative, or mimetic or mediated desire.

Everything Troilus says confirms the mimetic nature of his relationship to the Greeks. He certainly wants to acquire the talents and achievements that he admires in them. Which young man in love would not? The only way to proceed is to learn by imitation. Every single detail in my last quote reveals the urge to imitate. Unfortunately a Greek education – this is what it would amount to, really – would take too much time and patience to be feasible.

The one feature in his image of the Greeks that Troilus can imitate and duplicate with the greatest ease and perfection is one which the theoreticians of imitation always omit: the Greeks' desire for Cressida, the desire he attributes to them. The "jealous" desire of Troilus for Cressida is patterned after the Greek desire, and not the reverse.

This desire is imaginary. No doubt but it does not matter. Troilus vividly imagines how the Greeks will feel and speak and behave as soon as they discover this pretty Trojan woman in their midst. Give Cressida a few hours and this Greek desire for her will be real enough. The real mediator anyway is not the Greeks, nor even Diomed later on, but Cressida, who manipulates the desire of Troilus as skillfully as Pandarus earlier had manipulated both hers and his, in order to make them fall in love with one another.

In order to understand the importance of mimetic desire in *Troilus and Cressida*, we must remember Pandarus: we must pay some attention to the technique of Pandarus when he "sells" Troilus on Cressida and Cressida on Troilus.

The two lovers would never admit, of course, that Pandarus had anything to do with their falling in love with each other. However intelligent Cressida may be in comparison with Troilus, even she does not understand her uncle's role. When she exclaims:

> But more in Troilus thousand-fold I see
> Than in the glass of Pandar's praise may be
> (I. ii. 289–90)

she implies that the intensity of her desire is a guarantee of its authenticity. We are all naturally inclined, romantically inclined to believe the lovers.

In the first two scenes, we have lengthy samples of Pandarus's technique and much of it is so banal, predictable and heavy-handed that we feel almost embarrassed for him and for Shakespeare. Pandarus first showers Troilus with extravagant praise of Cressida and then he showers Cressida with extravagant praise for Troilus. How could this lecherous old fool influence two bright and handsome young people?

All this is window-dressing. The meaty part is the constant reference in both scenes to someone who plays a rather sinister role in the lives and deaths of just about everybody in the Greek and Trojan world of the play, Helen of Troy. To Troilus, Pandarus says that Cressida is just as desirable as Helen, more desirable perhaps:

> And her hair were not somewhat darker than Helen's – well, go to, there were no more comparison between the women.
>
> (I. i. 41–3)

A little later, feigning anger at Troilus for his supposed indifference to his "niece," Pandarus says:

> Because she's kin to me, therefore she's not so fair as Helen. And she were not kin to me, she would be as fair o' Friday as Helen is o' Sunday.
>
> (I. i. 74–7)

Much of the following scene, with Cressida, consists in stupid anecdotes about the Trojan court and, above all, Helen. Cressida does not have access to the "beautiful people," and she seems as thirsty for gossip as a contemporary television addict. There is something highly *bovaryque* about all her reactions.

Pandarus too is a dreadful snob, but his fascination for the royal palace can be used to arouse the desire of Cressida. One story refers to some occasion when the entire Trojan elite was gathered and Troilus, supposedly, dominated the scene. Helen in particular had eyes only for Troilus. She admired his complexion. She tickled his chin and she even counted the sparse hair on it. A witty exchange occurred with Helen, and Troilus came out the winner. All the applause was for him. Then, Pandarus adds: "I swear to you I think Helen loves him better than Paris" (I. ii. 108–9). A little later, once again, he says: "But to prove to you that Helen loves him . . ." (I. ii. 120). The phrase keeps coming back as a refrain: "But to prove to you that Helen loves Troilus –" (I. ii. 129–30).

The intrinsic value Troilus may have mattered less in the genesis of Cressida's desire than, true or false (in fact undoubtedly false), the rumor of his being desired by Helen. Why Helen? Because she is at the center of the Trojan war, its object or rather its pretext. Thousands and thousands of people have died, are dying, and will die for her, thousands of rival desires converge upon Helen.

As a magnet for countless desires, whatever Helen herself desires, especially in matters erotic, is likely to appear more desirable than it really is. As an inspirer of desire, Helen has more potential than anyone else.

All this prestige, however, is the result of a massive Pandarus-style operation called the Trojan war. The more people die for Helen's sake, the more valuable she appears and vice versa. This is a typical vicious circle of mimetic desire. The purely imitative, contagious, and irrational nature of Helen's prestige is discussed at length in the meeting of the Trojan general staff.

As long as Troilus believes that Cressida will reject him, he remains lucid about the whole process. Of the two armies fighting each other, he says, magnificently:

> Fools on both sides, Helen must needs be fair
> When with your blood you daily paint her thus.
>
> (I.i.90–1)

Shakespeare was probably too ignorant of primitive societies to know that in quite a few of them – including perhaps the ones that generated the myths behind the Homeric treatment of the Trojan war – the idols of sexuality and violence were often daubed with the blood of the faithful. But in two lines his genius can achieve what the enormous apparatus of modern research has not yet achieved: the understanding of the relationship between these phenomena and mimetic rivalry.

Can the erotic prestige of one woman really be transferred to someone else, or something else? Who are we to ask? Don't we live in a world of advertisers who resort to sultry women in order to sell even such products as aspirin and instant coffee? Decrepit actresses can also do, provided they have many trophies in their sexual war chest, half a dozen husbands at the least, and lovers by the hundreds.

Our boundless pretentiousness makes us believe that even the worst features of our world are entirely original to us, born yesterday with the electronic age. Far from being exclusively modern, sexiness by proxy is a most ancient trick. The medium and the message are not the same. The message came first, and Shakespeare could teach a thing or two to our specialists in communications.

Helen's prestige as a lover was of paramount importance in the case of Cressida, and so is the prestige of the Greeks in the case of Troilus. In both instances, the image of another desire has to be there in order to generate in the beholder a desire that duplicates the suggested image.

First Pandarus dangled in front of Cressida the "sweet bait" of a Helen madly in love with Troilus. This time, not Pandarus but Cressida dangles in front of Troilus the "sweet bait" of the adorable Greeks madly in love with herself.

In an act of retaliation for his indifference, of vengeful imitation, Cressida turned against Troilus the trick that Pandarus played on her. She has learned her lesson well. She can now act as her own Pandarus. She has become an expert.

And Troilus too, ironically, in his relationship with Cressida, becomes an involuntary Pandarus working against his own interests. Each performs for the other the function of the go-between. Troilus is so dazzled by the Greeks that he does his best, unconsciously, to dazzle her as well. And he succeeds beyond his wildest expectations.

Troilus turns "bawd and cuckold," as Joyce would say, in spite of himself, because of his mimetic fascination with his rivals. Pandarus is not working for money; he is driven by his own desire. His "business" can only be a more extreme manifestation of the mimetic process. He is so entranced with both Cressida and Troilus, the one and the other potential rivals as well as objects, more or less indifferently, that he must deliberately push them into each other's arms. A more *advanced* modality of mimetic desire will systematically engineer the kind of voyeuristic masochism that Troilus already ends up with, although against his conscious will.

*

A comparison between the erotic and the political games will provide additional evidence regarding the pervasive and unifying presence of mimetic desire in *Troilus and Cressida*.

In spite of many years of war and great losses on both sides, the conflict is a stalemate. Completely demoralized, the Greek army cannot mount any serious operation. In I.iii, the Greek general staff meets at great length and Ulysses, the best political mind, diagnoses the disease. Authority has disintegrated; factionalism is rampant.

Achilles, the most popular warrior, refuses to fight. His immense prestige has made him so "plaguy proud" that he finds it intolerable not to be first in all respects. Under his tent, with his mignon Patroclus, he mocks Agamemnon, whom he wants to replace as commander-in-chief.

One notch under Achilles stands Ajax, another great warrior, second only to Achilles in strength, popularity and vanity, and extremely envious as a result. To him, Achilles is too much of a model not to be an obstacle and vice versa, in the same sense that Achilles and Agamemnon are models and obstacles to one another. Agamemnon would like to be as popular as Achilles. Achilles would like to be Agamemnon. Ajax would like to be Achilles. Each man wants to *be* the other man without ceasing to be himself.

Ajax apes Achilles in every possible way. He, too, behaves like a coquettish woman; he too has withdrawn under his tent and refuses to fight. It cannot be doubted here that desire coincides with imitation. Shakespeare himself describes the whole process of rivalry as one of *imitation*:

> *Nestor:* And in the imitation of these twain,
> Who, as Ulysses says, opinion crowns
> With an imperial voice, many are infect.
> Ajax is grown self-will'd, and bears his head
> In such a rein, in full as proud a place
> As broad Achilles; keeps his tent like him . . .
>
> (I. iii. 185–90)

Nothing is more contagious, or mimetically attractive, than mimetic rivalry; and the behavior of Achilles serves as a model to the rank immediately below him and then down the entire hierarchic ladder, until the whole army is "infect" with mimetic desire.

> *Ulysses:* The general's disdain'd
> By him one step below, he by the next,
> The next by him beneath: so every step,
> Exampled by the first pace that is sick
> Of his superior, grows to an envious fever
> Of pale and bloodless emulation.
>
> (I. iii. 129–34)

Emulation is mimetic rivalry itself. It creates many conflicts but it empties them of all content. That is why it is called "pale and bloodless." At every turn in this text, one encounters descriptions of mimetic rivalry so explicit that they require no interpretation.

Ulysses seeks to remedy the situation and to restore authority. In such a desperate predicament, the disease itself is the only available medicine. To produce a soothing effect on the body politic, mimetic desire must be further inflamed in strategically sensitive areas.

Since the bad example and the greatest danger come from the top, Ulysses works at the top and he tries to cut Achilles down to size. How can it be done? A series of highly significant maneuvers are devised and implemented, at least in part.

The first maneuver consists in providing Achilles with a rival. He already has one, of course, but Ajax is not credible enough. He must be given more prestige. In response to a challenge by Hector, Ajax must be chosen as a champion.

Nestor had first suggested Achilles, but Ulysses showed him the error of his ways. If Achilles lost, the Greeks would be in terrible shape, deprived of their best man. If he won, he would be more insolent than ever.

Ajax is the man precisely because he is only second best. If he fails, not much is lost. A Trojan victory over Ajax would have little significance. But if Ajax won, his victory would mean a great deal not only against the Trojans, but against Achilles, whose prestige would suffer:

Ulysses: Among ourselves
> Give him [Ajax] allowance for the better man;
> For that will physic the great Myrmidon,
> Who broils in loud applause. . . .
> Ajax employ'd plucks down Achilles' plumes.
>
> (I. iii. 376–86)

If we compare this political maneuver of Ulysses with the vengeance of Cressida against her vain and indifferent lover, we can see that they are exactly the same. Cressida has decided to give Troilus some serious competition. At first she has merely mentioned "the merry Greeks," and the success has been such that she has picked a new lover as soon as she has arrived among the Greeks. She has given Troilus such rivals that she has attached him to her by chains heavier and stronger than any kind of marriage that societies have ever devised.

In the case of Ulysses and Achilles, this strategy is not successful. After some insignificant fighting, Ajax and Hector conveniently discover that they are distant relatives and they decide they should call it quits. Achilles is not disturbed. The only result is to make Ajax even more "plaguy proud" than before, just as insufferable as Achilles himself.

In II. iii, Ulysses renews his attempts to deflate the ego of Achilles. This hero once again has refused to participate in the fighting. He does not even bother with excuses. Painfully surprised, Agamemnon asks:

> Why will he not, upon our fair request,
> Untent his person, and share th' air with us?
>
> (II. iii. 168–9)

Achilles has become so puffed up with pride, Ulysses reports, that he will listen to no one. Agamemnon then proposes the following:

> Let Ajax go to him.
> Dear Lord, go you and greet him in his tent.
> 'Tis said he holds you well, and will be led
> At your request a little from himself.
>
> (II. iii. 179–82)

This illustrates perfectly what should *not* be done in such a case, in exactly the same way as Nestor's idea of picking Achilles as a champion of the Greeks in the previous episode. Here again the wrong proposal is made in order to provide Ulysses with an occasion for explaining why it is wrong. It reflects the illusions of mimetic desire which it can only reinforce:

> O Agamemnon, let it not be so!
> We'll consecrate the steps that Ajax makes
> When they go from Achilles. Shall the proud lord

That bastes his arrogance with his own seam
And never suffers matter of the world
Enter his thoughts, save such as do revolve
And ruminate himself – shall he be worshipp'd
Of that we hold an idol more than he? . . .
By going to Achilles.
That were to enlard his fat-already pride
And add more coals to Cancer when he burns
With entertaining great Hyperion.
This lord go to him? Jupiter forbid,
And say in thunder 'Achilles, go to him!'

(II. iii. 183–200)

The enormous self-assurance of Achilles looks like a kind of divinity, or at least a fact of nature, a permanent endowment that cannot be taken away from him. Literary critics would call it the "character" of Achilles. The Freudians would talk about his "narcissism."

Ulysses does not share this "essentialist" conception of Achilles' self-confidence. According to him, this formidable pride has no objective basis; it is the result of universal worship, of the huge amount of admiration and desire directed towards Achilles.

Achilles mistakes himself for a god because everybody worships him. If Ajax, whom the leaders "hold an idol more than he [Achilles]," shows himself inferior by going humbly to Achilles, he partakes in the cult; he strengthens everybody's faith in Achilles including Achilles' own, he feeds or "enlards" his "fat-already pride." One must not add more desire to the enormous mountain on which the hero is already perched, invulnerable, it seems, to the doubts and difficulties of lesser human beings.

If Ulysses is right, pride is only one more effect of mimetic desire. Achilles can desire himself not because he is objectively stronger or greater, but because of the mimetic desire that keeps flowing in his direction in huge quantities and that serves as a model for his own desire. By imitating the desires that converge upon him, Achilles desires himself. His pride inflates further and, as a result, innumerable fools worship him all the more. This enlarding of pride, or, in modern jargon, this feedback process, grows worse and worse.

If Ulysses is right, the whole Achilles cult, including Achilles' own role in it, is a mimetic system most impressive no doubt, but more fragile than it appears, because its stability results only from our own mimetic susceptibility. It must be possible to destabilize this system by deflecting the great stream of desire that always flows to Achilles and never away from him.

How can it be done? You can either set up a rival model, such as Ajax (but this has been tried without success); or you can pretend that you are no longer interested in Achilles, that you have only indifference for him and even contempt. You thus proclaim to the world that, as far as you are concerned, Achilles has lost his power as a mimetic magnet. You pretend to be your own model of mimetic desire, you proclaim to the world that you are more attracted to yourself than to Achilles.

Immediately after the preceding speech, Ulysses seeks to exploit the second possibility by organizing a spectacular display of studied indifference vis-à-vis Achilles. Here are his instructions to the Greek leaders who have gathered in the vicinity of the famous tent.

> Achilles stands i' th' entrance of his tent.
> Please it our general pass strangely by him
> As if he were forgot; and, princes all,
> Lay negligent and loose regard upon him.
> I will come last. 'Tis like he'll question me
> Why such unplausive eyes are bent, why turn'd on him.
> If so, I have derision medicinable
> To use between your strangeness and his pride,
> Which his own will shall have desire to drink.
> It may do good: pride hath no other glass
> To show itself but pride; for supple knees
> Feed arrogance, and are the proud man's fees.
> (III. iii. 38–49)

Even Agamemnon, now, sees the wisdom of this tactic and he promises that everybody will behave in the proper manner:

> We'll execute your purpose, and put on
> A form of strangeness as we pass along.
> So do each lord, and either greet him not
> Or else disdainfully, which shall shake him more
> Than if not look'd on. I will lead the way.
> (III. iii. 50–4)

Shakespeare insists too much on this little play within the play not to attach a great importance to it. And yet it is neither very dramatic nor truly comical. It does not lead to some great action. Its whole interest lies in what it reveals regarding the configuration of mimetic desire that the insane popularity of Achilles represents.

*

Now, if we go back to the erotic plot and ask ourselves if this second maneuver of Ulysses has some equivalent in the strategy of Cressida, no hesitation is possible. It corresponds to what Cressida had in mind, in her monologue, when she proudly proclaimed, "yet I hold off."

The little comedy in front of Achilles' tent is an example of the "hold off" strategy if I ever saw one. Cressida had obtained excellent results from that trick as long as she remained able to keep up the pretense of indifference. The intensity of Troilus's desire was brought to a quite satisfactory level, but then Cressida relented and destroyed her own work. That is why she had to resort to the second strategy; she had to give Troilus a powerful rival.

The same two strategies are used in the political realm and the erotic realm – but in the reverse order, because their success too is reversed, which means that in both realms the second strategy is more successful than the first. When the first one has failed, the second is tried, and succeeds.

Both strategies are applicable to both domains. The difference in the objects of desire does not matter much. The mimetic effects matter more; they determine which objects will be desired, and in which field, and both strategies are attempts to change the orientation of mimetic effects. The politics of eroticism and the politics of power are really one and the same.

Cressida, in the case of Troilus, and Ulysses, in the case of Achilles, try to shatter the excessive self-confidence of a rebellious partner by persuading him that the desire upon which he counts as a model for self-love is now denied to him, either because it is focused on someone else, a more successful rival, or because it is focused on no one but the desiring subject himself, which amounts to the same thing.

At first, Achilles believes the leaders have come once more to beg for his help in the fighting and he turns away haughtily. But when he and Patroclus realize that their haughtiness is repaid with haughtiness, they are both taken aback.

Patroclus contrasts the new attitude with the humility of the leaders in the past, when they would approach Achilles "as humbly as they used to creep to holy altars." Achilles says nothing at first but then, noticing that Menelaus himself pays no attention to him, he exclaims: "What, does the cuckold scorn me?" (III. iii. 64).

When Troilus first heard about "the merry Greeks" from Cressida's own mouth, his good mood abandoned him and he began to feel more and more worried and depressed. Now the same thing exactly is happening to Achilles, for very similar reasons:

> What, am I poor of late?
> 'Tis certain, greatness once fall'n out with fortune
> Must fall out with men too. What the declin'd is,
> He shall as soon read in the eyes of others
> As feel in his own fall . . .
>
> (III. iii. 74–8)

Achilles tries to fight this incipient fit of depression. He tries to reassure himself: with him, this decadence of most leaders cannot occur. His fame is such that he will never share the lot of the ordinary great men:

> But 'tis not so with me:
> Fortune and I are friends; I do enjoy
> At ample point all that I did possess,
> Save these men's looks; who do, methinks, find out
> Something not worth in me such rich beholding
> As they have often given.
>
> (III. iii. 87–92)

Achilles still has everything he had *save these men's looks*. Unfortunately, in his mimetic world, just as in our media-crazy world, nothing matters more than the looks of other men. These looks, and the desires they signal, must be visibly focused upon the proud man at all times, to keep his own desire well supplied with models of what becomes, for him, self-adulation. If these models disappear, if the looks of other men are withdrawn, the proud man's desire cannot circle back all the way toward himself and generate the phenomenon called pride.

Instead of the desires that would enlard his pride, Achilles now sees in the other men's eyes an indifference and a contempt no less irresistible as models of imitation than their opposite. All highly visible heroes – or artists, notably dramatists – can shift quite easily from self-adulation to self-contempt. The more inflated the balloon of their pride, the less of a pinprick it takes to deflate it.

Achilles is no longer the proud man he seemed to be but in reality never was in the sense of *being*. He was the beneficiary of a mimetic tidal wave so powerful and durable that everybody, including himself, mistook it for *being*. The illusion of *being* is only a product of mimetic desire. Mimetic desire seeks *being* and always finds it in the idol of the moment.

This illusion remains the same whether it is expressed in terms of Achilles' "character," by the old-style literary psychologists, in terms of a "narcissism" independent of how other people behave with the so-called "narcissist," or in terms of religious ritual. A poet will always prefer the latter language, which is more beautiful and closer to the truth of its own mimetic and violent genesis which it nevertheless distorts.

In order to rectify this distortion, a biblical perspective is needed – which is undoubtedly present in *Troilus and Cressida*, notably in the constant use of such words as *idol* and *idolatry*. If we regard the use of such words as naive and misguided because the world of *Troilus and Cressida* is supposed to be ancient paganism, we miss the whole point of the play, which is not a celebration but a formidable indictment of mimetic desire. The mimetic religion of violence and the sacred is a false religion which even in Shakespeare's own world threatens all human beings.

In spite of this temporary success with Achilles, the schemes devised by Ulysses all seem to fail in the end. Their outcome is hardly mentioned anyway.

The mimetic disease is so advanced in *Troilus and Cressida* that no coherent action is possible. Shakespeare does not seem interested in moving toward a dramatic climax. He is more interested in presenting Ulysses as a political Pandarus, a brilliant mind, no doubt, but too fascinated with the politics of desire, the very disease he is fighting, not to need himself some of his own medicine. Since this medicine and the disease are really one, all Ulysses does in the end, in his own sophisticated way, is to contribute to the general contamination. Lack of differentiation and chaos prevail everywhere. This is the great downfall of Degree – difference – so eloquently described by Ulysses himself.

From a dramatic standpoint, the two subplots do not really dovetail. But from the standpoint of the mimetic plague, they marvelously mirror each other. Which is exactly as it should be. The purpose of the play is really to show that lechery and war are one, just as Thersites claims; and you can actually verify this truth by showing that both subplots are symmetrically structured by the same twists and turns of the strategies generated by the mimetic process.

These two subplots should not be judged according to the habitual values of dramatic criticism. From that standpoint, the play fails miserably. There is no suspenseful action; there are no real heroes or villains, no "characters," no *catharsis* of any kind. The spectators cannot "identify" with anyone.

Shakespeare devised the various incidents for the purpose of creating circumstances favorable to the genesis and revelation of this or that configuration of mimetic desire. In that play, "good theater" is not the goal. The goal is an exploration of something which philosophy has always repressed and denied, and literary criticism as well, something which is simmering in the infrastructure of all great dramas and novels of the western world, and which, in the greatest, rises to the surface, *mimesis* as desire, and desire as *mimesis*. As a revelation of mimetic desire, *Troilus and Cressida* can only be described as stupendous.

This prevalence of mimetic desire accounts, I believe, for the importance of Pandarus, the go-between, the *mediator* of desire, who plays no political role but who nevertheless rightly appears as the symbol of everything in the play, the alpha and the omega of *Troilus and Cressida*. He is on stage at the beginning, and he is on stage again at the end. In his Rabelaisian epilogue he bequeaths to the spectators a venereal disease that had not been mentioned earlier, and that seems to turn him almost into an allegory of the contagious power of mimetic desire.

Note

1. All quotations from *Troilus and Cressida* are taken from the Arden Shakespeare edition, edited by Kenneth Palmer (London, 1982).

11

HARRY BERGER, JR

Psychoanalyzing the Shakespeare text: the first three scenes of the *Henriad*

Patriarchal ideology is shown in the *Henriad* to create deep tensions which are not dispelled, are often exacerbated, by its mechanisms of repression and displacement. This is partly because the problems inherent in the cultural constructions of "natural" or jural fatherhood are carried into the wider sphere of national and dynastic politics in two uneasily related forms of symbolic fatherhood: the Christian principle of divine paternity, and the aristocratic principle of what might be called heraldic genealogy. The name of the Father, God, is used to authorize the distribution of patriarchal power into two axes of "descent": the "vertical" axis of substitution called hierarchy, and the "horizontal" axis of succession, heraldic genealogy. In both axes, the formal "cause" or criterion is *mimesis*; but whereas, in the first, descent is organized in terms of declining resemblance to the Father, in the second, the Father ideally achieves genealogical immortality by reproducing its image in progenial replicas.[1] My emphasis in this essay will be on a certain disorder in the mimetic principle itself, a contradiction which, as Plato saw, causes the structure of genealogical mimesis to be contaminated by that of hierarchical mimesis.

The ideal of genealogical mimesis is appealed to early in *Richard II* by the Duchess of Gloucester, who reminds Gaunt that his father's seven sons "Were as seven vials of his sacred blood, / Or seven fair branches springing from one root" (I. ii. 12–13), and that his murdered brother, her late husband, "was the model of thy father's life" (28). Similarly, in II. i, York appeals to this ideal when he urges Richard to live up to the standards set by his father, reminding him that "His face thou hast, for even so look'd he" (176). A little later, he gives the principle its classic statement:

Is not Gaunt dead? and doth not Herford live?
Was not Gaunt just? and is not Harry true?
Did not the one deserve to have an heir?
Is not his heir a well-deserving son?
Take Herford's rights away, and take from time
His charters, and his customary rights;
Let not to-morrow then ensue to-day:
Be not thyself. For how art thou a king
But by fair sequence and succession?

(II. i. 191–9)[2]

Though these appear to be blandly constative articulations of the mimetic principle, they are being uttered in the face of its violation, and York's rhetoric is already charged with a sense of its fragility – a sense of the generational malaise which he will betray later in the play, and which may be imagined to motivate the blandness and the appeal of heraldic genealogy.

Consider, for example, the third and fourth lines: their chiasmic bonding does not quite efface the tension between the claims stated in the two separate rhetorical questions. Gaunt "deserves" an heir, not only because he was just, but also because he is dead. His son "deserves" to be an heir not only because he is true (we could read this mimetically as "true to his father," "in his image") but also because he is alive. The heir represents his father's death, the loss of authority, power, life – "no less than all" – and he can plead his right to this appropriation by appealing to the plague of custom and curiosity of nations.

Edmund's pungent if pathetic braveries – the clichés of knavery and folk cynicism – take on a different kind of life when transplanted to the soil of primogeniture and legitimate inheritance. For they clearly apply:

This seems a fair deserving, and must draw me
That which my father loses; no less than all:
The younger rises when the old doth fall.
(*King Lear*, III. iii. 23–5)

York tries to secure the rhetorical icon of the transmission he is defending by the chiasmus "one–deserve–heir–heir–deserving–son": "the one" re-appears at the end, but not quite, in "son"; mimesis implies and demands a difference which it tries to overcome by a mirroring that recuperates the lost identity, but the inversion that expresses the difference at the heart of the process also expresses opposition between the two orders of "the one" and "son."

The threat of external violation addressed by York in his protest to Richard thus reflects a problem lurking within the mimetic process itself, and may partially account for the ineffectuality of the protest. Such persuasions meet stiff competition in paternal criticism of sons, as exemplified by Gaunt early in *Richard II* and much later by Gaunt's son in *2 Henry IV*:

> O, had thy grandsire with a prophet's eye
> Seen how his son's son should destroy his sons,
> From forth thy reach he would have laid thy shame
> > (*Richard II*, II.i. 104–6)

> See, sons, what things you are
> (*2 Henry IV*, IV.v. 64)

The negative and positive sides of paternal ideology are expressed in the following two statements by Bolingbroke, the first to York, who has just disclosed his son's treason, and the second to Hal:

> O loyal father of a treacherous son!
> Thou sheer, immaculate and silver fountain,
> From whence this stream, through muddy passages,
> Hath held his current and defil'd himself,
> Thy overflow of good converts to bad
> > (*Richard II*, V.iii. 58–62)

> And now my death
> Changes the mood, for what in me was purchas'd
> Falls upon thee in a more fairer sort;
> So thou the garland wear'st successively.
> (*2 Henry IV*, IV.v. 198–201)

But the negativity and positivity of these utterances are complicated, and indeed challenged, as soon as they are contextualized.

Psychoanalytic criticism has tended to approach the problems adumbrated by these statements by resituating them within the network of explanations made available by the institutionalized lore of psychoanalysis. I propose as an alternative taking a scion from that root and grafting it onto a different explanatory network whose stock is the mimetic process. As I mentioned earlier, there is a disorder, a structural flaw, in the very notion of mimesis, and it is magnified by confusion in the paternal deployment of the genealogical principle. The father's desire for immortality may produce a desire to clone and control an endless series of identical replacements. This, incidentally, implicates a latent ideal of male parthenogenesis which may be expressed in the fear, scapegoating, and repression of the feminine. But this desire is crossed by the desire to overgo one's replacements, to be the unrepeatable archetypal eponymous progenitor whose all-giving cannot be matched. What the father then wants to reproduce are not replicas but images, imitations. It is of the nature of an imitation to be defective, to fall short of what it represents so that it can represent itself *as* the representation of an exemplar. A perfect imitation, as Derrida notes, "is no longer an imitation"; the tiny difference between imitated and imitation makes all the difference; imitation "is not what it is . . . unless it is in some way at fault or rather in default."[3] The paternal project entails the reduction of the son's difference, his otherness, to assure both the genealogical continuity of the paternal archetype and its hierarchic superiority to the weaker vessels that transmit its image. This is a project of symbolic filicide, and it is nourished by the desire of immortality, that is, by the fear of death which, projected onto the potential replacement, makes of a "true inheritor" a true competitor. In the space or gap of otherness which the act of paternity creates, and which symbolic filicide cannot efface, but can only render more alien, arises the answering project of symbolic parricide.

The centrality of this theme to the *Henriad* has often been recognized and discussed, but with two limitations which I shall try to confront in this essay. First, the burden of critical discussion has been placed on Henry IV as father; virtually no attention has been paid to him as son, and this will be the subject of the following interpretation. Second, I know of no serious attempts to correlate psychoanalytic criticism with the two other major lines of interpretation addressed to the *Henriad*, political and metatheatrical criticism. And while I do not have space to consider these in any detail, I shall illustrate and formulate a methodological hypothesis for connecting metatheatrical issues to the intratextual representation of political and generational conflict. For reasons that will become clearer as we proceed, a metatheatrical approach to the dramatic and theatrical dimensions of the "story" of the *Henriad* presupposes a standpoint outside the normative limits of what has been called "stage-centered" reading. It calls for a project that is doggedly textual in orientation, and is thus *anti*theatrical: it will generate readings that do not readily lend themselves to performance and that will necessarily draw fire from stage-centered critics. But that, in a perverse way, is my point: that the antitheatricality of the readings I shall give reflects an antitheatricality in the Shakespeare text. By calling that text "antitheatrical" I mean that it throws into question all the dramatic structures – narrative, episode, scene, character, and body – that theatrical performance privileges and the author of Shakespeare's plays clearly loves. I include among these structures the political and historical scenarios as embodiments of the patriarchal ideology with its two axes of hierarchy and orderly succession. I shall read the critique of drama and theater politically as a critique of that ideology, but what I am chiefly interested in is its relation not to the politics of the state but to that of father/son conflicts. I therefore view psychoanalytic, political, and dramatico-theatrical interpretation as closely intertwined strands of a single activity.

Mimesis is the common representational principle informing the organiza-

ical and hierarchic relationships, and of relationships among
matic narrative, and theatrical performance. Thus I assume
orming a critique of mimesis – and of its own mimetic status
of producing a mimesis. In exploring the critique I shall not
with its possible relevance for allegories of the playwright's literary or
psychological development. I prefer to seek within the dramatic community
and its generational conflicts for the motives that lead to the production and
critique of mimetic structures. What regulative and representational functions do these structures fulfill in relation to the father/son conflicts depicted
in the *Henriad*? And since "in the *Henriad*" here means in the language of the
play as it offers itself directly to readers rather than to actors, what functions
do those structures fulfill in relation to the text?

I consider these two questions to be the same question, and I shall respond
to it by exploring, in the interpretations that follow, a particular hypothesis:
that Shakespeare's mimetic structures – theater, drama, and the narrative
sequences they represent – are related to the text as manifest to latent
contents; they are explicitly and conspicuously presented as displaced,
condensed, and dramatized visualizations of latent textual meanings they
thereby repress. This hypothesis will now be tested by excavating from the
text of the first Act of *Richard II* the shadowy evidence of the first major
father/son conflict in the *Henriad*.

In the opening scenes of *Richard II*, the inflation of speech is no more
conspicuous than the silences it constitutes as hidden behind it. Participants
within the drama share with audiences and readerships an uneasy awareness
that the ceremonially dramatic but otherwise noncommittal language pushes
much into the background, that ritual speech is being used to hide, mystify, or
justify other motives than those expressed, and that no one knows exactly
what those motives may be – least of all, perhaps, in some cases, those whose
motives they are. Since the characters seem for the most part to be maneuver-
ing in the dark, it may be risky to venture into one of the more charged and
salient pockets of silence, the one that encloses what goes on between John of
Gaunt and his son. That pocket is peripheral to the more central one enclosing
what goes on between Richard and Bolingbroke; but since both pockets are
mediated, or set off, or circumscribed, by the more accessible relationship
between Richard and Gaunt, I shall observe due caution and begin there. The
Gaunt/Bolingbroke relation remains a mystery throughout the *Henriad*.
Bolingbroke's obsession with his relation to Richard crops up frequently in
the *Henry IV* plays, and his revisionary retrospects afford at least limited
access to what went on (or goes on) in *Richard II*. The relation between Gaunt
and Richard is resolved with considerable stridency by the time Act II, Scene i
of the first play is over.

The general tenor of Richard's attitude toward Gaunt may be caught by
trying to listen with Gaunt's ears to Richard's opening words:

> Old John of Gaunt, time-honoured Lancaster,
> Hast thou according to thy oath and band
> Brought hither Henry Herford thy bold son,
> Here to make good the boist'rous late appeal,
> Which then our leisure would not let us hear,
> Against the Duke of Norfolk, Thomas Mowbray?
> *Gaunt:* I have, my liege.

$$(\text{I.i. } 1-7)$$

The chiasmic patterning of name–title–title–name in the first and last lines works to Gaunt's detriment, since the last line lacks modifiers which Richard so pointedly uses in the first. The blunt and familiar opening, "Old John of Gaunt," edges the elegant variation that follows it with faint sarcasm. Richard pushes on the tonal difference between personal and ritual address, converts apposition into opposition, makes the second epithet sound like a euphemistic or mystified equivalent of the first. Then, turning from father to son, his alliterative coupling of "bold" with "boist'rous" reduces the ambivalent first term to its negative connotation: under the pressure of the meanings of "boisterous" (rough, coarse, clamorous, unskillful) "bold" shifts from "fearless" or "confident" to "presumptuous" or "forward." At the same time the combination of "son" and "boist'rous" tends to diminish Bolingbroke – to *boy* him – and to stress Gaunt's responsibility for his son's good behavior.

In the lines that follow the opening exchange, Richard continues to press on Gaunt's role as surety:

> *Richard:* Tell me, moreover, hast thou sounded him,
> If he appeal the Duke on ancient malice,
> Or worthily as a good subject should
> On some known ground of treachery in him?
> *Gaunt:* As near as I could sift him on that argument,
> On some apparent danger seen in him,
> Aim'd at your Highness, no inveterate malice.

$$(\text{I.i. } 8-14)$$

Although Richard's questions are clearly ceremonial, and therefore rhetorical, he puts them to aggressive use not merely in picking away at Gaunt's responsibility for the good faith of the appeal but also in trying to elicit a response that will reveal the extent of the knowledge, and perhaps complicity, Gaunt shares with his son. The response is evasive: not "*known* ground of treachery" but "*apparent* danger seen." The measured, heavily stopped blank verse of Gaunt's vague reply expresses the care he takes to dissociate himself from any appearance of complicity or knowledge. We hear much in later scenes about his view of Richard and England, but never a word about his relation to Bolingbroke's appeal – or, for that matter, about his relation to Bolingbroke. This is the subject which the following textual excavation aims to elucidate.

Bolingbroke prefaces his accusation of Mowbray with words in which, as the Arden editor observes, he "takes care to explain . . . the purity of his motives":

> In the devotion of a subject's love,
> Tend'ring the precious safety of my prince,
> And free from other misbegotten hate,
> Come I appellant to this princely presence.
>
> (I.i.31–4)

While "other misbegotten hate" answers to Richard's "ancient malice" and thus apparently has Mowbray as its object, the vagueness of both phrases gives them a wider sweep, for in the background of the appeal lies the murder of Gloucester which is the climactic and most heavily stressed of the three articles in Bolingbroke's accusations: "misbegotten hate" may refer to the family feud and the motive for revenge.

In the rhetorical climax of his accusation, Bolingbroke asserts that Gloucester's blood,

> like sacrificing Abel's, cries
> Even from the tongueless caverns of the earth
> To me for justice and rough chastisement;
> And, by the glorious worth of my descent,
> This arm shall do it, or this life be spent.
>
> (I.i.104–8)

His generational logic is less shaky than it seems, for why should Gloucester's blood be like the archetypal murdered *brother's*, and why should it cry to *him* to be God's surrogate in this affair, unless he is replacing the father whose consenting silence amounts to symbolic fratricide, and whose "unwilling tongue" (I.iii.245) diminishes "the glorious worth" of Bolingbroke's descent from Edward III? It is to these lines that Richard/Cain responds: "How high a pitch his resolution soars!" (109). A few lines later, assuring Mowbray of his impartiality, he redefines the lineal scheme to his own advantage:

> Were he my brother, nay, my kingdom's heir,
> As he is but my father's brother's son,
> Now by my sceptre's awe I make a vow,
> Such neighbour nearness to our sacred blood
> Should nothing privilege him
>
> (I.i.116–20)

As Kittredge observes, the second line is a "slighting antithesis to 'my kingdom's heir.'" Though the derogation of Gaunt is here only a move in the game of lineal checkers, the opening words of the play had already begun to establish Richard's disdain for his uncle, and this impression is situationally reinforced shortly after when Gaunt participates in the tactic Richard employs to frustrate Bolingbroke's justice. In jingling rhymes whose flippancy sharpens the calculated tone of affront, Richard makes Gaunt share the onus of his arbitrary interruption of the ritual: "Good uncle, let this end where it begun; / We'll calm the Duke of Norfolk, you your son" (158–9). Gaunt complies with a disingenuous aphorism that avails itself of Richard's opening, "Old John of Gaunt," to activate the weakling's plea, senility: "To be a make-peace shall become my age. / Throw down, my son, the Duke of Norfolk's gage" (160–1).

Bolingbroke directs his bitter refusal to Richard, and continues insulting Mowbray, but if in reading his words we pretend once again to be listening with Gaunt's ears, we may feel that his son's sentiments towards those two targets are not entirely displaced:

> O God defend my soul from such deep sin!
> Shall I seem crest-fallen in my father's sight?
> Or with pale beggar-fear impeach my height
> Before this out-dar'd dastard? Ere my tongue
> Shall wound my honour with such feeble wrong,
> Or sound so base a parle, my teeth shall tear
> The slavish motive of recanting fear,
> And spit it bleeding in his high disgrace,
> Where shame doth harbour, even in Mowbray's face.
>
> (I.i.187–95)

The second line contains the only verbal acknowledgment of his father's presence made by Bolingbroke in this scene. It is ceremonially correct: he salutes the immediate source of "the glorious worth of my descent" and states his unwillingness to dishonor the source by displaying cowardice before his father's eyes. Nevertheless, this line gives the whole speech the capacity to strike daggers into any ears pretending to be Gaunt's.

Since Gaunt commanded the display, the ritual force of the rhetorical question changes to "shall I let my father have the satisfaction of watching me perform the base act he and Richard urged on me?" The question that follows may then be heard as intensifying the speaker's sense of outrage: "Is this what you ask me to do, lower my crest by impeaching my height with a display of fear?" The parallelism of the prepositional clauses that end each question places Gaunt and Mowbray in the same position. This adds interest to "out-dar'd": it does not characterize Mowbray's behavior, and as a ritual insult it does not have to, but it can be applied with some justice to Gaunt who, unwilling to avenge or speak up for his brother himself, seconded the king's attempt to frustrate Bolingbroke's appeal "for justice and rough chastisement." His son's refusal to be infected with this shameful fear-bred silence challenges Gaunt's self-imposed tonguelessness: the amputated tongue symbolizes the father's "feeble wrong" ("Ere my [father] / Shall wound my honour"), and the hyperbolic violence directed at this ritual surrogate is at once masked and enabled by the careful emphasis of the final clause, "even in Mowbray's face." This displacement effectively makes the speech self-referential, for Bolingbroke is spitting his challenge to Gaunt in Mowbray's face.

Our evidence for decoding the meant or unmeant messages one character receives from another's words comes from the meant or unmeant meaning transmitted through his own words. Gaunt's words to the Duchess, which follow almost immediately after Bolingbroke's speech, register an uneasiness that suggests he is belatedly directing toward her the kind of lame excuse he might wish to make toward his son; yet at the same time they register more aggressive feelings:

> Alas, the part I had in Woodstock's blood
> Doth more solicit me than your exclaims
> To stir against the butchers of his life;
> But since correction lieth in those hands
> Which made the fault that we cannot correct,
> Put we our quarrel to the will of heaven,
> Who, when they see the hours ripe on earth,
> Will rain hot vengeance on offenders' heads.
>
> (I. ii. 1–8)

Gaunt is very careful here with his plural forms and shifters, and though we immediately identify "the butchers," "those hands," and "offenders," "they" in line 7 is less obvious – what divine, angelic, or human avengers pluralize "the will of heaven"? When will they judge the time to be ripe? And into what saving community of "we" does the first person of lines 1–2 vanish? If the apocalyptic excuse is meant to suggest a more legitimately sanctioned revenge than his son's effort, and one from which Gaunt will be spared, what could that possibly be? The vagueness of "offenders," lacking the article that would link it more closely to particular "butchers" and "hands," implies something not less encompassing and remote than the psalmist's wish for fire and brimstone, or the Last Judgment; it measures the sense of justified helplessness Gaunt encodes in the "we" of line 5; hence according to the logic of his argument those who wrongly attempt correction will join the offenders at the general doom. In I. i he had heard his son say that he would make his challenge to Mowbray "good upon this earth, / Or my divine soul answer it in heaven" (37–8), and buried in Gaunt's words to the Duchess is a protest against that arrogance.

The Duchess, however, does not let Gaunt slip off into the Elizabethan world picture, nor even into the sunset of his declining years: "Finds brotherhood in thee no sharper spur? / Hath love in thy old blood no living fire?" (9–10). She accuses him of something very like the "pale beggar-fear" and "feeble wrong" spat out by Bolingbroke:

> thou dost consent
> In some large measure to thy father's death
> In that thou seest thy wretched brother die,
> Who was the model of thy father's life.
> Call it not patience, Gaunt, it is despair;
> In suff'ring thus thy brother to be slaught'red,
> Thou showest the naked pathway to thy life,
> Teaching stern murder how to butcher thee.
> That which in mean men we intitle patience
> Is pale cold cowardice in noble breasts.
> What shall I say? to safeguard thine own life,
> The best way is to venge my Gloucester's death.
>
> (I. ii. 25–36)

In these words Gaunt could well hear Bolingbroke's allusion to symbolic fratricide repeated as a direct accusation, intensified by conversion to symbolic parricide.

He defends himself with an aggressive restatement of the Tudor ideology:

> God's is the quarrel – for God's substitute,
> His deputy anointed in His sight,
> Hath caus'd his death; the which if wrongfully,
> Let heaven revenge, for I may never lift
> An angry arm against His minister.
>
> (I. ii. 37–41)

These words both acknowledge his feeble wrong and register the need to justify it more fully by rejecting the Duchess's appeal to the vendetta ethic. The concluding lines use the Tudor theory to rationalize his own "patience," but they also imply a criticism of Bolingbroke's impatient arm. To Dover Wilson they seemed to "condemn in advance the usurpation of his son . . . after his death,"[4] but I think the observed connection to Bolingbroke is strengthened by being shifted from the prospective mode of dramatic irony to the retrospective mode of structural irony.

When Gaunt suggests that the Duchess should direct her complaint to "God, the widow's champion and defence," her reply is definitive, and Gaunt makes no answer to it:

> Why then, I will. Farewell, old Gaunt.
> Thou goest to Coventry, there to behold
> Our cousin Herford and fell Mowbray fight.
> O, sit my husband's wrongs on Herford's spear,
> That it may enter butcher Mowbray's breast!
> Or if misfortune miss the first career,
> Be Mowbray's sins so heavy in his bosom
> That they may break his foaming courser's back
> And throw the rider headlong in the lists,
> A caitive recreant to my cousin Herford!
> Farewell, old Gaunt; thy sometimes brother's wife
> With her companion, grief, must end her life.
> *Gaunt:* Sister, farewell; I must to Coventry,
> As much good stay with thee as go with me!
>
> (I. ii. 44–57)

The Duchess refuses to call Bolingbroke Gaunt's son. In the first of her three references to him he is "*Our* cousin" – she shares him equally with Gaunt in a general classificatory relation – and by the third, at l. 53, her possession has become singular. This shift destabilizes the modifier in the next line: we may read it either as "thy brother's sometimes wife" or as "the wife of thy sometimes brother," cut off from Gaunt not only by his death but also by the recreancy that would leave "sacrificing Abel" unavenged, i.e. "you are no longer of 'our faith,' and our extended kin group is now represented by our cousin, not by you; he has assumed your lapsed responsibility." But since the Duchess has already described that lapse as a wrong done to her husband, the implication is even stronger. "O, sit my husband's wrongs on Herford's spear": to replace Gaunt and to redress his wrong is to challenge him to combat. Once again, the "recreant" Mowbray is a ritual scapegoat, and the violent imagery of trial by combat provides a hyperbolic image, a melodramatic outlet, for the displaced expression of sentiments that might be less easy to entertain toward Gaunt.

The argument I have excavated from the tongueless caverns of the Duchess's language is that Bolingbroke has replaced – indeed, displaced – his father as the true son of Edward III and brother of Gloucester, and that some defensive and even resentful recognition of the argument is embedded in Gaunt's language. When I read "Hath love in thy old blood no living fire?" I recall and refocus Gaunt's "To be a make-peace shall become my age," seeing it now tinged by rueful and bitter, if resigned, acknowledgment of the trimmer's role he has assumed in others' eyes – tinged also by a more aggressive complement: "To be a troublemaker becomes his youth."

The Duchess names Gaunt four times in this scene: she calls him "Gaunt" twice in her opening speech when she still hopes to persuade him to action, but switches to "old Gaunt" after he has referred her to God, the widow's champion, and she turns instead to Herford for succor. I think the contexts in which the Duchess, Richard, and Gaunt himself refer to his age – whether in epithets, descriptions, or puns – almost always skewer the reference on the sharp sword of the father/son interaction: when his authority over Boling-broke is invoked or being called into question (I.i. 1, 160, 162–3); when – as here – Bolingbroke's challenge is contrastively related to his own ideologic-ally toned evasions; and when, after being party to his son's banishment, he complains to Richard that it will hasten his death (I.iii. 216–32).

Under the pressure of these contexts and their language, "old" and "gaunt" become Gaunt's defensive weapons in the struggle between father and son that marks the passage of patriarchal authority from predecessor to succes-sor, aged to young, old to new – it would be better to say the passage of phallic power, since my excavation leads me to conclude that the play's language characterizes Gaunt not only as pleading impotence, and not only as accused of it, but also as symbolically "castrated" by Bolingbroke's challenge. And this is the conclusion I want to carry as a hypothesis into the third scene of Act I: Bolingbroke's presence and behavior are a standing rebuke to Gaunt; he feels accused and challenged, replaced and excelled, by his son; Bolingbroke's innuendoes in I.i, reinforced by the Duchess's charges in I.ii, point toward a father who has been "deposed," or self-deposed, having allowed his son to "usurp" his place and function in the generational order; thus to see and be seen by his son ("in my father's sight") may not cause him unmitigated joy, and this occasions another speculation: will it cause him unmitigated grief to be relieved of that presence?

"As much good stay with thee as go with me": the limp sentiment with which Gaunt takes his leave hardly suggests that he is any more eager to rush off to Coventry than he is to linger on and hear the Duchess talk about it. The contrast to Bolingbroke is driven home in the opening lines of I.iii:

Mar: My Lord Aumerle, is Harry Herford arm'd?
Aum: Yea, at all points, and longs to enter in.

Bolingbroke does not immediately appear, however; Mowbray enters and speaks first. Ritual purists complain that the appellant should have preceded the defendant into the lists.[5] But the reversed order makes possible an interesting variation in Richard's two requests to the Marshall to administer the oath of justice. For Mowbray, he uses these words: "swear him in the justice of his cause." But for Bolingbroke the formula is significantly altered, and I think the significance is underlined by its contrast to the earlier request: "Depose him in the justice of his cause." Reading the word that names the central action of the play, I succumb to the charm of several temptations. First, of course, the pun invites a proleptic interpretation – as if Richard already sees Bolingbroke crowned and pronounces a curse ("Let him be deposed") that nevertheless reflects awareness of his own unjust regime. This implies a second alternative, "Depose *me* in the justice of his cause," from which I slide helplessly into the pleasure of imagining either or both statements as expressions of Gaunt's dilemma: "if my son is 'deposed' by Mowbray, his cause will be proved unjust, *ergo*, I shall be justified, but if his cause is just, I am 'deposed.'"

A similar temptation is dropped in my path by Richard's leavetaking of Bolingbroke:

> We will descend and fold him in our arms.
> Cousin of Herford, as thy cause is right,
> So be thy fortune in this royal fight!
> Farewell, my blood; which if to-day thou shed,
> Lament we may, but not revenge thee dead.
>
> (I. iii. 54–8)

In the first line I see not only a foreshadowing of the deposition scene but a condensed visualization of Richard's latent project as it unfolds through the play, here displaced to the physical circumstance of a ceremonial gesture. The rhythm accentuates the *will* to descend; the second phrase is a kinesic hyperbole that mimes the desire coupling Richard to Bolingbroke in their dance toward deposition and regicide, and toward the subsequent regime, when the embrace gradually becomes a stranglehold. This line chimes with "Depose" and with the odd reference to "royal fight" as an element of the proleptic rhetoric threading glints of the latent project through the first and third scenes of the play.

The second couplet adds another element: Richard's message is that if Bolingbroke loses he will unjustly have shed the "high blood" his royal kinsman shares, but his language also lets the alternate message, "if you kill me," flicker briefly before us. In the final line, the alert excavator might discern another displacement. While the statement is sardonic in Richard's mouth – as if he might be expected to avenge his kinsman and has to explain that he won't – it crisply epitomizes the attitude Gaunt expressed in I. ii: "Lament" = "Alas, the part I had in Woodstock's blood"; "but not revenge" = "I may never lift / An angry arm," since Mowbray will have proved to be heaven's minister.

In the balanced duplicity of these lines Richard flaunts his mastery of the rhetorical tease. He (con)descends to favor Bolingbroke with a hug and a word of tepid encouragement (by the judicial logic of trial by combat, "as" in l. 55 must mean "if," not "since"), then devotes the last line and a half to harping on his possible defeat. Rhymes, end-stopping, and echoing caesuras add bite to his wicked tongue – the finality, certainty, and witty detachment of aphoristic or recited speech. This is political, not merely poetic, mastery. Even as he folds the successor-to-be in his arms, he sends the usurper-to-be off with a dry-eyed mock. Bolingbroke parries the mock in answering couplets that are more forceful but less balanced and assured:

> O, let no noble eye profane a tear
> For me, if I be gor'd with Mowbray's spear!
> As confident as is the falcon's flight
> Against a bird, do I with Mowbray fight.
>
> (I. iii. 59–62)

This begins well with "profane a tear"; the lament would be profaned not only by his unworthiness but also because it would indubitably be feigned. Yet the expansive energy of his heroic clichés flags suddenly at the end of each enjambment. The falcon comes down on its prey more confidently than the figure does on "a bird." The trajectory of Bolingbroke's career, its brief upward surge and long anticlimax, is epitomized in this rhythm. His real contest is not the physical encounter with Mowbray but the verbal encounter with Richard, and, behind that, the silent encounter with Gaunt. The putative referent of the words – the anticipated fight with Mowbray – is actually the signifier of the present power struggle that goes on, and will continue to go on, within the "fair designs" of the rhetorical lists.

After two unrhymed lines of farewell to Richard and Aumerle, and a summary couplet broadcasting his self-assurance, Bolingbroke winds up for the climax of his speech – his farewell to Gaunt – with an odd simile: "Lo, as at English feasts, so I regreet / The daintiest last, to make the end most sweet" (I. iii. 67–8). The figure implies that these "ceremonious" farewells and salutes are things to be savored, things to be consumed. The farewell salute to Gaunt will be the tastiest morsel. Bolingbroke's emphasis is on rhetorical pleasure and performance rather than on the illocutionary force of the sentiment; he will confect a filial dessert of sweetly end-stopped pieties. Yet, once again, the language writhes out of his control and serves up a more disconcerting message:

> O thou, the earthly author of my blood,
> Whose youthful spirit in me regenerate
> Doth with a twofold vigour lift me up
> To reach at victory above my head,
> Add proof unto mine armour with thy prayers,
> And with thy blessings steel my lance's point,
> That it may enter Mowbray's waxen coat,
> And furbish new the name of John a Gaunt,
> Even in the lusty haviour of his son.
>
> (I. iii. 69–77)

The frame or crust of this trifle is a request for blessing; the filler is a respectful *æmulatio*. But from under the mock modesty of the fourth line something interesting begins to bubble forth. "To reach . . . above my head" can hardly refer to victory over Mowbray; whatever the speaker intends, the words are steeled (or stolen) by another sky-aspiring proleptic allusion: they point toward Richard. Then, with "furbish," they become more abrasive as their lance passes almost too easily from Mowbray's waxen coat to Gaunt's rusty name. Ure makes a good case for preferring the Quarto's "furbish" to the Folio's "furnish"; "Besides its more general meaning of 'clean up,' *furbish* means 'scour the rust from armour' . . . so Gaunt's 'name' (honour, repute) is also his armour, and the metaphor continues the references to arms and armour in the preceding lines."[6] But it also joins with "new" to scratch away at the film of self-apology Gaunt has coated his name with – "*Old* John of *Gaunt*." It is the *former* spirit of Gaunt's youth that Bolingbroke invokes to help the falcon soar to the height of his heavenly author's quarrel; a spirit that died and now revives only in the "lusty haviour" of the son whose angry arm will "scour the rust" from his earthly author's (and his family's) once untarnished honor.

   Bolingbroke's English confection thus concludes as a challenge to Gaunt to support his cause: the son's victory will clear his father's name. The name-clearing problem places Gaunt in a classic double bind, since he also seems to want a clear name in the court's eyes and those of God's anointed deputy. This problem comes into focus after the interruption when Richard reminds him that his "tongue a party-verdict gave" to his son's banishment (I. iii. 234). Gaunt's rueful reaction to the verdict and to his share in it is troubled by his strident protest of non-responsibility. But I think it is also troubled by the deceptively truistic distinction with which he justifies himself:

> You urg'd me as a judge, but I had rather
> You would have bid me argue like a father.
> O, had it been a stranger, not my child,
> To smooth his fault I should have been more mild.
> A partial slander sought I to avoid,
> And in the sentence my own life destroy'd.
> Alas, I look'd when some of you should say
> I was too strict to make mine own away;
> But you gave leave to my unwilling tongue
> Against my will to do myself this wrong.
>
> (I. iii. 237–46)

The first couplet says that if he had been arguing as a father he would have been more mild. The second couplet says that if he had been arguing as a non-father he would have been more mild. The first couplet implies that he argued as a non-father in order to avoid the charge of prejudice. The second couplet implies that being less mild in order to avoid the charge of prejudice is acting like a father. But consider also the following variation: "Because it was no stranger but my child, / I could not smooth his fault or be more mild." This more directly conveys the message that the partiality of the loving father is not toward any child but toward a guilty child. Gaunt acknowledges his son's fault, confesses to a father's impulse to overlook it (only a "child," after all), and goes on to lament the strictness of the loyal and obedient subject forced to suppress the impulse in the interest of justice. In this parable, the primary focus of self-presentation is on the trials of the good father. Gaunt is smoothing faults all around – Richard's, his own – and the smoothness penetrates the syrupy rhymes and rhythms of his speech.

What the speech actually suppresses is the fear and guilt of the bad father, who pleads the avoidance of partiality to cover other motives for being less mild to a son than to a stranger. He blames others for letting himself destroy his life and for not telling him "I was too strict to make mine own away." The elliptical strain of this phrase betrays the pressure of his not mentioning what he is doing to his "child": insofar as "make . . . away" is apposite to "my own life destroy'd," it means "do away with"; but insofar as it refers to Bolingbroke's exile it means "send away." In the blurring together of these senses, "mine own" opens up to include not only his upright self-sacrifice but also the sacrifice of his son that enables him to avoid a partial slander. "Mine own" justifies both sacrifices, because it suggests that his son, like his life, is his possession, to dispose with as he judges right. This judgment, he explains, is the source of his grief. Yet further reflection will show that it is also the effect of his guilt, which it reinforces.

Since Gaunt's conversation with the Duchess established his interest in making himself and others believe that it is wrong to oppose the king, we can imagine him seeing Bolingbroke's *de facto* challenge to Richard through the medium of Mowbray as a fault in which he could easily be implicated as an accomplice to a plot fomented by the Gloucester faction. This changes the import of "partial slander" from "accusation of leniency" to "accusation of complicity": it would have been easier for him to smooth the fault of a stranger whose questionable motives did not glance at him. What could make his party-verdict doubly painful is his sense that he has sacrificed his son to clear himself. His behavior constitutes a betrayal of Bolingbroke and his cause; worse than that, it expresses a desire to betray his son. He looked in vain for others to temper this ignoble impulse. The unstable syntax of the final couplet betrays the effect of their failure. Construed as a redundant negative construction, it says that both he and his tongue were unwilling to do himself the injury of voting for his son's exile, or to inflict on his son the injury he ignobly desired to inflict. But construed as an antithetical construction – "[my unwilling tongue] / Against [my will to do myself this wrong]" – it says that he had a will, a desire, to do this wrong, that he was unwilling to actualize the desire in speech, but that Richard's urging prevailed upon him.

The conclusion of this strenuous excavation of Gaunt's lines is that they betray his fear of being contaminated by Bolingbroke's action; his reluctant agreement to the sentence of exile in response to that fear; the desire to defeat the son who challenges him; the guilt occasioned in him by that desire and by an agreement that sacrifices his son's interest to his own; and the attempt to assuage that guilt by blaming his party-verdict on others, an attempt that could only increase the corrosive power of self-despite. What destroys his life, then, what makes him gaunt for the grave, is not merely grief at being separated from his son, perhaps forever, but guilt at having willed to do his son that wrong. On Bolingbroke's side, the father/son conflict is concealed, enabled, exacerbated by a double displacement: from Gaunt to Richard to Mowbray; from father to king to peer. Mowbray serves as the medium in which are condensed Bolingbroke's darker purpose, to accuse the king, and his darkest purpose, to rebuke his father.

The centrality of this conflict in the *Henriad* is obvious and has often been noted, but never with reference to Gaunt and Bolingbroke. As I stated at the beginning of the essay, my purpose in excavating their relationship has been to situate an interpretation in the most antitheatrical reaches of the text in order to position myself "outside" the politico-historical and dramatico-theatrical narrative privileged by stage-centered criticism. This positioning (or positing) allows me to interpret the emergence of that narrative in functional terms as a defensive transformation of latencies in the text, and to explore the dialectic by which Shakespeare represents the meaning of theatrical drama in those terms. I conclude with a brief reading of a passage that will open up onto a summary overview of the process I have been discussing.

Early in the play Richard commands the appearance of Bolingbroke and Mowbray in characteristically tortured syntax:

> Then call them to our presence; face to face,
> And frowning brow to brow, ourselves will hear
> The accuser and the accused freely speak.
>
> (I.i.15–17)

"Face to face, / And frowning brow to brow": leading off thus with a pair of unbound modifier phrases frees them up for serial redefinition. In a first fleeting mirage they seem to describe Richard confronting the other two as *his* antagonists and/or appellants. This gives way to a second when the strangely pluralized royal plural suggests that he confronts and/or accuses himself. Finally, the opposed selves are bound to their proper ritual representatives in l. 17, and their proper ritualized representation in ll. 18–19, an event celebrated with the play's first rhymed couplet: "High-stomach'd are they both and full of ire, / In rage, deaf as the sea, hasty as fire."

The shift in these six lines from enjambed, internally stopped blank verse to end-stressed rhymed verse reinforces the shift from uncertain syntax and rapidly changing impressions to the too predictable formulas of chivalric rhetoric, which in this case produces an oxymoronic relation between what is said and how it is said: the analogies of nature are clichés of art; the reported unruliness of the combatants is overruled by the measured rhythm of the report, by its discountable literary hyperboles. And there is a sense in which their rage will be as artificial and literary as the language, a sense in which the "report" is actually a self-fulfilling stage direction that prescribes the emotions and behavior appropriate to culturally prefabricated roles embedded in a certain institutional narrative. The rage will also be artificial because it will be ritually displaced and misdirected.

The shifts described above combine to mark the most fundamental process that structures this drama: the passage and transformation of conflict from the tongueless caverns of some "hidden imposthume" to the safety of the sanctioned artifice and "fair designs" of ritualized combat and behavior. In the *Henriad* the equivalents of Hamlet's phrase are, like his, carefully vague, as if keeping their distance from the miasma they fear to touch: "buried fear," "some other grief," "inward wars." The passage from this latent content to the manifest fictions of ritual embodiment is perfectly described by Lafew in *All's Well That Ends Well*: "we make trifles of terrors, ensconcing ourselves into seeming knowledge when we should submit ourselves to an unknown fear" (II. iii. 3 ff.). A sconce is a fortress, and in *Richard II* the conspicuous trifles, the stiff and stilted formulas, of ritual are the palisades that impose quarantine against the miasma:

> I'll answer thee in any fair degree
> Or chivalrous design of knightly trial
> > (I. i. 80–1)

> On pain of death, no person be so bold
> Or daring-hardy as to touch the lists,
> Except the marshall and such officers
> Appointed to direct these fair designs.
> > (I. iii. 42–5)

The textual confusions buried in Richard's call to the combatants resonate with obscure, labile, and dangerous power struggles – rooted in fear, guilt, aggressivity, self-contempt, and Janus-faced desire – that defy closure and shun exposure; his final couplet visualizes the dramatic form in which they can find legitimate heroic expression and narrative resolution.

Trial by combat displaces, condenses, dramatizes, and thereby at once represses and represents such "inward wars" as those that divide a father from his son and from himself. Shakespeare's achievement lies in making the "fair designs" represent and be touched by the miasma they eschew. The prescribed rhetoric of ritual speech and action is shown to be inadequate to deal with or represent whatever "other grief" is buried in the language of the dramatic community. It is precisely its inadequacy, its parodic and artificial character, that lets the ritual function as a mode of concealment enabling the hidden struggles to continue. To borrow René Girard's terms, if trial by combat is a caricature of *differentiation*, Shakespeare presents it as such by encouraging us to search his text for the undifferentiating forces that produce the caricature as its instrument. Cutting across the differentiating boundaries of the nominal combatants and subjects of dispute, the text throws anamorphic shadows that bathe the empty glitter of ceremonial speech in a rich chiaroscuro.

Girard's distinction was formulated not for the analysis of a particular ritual but for all ritual, including what he refers to as the "surface play," and I have argued elsewhere that the surface play is the one privileged by theatrical performance.[7] My concluding incautious generalizations are that the preceding comments on trial by combat apply to Shakespeare's representation of the "fair designs" of theatrical performance on its audience; apply to dramatic fiction, whether staged or not; apply to any transformational interaction between the excavated meanings of the text and the speech assigned to names we conventionally reify and imagine as persons. They apply wherever language is distributed among the embodied subjects who speak it. The *meta*morphosis of text into bodies produces conspicuous *ana*morphosis that has the same function and effects as those of the "fair designs" of trial by combat. Socially or culturally produced structures of embodiment – of presences, subjects, characters, roles, individuals – are quarantines against the "discourse of the Other" (Lacan) that smokes the edges of clear visualization and ambiguates simple location. The plastic design behind that mode of production is to *pre-vent* "bad humors" by providing identities and stories the actors can live with, narratives that enable them to discharge those humors while preserving unawareness and self-esteem. The embodiment of presence is thus the building of Lafew's sconce.

Shakespeare's text, then, is not the representation of drama *per se* but rather the representation of its construction *out of* the text's discourse of the Other and *against* that discourse – the representation and, in the positive sense, the critique of the self-concealing motivational conditions of embodiment. Insofar as theatrical performance is the ritual reinforcement of the drive to embodiment, its actualization in living bodies, it intensifies the defensive flight of drama from text, imposing itself on the contours of drama like a template that masks its underlying textuality. Shakespeare's metatheatrical critique of theater is, as we know, contained within his metadramatic critique of drama. These are enabling, not inhibiting, critiques: they support his production of dramatic fictions and theatrical performances in a transgressive manner, that is, by clearly signaling their limits, laying bare the motives behind their production, adumbrating a textual dimension at once implicit in them and beyond them. To represent performed drama *as* a flight from text is to enrich it with the transcendent fringe of meanings, the signifying nothing conspicuously concealed by the sound and fury of the words, conspicuously frustrated by the splendors of embodiment. The fury, splendor, and frustration can be experienced together only in performance; we have to feel the presence and pressure of the theatrical template, submit to its fair designs, in order to measure both *its* power and the shadowy counterforce of the power it represses. The politics of that repression cannot be borne home to us in any other way. But the fury, splendor, frustration, and politics can only be understood and evaluated by the excavation that psychoanalyzes the text.

Notes

1. Property interests may not account for all aspects of the appeal of primogeniture. Both the hierarchic and the genealogical principles of mimesis surely contribute something. The father wishes to replicate *himself*, not *himselves*. There is support for the primacy of the firstborn as *image* in both Testaments.
2. All passages of the play are quoted from the New Arden Shakespeare edition: *King Richard II*, ed. Peter Ure, 5th edn (London, 1961). Passages from 2 *Henry IV* and *King Lear* are quoted from the New Arden Shakespeare editions: *King Henry IV Part 2*, ed. A. R. Humphreys (London, 1966); *King Lear*, ed. Kenneth Muir (London, 1972).
3. "Plato's pharmacy," in *Dissemination*, tr. Barbara Johnson (Chicago, 1981), 139.
4. *The Life and Death of King Richard the Second*, ed. Matthew W. Black, in *A New Variorum Edition of Shakespeare*, 27 (Philadelphia, 1955), 44.
5. *Variorum*, 50 f. Another complaint is that Mowbray should have been summoned by a herald, not by "the appellant's trumpet" (4). It is as if a second trial, a shadow trial, is being conducted, with the appellant usurping the function of the "officers / Appointed to direct these fair designs" (44–5), but doing so to peculiar effect, since Mowbray and whomever he represents (Richard? Gaunt?) thereby usurp Bolingbroke's role as appellant and are placed in a position to accuse him. And this, in short, is the story of Henry Bolingbroke in the *Henriad*.
6. Arden edn, 26.
7. "Text against performance in Shakespeare: the example of *Macbeth*" (*Genre*, 15 (1982), 49–79). See also René Girard, *Violence and the Sacred*, tr. Patrick Gregory (Baltimore, 1977).

12

THOMAS M. GREENE

Pitiful thrivers: failed husbandry in the Sonnets

Sonnet 125 of Shakespeare's collection ("Wer't ought to me I bore the canopy") is the penultimate poem in the series addressed to the male friend. It is the last complete sonnet in this series, and in comparison with its somewhat slighter successor, 126, it appears to offer a more substantial, dense, and conclusive instrument of retrospection. It opens by distinguishing the poet from those who court his friend's love by means of external gestures, "dwellers on forme and favor," but who see their calculations fail and are condemned to admire the young man from a distance: "Pittifull thrivors in their gazing spent." The poet's own devotion, he claims, consists purely of uncalculated internal gestures and it leads to a genuine, unmediated exchange.

> Noe, let me be obsequious in thy heart,
> And take thou my oblacion, poore but free,
> Which is not mixt with seconds, knows no art,
> But mutuall render onely me for thee.[1]

The couplet dismisses a "subbornd *Informer*," a slanderer who might accuse the poet himself of dwelling on form. But despite this calumny, the affirmation of the "mutuall render" between the two men acquires in the context of the whole collection a peculiar resonance. It can be regarded as a culminating moment in the twisting history of their relationship, and our understanding of the outcome of the "plot" in Sonnets 1–126 depends in part on our interpretation of this phrase. Contrariwise, fully to grasp the implications of the phrase and the sonnet requires consideration of all that precedes, and even to some degree what follows. An informed reading will necessitate a long swing backward before returning to 125.

Within its immediate context, this is the third of three successive sonnets affirming that the poet's love for his friend is untouched by external accidents. This succession (123–5) needs to be read in the light of an earlier group (109–12) alluding to the poet's shameful and scandalous conduct and another group (117–21) alluding to the poet's apparent neglect and betrayal of the friend. Thus, if one attributes validity to the Quarto sequence, the three protests of uncalculating devotion follow almost directly an experience of partial rupture, and they attempt to cement a reconciliation which has been to some degree in doubt.

But from a wider perspective, Sonnet 125 is responding to problems raised from the very opening of the collection. Its resolution of pure exchange could be said to respond to the anxiety of cosmic and existential economics which haunts the Sonnets and which marks their opening line: "From fairest creatures we desire increase." The paronomasia which links the two nouns translates phonetically the poet's obsessive concern with metaphorical wealth, profit, worth, value, expense, "store," "content." The "pittifull thrivors" of 125 take their place in a line of disappointed or misguided would-be thrivers distributed throughout the work. The "mutuall render," if in fact it is successful, would thus bring to a happy conclusion a quest for an adequate economic system which would avoid the "wast or ruining" and the excessive "rent" which burden those in 125 who vainly spend themselves. Up to the climactic reciprocity at the close of that sonnet, the sequence to the young man has provided very little by way of stable exchange systems.

The first of the pitiful thrivers is the onanistic friend as he appears in the opening 17 "procreation" sonnets. By refusing to marry and to beget children, he "makst wast in niggarding" (1); he becomes a "profitles userer" "having traffike with [him] selfe alone" (4). The procreation sonnets display with particular brilliance Shakespeare's ability to manipulate words which in his language belonged both to the economic and the sexual/biological semantic fields: among others, "increase," "use," "spend," "free," "live," "dear," "house," "usury," "endowed," along with their cognates. The umbrella-pun which covers them all, and which establishes a semantic node for the whole collection, lies in still another word: "husbandry":

> For where is she so faire whose un-eard wombe
> Disdaines the tillage of thy husbandry? (3)

The *ad hoc* meaning "marriage" joins the traditional meanings of "thrift," "estate management," "agriculture," and, by means of a conventional metaphor, coition as ploughing. When the pun returns ten sonnets later, the dominant meaning will emerge as management:

> Who lets so faire a house fall to decay,
> Which husbandry in honour might uphold,
> Against the stormy gusts of winters day
> And barren rage of deaths eternall cold? (13)

"House" means both the friend's body (the *banhus*, "bonehouse," of the Anglo-Saxon kenning) and the family line. The bourgeois poet accuses the aristocratic friend of a dereliction of those responsibilities incumbent on the land-owning class. The apparent implication is that through marriage the friend could "live" (4), could make a profit by perpetuating his family.

But if, in the procreation sonnets, thriving seems ostensibly within the young man's grasp, one must recognize nonetheless the disproportionate force of the thwarting power, the "barren rage of deaths eternall cold." Procreation progressively comes to appear as a desperate defense, a final maneuver against a principle which is ultimately irresistible.

> And nothing gainst Times sieth [scythe] can make defence
> Save breed to brave him, when he takes thee hence. (12)

The recurrent terror of "winters wragged hand" (6), particularly notable in this opening group, comes to cast doubt on the viability of marriage. Or rather, in view of the threatening "barenes everywhere" (5), husbandry emerges as a universal, existential concern that transcends the addressee's marital status. It even becomes a concern of the poetry we are reading, which alternately promises to "ingraft" the friend anew in the war with Time (15) only to describe itself as "barren" in the sequel (16). The friend, "making a famine where aboundance lies" (1), may after all be closer to the governing principle of the world, in which case the poet and his poetry are left in a confusing limbo.

Thus a terrible fear of cosmic destitution overshadows the husbandry of the procreation sonnets, a fear in excess of the announced argument, not easily circumscribed, rendering the bourgeois desire for "store" more urgent, eccentric, and obsessive. In the main body of the sonnets to the young man (18–126), this fear continues to find frequent expression but it is also localized much more explicitly in the poet's feelings about himself. The poetry reflects a sense of inner depletion, emptiness, poverty, which the friend is asked or stated to fill up; elsewhere it reflects a nakedness which the friend is asked to clothe. Sometimes the language evoking the friend's role might suggest literal patronage; elsewhere it might suggest a literal filling up through sex; but each of these literalizations taken alone would reduce the quality of the expressed need. The sense of depletion is more radical and more diffuse, and it is inseparable from feelings of worthlessness and deprivation. Sonnet 29 ("When in disgrace with Fortune . . .") represents the speaker

> Wishing me like to one more rich in hope,
> Featur'd like him, like him with friends possest,
> Desiring this mans art, and that mans skope,
> With what I most inioy contented least. . . .

The language faintly underscores the economic character of this despondency. Friends, if they existed, would be possessed. "Rich in hope" means both "endowed with hope" and "rich in prospect." "Inioy" here means "possess" as well as "take pleasure in" (Booth), thus justifying a secondary reading of "contented least": "poorest in whatever I own of worth." This privation is only relieved by thoughts of the friend: "thy sweet love remembred . . . welth brings," and this transfer is dramatized by the imagistic wealth of the lark simile interrupting the rhetorical bareness of the octave. In the following sonnet, 30 ("When to the Sessions . . ."), the poet laments the deaths of precious friends, moans the expense of many a vanished sight, pays anew "the sad account of fore-bemoned mone," until with remembrance of his friend "all losses are restord, and sorrowes end." In 26 ("Lord of my love . . ."), the poet sends his naked poetry as an offering to his liege lord, hoping that the friend will dress the drab language in "some good conceipt of thine," will "[put] apparell on my tottered loving." Dressing the tottered (tattered) loving might mean making the poet more eloquent or more rich or more accomplished as a lover, but the nakedness seems finally to transcend rhetoric or money or seductiveness. In 38 ("How can my Muse . . ."), the friend is once again filling a void:

> How can my Muse want subiect to invent
> While thou dost breath that poor'st into my verse
> Thine own sweet argument?

The friend plays the masculine role, pouring his worth into the otherwise barren verse, leaving the poet with the travail of giving birth but rightly taking credit for any success: "The paine be mine, but thine shal be the praise." In this economic system, all value seems to reside in the friend, or in *thoughts* of the friend, and the poet seems to be a leaky vessel constantly in need of replenishing, his personal and linguistic poverty never definitively abolished.

This system, however, rests on a shaky basis. The worth of the friend may reside after all in the poet's own fancy, as at least one passage may be understood to suggest:

> So then I am not lame, poore, nor dispis'd,
> Whilst that this shadow doth such substance give,
> That I in thy abundance am suffic'd. (37)

The substance of abundance may actually derive from the shadow of projection. This doubt becomes more plausible as fears of betrayal mount

> Thou best of deerest, and mine onely care,
> Art left the prey of every vulgar theefe. (48)

and as the fears are realized in the young man's affair with the poet's mistress (40–2): "Both finde each other, and I loose both twaine" (42). In other sonnets apparently free of jealousy, a threat to the friend's worth looms from the cosmic mutability already evoked in the procreation sonnets, and now an alternative economic system situates the source of value in the poetry of the Sonnets. The poetry, elsewhere naked, becomes in these poems an artifact that successfully resists time and death, assures eternal life to the one it celebrates, distills his truth for the ages, acts as a perpetuating force against "mortall rage" (64). In the sonnets which affirm this source of value, the young man is represented as a potential victim, helpless against the cosmic principle of destruction, passive, disarmed, doomed without the saving power of "my verse." Verse preserves, engrafts, refurbishes; it seems informed with a masculine force the friend lacks. He remains in this system the beneficiary of a gift his worth draws to itself, but this worth is not otherwise active. "Where alack, shall times best Iewell from times chest lie hid?" (65). The young man's excellence is a plunderable commodity, as it is elsewhere perishable; inert as a precious stone, it belongs to the world of basic elements in flux, "increasing store with losse, and losse with store" (64). The alleged source of genuine "store" in this class of sonnets is the poetry.

Yet it is noteworthy that the affirmations of this linguistic power tend to appear in the couplets of these sonnets (15, 18, 19, 54, 60, 63, 65; exceptions are 55 and 81). The couplets, moreover, tend to lack the energy of the negative vision in the 12 lines that precede them. The final affirmation in its flaccidity tends to refute itself; the *turn* fails to reverse the rhetorical momentum adequately, as the language loses its wealth and its potency while asserting them.

> His beautie shall in these blacke lines be seene,
> And they shall live, and he in them still greene. (63)

> O none, unlesse this miracle have might,
> That in black inck my love may still shine bright. (65)

The turn toward restoration can be read as a desperate bourgeois maneuver, struggling to shore up the cosmic economy against the mutability which instigates true verbal power. The poetry arguably fails to celebrate, refurbish the worth of the young man. The worth remains abstract, faceless, blurred, even when it is not tainted.

Thus we are left with two distinct sources of alleged value, the friend and the poetry, each the basis for a rudimentary economic system, each vulnerable to skepticism. The presence of each system tends to destabilize the other by casting doubt on the kind of value it attempts to establish. To cite the poetic convention behind each system does not adequately deal with its constituent presence in this work. At stake in this conflict of systems is the status and force of the poetic word, which alternately shares its maker's hollowness and serves his (narcissistic?) fantasies of power. The one system, the one relationship which is *not* to be found before the last sonnets to the friend is equal, direct, unmediated reciprocity. Reciprocity is unattainable partly because of the poet's social inferiority and, so to speak, his felt "human" inferiority, because the friend frequently appears in thought, fantasy, or memory rather than in the flesh, because the adulatory style intermittently gives way to suspicion, resentment, fear, anger (33–5, 40–2, 57–8, 67, 69, etc.) which militate negatively against equality, because the friend as an individual remains a "shadow," undescribed, voiceless, hazy, dehumanized by the very superlatives he attracts, and because the poetry, however unclear its status, is repeatedly presented as the binding agent of mediation, an essential go-between. It is not clear whether *any* of the sonnets is to be read as a spoken address, a dramatic monologue, rather than as a written communication. Many of them refer to themselves as written, refer to paper, ink, pens, and to poetic style. They may occasionally affirm a closeness between poet and friend, but their very existence suggests a distance which has to be crossed. We are never allowed to envision unambiguously the poet in the presence of his friend, as we are in love poems by Wyatt, Sidney, Spenser, and Donne.

The conflicting representations of the poetry's power (potent or weak?), its gender (male or female?), its durability (perennial or transient?) together with its mediating function between the two men raise questions about what might be called its rhetorical economics. The poetry is distinguished by its super-charged figurative density, its inexhaustible ramifications of suggestion, its insidious metaphoric multiplications, a superfetation which might have been accumulated to avoid at all cost the alleged danger of nakedness. The poetry could be working to refute its own self-accusations of dearth and repetition.

> Why is my verse so barren of new pride?
> So far from variation or quicke change? . . .
> So all my best is dressing old words new,
> Spending againe what is already spent. (76)

As though to adorn the monotony, every rift is loaded with ore, to the degree that the rhetorical density can be read as an extraordinary effort to exorcize that stylistic poverty the poetry imputes to itself. The poet may feel himself to be depleted, but he evidently owns enough wit to spend it extravagantly. Yet this very supercharging of language tends to heighten a certain impression of linguistic slippage. Metaphors are mixed, replaced by others, recalled, jostled, interfused, inverted, disguised, dangled, eroded, in ways which blur meanings as they are enriched.

> Nativity once in the maine of light,
> Crawles to maturity, wherewith being crown'd,
> Crooked eclipses gainst his glory fight,
> And time that gave, doth now his gift confound. (60)

The enriching of metaphor, a putative demonstration of the poet's real potency, is indistinguishable from a mutability of metaphor, a fragmentation which might be said to demonstrate instability. By this reading the process of verbal enrichment would coincide with a process of deterioration; indeed the enrichment might be perceived as leading to the slippage, "increasing store with losse, and losse with store." The poetry would then come to resemble a pail of the Danaids, and the questions regarding the poet's potency would remain open.

That poetic potency is related here to sexual potency is made clear beyond cavil by the rival poet group (78–80, 82–6). The other poet is a rival both for patronage and for sexual favors, and his rhetorical brilliance (or bombast) is associated with his glittering seductiveness. Thus the poetic speaker is doubly threatened by "the proud full saile of his great verse, bound for the prize of (al to precious) you" (86). The revealing word here is *proud*, which meant "lecherous" as well as "stately" and "ostentatious." Cognate forms have already appeared in 80, which constitutes a tissue of sexual double meanings and interweaves poetic competition inextricably with erotic:

> O how I faint when I of you do write,
> Knowing a better spirit doth use your name,
> And in the praise thereof spends all his might,
> To make me toung-tide speaking of your fame.
> But since your worth (wide as the Ocean is)
> The humble as the proudest saile doth beare,
> My sawsie barke (inferior farre to his)
> On your broad maine doth wilfully appeare.
> Your shallowest helpe will hold me up a floate,
> Whilst he upon your soundlesse deepe doth ride,
> Or (being wrackt) I am a worthlesse bote,
> He of tall building, and of goodly pride.
>   Then if he thrive and I be cast away,
>   The worst was this, my love was my decay.

So many words have sexual meanings ("use," "spends," "proudest," "saucy," "wilfully," "ride," "pride" – by attraction, "tall building") that the reader is tempted to interpret the sonnet primarily in erotic terms. But it opens with a contrast of the rivals as writers before shifting in ll. 11–12 to a presumptive contrast of physical endowments. It is true that the analogy of the possibly promiscuous love object with the ocean will return more crudely and unambiguously in the dark lady group (134). But if language is presented in 80 as a means to seduction, seduction on the other hand may consist simply of verbal overpowering. "Love" and poetic language are linked so closely that the primary meaning of the final clause would seem to be "my inadequate verse has led to my rejection." The contrast of the rivals underscores what the speaker will shortly call his *penury*, a word which brings together his financial, poetic, and sexual shortcomings but which leaves uncertain what is figure and what ground. At any rate the rival, however we regard his challenge, introduces a complicating factor in the economics of the Sonnets, by appearing to "thrive" (80, l. 13) while the speaker is ruined. In spending more, verbally, sartorially, and sexually, he may get more. Yet in the end he and his new patron will be revealed as devalued, the one by the vulgarity of his praise and the other by the vulgarity of the pleasure he takes in it. They are pitiful thrivers both. So at least the poet suggests, and he follows the rival poet group with a temporary kiss-off, not without sarcasm:

> Farewell thou art too deare for my possessing,
> And like enough thou knowst thy estimate. (87)

Farewell also to the theme of poetry's immortalizing power: with two brief exceptions (100, 107), it will disappear from the collection.

The rival poet group is of interest because it confirms the implicit linkage between monetary, verbal, and sexual "pride," and because it complicates the linkage between these forms of power and deeper, vaguer intrinsic "worth." The group is equally of interest because it throws up, almost incidentally, a revealing formulation of the Sonnets' essential vulnerability, a formulation which will prove useful when we return to our starting point in Sonnet 125:

> Who is it that sayes most, which can say more,
> Then this rich praise, that you alone, are you,
> In whose confine immured is the store,
> Which should example where your equall grew,
> Leane penurie within that Pen doth dwell,
> That to his subiect lends not some small glory,
> But he that writes of you, if he can tell,
> That you are you, so dignifies his story.
> Let him but coppy what in you is writ. (84)

The pen is penurious which cannot add to its subject, but a praiser of the friend is subject to this penury, since in him "are locked up all the qualities needed to provide an equal example."[2] The friend's alleged excellence is such that no metaphors are available, no imagistic equivalent is possible, and the authentic praiser will limit himself to pure representation ("Let him but coppy"). Only by representing accurately, achieving a perfect counterpart of the young man, will the poet overcome penury, "making his stile admired every where." But this last solution, in its context, proves to be unsatisfactory on several grounds. First it fails to escape epideictic drabness, by the poet's own showing. It leaves the poetry "barren of new pride," spending again the respent, "keep[ing] invention in a noted weed" (76). Second, he who is to be copied proves to be less of a Platonic idea than a changeable and fallible human; for that revelation we need go no further than the couplet of this sonnet (84), with its malicious glance at the rival's demeaning flattery.

> You to your beautious blessings adde a curse,
> Being fond on praise, which makes your praises worse.

A certain pathology of praise can infect both parties. But the third and most momentous reason why the copy solution fails is that pure representation in language is not of this world. Poetry depends on figuration, but precise figural adequation is unattainable. What is said with ostensible hyperbole in the opening quatrain – that no "example" can serve as "equall" to the young man – is universally true. To attempt not to add to one's subject may court penury, as Sonnet 84 argues, but the real failure lies in the necessity of accepting addition, of employing "compounds strange" (76), as the Sonnets most decidedly do and as all poetry does. Poetry as representation will always be vulnerable, because in its shifting mass of meanings it can never copy with absolute precision and because that which is copied changes, gains, and loses value. The economics of copying reserves its own pitfalls for aspirant thrivers; the pen is bound to be penurious.

Sonnet 105 betrays a similar vulnerability:

> Let not my love be cal'd Idolatrie,
> Nor my beloved as an Idoll show,
> Since all alike my songs and praises be
> To one, of one, still such, and ever so.
> Kinde is my love to day, to morrow kinde,
> Still constant in a wondrous excellence,
> Therefore my verse to constancie confin'de,
> One thing expressing, leaves out difference.
> Faire, kinde, and true, is all my argument,
> Faire, kinde and true, varrying to other words,
> And in this change is my invention spent,
> Three theams in one, which wondrous scope affords.
>   Faire, kinde, and true, have often liv'd alone.
>   Which three till now, never kept seate in one.

This appears to be another apology for an allegedly plain style. (I follow Ingram and Redpath in interpreting "since" in l. 3 as introducing the reason for the accusation, not its defense; the latter begins in l. 5.) Although the poet claims to hew singlemindedly to a unique theme with the same constant language, he cannot, he says, be accused of idolatry because the friend, in his inalterable generosity, deserves no less. The poetry "leaves out difference," spending its invention by varying three words in others. One might argue that *some* difference is already present in this variation. But there are differences in the word "difference" itself, as one learns from a glance at Booth's paragraph on the word; among its relevant meanings are "variety," "anything else," "disagreement," "hostility." *Constant* means both "invariable" and "faithful"; *kinde* means both "generous" and "true to his own nature"; *spent*, that ubiquitous word, means both "used" and "exhausted." The Sonnets escape the charge of idolatry, not because the man they celebrate remains correspondingly unchanging (he is nothing if not inconstant, in both senses), but because they fail to express one thing and systematically admit difference. They alternately valorize and deplore a plain stylistic constancy which they cannot achieve.

The problem of "difference," like the related problem of accurate representation, is pertinent to the affirmation of mutuality which concludes the long section of sonnets to the young man. Before we reach that affirmation, we hear of derelictions on both sides, derelictions grave enough to undermine the fragile economic systems in force earlier. The falsity of the friend, a mansion of vices (95), produces a policy of husbandry the precise reverse of that recommended in the procreation sonnets; now it is those who remain aloof from others like a stone who "husband natures ritches from expence" (94). The poet for his part has made himself a motley to the view, "sold cheap what is most deare" (110), blemished himself and his love. We have already noted the waning of poetry's asserted power as an immortalizing agent. As the Sonnets spiral downward in a vortex of betrayal, counter-betrayal, and justifications not untouched with sophistry, we look for an economic alternative to mere self-deception, that "alcumie . . . creating every bad a perfect best" (114). Something like this alternative can be glimpsed briefly in 120, where the mutuality of suffering and dishonor might produce mutual guilt in compassion and lead to an exchange of quasi-Christian redemption:

> But that your trespasse now becomes a fee,
> Mine ransoms yours, and yours must ransome mee.

This glimpse of reciprocity in shared weakness fades, however, and leads to the group of three (123–5) with which we began, a group essentially protesting the poet's freedom from self-interest and the enduring purity of his feelings, which will never flag and can dispense with ostentatious demonstrations. The last of this group culminates in the proffered "mutuall render" between poet and friend, before the very last poem to the friend, 126, returns to the theme of time and anticipates nature's final, mortal settling of accounts: "her *Quietus* is to render thee."

A skeptical reading of these concluding gambits would represent them as repressing artificially the pain and guilt which have already surfaced, and which will surface even more harshly in the dark lady group to follow. In their context these protests of fidelity, which "nor growes with heat, nor drownes with showres" (124), could be regarded as attempts to mask the real bankruptcy of the relationship. The negative stress of 123–5, lingering over that change (123), "policy" (124), form (125) the poet abjures, might well be read as symptomatic of a bad conscience whose spokesman would be the (internal) accusatory informer of 125. This repressive character of the final sonnets could plausibly be linked to their return to a relatively aureate style after the burst of directness earlier (as in 120 – "y'have past a hell of Time"). This *suspicion* of the excessive protest does hang over the concluding group, deepened by their conspicuous discontinuity with their context. Yet a purely cynical reading would strain out that element of real wishing which is also present. The reader can recognize the implausibility of the asserted constancy while regarding the struggle to hope, the conative pathos, with respect.

The crucial sonnet in this group is 125, since it seems to offer at last the possibility of a stable existential economics, a definitive end to penury, a compensation for the expense of living and feeling, even though it does this like its predecessors in large part by exclusion:

> Wer't ought to me I bore the canopy,
> With my extern the outward honoring,
> Or layd great bases for eternity,
> Which proves more short then wast or ruining?
> Have I not seene dwellers on forme and favor
> Lose all, and more by paying too much rent
> For compound sweet; Forgoing simple savor,
> Pittifull thrivors in their gazing spent.
> Noe, let me be obsequious in thy heart,
> And take thou my oblacion, poore but free,
> Which is not mixt with seconds, knows no art,
> But mutuall render onely me for thee.
> > Hence, thou subbornd *Informer*, a trew soule
> > When most impeacht, stands least in thy controule.

Lines 1–12 are ostensibly responding to the calumny of the unidentified informer of l. 13, a calumny whose content we can determine only through its refutation. This consists in a repudiation of what might be called affective formalism, external gestures of dutifulness like the carrying of a canopy of state over a monarch's head. Suitors who employ such external gestures may believe that they prepare in this way for an everlasting intimacy with him whose favor they court, but the intimacy "paradoxically turns out to be briefer than the time required to run through an estate by extravagance" (Ingram and Redpath). We have still another example of failed husbandry, combining formalism with the kind of decadent sophistication which would prefer cloying elaborate sauces ("compound sweet") to the familiar taste of homely fare. *Forme* (l. 5) brings together the young man's physical figure, the ceremonial of line 1, exaggerated courtesy, hollow gestures of servility, and the craft which produces "compound sweet," artificial confections of any sort, but which is allegedly absent from the poet's oblation. "Compound sweet" recalls the poetic "compounds strange" of 76, which the poet there reproached himself for omitting from his own verse. This suggests that dwellers on form are also ambitious poets whose style is overwrought. The image of the projected manor house (l. 3) is faintly sustained by "ruining" (l. 4), "dwellers" (l. 5), "rent" (l. 6), and the possible allusion to compound and simple interest (l. 7). This version of negative formalism ends with the loaded word "spent" (l. 8), in which so much meaning has sedimented throughout the work; here it means "bankrupted," "exhausted," "failed," ironically "summed up" in reliance on visual externals, and doubtless also "drained of semen," as the suitors' sexual designs are reduced to voyeurism. Unsuccessful entrepreneurs, with only the groundworks built of their mansion of love, the failure of their misguided, formalist generosity is symbolized by the suitors' symbolic distance from their prize, observable but not touchable.

Lines 9–12 supply the poet's redemptive version of erotic ceremonial, which substitutes the eucharistic oblation for the canopied court procession. In this secularized sacrament, the dutiful ("obsequious") poet freely makes an offering intended to manifest the inwardness and simplicity of his own devotion, knowing, or thinking that he knows, that his oblation will win him the unmediated, inner reciprocity which is his goal. The oblation which "knows no art," free from the charge of formalism, is that poetry which, as in 105, is confined to constancy, "to one, of one, still such, and ever so." Just as in 105 it "leaves out difference," in 125 it "is not mixt with seconds." Yet ironically and pathetically, the word "oblacion" is mixed with a transcendent "second," the deity of the communion service, so that the metaphor can only be regarded as a very strange, and somewhat ambiguous, compound. The use of the sacramental term leaves the reader uncertain just how much weight to accord it, and, by introducing the unbridgeable hierarchy of human and divine, would seem to annul in advance the pure reciprocity of the "mutuall render." To deny the operation of art requires art, and this art will prohibit the reciprocal affective mutuality toward which the whole work has seemed to want to move. To compose poetry is expensive, just as loving is expensive, and the unformulated implication of the work as a whole seems to be that expense is never truly recuperated. The increase we desire from fairest creatures never materializes. Spending leaves one spent, and it fails to buy immediacy; it places a residue of compound feeling and compound language between lover and beloved. Here in 125 the very word "seconds" is a compound. It means primarily "merchandise of inferior quality," but it associates itself with the "compound sweet" and thus with that formalist craft from which the oblation is supposedly pure. But banning "seconds" from his poetry, the poet introduces a "second," which is to say a metaphor, and one which is complicated with still more implications. Language is condemned to be compound; poetry *is* art; it shapes and forms and distorts; it introduces inequalities, like the inequality between an offering and an exchange, or the inequality between a secular offering and the sacramental body of Christ.

Thus neither a "pure" offering (Booth discerns this "second" meaning in the word "poore") nor a pure mutuality is possible in a relationship which depends on the word; still less is it possible when the word, as here, is always presented as written. In a curious sonnet which immediately precedes the group 123–5, the poet reports that he has given away a gift he had received from the friend. This gift had been a notebook, "tables." It is unclear whether the notebook contained writing by the friend or memorials of the relationship by the poet, or had been so intended by the giver but been allowed to remain blank. The stress in any case falls on the superior retentiveness of the poet's mind and heart, in contrast to the limits of the "tables":

> That poore retention could not so much hold,
> Nor need I tallies thy deare love to skore. (122)

To dispose of the notebook which contained or might have contained a written record suggests a deep dissatisfaction with language as a mediating instrument. The verb "to skore," to keep a tally, is used contemptuously, as though to insinuate that writing involves a petty arithmetic of feeling. What is striking is that the writing before us has done precisely that, has supplied us with the tallies of an intimate cost accounting. The phrase in 122 may be scornful, and yet both inside and outside the poetic fiction the language of the poetry is all we have, keeping the score and keeping an ambiguous distance open between the tarnished lovers. As that space widens, the poet begins to look like the dwellers on form and favor, spent in his gazing across a distance. He and perhaps the friend as well become pitiful thrivers, barred from the absolute immediacy at least one of them yearns for, because poetry can never be idolatrously one and can never find the metaphor, the "example," which knows no difference. The poet's real enemy is not the "informer" as slanderer, but the voice within himself through whose forming action feeling comes into being.

In the sonnets to the dark lady that follow, poetic language is thematized less prominently; the poet's sense of inner poverty modulates to self-contempt; the physiological meanings of such words as "expense" and "will" are foregrounded. The mistress, who has "robd others beds revenues of their rents" (142), is perhaps the one thriver in the work who is not pitiful. Her role is antithetical to the young man's of the procreation sonnets; she is a "usurer that put'st forth all to use" (134) and her wealth is like the ocean's:

> The sea all water, yet receives raine still,
> And in aboundance addeth to his store,
> So thou beeing rich in *Will* adde to thy *Will*,
> One will of mine to make thy large *Will* more. (135)

But this inflationary economy leads to a depreciation of all values, and the only feasible policy apparently lies in a Christian husbandry:

> Why so large cost having so short a lease,
> Dost thou upon thy fading mansion spend? . . . .
> Buy tearmes divine in selling houres of drosse:
> Within be fed, without be rich no more. (146)

By the close of the sequence, however, the poet does not seem to have adopted this policy. In his disgust with sexuality and his own revolting entrapment in it, the poet tries systematically to subvert his own authority as poet and his perception of metaphoric congruence:

> O Me! what eyes hath love put in my head,
> Which have no correspondence with true sight. (148)

Language is systematically vulgarized, "abhored," and in the last regular sonnet to the mistress (152) the coherence of the poetic consciousness and the integrity of the poetic statement are simultaneously denied, as though the poetry had no legitimate source:

> For I have sworne thee faire; more periurde eye,
> To swere against the truth so foule a lie.

The "eye" is perjured, but also the "I" and the "aye," the capacity to affirm. "Loves eye is not so true as all mens: no" (148). It is as though the pitiless obscenity, love-denying and love-blaspheming, had to expose the *pudenda* of language to register the meanness of the seamy loyalties and tawdry bargains.

The Sonnets can be read to the end as attempts to cope with progressively powerful and painful forms of cost and expense. The bourgeois desire to balance cosmic and human budgets seems to be thwarted by a radical flaw in the universe, in emotion, in value, and in language. This flaw is already acted out at the beginning by the onanistic friend who "feed'st thy lights flame with selfe substantiall fewell" (1). In Sonnet 73, the metaphoric fire lies in its ashes as on a deathbed, "consum'd with that which it was nurrisht by." This becomes, in the terrible Sonnet 129, "a blisse in proofe and proud and very wo," a line always, unnecessarily, emended. The vulnerability of the Sonnets lies in their ceaselessly resistant reflection of this flaw, their stubborn reliance on economies incapable of correcting it, their use of language so wealthy, so charged with "difference," as to be erosive. The vulnerability of the Sonnets might be said to resemble that nameless flaw that afflicts their speaker, but in their case the flaw is not ultimately disastrous. They are not consumed by the extravagant husbandry that produced them. Their effort to resist, to compensate, to register in spite of slippage, balances their loss with store. They leave us with the awesome cost, and reward, of their conative contention. The vulnerability is inseparable from the striving that leads us to them: the "poet's" expense and Shakespeare's expense.

Notes

1. All quotations from the Sonnets are taken from the reproduction of the Quarto text in *Shakespeare's Sonnets*, ed. Stephen Booth (New Haven and London, 1980). I have normalized the usage of u/v. The glosses by Booth occasionally cited are taken from the compendious notes to this edition. I have also had occasion to cite glosses from the edition by W. G. Ingram and Theodore Redpath, *Shakespeare's Sonnets* (New York, 1965).
2. William Shakespeare, *Sonnets*, ed. Douglas Bush and Alfred Harbage (Baltimore, Md, 1967).

13

STANLEY CAVELL

"Who does the wolf love?": *Coriolanus* and the interpretations of politics

Something that draws me to *Coriolanus* is its apparent disdain of questions I have previously asked of Shakespearean tragedy, taking tragedy as an epistemological problem, a refusal to know or to be known, an avoidance of acknowledgment, an expression (or imitation) of skepticism. Coriolanus's refusal to acknowledge his participation in finite human existence may seem so obviously the fact of the matter of his play that to note it seems merely to describe the play, not at all to interpret it. It may be, however, that this lack of theoretical grip itself proposes a moral, or offers a conclusion, namely that *Coriolanus* is not exactly to be understood as a tragedy, that its mystery – supposing one agrees to something like a mystery in its events – will be located only in locating its lack or missing of tragedy, hence its closeness to tragedy.

But systematically to pursue this possibility would require – from me – following out a sense that this play presents a particular interpretation of the problem of skepticism as such (skepticism directed toward our knowledge of the existence of others), in particular an interpretation that takes skepticism as a form of narcissism. This interpretation does not in itself come to me as a complete surprise, since a book I published a few years ago – *The Claim of Reason* – begins with an interpretation of Wittgenstein's *Philosophical Investigations* which takes his move against the idea of a private language (an idea which arises in his struggle against skepticism) as a move against a kind of narcissism, a kind of denial of an existence shared with others; and my book ends with a reading of *Othello* as a depiction of the murderous lengths to which narcissism must go in order to maintain its picture of itself as skepticism, in order to maintain its stand of ignorance, its fear or avoidance of knowing, under the color of a claim to certainty.[1] What surprised me more in *Coriolanus* was its understanding of narcissism as another face of incestuousness, and of this condition as one in which language breaks down under the sense of becoming incomprehensible, of the sense of oneself as having lost the power of expression, what I call in *The Claim of Reason* the terror of inexpressiveness; together with the thoroughness with which Narcissus's fate is mirrored in the figure of Coriolanus, a figure whose every act is, by that act, done to him so perfectly that the distinction between action and passion seems to lose its sense, a condition in which human existence becomes precarious, if perhaps transcendable. I mention these connections with the philosophical issue of skepticism, not because I pursue them further in the essay to follow, but only to attest my conviction that a work such as a play of Shakespeare's cannot contribute the help I want from it for the philosophical issues I mention, unless the play is granted the autonomy it is one's power to grant, which means, seen in its own terms. What does this mean? What is a play of Shakespeare's? I will try to say something about these questions.

Something else also draws me. The way I have been understanding the conflicts engendered by the play keeps sending me back over paths of thought that I believe many critics have found to be depleted of interest, or conviction; three paths, or branches of paths, in particular: (1) those that look in a Shakespearean play for something like an idea of theater, as it were for the play's concept of itself; (2) those that sense Christian stirrings and murmurings under the surface of the words; and (3) even those paths of thought that anticipate something you might call the origins of tragedy in religious ritual. I am, I suppose, as drawn to critical paths that others find empty as some poets are to words that others find flat. But to say fully why one is drawn to a work, and its work of interpretation, can only be the goal of an interpretation; and the motive of an interpretation, like what one might call the intention of the work it seeks, exists fully only in its satisfaction.

I expect, initially, general agreement on two facts about *Coriolanus*. First, compared with other Shakespearean tragedies, this one lacks what A. C. Bradley called "atmosphere" (in his British Academy lecture on the play, the decade after his *Shakespearean Tragedy*). Its language, like its hero, keeps aloof from our attention, as withdrawn, austere, as its rage and its contempt permit. Second, the play is about the organization of the body politic and about how that body is fed, that is, sustained. I expect, further, that readers from opposed camps should be willing to see that the play lends itself equally, or anyway naturally, to psychological and to political readings: both perspectives are, for example, interested in who produces food and in how food is distributed and paid for. From a psychological perspective (in practice this has in recent years been psychoanalytic) the play directs us to an interest in the development of Coriolanus's character. From a political perspective the play directs us to an interest in whether the patricians or the plebeians are right in their conflict and in whether, granted that Coriolanus is unsuited for political leadership, it is his childishness or his very nobility that unsuits him.

In the critical discussions I have read so far, the psychoanalytic perspective has produced more interesting readings than the political. A political reading is apt to become fairly predictable once you know whose side the reader is taking, that of the patricians or that of the plebeians; and whose side the reader takes may come down to how he or she sees Menenius's fable of the organic state, the Fable of the Belly, and upon whom he or she places the blame for Coriolanus's banishment. If few will consider it realistic to suppose that Coriolanus would have made a good political leader, fewer will deny that in losing him the city has lost its greatest hero, and that this loss is the expression of a time of crisis in the state. It is a time of famine in which the call for revolt is made moot by the threat and the fact of war and invasion, followed by a time in which victory in the war, and bitterness over its conduct, creates the call for counter-revolt by the state's defender and preserver. In such a period of crisis everyone and no one has good arguments, everyone and no one has right on their side. In Aufidius's great description of Coriolanus at the end of Act IV, he summarizes as follows:

> So our virtues
> Lie in th'interpretation of the time. . . .
> One fire drives out one fire; one nail, one nail;
> Rights by rights falter, strengths by strengths do fail.
> (IV. vii. 49–55)

One might say that just this division of fire and right is the tragedy; but would that description account for the particular turns of just these events, as distinct from the losses and ironies in any revolutionary situation? Even the most compelling political interpretation – in my experience this is given in Bertolt Brecht's discussion with members of his theater company of the opening scene of the play[2] – seems to have little further to add, in the way of interpretation, once it makes clear that choosing the side of the plebeians is dramatically and textually viable. This is no small matter. It shows that Shakespeare's text – or what we think of as Shakespeare's humanity – leaves ample room for distinctions among the "clusters" of citizens, and it shows the weight of their common position in opposition to that of the patricians. And I take this in turn to show that the politics of the play is essentially the politics of a given production, so that we should not expect its political issues to be settled by an interpretation of what you might call "the text itself."

Exactly the power of Brecht's discussion can be said to be its success in getting us *not* to interpret, not, above all, to interpret food, but to stay with the opening fact of the play, the fact that the citizens of Rome are in revolt because there is a famine (and because of their interpretation of the famine). They and their families are starving and they believe (correctly, for all we know) that the patricians are hoarding grain. Not to interpret this means, in practical or theatrical terms, that we come to see that this cluster is of human beings, individual human beings, who work at particular trades and who live in particular places where specific people await news of the outcome of their dangerous course in taking up arms. This fact of their ordinary humanity is the most impressive fact that can be set against the patricians' scorn of them – a fact that ought not to be visible solely to a Marxist, a fact that shows up the language of the leaders as mysterious and evasive, as subject to what one may think of as the politics of interpretation.

Yet we also feel that the pervasive images of food and hunger, of cannibalism and of disgust, do mean something, that they call upon us for some lines of interpretation, and that the value of attending to this particular play is a function of the value to individual human beings of tracing these lines.

Psychoanalysts naturally have focused on the images of food and feeding that link Coriolanus and his mother. In a recent essay,[3] Janet Adelman has given so clear and fair an account of some two decades of psychoanalytic interpretations of food and feeding in the play, in the course of working out her further contributions, that I feel free to pick and choose the lines and moments bearing on this aspect of things that serve my somewhat different emphases.

Twice Volumnia invokes nursing. Early she says to Virgilia, rebuking her for worrying about her husband:

> The breasts of Hecuba
> When she did suckle Hector, look'd not lovelier
> Than Hector's forehead when it spit forth blood
> At Grecian sword contemning.
>
> (I. iii. 40–3)

And in her first intercession with her son:

> Do as thou list.
> Thy valiantness was mine, thou suck'st it from me,
> But owe thy pride thyself.
>
> (III. ii. 128–30)

Both invocations lead one to think what it is this son learned at his mother's breast, what it is he was fed with, particularly as we come to realize that both mother and son declare themselves to be starving. It is after Coriolanus's departure upon being banished, when Menenius asks Volumnia if she'll sup with him, that she comes out with:

> Anger's my meat: I sup upon myself
> And so shall starve with feeding.
>
> (IV. ii. 50–1)

248

As Coriolanus mocks and resists the ritual of asking for the people's voices, his being keeps revolting, one time as follows:

> Better it is to die, better to starve,
> Than crave the hire which first we do deserve.
>
> (II. iii. 112–13)

I say that mother and son, both of them, *are* starving, and I mean throughout, always, not just when they have occasion to say so. I take Volumnia's vision of supping upon herself to be a picture not simply of her local anger, but of self-consuming anger as the presiding passion of her life – the primary thing, accordingly, that she would have to teach her son, the thing he sucked from her, of course under the name of valiantness. If so, then if Volumnia and hence Coriolanus are taken to exemplify a Roman identification of virtue as valor, they should further be taken as identifying valor with an access to one's anger. It is "In anger, Juno-like," godlike, that Volumnia laments (IV. ii. 53); and it is this anger that the tribune Sicinius is remarking as, in trying to avoid being confronted by her, he says, "They say she's mad" (IV. ii. 9). Along these lines, I emphasize Coriolanus's statement about deserving rather than craving not as

> Better it is to *die*, better to *starve*,
> Than crave

as if he is asserting the rightness of a particular choice for the future; but as

> *Better* it is to die, *better* to starve,
> Than crave

as if he is reaffirming or confessing his settled form of (inner) life. I expect that the former is the more usual way of emphasis, but I find it prejudicial.

Coriolanus and Volumnia are – I am taking it – starvers, hungerers. They manifest this condition as a name or a definition of the human, like being mortal. And they manifest this as a condition of insatiability (starving by feeding, feeding as deprivation). It is a condition sometimes described as the infiniteness of desire, imposing upon the finiteness of the body. But starving for Volumnia and her son suggests that this infiniteness is not the cause of human insatiability but is rather its effect. It is the effect not of an endless quantity, as though the self had, or is, endless reserves of desire; but of an endless structure, as though desire has a structure of endlessness. One picture of this structure is given by Narcissus, for whom what is longed for is someone longing, who figures beauty as longing. Starving by feeding presents itself to Coriolanus as being consumed by hunger, and his words for hungering are desiring and craving. And what he incessantly hungers for is ... not to hunger, and not to desire, that is, not to be mortal. Take the scene of interview by the people:

Coriolanus:	You know the cause, sir, of my standing here.
Third Citizen:	We do, sir; tell us what hath brought you to't.
Coriolanus:	Mine own desert.
Second Citizen:	Your own desert?
Coriolanus:	Ay, but not mine own desire.
Third Citizen:	How, not your own desire?

(II. iii. 64–69)

If you desire to be desireless, is there something you desire? If so, how would you express it; that is, tell it; that is, ask for it? Coriolanus's answer to this paradox is to become perfectly deserving. Since to hunger is to want, to lack something, he hungers to lack nothing, to be complete, like a sword. My speculations here are an effort to do justice to one's sense of Coriolanus as responding not primarily to his situation with the plebeians, as if trapped by an uncontrollable disdain; but as responding primarily to his situation with himself, as befits a Narcissus, trapped first by an uncontrollable logic. While I will come to agree with Plutarch's early observation or diagnosis in his *Life of Caius Martius Coriolanus* that Coriolanus is "altogether unfit for any man's conversation," I am in effect taking this to mean not that he speaks in anger and contempt (anger and contempt are not unjustifiable) but that, while under certain circumstances he can express satisfaction, he cannot express desire and to this extent cannot speak at all: the case is not that he will not ask for what he wants but rather that he can want nothing that he asks. His solution amounts, as both patricians and plebeians more or less note, to becoming a god. What god? We have to get to this.

Let us for the moment continue developing the paradox of hungering. To be consumed by hunger, to feed upon oneself, must present itself equally as being fed upon, being eaten up. (To feed means both to give and to take nourishment, as to suckle means both to give and to take the breast.) So the other fact of Coriolanus's and Volumnia's way of starving, of their hunger, is their sense of being cannibalized.[4]

The idea of cannibalization runs throughout the play. It is epitomized in the title question I have given to these remarks: "Who does the wolf love?" Menenius asks this of the tribunes of the people at the opening of Act II. One of them answers, with undeniable truth: "The lamb." And Menenius, ever the interpretative fabulist, answers: "Ay, to devour him, as the hungry plebeians would the noble Martius." The other tribune's answer – "He's a lamb, indeed, that baes like a bear" – does not unambiguously deny Menenius's interpretation. The shock of the interpretation is of course that it is from the beginning the people, not the patricians, and least of all Coriolanus, who are presented as lambs, anyway as food for patrician wolves. In Menenius's opening effort to talk the people out of revolt, he declares that "The helms o'th' state . . . care for you like fathers," to which the First Citizen replies,

"Care for us? . . . If the wars eat us not up, they will; and there's all the love they bear us." This fantasy is borne out when the general Cominius speaks of Coriolanus's coming to battle as to a feast (I.ix.10). And the idea of the warrior Coriolanus feeding on a weaker species may be raised again in the battle at Corioli in his threat to any soldier who holds back, "I'll take him for a Volsce, / And he shall feel mine edge," allowing the suggestion of his sword as a piece of cutlery. The idea of an ungovernable voraciousness is furthered by Volumnia's association of her son with his son's tearing apart a butterfly with his teeth. On the other hand, when Coriolanus offers himself to Aufidius at Antium he expresses his sense of having been devoured, with only the name Caius Martius Coriolanus remaining, devoured by "The cruelty and envy of the people" (IV.v.75). And Menenius, whose sense of justice is constricted by, among other things, his fear of civil disorder, is accurate in his fears, in the consequences they prophesy for Rome, and he will repeat his vision of civil cannibalism:

> Now the good gods forbid
> That our renowned Rome, whose gratitude
> Towards her deserved children is enroll'd
> In Jove's own book, like an unnatural dam
> Should now eat up her own!
>
> (III.i.287–91)

All readers of this aspect of the play will recognize in this description of Rome as potentially a cannibalistic mother an allusion to Volumnia; and the identification of Volumnia and Rome is enforced in other ways, not least by Volumnia herself when in the second and final intercession scene she says to her son:

> thou shalt no sooner
> March to assault thy country than to tread –
> Trust to't, thou shalt not – on thy mother's womb
> That brought thee to this world.
>
> (V.iii.122–5)

It is very much to the point to notice that, in Menenius's vision of Rome as an "unnatural dam," an identity is proposed between a mother eating her child and a mother eating herself: if Rome eats up all Romans there is no more Rome, for as one of the tribunes asks, "What is the city but the people?" (III.i.197).

The paradox and reciprocity of hungering may be found registered in the question "Who does the wolf love?" If the question is asking for the object of the wolf's affection, the more nearly correct grammar would seem to be: "Whom does the wolf love?"[5] But this correctness (call it a patrician correctness, a refinement in which the plebeians apparently do not see the good) would rule out taking the question also in its opposite direction, grammatically strict as it stands, namely as asking whose object of affection the wolf is. (Who does love the wolf?) The answer given directly, "The lamb," does not rule out either direction but, as the ensuing discussion demonstrates, the direction will be a function of what or who you take the lamb to be, and hence what the wolf. Both directions, the active and the passive constructions of the play's focal verbs, are operative throughout the action. I have mentioned this explicitly in the cases of feeding and suckling. But it is, I find, true less conspicuously, but pertinently, in such an odd moment as this:

> *Coriolanus:*   Let them hang.
> *Volumnia:*   Ay, and burn too.
>
> (III. ii. 23–4)

One of the functions in providing Volumnia with this amplification here strikes me as suggesting her sense of the inevitable reflexiveness of action in their Rome: are hanging and burning actions done to someone, or something "they" are, or will be, doing?

The circle of cannibalism, of the eater eaten by what he or she eats, keeps being sketched out, from the first to the last. You might call this the identification of narcissism as cannibalism. From the first: at the end of Coriolanus's first long speech he says to the citizens:

> You cry against the noble Senate, who
> (Under the gods) keep you in awe, which else
> Would feed on one another.
>
> (I. i. 185–7)

And at the last: Rome devouring itself is the idea covered in the obsessive images of Coriolanus burning Rome. It was A. C. Bradley again who, at the end of his British Academy lecture, pointed up the sudden and relentless harping, principally after the banishment, on the image of fire, of Rome burning. Bradley makes nothing further of the point; but it is worth noting, in view of the theme of starving and cannibalism, that fire in this play is imagined under the description of it as *consuming* what it burns.

You may say that burning as a form of revenge is Coriolanus's projection onto Rome of what he felt Rome was doing to him. This cannot be wrong, but it so far pictures Coriolanus, in his revenge, to be essentially a man like Aufidius, merely getting even; the picture requires refining. Suppose that, as I believe, in Coriolanus's famous sentence of farewell, "I banish you!" (III. iii. 123), he had already begun a process of consuming Rome, incorporating it, becoming it. Then when the general Cominius tried in vain to plead with him to save Rome, and found him to be sitting "in gold, his eye / Red as 'twould burn Rome" (V. i. 63–4), he somewhat misunderstood what he saw. He took Coriolanus to be contemplating something in the future, whereas

Coriolanus's eye was red with the present flames of self-consuming. Consuming the literal Rome with literal fire would accordingly only have been an expression of that self-consuming. Thus would the city understand what it had done to itself. He will give it – horribly – what it deserves. Thus is the play of revenge further interpreted.

These various understandings of cannibalism all illustrate the ancient sentiment that man is wolf to man. (The Roman Plautus, to whom Shakespeare is famously indebted, is credited with being the earliest nameable framer of the sentiment. A pertinent modern instance occurs in Brecht's *Threepenny Opera*.) But the question "Who does the wolf love?" has two further reaches which we must eventually consider. First, there is the repetition of the idea that devouring can be an expression of love. Second, if, as I think, there is reason here to take the image of the wolf as the figure of the mythical animal identified with Rome, the one who suckled the founders of Rome (Volumnia is the reason), there is reason to take the lamb it is said to love (or that loves it) as the mythical animal identified with Christ.

Before this, I should make explicit a certain way in which the account of Coriolanus's motivation I have been driving at is somewhat at odds with the direction of psychoanalytic interpretation summarized and extended by Janet Adelman. She understands Coriolanus's attempt to make himself inhumanly independent as a defense against his horror of dependence, and his rage as converting his wish to be dependent against those who render him so. A characteristic turn of her argument consists of a reading of some lines I have already had occasion to quote:

> The breasts of Hecuba
> When she did suckle Hector, look'd not lovelier
> Than Hector's forehead when it spit forth blood
> At Grecian sword contemning.

Adelman reads as follows:

> Blood is more beautiful than milk, the wound than the breast, warfare than peaceful feeding. . . . Hector is transformed immediately from infantile feeding mouth to bleeding wound. For the unspoken mediator between breast and wound is the infant's mouth: in this imagistic transformation, to feed is to be wounded; the mouth becomes the wound, the breast the sword. . . . But at the same time as Volumnia's image suggests the vulnerability inherent in feeding, it also suggests a way to fend off that vulnerability. In her image, feeding, incorporating, is transformed into spitting out, an aggressive expelling; the wound once again becomes the mouth that spits. . . . The wound spitting blood thus becomes not a sign of vulnerability but an instrument of attack.[6]

This is very fine and it must not be denied. But the transformation of

Hector's mouth into a wound must not in turn deny two further features of these difficult lines. First, when Hector contemns Grecian swords, he is also to be thought of as fighting, as wielding a sword, so the mouth is transformed into, or seen as, a cutting weapon: the suckling mother is presented as being slashed by the son-hero, eaten by the one she feeds. Suffering such a fantasy would constitute some of Volumnia's more normal moments. Second, the lines set up an equation between a mother's milk and a man's blood, suggesting that we must understand the man's spitting blood in battle not simply as attacking but equally, somehow, as providing food, in a male fashion. But how? Remember that Coriolanus's way to avoid asking for something, that is, to avoid expressing desire, is by what he calls deserving the thing. His proof of desert is his valiantness, so his spitting blood in battle is his way of deserving being fed, that is to say, being devoured, being loved unconditionally. (War and feeding have consistently been joined in the words of this play. A plebeian says: "If the wars eat us not up, they will" (I.i.84). And Cominius: Coriolanus "cam'st . . . to . . . this feast, / Having fully din'd before" (I.ix.10–11); but again Cominius does not get the connection complete.) To be fed by Volumnia is to be fed *to* her. But since the right, or effective, bleeding depends (according to the equation of blood and milk) upon its being a form of feeding, of giving food, providing blood identifies him with his mother. His mother's fantasy here suggests that the appropriate reciprocation for having nourished her son is for him to become her, as if to remove the arbitrariness in her having been born a woman; and since it is a way of putting her into the world, it is a way of giving birth to her. Her son's companion fantasy of reciprocation would be to return Rome's gift, to nurse Rome with the valiantness he sucked from it.

This fantasy produces contradictions which are a match for the fury of contradictions one feels in Coriolanus's position (for example, between the wishes for dependence and for independence). For he can only return his nourishment if Rome – taken as the people – deserves it. Hence the people's lack of desert entails his lack of desert, entails that he cannot do the thing that acquires love; he is logically debarred from reciprocating. The fact that he has both absolute contempt for the people and yet an absolute need for them is part of what maddens him. (This implies again that I cannot understand Coriolanus's emotions toward the people as directed simply to, say, their cowardice, their being poor fighters. I am taking it that he needs their desert for, so to speak, private reasons as much as public.) The other part of what maddens him is that neither the people nor his mother – neither of the things that mean Rome – will understand his position. Neither understands that his understanding of his valiantness, his virtue, his worth, his deservingness, is of himself as a provider, and that this is the condition of his receiving his own sustenance. (This assumes that he shares his mother's fantasy of the equation of milk and blood – as if there is nothing in her he has not taken in.) The people, precisely on the contrary, maddeningly accuse him of *withholding* food; and his mother precisely regards his heroism purely as toughness, devoid of tenderness; or pure fatherhood devoid of motherhood; and as deserving something more than acknowledging what he provides, more than the delicate balance of his self-account, as if being made consul were indeed something more. ("Know, good mother, / I had rather be their servant in my way / Than sway with them in theirs" (II. i. 200–2).) In these misunderstandings they have both already abandoned him, weaned him, before the ritual of being made consul comes to grief and he is formally banished. This prior rejection, not just once but always, inherently, would allow the understanding of his anger as his mother interprets anger, that is, as lamentation ("Anger's my meat . . . lament as I do, / In anger, Juno-like"). We may not contradict her interpretation, though we may interpret it further. We might go on to interpret it as depression.

I might characterize my intention in spelling out what I call these fantasies as an attempt to get at the origin of words, not the origin of their meaning exactly but of their production, of the value they have when and as they occur. I have characterized something like this ambition of criticism variously over the years, and related it to what I understand as the characteristic procedure of ordinary language philosophy.[7] And do my spellings out help? Do they, for example, help comprehend Coriolanus's subsequent course – how he justifies his plan to burn Rome and how he is talked out of his plan by his mother? It is not hard to encourage oneself in the impression that one understands these things. To me they seem mysteries. I will sketch the answers I have to these questions and then conclude by indicating how these answers serve to interpret our relation to this play, which means to me, to understand what a Shakespearean play is (as revealed in this instance).

I pause, in turning to these questions, to make explicit an issue that at any time may nag our consciousness of the play. The mother-relation is so overwhelmingly present in this play that we may not avoid wondering, at least wondering whether we are to wonder, what happened to the father. The play seems to me to raise this question in three ways, which I list in decreasing order of obviousness. First, Menenius is given a certain kind of fatherly role, or a role as a certain kind of father, but the very difficulty of conceiving of him as Coriolanus's real father, which is to say, as Volumnia's husband and lover, keeps alive our imagination of what such a figure might look like. Second, Coriolanus's erotic attachment to battle and to men who battle suggests a search for the father as much as an escape from the mother. This would afford an explanation for an otherwise, to me, insufficiently explained use in the play of the incident from Plutarch's *Life* in which Coriolanus asks, exhausted from victorious battle, that a man in the conquered city of Corioli be spared slavery on the ground that Coriolanus "sometime lay at the poor man's house," a man whose name Coriolanus discovers he has forgotten. The vagueness of the man's identity and Coriolanus's expression of confusion in the Shakespeare – distinct differences from the occurrence of the incidents in Plutarch – suggest to my mind that the unnamed figure to whom Coriolanus wishes to provide reparation is, vaguely, transiently, an image of his father.[8]

Third, and so little obvious as to be attributable to my powers of hallucination, Coriolanus's efforts at mythological identification as he sits enthroned and entranced before Rome is an effort – if one accepts one stratum of description I will presently give of him – to come unto the Father. (I will not go into the possibilities here, or fantasies, that a patrician matron is simultaneously father and mother, or that, in replacing his father, he becomes his own father.)

I was about to ask how we are to grasp Coriolanus's return and his change of heart. My answer depends on plotting a relation between him and the other sacrificial lamb I have mentioned, the lamb of god, Christ. I say plotting a relation between the figures, not at all wishing to identify them. I see Coriolanus not so much as imitating Christ as competing with him. These are necessarily shadowy matters; and, while everything depends on accuracy in defining this relation, all I can do here is note some elements that will have to figure in the plotting.

Earlier I spoke of Coriolanus's solution to the paradox of hungering not to hunger, of wanting not to want, of asking not to ask, as one of becoming a god. Now we may see that Christ is the right god because of the way he understands his mission as providing nonliteral food, food for the spirit, for immortality; and because it is in him that blood must be understood as food. If one is drawn to this as a possibility, one may find surprising confirmation for it in certain of Coriolanus's actions and in certain descriptions of his actions. (I am interested not in claiming that Coriolanus is *in some sense* a scapegoat, the way perhaps any tragic hero is, but in claiming that he is a specific inflection of *this* scapegoat.)

First his actions, two especially. First is his pivotal refusal to show his wounds. I associate this generally with the issue of Christ's showing his wounds to his disciples, in order to show them the Lord – that is, to prove the resurrection – and specifically with his saying to Thomas, who was not present at the first showing and who made seeing the wounds a condition of believing, that is, of declaring his faith, "Thomas, because thou hast seen me, thou believest: blessed are they that have not seen, and have believed" (John 20:29). (Thomas would not believe until he could, as he puts it and as Jesus will invite him to, "put mine hand into his side"; Aufidius declares the wish to "Wash my fierce hand in's heart" (I.x.27). I make no further claims on the basis of this conjunction; I can see that some good readers may feel that it is accidental. I do claim that good reading may be guided, or inspired, by the over-excitement such conjunctions can cause.) The second action is the second intercession, in which Volumnia, holding her son's son by the hand, together with Virgilia and Valeria, appears to Coriolanus before Rome. I take this to invoke the appearance, while Christ is on the cross, of three women whose names begin with the same letter of the alphabet (I mean begin with Ms, not with Vs), accompanied by a male he loves, whom he views as his mother's son (John 19:25–7). (Giving his mother a son presages a mystic marriage.)

I do not suppose that one will be convinced by these relations unless one has antecedently felt some quality of – what shall I say? – the mythic in these moments. This is something I meant in calling these relations "shadowy matters": I meant this not negatively but positively. It is a way to understand Volumnia's advice to Coriolanus that when he makes his appeal to the people he act out the meaning of his presence:

> for in such business
> Action is eloquence, and the eyes of th'ignorant
> More learned than the ears
>
> (III. ii. 75–7)

I accept this as advice Shakespeare is giving to his own audience, a certain hint about why the words of this particular play may strike one as uncharacteristically ineloquent.

The second source of confirmation for Coriolanus's connection with the figure of Christ lies, I said, in certain descriptions of his actions. I specify now only some parallels that come out of Revelation. In that book the central figure is a lamb (and there is also a dragon), and a figure who sits on a special horse and on a golden throne, whose name is known only to himself, whose "eyes were as a flame of fire," and who burns a city which is identified as a woman; it is, in particular, the city (Babylon) which in Christian tradition is identified with Rome. And I associate the opening of Coriolanus's opening diatribe against the citizens, in which he rebukes their wish for "good words" from him – glad tidings – accusing them of liking "neither peace nor war," with the message Christ dictates to the writer of Revelation: "I know thy works, that thou art neither cold nor hot. . . . Therefore, because thou art luke warm, and neither cold nor hot, it will come to pass that I shall spew thee out of my mouth" (Revelation 3:15–16). (An associated text from Plutarch would be: "So Martius, being a stowte man of nature, that never yelded in any respect, as one thincking that to overcome allwayes, and to have the upper hande in all matters, was a Token of magnanimities, and of no base and fainte corage, which spitteth out anger from the most weake and passioned parte of the harte, much like the matter of an impostume: went home." Whatever the ambiguities in these words, the general idea remains, indelibly, of Coriolanus's speech, when angry, as being the spitting forth of the matter of an abscess.[9] This play about food is about revolted-ness and disgust. *Coriolanus* and Revelation are about figures who are bitter, disgusted by those whom they have done good, whose lives they have sustained.)

Conviction, or lack of it, in these relations is something one has naturally to assess for oneself. Granted that they are somehow at work, they work to make comprehensible what Coriolanus's identification with the god is (they are identified as banished providers of spiritual food) and what his justification for destruction is (the people lack faith and are to suffer judgment) and why he changes his mind about the destruction. It is, I think, generally felt that his mother prevails with him by producing human, family feeling in him, in effect showing him that he is not inhuman. This again cannot be wrong, but first of all he has his access of family feeling the moment he sees the four figures approaching (a feeling that does not serve to carry the day), and, second, his feeling, so conceived, does not seem to me to account for Coriolanus's words of agony to his mother as he relents and "Holds her by the hand, silent":

> O mother, mother!
> What have you done? Behold, the heavens do ope,
> The gods look down, and this unnatural scene
> They laugh at. O my mother, mother! O!
> You have won a happy victory to Rome;
> But, for your son, believe it, O, believe it,
> Most dangerously you have with him prevail'd,
> If not most mortal to him. But let it come.
>   (V. iii. 182–9)

I say these are words of agony but, so far as I recall, no critic who cites them seems to find them so. I feel here especially at a disadvantage in never having been at a performance of *Coriolanus*. But I find on reading this passage, or rather in imagining it said (sometimes as by specific actors; Olivier, of course, among them, and the young Brando), that it takes a long time to get through. Partly that has to do with the fact of the repetition of words in the passage; partly with the specific words that are repeated, "O," "mother," and "believe it." It has further to do, I feel sure, with my uncertainty about how long the silences before and within this speech are to be held – a speech which may be understood as expressing the silence with which this son holds, and then relinquishes, his mother's hand. Suppose we try imagining that he does not relinquish her hand until just before the last sentence, "But let it come" – as if what is to come is exactly expressive of their separating, or say the separating of Rome from Rome. Then how far do we imagine that he goes through the imagining of what is to come, and how long would the imagining take, before he takes upon himself the words that invite its coming? What it means to say that she may be "most mortal" to him cannot be that he may be killed – the mere fact of death is hardly what concerns this man. He must mean somehow that she has brought it about that he will have the wrong death, the wrong mortality, a fruitless death. Has she done this by showing him that he has feelings? But Christ, even by those who believe that he is the Lord, is generally held to have feelings. Coriolanus's speech expresses his agonized sense that his mother does not know who he is, together with an agonized plea for her belief. She has deprived him of heaven, of, in his fantasy, sitting beside his father, and deprived him by withholding her faith in him; for if she does not believe that he is a god then probably he is not a god, and certainly nothing like the Christian scenario can be fulfilled, in which a mother's belief is essential. If it were his father who sacrificed him for the city of man, then he could be a god. But if it is his mother who sacrifices him, he is not a god. The logic of his situation, as well as the psychology, is that he cannot sacrifice himself. He can provide spiritual food but he cannot make himself into food; he cannot say, for example, that his body is bread. His sacrifice will not be redemptive, and hence one may say his tragedy is that he cannot achieve tragedy. He dies in a place irrelevant to his sacrifice, carved by many swords, by hands that can derive no special nourishment from him. It is too soon in the history of the Roman world for the sacrifice to which he aspires and from which he recoils.

And perhaps it is too late, as if the play is between worlds. I know I have been struck by an apparent incorporation in *Coriolanus* of elements from Euripides' *Bacchæ*, without knowing how or whether a historical connection is thinkable. Particularly, it seems to me, I have been influenced in my descriptions by feeling under Coriolanus's final plea to his mother the plea of Pentheus to his mother, outside the city, to see that he is her son and not to tear him to pieces. The *Bacchæ* is about admitting the new god to the city, present in one who is returning to his native city, a god who in company with Demeter's grain brings nourishment to mankind, one who demands recognition in order to vindicate at once his mother's honor and his being fathered by Zeus; the first in the city to acknowledge his divine descent are two old men. My idea is that Coriolanus incorporates both raging, implacable Dionysus and raging, inconstant Pentheus, and that Volumnia partakes both of the chaste yet god-seduced Semele and of the mad and murderous Agave. Volumnia's identifying of herself with Juno (specifically, with Juno's anger) may thus suggest her sensing herself as the cause of her curse. It is not essential to my thought here that Shakespeare knew (of) Euripides' play. It is enough to consider that he knew Ovid's account of Pentheus's story, and to suppose that he took the story as Euripides had, as about the kind of son (one unable to express desire) to whom the failure of his mother's recognition presents itself as a sense of being torn to pieces.

What is the good of such a tragedy of failed tragedy? Which is to ask: What is this play to us? How is it to do its work? This is the question I have been driving at, and now that it is before us I can only state flatly, without much detail, my provisional conclusions on the topic.

Those conclusions can by now be derived from certain considerations about Menenius's telling of the Fable of the Belly in the opening scene of the play. Every reader or participant has to make something of this extended, most prominently placed event. Until recent times, most critics have assumed that Menenius is voicing a commonplace assumption of the times in which Shakespeare wrote and one that represents Shakespeare's view of the state – the state as a hierarchic organism, understandable on analogy with the healthy, functioning body. It is my impression that recent critics have tended not to dwell on the fable, as though the conservative way is the only way to take it and as though that vision is no longer acceptable, or presentable. But this seems to me to ignore what I take to be the three principal facts about Menenius's telling of the tale, the facts, one may say, of the drama in the telling. (1) The fable has competing interpretations. What the First Citizen calls its "application" is a *question*. He and Menenius joke about whether the people or the patricians are better represented by the belly. (2) The fable is about food, about its distribution and circulation. (3) The fable is told (by a patrician) to citizens who are in the act of rising in revolt against a government they say is deliberately starving them, and hence the patrician can be said to be giving them words *instead* of food. The first mystery of the play is that this seems to work, that the words stop the citizens, that they stop to listen, as though these citizens are themselves willing, under certain circumstances, to take words for food, to equate them.

Coriolanus's entrance at the end of the argument over the application of the fable confirms this equation of words and food: he has from the early lines of the play been identified as the people's chief enemy, here in particular as chief of those who withhold food; and his opening main speech to them, after expressing his disgust with them, is to affirm that he does withhold and will go on withholding "good words" from them. Accordingly, every word he speaks will mean the withholding of good words. He will, as it were, have a sword in his mouth. There are other suggestions of the equation of words and food in the play (for example, the enlivening of the familiar idea that understanding is a matter of digesting); but this is enough for me, in view of my previous suggestions, to take the equation as part of the invocation of the major figure of our civilization for whom words are food. The word made flesh is to be eaten, since this is the living bread. Moreover, the parables of Jesus are characteristically about food, and are always meant as food. The words/food equation suggests that we should look again at Volumnia's intercession speeches, less for their content than for the plain fact of their drama: that they are much the longest speeches Coriolanus listens to, that they cause his mother to show him her undivided attention and him to give her his silence; he is as if filled up by her words. It pleases me further to remember that

Revelation also contains a vision of words that are eaten: there is a book the writer swallows that tastes as sweet as honey in the mouth but bitter in the belly (10:10), as if beauty were the beginning of terror, as in, for example, a play of Shakespeare's.

My conclusion about the working of the play, about what kind of play it is, adds up then as follows. I take the telling of the Fable of the Belly as a sort of play within the play, a demonstration of what Shakespeare takes his play – named for Coriolanus – to be, for *Coriolanus* too is a tale about food, with competing interpretations requiring application, told by one man to a cluster (call this an audience), causing them to halt momentarily, to turn aside from their more practical or pressing concerns in order to listen. Here is the relevance I see in the fact that the play is written in a time of corn shortages and insurrections. The fact participates not just in the imagery of the play's setting, but in the question of the authority and the virtue of portraying such a time, at such a time, for one's fellow citizens; a question of the authority and the virtue in being a writer. I see in Shakespeare's portrayal of the Fable of the Belly a competition (in idea, perhaps in fact) with Sir Philip Sidney's familiar citing of the fable in his *Defence of Poetry*, or a rebuke of it.[10] Sidney records Menenius's application of the tale as having "wrought such effect in the people, as I never read that only words brought forth but then, so sudden and so good an alteration; for upon reasonable conditions a perfect reconcilement ensued." But in casting his partisan, limited Menenius, as the teller of the tale, and placing its telling at the opening of the play, where we have minimal information or experience for judging its events, Shakespeare puts into question both the nature of the "alteration" and the "perfection" of the reconciliation. Since these are the two chief elements of Sidney's defense of poetry, this defense is as such put into question; but hence, since Shakespeare is nevertheless giving his own version of the telling of the fable, making his own story about the circulation of food, he can be understood as presenting in this play his own defense of poetry (more particularly of plays, which Sidney particularly attacks). It is in this light noteworthy that Sidney finds "Heroical" poetry to be most "[daunting to] all back-biters," who would "speak evil" of writing which presents "champions . . . who doth not only teach and move to a truth, but teacheth and moveth to the most high and excellent truth." But since "the image of such worthies" as presented in such works "most inflameth the mind with desire to be worthy," and since *Coriolanus* is a play that studies the evil in such an inflammation, Shakespeare's play precisely questions the ground of Sidney's claim that "the Heroical . . . is not only a kind, but the best and most accomplished kind of Poetry."

What would this play's defense of poetry be, I mean how does it direct us to consider the question? Its incorporation of the Fable of the Belly I understand to identify us, the audience, as starvers, and to identify the words of the play as food, for our incorporation. Then we have to ask of ourselves, as we have to ask of the citizens: Why have we stopped to listen? That is, what does it mean to be a member of this audience? Do we feel that these words have the power of redemption for us?

They are part of an enactment of a play of sacrifice; as it happens, of a failed sacrifice. And a feast-sacrifice, whether in Christian, pre-Christian, Nietzschean, or Freudian terms, is a matter of the founding and the preserving of a community. A community is thus identified as those who partake of the same body, of a common victim. This strikes Coriolanus as our being caught in a circle of mutual partaking, incorporating one another. And this is symbolized, or instanced, by speaking the same language. A pervasive reason Coriolanus spits out words is exactly that they *are* words, that they exist only in a language, and that a language is metaphysically something shared, so that speaking is taking and giving in your mouth the very matter others are giving and taking in theirs.

It is maddeningly irrevelant to Coriolanus which party the belly represents. What matters to him is that, whoever rules, all are members, that all participate in the same circulation, the same system of exchange, call it Rome; that to provide civil nourishment you must allow yourself to be partaken of. This is not a play about politics, if this means about political authority or conflict, say about questions of legitimate succession or divided loyalties. It is about the formation of the political, the founding of the city, about what it is that makes a rational animal fit for conversation, for civility. This play seems to think of this creation of the political, call it the public, as the overcoming of narcissism, incestuousness, and cannibalism; as if it perceives an identity among these relations.

In constructing and contesting with a hero for whom the circulation of language is an expression of cannibalism, *Coriolanus* takes cannibalism as symbolic of the most human of activities, the most distinctive, or distinguished, of human activities. (Sidney cites the familiar conjunction: "Oratio, next to Ratio, . . . [is] the greatest gift bestowed upon mortality.") Coriolanus wishes to speak, to use words, to communicate, without exchanging words; without, let us say, reasoning (with others); to speak without conversing, without partaking in conversation. Here is the conversation for which he is unfit, call it civil speech. Hence I conceive *Coriolanus* to be incorporating Montaigne's interpretation of literal cannibalism as more civilized than our more sophisticated – above all, more pervasive – manners of psychological torture, our consuming others alive.[11] Montaigne's "On cannibals" is more specifically pertinent to this play: its story of a cannibal prisoner of a cannibal society valorously taunting his captors by reminding them that in previous battles, when he had been victorious over them, he had captured and eaten their ancestors, so that in eating him they will be consuming their own flesh – this is virtually the mode in which Coriolanus addresses himself to the Volscians in putting himself at their mercy. And more variously pertinent: the essay interprets cannibalism as revenge; and it claims (in one of those moods of measured hilarity) that, when three men from a cannibal society visited Rouen and were asked what they found most amazing about the ways of Montaigne's countrymen, one of their responses was as follows (I will not comment on it but quote in Frame's translation):

> Second (they have a way in their language of speaking of men as halves of one another), they had noticed that there were among us men full and gorged with all sorts of good things, and that their other halves were beggars at their doors, emaciated with hunger and poverty; and they thought it strange that these needy halves could endure such an injustice, and did not take the others by the throat, or set fire to their houses.

Within the experience of such a vision of the circulation of language a question, not readily formulatable, may press for expression: to what extent can Coriolanus (and the play that creates him and contests with him) be understood as seeing his salvation in silence? The theme of silence haunts the play. For example, one of Coriolanus's perfectly cursed tasks is to ask for "voices" (votes) that he exactly wishes not to hear. Again, the words "silent" and "silence" are beautifully and mysteriously associated, once each, with the women in his life: with his wife ("My gracious silence, hail!"), and with his mother ("He holds her by the hand, silent"). Toward both, the word of silence is the expression of intimacy and identification; but in his wife's case it means acknowledgment, freedom from words, but in a life beyond the social, while in his mother's case it means avoidance, denial, death, that there is no life beyond the social. The ambiguities here are drilled through the action of the play by the repeated calls "Peace, peace" – hysterical, ineffective shouts of this particular word for silence. The play literalizes this conventional call for silence by implying that speech is war, as if this is the reason that both words and war can serve as food. But the man for war cannot find peace in peace – not merely because he, personally, cannot keep a civil tongue in his head, but because a tongue is inherently uncivil (if not, one hopes, inveterately so). Silence is not the absence of language; there is no such absence for human beings; in this respect, there is no world elsewhere.

Coriolanus cannot imagine, or cannot accept, that there is a way to partake of one another, incorporate one another, that is necessary to the formation rather than to the extinction of a community. (As he cannot imagine being fed without being deserving. This is his precise reversal of Christ's vision, that we cannot in ourselves deserve sustenance, and that it is for that reason, and in that spirit, that we have to ask for it. Thus is misanthropy, like philanthropy, a certain parody of Christianity.) The play *Coriolanus* asks us to try to imagine it, imagine a beneficial, mutual consumption, arguing in effect that this is what the formation of an audience is. (As if *vorare* were next to *orare*.)

It seems to me that what I have been saying demonstrates, no doubt somewhat comically, the hypothesis of the origin of tragedy in religious ritual – somewhat comically, because I must seem rather to have deflated the problem, implying that whether the hypthesis is true depends on what is meant by "tragedy," what by "origin," and which ritual is in mind.[12] I have, in effect, argued that if you accept the words as food, and you accept the central figure as invoking the central figure of the eucharist, then you may accept a formulation to the effect (not that the play is the ritual of the eucharist, but to the effect) that the play celebrates, or aspires to, the same fact as the ritual does, say the condition of community. Eucharist means gratitude, precisely what Coriolanus feels the people withhold from him. This is another way to see why I am not satisfied to say that Coriolanus is enraged first of all by the people's cowardice. Perhaps one may say that to Coriolanus their cowardice means ingratitude. As for the idea of origin, we need only appeal to Descartes's idea that the origin of a thing is the same thing that preserves it. What preserves a tragedy, what creates the effect of a certain kind of drama, is the appropriation by an audience of this effect, our mutual incorporation of its words. When the sharing of a sacrifice is held on religious ground, the ritual itself assures its effectiveness. When it is shifted to aesthetic ground, in a theater, there is no such pre-existing assurance; the work of art has to handle everything itself. You might think of this as the rebirth of religion from the spirit of tragedy. A performance is nothing without our participation in an audience; and this participation is up to each of us.

To enforce the necessity of this decision to participate (a decision which of course has its analogue for the individual reader with the script in his or her hands) is the way I understand the starkness of the words of this play, their relative ineloquence, their lack of apparent resonance. The play presents us with our need for one another's words by presenting withholding words, words that do not meet us halfway. It presents us with a famine of words. This way of seeing it takes it to fulfill a prophecy from the Book of Amos (8:11): "Behold, the days come, saith the Lord God, that I will send a famine in the land, not a famine of bread, nor a thirst for water; but of hearing the words of the Lord."

Postscript

It may be felt, it should be felt, that my account of Coriolanus's disgust by language has studiously had to avoid a more obvious, or equally obvious, if less explicit understanding than I have given of it. I said that he has a horror of putting in his mouth what (as in his fantasy) comes out of the mouths of others; and I gave that as a reason why it is irrelevant to Coriolanus whether the Fable of the Belly is interpreted with the patricians or with the plebeians as the belly, or as the tongue, or as any other part. What alarms him is simply being part, one member among others, of the same organism. But there is a different way of characterizing his reason for alarm, a different manner of taking the parable from the beginning.

This way is one that rather literalizes the parable, one that takes its joking not to turn merely, or primarily, on an ambiguity over whom the belly represents, over who does the providing to whom, but on an ambiguity over what the product is that the belly provides, over what there is to be provided, on this organic view of the state. This further ambiguity concerns what we might think of as the direction in which the giving or returning done by the belly is imagined to happen. Is the belly's process and product directed back toward the body of which it is part, or out toward the earth which it shares, and of which it partakes? In the latter case disgust is a function of imagining that in incorporating one another we are asked to incorporate one another's leavings, the results or wastes of what has already been incorporated.

On this reading, two features of the Fable of the Belly find a better home than I was able formerly, concentrating on words as food, to provide for them: the First Citizen's image or fantasy of the belly as "the sink o'th' body" (I.i.121), its sewer; and Menenius's offering as the belly's taunting reply to the accusation against it of the rebel parts of the body, what he calls "a kind of smile, / Which ne'er came from the lungs, but even thus –" (I.i. 106–7). I do not insist that you must conceive Menenius here as figuring the answering smile as a noise, say a kind of laugh, or a cheer; but only that *if* you find yourself figuring it so, you must be unsure whether the noise comes from above or from below.

The outward direction of circulation is as familiar in this period of Shakespeare as the inward. From *Antony and Cleopatra*: the man at the beginning is saying, "Kingdoms are clay: our dungy earth alike / Feeds beast as man; the nobleness of life / Is to do thus"; and the woman at the ending, "and it is great / To do that thing that ends all other deeds, . . . / Which sleeps, and never palates more the dung, / The beggar's nurse, and Caesar's." These imaginings of the earth as feeding its inhabitants, in reciprocation with the imagining of its being nourished by the leavings and remains of those it feeds, for example, by us humans, are in each case here expressions of a mind in exaltation, hence somewhat reductive of its environment; minds in a mood that seeks transcendence of the common lot of humanity. But this means that neither Cleopatra nor Antony is seeking to deny – the thing it is Coriolanus's mission to deny – that this circulation *is* common, is even *what* is common, along the scale of living kinds and the degrees of human ranks. I suppose that these late Roman plays exist on this axis in what Norman Rabkin has called a relation of complementarity. It accordingly suggests itself that the two directions of the circulation of nourishment are kept, in healthier imaginations, in healthier appetites, from crossing; that the imagination of what the mouth receives as food is normally mediated by passing it through nature, so to purify the contribution made to the process by other, let us say, human beings.

In suggesting that in Coriolanus the imagination has collapsed upon itself, that his fantasy is that he is asked to feed directly on the leavings of others, I am not retracting, but further glossing, his sense of disgust at the words that exit from their mouths, glossing what it is he thinks words are, and what food is or, you may say, the chain of food. Keeping one's critical balance in this matter, not allowing one's imagination to collapse upon itself, could hardly be trickier. The very suggestion of the element this postscript invokes is apt to stifle what the body of my essay takes – correctly, I persist in thinking – as fundamental in the play, namely the circulation from mouth to mouth of language. The trick is to let this fact be challenged, and not overthrown, by the suggestion that language is at the same time something retained, which perhaps means hoarded, for expulsion, or banishment, a way of conceiving of writing, physically altering the world.

The suggestion makes its way, in the part of the world I know, mostly in slang, or jokes, as when E. E. Cummings has his erring Olaf say, "There is some s. I will not eat," and in expressions rejecting the words of others by asking what they are trying to hand you, or by naming the product as the droppings of horses or bulls. And the idea presents a link with the ideas associating the circulation of food with that of the circulation of words and with that of money (cf. note 11). Here the connection is primarily through the senses of "superfluity," as for example when the First Citizen says, "What authority surfeits on would relieve us. If they would yield us but the superfluity while it were wholesome, we might guess they relieved us humanely; but they think we are too dear: . . . our sufferance is a gain to them" (I.i.15–21). And the connection of words through grain to money is enforced in the same citizen's longest speech after Menenius enters: "They ne'er cared for us yet. Suffer us to famish, and their storehouses crammed with grain; make edicts for usury, to support usurers" (I.i.78–81). To my ear, Shakespeare's lines here do not simply cite usury as a second, historically accurate cause for a second (earlier) revolt, but put as it were the two revolts in apposition, so that usury and hoarding are metaphors for one another. Without insisting on this, I wish to invoke here Marc Shell's rehabilitation of the concept of "verbal usury," for his extraordinary essay on The Merchant of Venice, a concept he characterizes as referring "to the generation of an illegal – the church fathers say unnatural – supplement to verbal meaning by use of such methods as punning and flattering."[13] It is as if Coriolanus finds the barest use of words usurious, while the citizens accuse him of a kind of verbal miserliness, depriving them of all credit. The feeling in the citizens' speeches is not alone of their physical pain in suffering want, but of the insufferable *meaning* of this pain, that it is inflicted, that it communicates the contempt in which the patricians hold them. (In saying that grain forms a link between words and money, I take for granted the connection, on either Marxian or Freudian grounds, of money with excrement. The folk character of the connection, hence preparation for its convincingness to me, is present in a joke circulated my way by my father, who once remarked that they must be teaching me chemistry in college because I had learned so well to take money and make dreck out of it.)

In responding to Paul Alpers's query concerning a sense of the comic underlying my entire reading of *Coriolanus* (reported in note 12), I should have pointed to the belly's smile as well as to the gods' laughter. Then what is the joke? Who could laugh at it? Freud has some helpful words:

> There are yet other means of making things comic which deserve special consideration and also indicate in part fresh sources of comic pleasure. . . . Caricature, parody and travesty (as well as their practical counterpart, unmasking) are directed against people and objects which lay claim to authority and respect, which are in some sense "*sublime*." They are procedures for *Herabsetzung* [degradation] as the apt German expression has it. . . . When . . . the procedures . . . for the degradation of the sublime allow me to have an idea of it as though it were something commonplace, in whose presence I need not pull myself together but may, to use the military formula, "stand easy," I am being spared the increased expenditure of the solemn restraint . . . the difference in expenditure . . . can be discharged by laughter.
>
> Under the heading of "unmasking" we may also include . . . the method of degrading the dignity of individuals by directing attention to the frailties which they share with all humanity, but in particular the dependence of their mental functions on bodily needs. The unmasking is equivalent here to an admonition; such and such a person, who is admired as a demigod, is after all only human like you and me.[14]

But the comic pleasure in discovering Coriolanus's vulnerabilities, to us who are neither gods nor just bellies, does not get much beyond the cold comfort of an ironic awareness of the viciousness of his virtue, the uselessness in his usefulness. I think back to my suggestion that the formation of a society depends on there being, on our achieving, a partaking of one another that is beneficial, creative, not annihilating, as if our mutual cannibalism is a parody of what we might be, that we are standing jokes on ourselves, wishing to transcend what would no longer deserve to be transcended if we could mutually give up the wish (as if needing one another's hands meant that human beings are fated to accept what they have so far learned to hand one another). Instead we feel deprived, hence vengeful, feel fated as things stand not to get as good as we give. (The comic necessity in these feelings, or tragic contingency, will want pursuing into the bearing of the Fable of the Belly on the full appeal of the idea of the body politic, as though the belly is smiling at all theorizing that leaves the state, or say sovereignty, organic. And does political thinking know itself to be free of this appeal, of, let us say, the idea of the citizen's two bodies, or it may be more; or is it better to think of each of us as of two or more minds?)

In broaching the subject of this postscript, I said that the anality in the play is less explicit than the orality I had confined myself to in the, as it were, body of my essay, implying that its being mostly implicit in the words of the play is hardly a sufficient reason for leaving it inexplicit in a stretch of criticism. But one may well take, as Kenneth Burke has taken, the issue to be given full explicitness in the play's, and its hero's, name. In the section headed "Comments" that follows, or concludes, Burke's masterful essay "*Coriolanus* and the delights of faction," he remarks:

> Though the names are taken over literally from Plutarch, it is remarkable how tonally suggestive some of them are, from the standpoint of their roles in this English play. . . . And in the light of Freudian theories concerning the fecal nature of invective, the last two syllables of the hero's name are so "right," people now often seek to dodge the issue by altering the traditional pronunciation (making the *a* broad instead of long).[15]

But how are we to specify what is "right" about the name? Granted the intentionality of Shakespeare's play's attention to the name, he may in it be seeking a heavenly horse-laugh at language's vengeance in distributing one and the same sound equally to a suffix that encodes a name's military honor and to the name of the shape of a sphincter; as if noting a kind of poetic justice. (Another point of justice is perhaps noted in Burke's suggesting "excess" as well as "pride" as a translation of *hubris*.)

Burke is immensely tactful in mentioning the subject, in his essay here and elsewhere, and while on the occasions of delivering versions of my essay as talks I would allude to the fecal issue as something to be considered, I did not see how to consider it well in unprotected prose. Whatever I wrote down seemed to me either too explicit or too implicit, brazen or hidden. I could understand part of my difficulty to be quite inescapable; one cannot readily rise above the level of one's civilization's sense of humor. As in other matters, I take *Walden* as a touchstone for this issue. Thoreau's recurrent allusions in that book to eating and elimination are expressions of his bursting admiration for the capacity of (especially Indian) scriptures to name the organs and functions of the body as plain facts of cosmic rhythms; as facts; without invoking or evading attitudes toward them, as if to suppose them so much as good or bad were presumptuous. It is a capacity to name them, and to make recommendations with respect to them with, let me say, detachment; to name philosophically. Thoreau did not think us westerners capable of this, as a culture, yet. You might think of philosophical naming as something the serious writing of a culture holds out to it.

It was in coming to see more unprotectedly that Shakespeare's *Coriolanus* is itself exactly in struggle with this question of explicitness and naming, or that it is internal to the way I have proposed taking the play, as a study of the shunning of voices, hence the craving of them, that I was shamed into making my embarrassment (of style, say) more explicit in this note. The implication is that to avoid risking one's critical balance in traversing this play is to avoid a measure of participation in the play's assessment of the balance civilization exacts. Call it the exaction of civility. To what extent can the powers of a city reciprocate in civility and remain powers? To what extent can they withhold reciprocation without naming a state of war, directed inward or outward?

I hope I have sufficiently indicated in my essay why a study of voices goes into a study of the formation of human society, of the recognition of others as, so to speak, *my* others. The idea of a social contract as expressing one's consent to be governed, to be civil, is a demand, as I have had reason to insist, for explicitness, however hard it may be to establish what must constitute an original explicitness.[16] For think of it this way. The consent to be governed must express the desire to be governed, governed by consent, and hence to participate in the city. To express desire inexplicitly is an act of seduction, hence one that exists only in a medium of prohibition and conspiracy. It may be that human sexual life will continue to require this medium and its struggles for the foreseeable future, say for as long as our politics does not create a more perfect public medium, unfailingly intelligible, reciprocal, and nourishing. Without this, we will continue to interpret privacy as inexplicitness, and on this ground the private will continue to look like the natural enemy of the political, as in opposite ways it is shown to be, to our distress, in *Antony and Cleopatra* and in *Coriolanus*. Who cares whether the unjust can be happy when we still do not know whether the demand for happiness is survivable?

And the idea of the recognition of others as mine, implying the acknowledgment of human beings as human, things that think, is a matter of putting body and soul together, of connecting perception and imagination I have sometimes said, whatever these are. Philosophers have made problems, as well they might, about what it is to know that others have minds. I am in effect taking *Coriolanus* to raise the question, as well we might, what it is to know that others, that we, have bodies. According to the line of thought in this postscript it is to know that, and perhaps know why, the body has (along with the senses) two openings, or two sites for openings, ones that are connected, made for each other, a top and a bottom, or a front and a back, outsides and insides. But what is the expression of this knowledge, what acknowledges it; I mean, what is the expression of a knowledge of its commonness, for example as between us? Harping on the idea (perhaps as Swift did) seems to miss its commonness, or ordinariness. But how do you know that remaining silent about it isn't denying it? And does Descartes's metaphysical insistence that we are essentially minds deny the universal accident that we are (connected to) bodies? And does Nietzsche's metaphysical insistence that we are bodies deny the grandeur of the mind?

If we say that noting the connection of the body with itself wants tact, we may say that Coriolanus traces the costs of the absence of this tact of civility. While his case is more extreme than ours, our satisfaction in ridding ourselves of him attests to our representation by him, that we make him our agent. Our differences from his case are that we demand less of our honor than he of his, and that social divisions among us are less, differences which at best speak of our fortune, or belatedness, not of our credit. So I gather that no one is in a position to say what the right expression is of our knowledge that we are strung out on both sides of a belly. Then the issue is whether we have to know this before we can know the partaking that makes a city good, or whether the city, in its poverty of goodness, can provide itself with individuals, or clusters, who know such a thing, and whether it can then stop and take in what they have to say, whether it can tolerate the voice of its own language.

Notes

This essay is excerpted from: *Themes Out of School: Effects and Causes*, copyright © 1984 by Stanley Cavell. Published by North Point Press and reprinted by permission.

All quotations from *Coriolanus* are taken from the Arden Shakespeare edition, ed. Philip Brockbank (London and New York, 1976).

1. Stanley Cavell, *The Claim of Reason* (New York and Oxford, 1979). The subject was broached in "The avoidance of love: a reading of *King Lear*," in Stanley Cavell, *Must We Mean What We Say?* (Cambridge, 1976).
2. See Bertolt Brecht, *Collected Plays*, 9, ed. Ralph Manheim and John Willett (New York, 1973), 378–94.
3. Janet Adelman, "'Anger's my meat': feeding, dependency and aggression in *Coriolanus*," in *Representing Shakespeare*, ed. Murray Schwartz and Coppélia Kahn (Baltimore, 1980).
4. "There seems to be some question whether one's knowing oneself is something active, something one does . . . or rather something one suffers, something that happens to one" (Cavell, *The Claim of Reason*, 352).
5. A point emphasized in remarks by Professor Harry Berger, chairman of the *Coriolanus* panel at the Humanities Institute meetings at Stanford University, September 10–12, 1982, at which a version of the present essay was read.
6. Adelman, op. cit., 131.
7. One such effort enters into the opening pages of "The avoidance of love" (Cavell, *Must We Mean What We Say?*).
8. This is not meant as an alternative to but as an extension of the fine perception in the last note to I. ix by the editor of the Arden edition (Philip Brockbank) that "One name is found in the scene and another lost." My thought is that both are names held by Caius Martius Coriolanus. I suppose I am influenced in this thought by a further change Shakespeare makes in Plutarch's characterization of

the man. In Plutarch, Coriolanus speaks of the man as "an old friend and host of mine"; it is at the analogous moment in Shakespeare that Coriolanus speaks of the man as one at whose house he lay. The opening words of Plutarch's *Life* are "The house of the Martians," where "house" of course means "family," a phrase and passage employed by Shakespeare at the end of Act II where the tribunes invoke Coriolanus's biological descent as if to their sufficient credit for having considered it but to Coriolanus's insufficient credit for election to consul.

9. I quote from North's translation of Plutarch's biography of Coriolanus, which is given in an appendix to the Arden edition of *Coriolanus* (London, 1976). The "impostume" passage occurs on p. 133.

Coriolanus's sense of disgust with the people is more explicitly conveyed by Shakespeare through the sense of their foul smell than of their foul taste. Shakespeare does use the idea of spitting twice: once, as cited, to describe Hector's forehead bleeding in battle, and the second time in Coriolanus's only scene of soliloquy, disguised before Aufidius's house: "Then know me not; / Lest that thy wives with spits, and boys with stones, / In puny battle slay me" – so that both times spitting is linked with battle and with food. As I have implied, I understand Coriolanus's vision of his death in Antium at the hands of wives and boys as a prophecy of the death he actually undergoes there, spitted by the swords of strange boys.

10. The following remarks on Sidney's tract were reintroduced, expanded from an earlier set on the subject that I had dropped from the paper, as a result of an exchange with Stephen Greenblatt during the discussion period following my presentation at Stanford.

11. Finding the words/food representation so compelling, I am ignoring here the path along which the circulation of words also registers the circulation of money (as in "So shall my lungs / Coin words" (III.i.76–7); and in "The price is, to ask it kindly" (II.iii.75)). The sense of consuming as expending would relate to Coriolanus's frantic efforts to deny that his actions can be recompensed ("better to starve than crave the hire" – for example, of receiving voices *in return*). Money depends upon the equating of values; Coriolanus on their lack of equation, on measurelessness, pricelessness.

12. In the discussion period at Stanford, Paul Alpers noted that I seemed to find something like a comic perspective of the play to be more extensive than just here where I am making it explicit, and he asked how far I wished to go in seeking this perspective. I find this a true response to my reading, but it goes beyond anything I can explore now. I mentioned then what I take to be a starting point to such an exploration, Coriolanus's sense that as he and his mother stand silent together, "The gods look down, and this unnatural scene / They laugh at." Does he feel the gods laugh because mother and son are too close or too distant with one another? At least the scene is unnatural because it is social, and because the social is the scene of mazes of meaning as dense as poetry, in which its poor, prosaic, half-human creatures are isolated. The comedic perspective I seek presents itself to me as a totalization, or a kind of transcendentalizing, of dramatic irony – where the omen or allusion is not of some specific, future event, but of the totality of the present, of events as they are, without our being able to specify in advance what individuates or what relates these events.

13. Marc Shell, "The wether and the ewe," in *Money, Language, and Thought* (Berkeley and Los Angeles, 1982), 49. I knew that my debt to Marc Shell went beyond the writing of his I can cite, since, among other matters, he attended the seminar in which I first broached my sense of *Coriolanus*, and it was often his

questions that kept me moving. But it was not until after completing not only the body of this essay but also this postscript that I returned to complete my reading of the essays in his *Money, Language, and Thought,* and there I find that I have incurred, or would like at once to incur, a new debt. The second essay of the book, "The blank check: accounting for the Grail," which for some reason Shell did not press upon me on hearing my *Coriolanus* material, suggests to my mind that the story I have told, including its extension into this postscript, has to be extended further to incorporate the scene and action of Shakespeare's *Coriolanus* into a telling of (hence, as suggested by my account, a competition with) the dearth and plenitude as recounted in the legends of the Holy Grail. I assemble a packet of quotations from Shell's essay to indicate my sense of the issue:

"The infinitely large gift and the free gift (one given gratis, without intending to obligate the recipient to reciprocate and without making him feel obligated to do so) may well be impossible in everyday exchange. . . . The hypothesis of the infinitely large gift, for example, appears as the cornucopia, and the hypothesis of the free gift, as Pauline grace. . . . [T]owards the end of the medieval era . . . the first widespread vernacular literature told of a cornucopian grail, an extraordinary gift both infinitely large and free, which was said to be able to lift men out of the ordinary world of exchange into a world in which freedom and totality were possible. . . . The grail legends depict a wasteland to which the limitless production of material and spiritual goods stands as a defining and conceptually unique limit." (24–5)

"Chrétien is a poet-sower who must consider the relationship of the fertility of his seed both to the relative spiritual sterility of his audience and to the material sterility of the wasteland of which he would tell them. Spiritual fertility varies from person to person, so that Chrétien must speak on several levels at the same time. . . . All the grail tales claim the status of riddle." (25)

"Like the apostle's inkhorn (*cornu*) . . . the word *graal* operates in the grail tales as a 'cornucopia of words,' just as the grail itself operates as a plentiful cornucopia of nourishing food." (26–7)

"At the beginning of Chrétien's *Account,* for example, the hero Perceval is presented as a typical hungry adolescent who seeks food from his mother, expects food at the tent he mistakenly believes to be a chapel, demands food from the God he believes to live in the tent-chapel, and finally receives earthly food. Only divine nourishment, however, can satisfy the desire of this questing man. Perceval learns about the kind of food God provides when a hermit tells him on Good Friday that the food he failed to ask about at the grail castle was 'real.'" (27)

"The kind of men who do not have good food to go into their mouths do not have good words to come out of their mouths." (29)

"The free sacrifice of a woman helps to resolder the broken sword of the realm. . . . [T]here is in many stories this identity of sword and person." (33, and n.)

14. Sigmund Freud, *Jokes and Their Relation to the Unconscious,* tr. J. Strachey (New York, 1960), 200–1, 202.

15. Kenneth Burke, *Language as Symbolic Action* (Berkeley and Los Angeles, 1966), 96.

16. I have in mind *The Claim of Reason,* 22–8.

IV
The question of *Hamlet*

14

ROBERT WEIMANN
Mimesis in *Hamlet*

In view of recent revisions of the concept of "mimesis" and the thorough-going critique of "representation,"[1] Shakespeare criticism faces a number of challenging propositions which cut deep into its (largely unformulated and rarely questioned) assumptions of continuity and congruity between the act of interpretation, its cultural function, and its unique object, the Shake-spearean text in the theater. What the newest criticism seeks to undermine is the validity of a critical tradition according to which the "meaning" of Shakespeare, then and now, used to be read in terms of a privileged representativity and a given authority inherent in the act of representation (and interpretation) itself. In the light of this tradition the work of the poet, the voice of the actor, the response of the spectator or reader were taken to share in a cultural language and purpose whose legitimation was established through generally available and relatively stable links between language and meaning, signifier and signified. The argument against this tradition by now is powerfully familiar; and although there is no space here to interrogate the theoretical objections on the level of social ideology and cultural politics, yet it would be possible to suggest (although the oversimplification is obvious) that behind this argument there is a genuine sense of crisis in the continuity of the liberal tradition in both criticism and the theater. If, in western critical discourse, the humanistic education has ceased to be able to revitalize its sense of vocation and continuity on traditional grounds and if, in many theatrical productions, the contradictions between past functions and present uses of Shakespeare's plays have become too painful to provide a source of strength and coherence, then indeed there is some urgency in the necessary attempt to look more critically at those traditional premises on which concepts of representation and mimesis have in the past been applied to the plays of Shakespeare.

But which are the alternatives? How to cope with the liabilities of the old mimesis and from where to proceed towards a "new mimesis"? After the splitting of the sign, the rupture between thought and language, signification and figuration, traditional theories of mimesis (classical, neoclassical, even modern versions such as those by Lukács and Auerbach) have indeed revealed a number of theoretical limitations. Only, while it is easy today to point to the Platonic and generally idealistic nature of the classical version of mimesis (the naturalizing of the sign, the unacknowledged presence of authority and hierarchy in the "mirror" metaphor, the privileged focus on *Produktions-ästhetik*, the harmonizing language of unity and homogeneity),[2] it seems much more difficult even to begin to conceive of a practicable alternative, especially if this is to be based on a nonrepresentational theory of Shakespearean mimesis.[3] The reasons for that seem fairly obvious; although this is not the place to confront the poststructuralist challenge on an epistemological level,[4] the question needs to be asked whether or to what extent the textualizing methodology of deconstruction can provide a satisfactory framework within which the whole complex question of mimesis in Shakespeare can at all be adequately reopened.

As we all know, Shakespeare's plays were written for a theater which cannot satisfactorily be defined in reference to either a purely literary or an exclusively neoclassical tradition of mimesis. Even when deeply indebted to the humanist poetics of inscribed language, these plays remained close to a culture of voices, a civilization of oral signs and practical privileges where blindness itself (and the unliterary spectator) could be told to "look with thine ears." In other words, a theatrical institution in which *oratio* could precede so much *ratio* cannot lend itself easily to those semiotic and deconstructive methods which take as their starting point a purely literary definition of the sign or some exclusively textualized concept of language. Rhetoric, in this Elizabethan context, cannot be derived from the inscribed forms of language; nor can the wounding, healing, affectional power of the performed word be abstracted from the existential realities of theatrical representation.

Even more important, in one vital respect (let us conveniently call it the ritual or carnival dimension) the Shakespearean theater precedes the very premises upon which the recent critique of the classical modes of mimesis and representation are based. As soon as we look at the actual forms and functions of mimesis in the plays themselves (and *Hamlet* here can serve only as a paradigm), Shakespeare's theater appears to sustain a multiplicity of social and cultural functions in the light of which principles of homogeneity, "closure," and authority in representation are constantly undermined and subverted. If "representation" is said to homogenize textual production, stabilize hierarchies and privileges (and so void the text of contradictions and interrogations), then, indeed, the dramatic representations of Shakespeare may well be shown not to exhaust their mimetic potential under these modes of closure and plenitude. On the contrary, although the specular reading or viewing of the plays can of course fix the reader or viewer in the plenitude of some false consciousness, there is ample evidence that, over and beyond its stabilizing functions, Shakespearean mimesis comprehends a self-conscious subversion of authority in representation. In fact, a reconsideration of Shakespeare's uses of mimesis may lead to the conclusion that what is (or is not) represented in his plays is a major, open issue which the deconstruction- ist project is not well equipped to illuminate.

There is, in *Hamlet* as in at least some of the other tragedies and problem plays, a deeply disturbing gulf between what is represented and what is representing (i.e. the Shakespearean activity in the text plus the performative action on the stage). If there is room for authority in representation, then this authority is not, as in the contemporary political discourse of, say, William Lambarde, "already given."[5] For Shakespeare the issue of authority in representation is surprisingly unpredetermined. What his plays reveal (at least up to and including *King Lear*) is an increasing readiness critically to explore the sources of authority, its precariously personal or socially divided manifestations. As in *Measure for Measure*, authority emerges as a "demi- god" (I. ii. 114), a profoundly ambivalent instance, not as providing a closed relationship between signifier and signified. On the contrary, whenever "madness in discourse" is allowed to surface, there results an unprecedented interrogation and, in one case, splitting of authority which tends to subvert all logocentric standards:

> O madness of discourse,
> That cause sets up with and against itself!
> Bifold authority!
> (*Troilus and Cressida*, V. ii. 139–41)[6]

The absence of stability in the links between the rhetoric and the figures of authority is as remarkable as the rupture between its signs and its signifi- cations, between what "authority" or "ceremony" presumes to represent and what in actuality is represented by it. Eventually, this rupture seems to infest the whole drama of authority itself, the vulnerability of its dramaturgy, the unsuspected disclosure of brutally privileged power in the signified it- self. Note how Lear projects his own madness through the blindness of Gloucester'

Lear: What, art mad? A man may see how this world goes with no eyes. Look with thine ears. See how yond justice rails upon yond simple thief. Hark, in thine ear: change places and, handy-dandy, which is

> the justice, which is the thief? Thou hast seen a farmer's dog bark at
> a beggar?
>
> *Glo.:* Ay, sir.
> *Lear:* And the creature run from the cur? There thou mightst behold the
> great image of authority: a dog's obey'd in office.
>
> (IV. vi. 144–59)

This tragic "image of authority" contradicts the politics of Elizabethan rhetoric and is subversive by all standards of classical representation. Here is a mirror of topsy-turvydom, distorted as well as distorting, designed for "no eyes," with "matter and impertinency mix'd" (176). If in *King Lear* the mimesis of authority has reached a state of profound crisis, that crisis equally affects the authority of mimesis. But the "handy-dandy" mode of "change places" creates more than ambivalence; it creates a mimetic mode of so inverting the representativity of verbal images that the signifier ceases to stabilize the privileged signified (as in the imagery of "Robes and furr'd gowns," 165), impertinently turns its hierarchies upside down, and thus in the text helps to constitute the perspective of the victims rather than that of the spokesmen of "authority."

Lear utters these words in madness. Madness, there, is a pertinent object of representation, and as such it has plenty of classical sanctions, such as Seneca's *Hercules furens* and related drama. But on the Elizabethan stage madness not only constitutes an *object* of representation but also forms a (nonclassical) *mode* of representing, as associated with the element of clowning, punning, and "impertinency," the tradition of topsy-turvydom and the "mad" nonsensical Vice.[7] In other words, Shakespeare's plays represent the triumphs and defeats of authority, but at the same time the divisions and suspensions of authority are written large into their composition and performance, into their mode of representation, the activity behind the mimesis itself. Thus, the crisis of authority itself informs the contradiction between what is representing and what is represented, and in the midst of this contradiction the multiple uses of Shakespearean mimesis find their most complex function, one which does not necessarily stipulate either closure or rupture, naturalization or heterogeneity.

What, then, this hurried introduction to the problem of authority and representation in Shakespeare suggests is that his uses of mimesis cannot be formulated in (let alone reduced to) either a representational or nonrepresentational theory of dramatic language. As the following study of *Hamlet* attempts to show, Shakespearean mimesis comprehends so many functions that neither the traditional or classical nor the poststructuralist approach to mimesis can do justice to them all. To say this is not to dismiss the poststructuralist perspective out of hand; on the contrary, Geoffrey Hartman is surely right when he notes that "a restored theory of representation should acknowledge the deconstructionist challenge as necessary and timely."[8] Even when Derrida's "antitheatrical prejudice" (as Hartman calls it) as well as related stances in the anti-representational position of critics such as Michel Foucault and even René Girard, may have to be rejected, the poststructuralist direction in criticism is broad enough to have room for perspectives such as those developed by Bernard Pautrat and Philippe Lacoue-Labarthe. As the latter (responding to René Girard's definition of mimesis as a primordial pattern of desire, conflict, and appropriation[9]) reminds us,

> the oldest and most constant gesture vis-à-vis mimesis . . . is . . . to put it on stage and theatricalize it in order to try to catch it in the trap of *sa-voir*, of in-sight. Far from covering up or masking mimesis, theatricality "reveals" it – which means that it fixes it, defines and "presents" it as that which, in all events, it never is on its "own."[10]

If this is so, then mimesis in Shakespeare can neither be conceived as a re-presentation or rewriting, in a text or fiction, of an object which is known and agreed upon in advance nor can it be defined as – in the way of René Girard – a primordial act of desire desiring desire. The question is where to go beyond this unacceptable alternative between discursive and nondiscursive definitions of mimesis. Is there perhaps any basis in the Shakespearean text itself on which to redefine "mimesis" without necessarily opting for either the privileges or the repression of representation, and on which the issue of authority *in* representation need not necessarily preclude its deconstruction *through* representation?

*

In *Hamlet*, more than anywhere else in Shakespeare, the question of mimesis is central. The play contains the most sustained theoretical statement on the subject that we have in Shakespeare's whole *œuvre*; what is more, the links as well as the gaps between mimetic theory and mimetic practice are used in dramaturgy as well as thematically to such an effect that mimesis emerges in both its discursive and nondiscursive dimensions. The theory itself, through its dramatized application in and to the play within the play, becomes a matter of practical theatrical consequence. Since mimesis is associated and, in fact, identified with the conjuncture of discursive and nondiscursive activity ("Suit the action to the word, the word to the action"), the arrival of the players, the preparation and actual presentation of the play within the play, assume a pivotal function in correlating dramatic process and dramatic product: *The Mousetrap* itself becomes a peculiar "trap of *sa-voir*," a self-conscious vehicle of the drama's awareness of the functional and thematic heterogeneity of mimesis itself. Such mimesis of mimesis *dramatically* helps to establish the links between dramaturgy and theme, and in doing so provokes differing levels of contradiction, such as that between speaking and acting, or that between theory and practice which, in their turn, link up with the thematic conflict, associated with the central figure of the play, between discourse and action, conscience and revenge.

In order to unravel these complexities in Shakespeare's uses of mimesis, let us first of all look at the *locus classicus*, Hamlet's advice to the players:

> Speak the speech, I pray you, as I pronounced it to you, trippingly on the tongue. . . . Nor do not saw the air too much with your hand, thus, but use all gently. . . . For anything so o'erdone is from the purpose of playing, whose end, both at the first and now, was and is to hold as 'twere the mirror up to nature; to show virtue her feature, scorn her own image, and the very age and body of the time his form and pressure.[11]

Even the incomplete quotation reveals some significant relationship between mimetic theory and practice. The theoretical statement of poetic principle is rendered in the form of some well motivated practical advice to the actors. The trajectory of the speech, meandering between recommendation and disapproval, is (1) from a discussion of the actor's rhetoric and delivery to (2) some general outline of the "purpose of playing." Mimesis, in this connection, is defined in relation not to a dramatic text but to the work of the actors (who, once deficient in their "accent" and "gait," are said to have "imitated humanity so abominably" (35)). What Hamlet's advice emphasizes, then, is voice and performance rather than any purely literary, let alone textual, consideration. The emphasis on things theatrical is confirmed when the speech moves on to (3) projecting varying types of audience response ("though it makes the unskilful laugh, cannot but make the judicious grieve") and some unwelcome forms of actors/audience contact, which finally (4) are rejected in the interests of the self-contained drama of the Renaissance whose presumed unity does not allow that "in the meantime some necessary question of the play" be neglected (42–3).

The discussion of mimesis, then, itself serves a "necessary question of the play" in so far as it touches upon (and is made to prepare for) the requirements of a theatrical production within that other production which is the play at large. As Hamlet with great facility moves from precept to practice and again from practical matters to aesthetic scruples, the text of his whole speech reveals itself as a highly heterogeneous one. Its theme is neither exclusively that of Renaissance rhetoric or neoclassical poetics nor that of Elizabethan theatrical practice, but one in which the demands of the former are viewed as in relation to, or in collision with, the latter. What we have at the center is the tension (at least as strong as the attempt to achieve some balance) between poetic theory and theatrical practice, between drama as defined by the humanists (editors easily note echoes of Quintilian and Cicero via Donatus), and theater as practiced in the hands of traveling actors. The dramatized relationship between the two is such that it allows for important areas of concurrence, but it is precisely through the tensions remaining between neoclassical theory and Elizabethan practice that the utterance becomes *dramatic* and the whole speech achieves its self-motivated sense of urgency as well as its structuring significance within the play as a whole.

Hamlet, in this sense, can be seen to rehearse one basic contradiction in the history of the Elizabethan theater: the precariously achieved synthesis, maturing in Kyd and Marlowe, between humanist learning and native spectacle (including histrionic practice)[12] is significantly used and, as it were, interrogated within the play itself. For that, the players' scenes provide a scenario, in which the element of tension between neoclassical theory and theatrical practice (as articulated in Hamlet's repeated warnings, discouragements, and disapprovals) must be acknowledged as dramaturgically as well as thematically most consequential. Although the players' scenes have more often than not been treated as merely marginal or topical in their interest, they in their own way provide a dramatized version of the problematic relationship between language and action, and they adumbrate some deeply disturbing incongruity between what represents and what is represented. (I shall return to Ophelia's puzzlement over the dumb-show with its "miching malicho.") The resulting irresolutions (and the tragic quality of the resolutions) must ultimately be connected with that thematized conflict between discursive and nondiscursive activities which culminates in the hero's dilemma between the verbal promptings of his conscience and the violent acts of revenge. What in the present context needs to be emphasized, however, is that elements of both conflict and synthesis inform the mimetic statement on mimesis which we have in the play. For, in Hamlet's words of advice, humanist theory serves as an aristocratic touchstone of histrionic practice, while (less immediately so, but no less effectively) theatrical practice, including the dramatized image of both this theory and practice, serves as a testing ground for Renaissance poetic theory.[13] The relationship between mimetic theory and histrionic practice is not representational, then, in the sense that the former serves as a mere inscription (or prescription) of the latter. What we have, rather, is a correlation as well as an interrogation and, finally, a gap in communication between those who prescribe representations and those who practice them.

Thus, the mimesis of mimesis (which the players' scenes and the play within the play project) helps to underline the problematic of representation itself, and it accentuates the heterogeneity in the links between what is representing and what is represented. This heterogeneity marks the strategic contradiction between the signifying "image of a murder done in Vienna" (III. ii. 233) and the signified re-enactment of Claudius's crime. A similar element of incongruity suffuses the "miching malicho" (135) and Ophelia's puzzled response to the dumb-show and the Prologue: "Will a tell us what this show meant?" (139). Hamlet's obscene reply ("Ay, or any show that you will show him. Be not you ashamed to show, he'll not shame to tell you what it means") may be read as an impertinent paraphrase of such heterogeneous uses of presentation and representation: the rupture as well as the interaction between what is shown and what is meant (what "passes show"), between what is presenting and what is presented, are central to the whole relationship between the play and the play within the play. The mimesis of mimesis is deeply built into the play at large. More specifically, beginning with the Player's speech, the self-enacted multiple forms of mimesis provide a locus and a mode of "reproduction of the play's basic motifs in exaggerated form,"[14] such as the death of fathers, exemplified in Priam, the "tale" of their "slaughter," the grief of widowed queens, etc.

But while this self-engendering and self-reflexive mimesis serves in a metarepresentational function (transcribing and, thereby, intercepting at least part of the play's primary presentation), its most vital medium and ubiquitous sponsor – the figure of Hamlet – is itself so cast into multiple functions of mimesis that what the "character" throughout reveals is some profound crisis in representativity. This crisis has a lot to do with the rupture, in Hamlet himself, between what is shown and what is meant, and his related capacity for both dissociating and associating his own feigning and his "I know not seems." Perhaps it can be said that the presentation of Hamlet itself is affected by (just as it helps to sustain) the element of heterogeneity in the dramaturgy of the play. The multiplicity in the forms of mimesis used in his "characterization" is stronger than any consistency in the social and psychological attributes of the "character" himself. It is true that his words of advice to the actors may, temporarily, be in character, in that they reflect the neoclassical preference of humanist and courtly taste. But there is a tension between Hamlet the representative of the court, Maecenas and theoretician, and the rest of what he says and does, and this tension is at the center of the contradiction, so important in the play, between the privileged assertion and the subversive suspension of authority in representation. The contradiction is most consequential between Hamlet the representative "glass" of courtly fashion and the nonrepresentational madness and release of his "antic disposition," but at the same time a similar and corresponding tension informs the irresolutions and inconsistencies of Hamlet's mimetic theory. As Roy W. Battenhouse has pointed out, Hamlet's theory is so tested in the orbit of the play's total action that what we have is not only a Hamlet who violates his own rules but one who makes us realize what intolerable drama we would have if he did not.[15] In other words, the figure of the hero constitutes itself through highly variegated uses of mimesis which at least in part transcend the privileged representativity and self-declared authority of Hamlet the humanist courtier and Maecenas. But what, over and beyond his privileged status, is challenged is the authority of the whole neoclassical theory of representation as a strategy of verisimilitude, in accordance with which Hamlet would serve purely as a character or role, never as an actor, always as the *product* of characterization, never as a *process* of bringing it out.

To illustrate these conflicting uses of mimesis, let us recall the extraordinary amount of incongruity between Hamlet's (the aristocratic character's) theory, his pleading for the neoclassical poetics of that "excellent play, well digested in the scenes" which was "caviare to the general" (II. ii. 433 ff.) on the one hand, and his own mimetic action, his actual histrionic practice, on the other. Without spending too much time on marshaling these incongruous levels of Hamlet's association with mimetic theory and practice, we can distinguish at least half a dozen differing uses of mimesis which Hamlet relates to. These involve (1) his role as theoretician, in which he recommends the *imitatio vitæ* topos to the players, and (2) that as theater critic, in which he artfully reviews the production of that unpopular neoclassical play ("as wholesome as sweet, and by very much more handsome than fine"), together with those altogether different practical activities by which Hamlet himself pursues the business of (3) dramatist, (4) director, (5) chorus, and, of course, (6) actor. After Hamlet, as author, offers to contribute to the play within the play "some dozen or sixteen lines, which I would set down and insert in't" (II. ii. 535–6), he actually proceeds not only to arrange for the production of "*The Mousetrap*" (III. ii. 232) but to serve, in Ophelia's words, "as good as a chorus" (240) and altogether manages in such professional fashion that, almost triumphantly, he asks Horatio, "Would not this, sir, . . . get me a fellowship in a cry of players?" (269 ff.).

But Hamlet's association with the plebeian world of popular theater goes deeper than his playfully revealing self-consciousness suggests. As an actor, he can actually perform and be praised for the "good accent and good discretion" (II. ii. 462–3) with which he speaks the opening 13 lines of the Player's speech. But while in this one instance he assumes the role of actor, there is over and beyond this brief performance an extended dimension of antic role-playing which is only partially consonant with the privileged representativity (and neoclassical verisimilitude) of his own mimetic theory and authorship. Perhaps it can be said that the "antic disposition" itself conveys profoundly ambivalent uses of mimesis in the play: in his feigned madness Hamlet still represents a *role*, a motivated, time-serving response to his perilous position as a genuine perceived threat to Claudius. (Such "representation of madness" is of course anticipated in Shakespeare's oldest sources, where it already serves as some means of self-preservation, in the sense that young Amleth, fearful for his own safety, takes refuge in feigned stupidity and imbecility.) But, at the same time, the "antic disposition" ambivalently defeats and subverts its purely defensive representational functions. Although motivated from within the needs of the self-contained play, Hamlet's madness constantly serves to subvert the representational logic of his own role in the play: in a strictly representational context, Hamlet's antic pose arouses rather than allays suspicion. Madness and folly can (as in Euripides and Seneca) serve as an object of representation, but they do not themselves properly represent social station or consciousness. Madness as a "method" of mimesis dissolves important links between the representer and the represented, and can only partially sustain a logical or psychological motivation. What, especially in the court scenes, the "antic disposition" involves is another mode of release from representativity. Such release is at the center of a nonrepresentational dramaturgy as manifested in the achieved strategy of dissociating Hamlet from the courtly world of dramatic illusion and aristocratic decorum, the strategy of distancing this privileged world through proverb, pun, aside, "impertinency," and, most important, the use of the play metaphor.

As an illustration, take the impertinent irony of Hamlet's evasion from the representational logic of a discussion of his privileges:

> *Ros.:* Good my lord, what is your cause of distemper? You do surely bar the door upon your own liberty if you deny your griefs to your friend.
>
> *Ham.:* Sir, I lack advancement.
>
> *Ros.:* How can that be, when you have the voice of the King himself for your succession in Denmark?
>
> *Ham.:* Ay, sir, but while the grass grows – the proverb is something musty.
>
> (III. ii. 328–35)

Hamlet's answers are profoundly ambivalent in the way that they link representational and nonrepresentational planes of mimesis. Read as an allusion to a common complaint among scholars in late Elizabethan England,[16] Hamlet's "I lack advancement" serves to extend the play world into the real world and so intensifies the tensions between role and actor. But from the point of view of the dramatic illusion of conversation, Hamlet teases his false friend by both provoking his suspicions and exposing his purposes. In his second response ("but while the grass grows") he dissociates himself more radically from any authority and responsibility in the representation of his privileges: the degree of his impertinence reflects the distance (rendered in the form of a popular proverb) from any courtly (and representational) authority. Here, again, Hamlet refuses to heed Guildenstern's admonition: "Good my lord, put your discourse into some frame, and start not so wildly from my affair" (III. ii. 300). But indirectly (and this again illustrates the ambivalent uses of his mimesis of madness) Hamlet does refer the antic mode of his replies to the representational "frame" of the "affair" given: the proverb boldly suggests an incessant race between revenge and perfidy, illustrated by the grass growing under Hamlet's feet. Thus, there is not only (dramaturgic) "method" in his "madness" (II. ii. 205), but what we have is an intricate interplay and "mixture" between representational "matter" and post-ritual "impertinency."

Such "impertinency" reflects a distance (as well as its spatial correlative on the platform stage[17]) from the affairs of privilege and courtly decorum, which distance, in Hamlet's first words spoken in court, can fortify itself through an aside: "A little more than kin, and less than kind" (I. ii. 65). Again, the allusion to a proverb (to be complemented by a pun: "I am too much in the sun," 67) helps to elude the constraints which this privileged position of representativity would otherwise have bestowed on Hamlet. As this, again, is uttered as an aside (which by itself inverts the representational standards of dialogue as an image of dramatic conversation or "glass" of courtly behavior), the more representative characters on the planes of verisimilitude and *imitatio vitæ* neither "hear" nor respond to this mode of "impertinency." The element of subversion involved in it is obvious; it has its analogies in an oral and prerational culture of topsy-turvying misrule, and is worlds removed from any deconstructable discourse in the forms of textualized logocentricity. Hamlet's nonrepresentational stance in "dialogue" is rooted in preliterary convention of the theater, as handed down in the tradition of the post-ritual Vice. Ultimately, it is within this tradition that Hamlet as *actor-character* revitalizes, on the dramatized plane of stylized art, the legacy of the Vice actor as director and master of ceremonies theatrical.[18]

Although it is dangerous to overemphasize (or isolate) this theatrical tradition in *Hamlet*, yet its continuing vitality must be recognized when the conflicting quality of the uses of mimesis in Hamlet's own discursive (and nondiscursive) practice are to be fully appreciated. Take, for instance, Hamlet's theoretical insistence not to "tear a passion to tatters, to very rags, to split the ears of the groundlings" (III. ii. 10–11). But the "temperance" and "smoothness" which he positively recommends are conspicuously absent in such scenes as his encounter with his mother or his violent confrontation with Laertes in Ophelia's grave ("Woo't weep, woo't fight, woo't fast, woo't tear thyself, . . . I'll rant as well as thou" (V. i. 270–9)). Or take, as opposed to his condemnation of "inexplicable dumb-shows and noise" (III. ii. 12), the arrangement of his own dumb-show which, at least to Ophelia ("What means this, my lord?"), remains inexplicable throughout (134, 139).

But the contradiction is such that these conventions of "noise," mad speech and antic acting can either subvert or, at least as often, integrate neoclassical precept. In that case, heterogeneous modes of mimesis are linked: their interaction results in that peculiar balance between theatrical illusion and reality which informs the play metaphor in *Hamlet* (the use of words like "act," "perform," and "play the part") and, thereby, serves to connect the world of the audience with that of the play, but on a more subtle level than the purely nonrepresentational thrust of extra-dramatic address or aside would allow.[19]

As a characteristic stance, Hamlet's "O what a rogue and peasant slave" speech may appear especially revealing. For the Prince to address himself to the activity of an actor as a model of purposive action points to yet another use of the mimesis of mimesis:

> What would he do
> Had he the motive and the cue for passion
> That I have? He would drown the stage with tears,
> And cleave the general ear with horrid speech.
>
> (II. ii. 554–7)

As the traveling player's mimesis is imaginatively transposed into the requirements of Hamlet's situation, the Prince himself, by contrasting his own inactivity with the discursive practice of the actor, moves beyond his own previously upheld principles of "temperance" and "smoothness." What the comparison implies is a sense of the superiority of the very strategy which, more effectively, will "tear a passion to tatters, to very rags" and which, in fact, does manage "to split the ears of the groundlings." It is by waiving his neoclassical reservations against just this that, for Hamlet, to "cleave the general ear with horrid speech" now appears far from being distasteful. Thus, Hamlet's self-understanding of the uses of mimesis is complex in that it combines representational functions (as in reference to his *role* within the fictional situation in the court of Denmark) with a nonrepresentational awareness of the real requirements of an actor's success in the public theater.

But although the balance and, even, integration of varying modes of mimesis can be achieved in the teeth of their contradiction, the heterogeneity among them is such that it cannot quite be contained within the orbit of the self-contained Renaissance play. The gulf between the heritage of ritual and the poetics of representation becomes unbridgeable when Hamlet, Prince of Denmark, is made to consider the "self-resembled show" of the clowning actor who *embodies* (rather than *representing* any fictional *role*) whatever *reality* the direct actor/audience contact in the late Elizabethan theater can claim to possess.

> And let those that play your clowns speak no more than is set down for them – for there be of them that will themselves laugh, to set on some quantity of barren spectators to laugh too, though in the meantime some necessary question of the play be then to be considered.
>
> (III. ii. 38–43)

Hamlet's warning against the extemporal wit and the nonrepresentational acting of the clown seems unambiguous enough; and yet there is an ironic inversion in the prehistory of this warning, since in Q_1 the actor impersonating Hamlet himself proceeds to speak "more than is set down" for him, thereby providing an instance of the thing complained of.[20] What this player, in corrupting his own text, brings to life is a nonrepresentational version of mimesis in which the actor is not entirely absorbed by his role. Here at last the conflict between what in the play is supposed to be represented and what the player in actuality is embodying comes to a head. For the voice of the actor to assert itself at the very moment of its deletion is not without a certain consistency, not only because – as we have seen – the role of Hamlet elsewhere transcends the norms of self-contained representation but also, and in a wider sense, because the polemic against the witty clown is one which is directed against a tradition to which, from Tarlton to Kempe, Shakespeare's plays were of course deeply indebted.

The nonrepresentational uses of mimesis in this tradition are taken to task when Hamlet refers to the nondiscursive practice of those actors "that will themselves laugh." What Hamlet, in his role as Prince, refers to polemically (and what the actor behind the role in Q_1 proceeds to perform positively) is the post-ritual convention of Elizabethan actors laughing with their audience.[21] It is the same convention to which Joseph Hall refers, sarcastically enough, in his couplet about the "goodly hotch-potch" in Elizabethan popular drama:

> When each base clown, his clumbsie fist doth bruise,
> And show his teeth in double rotten row
> For laughter at his self-resembled show.[22]

A self-resembling show was of course part and parcel of that nonrepresentational version of mimesis by which the voice of the actor, re-enacting his own clowning self, predominated over the inscribed role. Although Shakespeare, for obvious reasons, repressed the wantonness of those "that will themselves laugh," yet the art of his comedy again and again rehearsed a situation where the audience laughed *with* the actor, rather than *at* his role. Even in his mature tragedies, the tradition of post-ritual self-enactment was far from dead: the porter in *Macbeth*, the Fool in *King Lear*, and of course the clowns in *Hamlet* witnessed the highly effective uses to which the nonrepresentational mode of mimesis continued to be put. Even more important, the contradiction between the representational and the ritual functions of mimesis suffused the uses of the language in which Lear's madness just as Hamlet's antic disposition was rendered. Their madness, together with the saturnalian voices of clown and fool, perpetually tended to re-embody the chaos before and beyond representation, whether tragically or as a comic resolution to the unbearable logic of an ordered/disordered world in theatrical representation.

Since Hamlet's preoccupation with mimesis has become so complex that it cannot be subsumed under *either* neoclassical and/or discursive *or* an exclusively histrionic and/or nondiscursive connection, the question must be faced in conclusion: is there any one consideration broad enough, any frame of reference flexible enough to serve as a more comprehensive angle for conceptualizing the areas of both concurrence and contradiction between the varying uses of mimesis? If, as a tentative answer, the concept of "appropriation" may finally be introduced in this connection,[23] the most stringent link with Hamlet's mimetic theory and practice is provided by the fact that Hamlet is both a product and, as it were, a producer of mimesis, a character performed in a role and one who himself performs and commissions a performance. Hamlet, through his own histrionic knowledge and activity, is both a product of mimesis, an object of mimetic appropriation to his audience in the theater of the world *and* an agent of mimesis, a *Subjekt* of appropriation, i.e. one who attempts to assimilate a theatrical situation (including a fictional audience) in the world of his own theater. There is in all likelihood no other character in Shakespeare and Elizabethan drama at large where the tension between what, in the theater, is appropriated and what, theatrically, is appropriating is so deliberately dramatized and so much at the heart of the dramatic potential of the contradiction between signified and signifier. If, then, the appropriation of the world in the play and the appropriation of the play in the world (by some actually existing audience) can at all be viewed together as well as in separation, the nonsymbolic gaps as well as the symbolizing links between them may so be correlated that what results can be defined neither by concepts of closure nor by those of rupture. What the product-as-process quality of these multiple functions of mimesis achieve is a simultaneity in the awareness of life in the theater, and the theater as a supreme form of life: the indivisibility, that is, of the appropriation of the world through and on the stage and the appropriation of the stage through and in the world. Thus, Hamlet's production of *The Mousetrap* can be seen as some dramatized metaphor of the appropriation of the world of the play through mimesis, which appropriation – as it affects Hamlet's position in the play – is itself turned into drama.

Here to introduce the concept of "appropriation" in such sweeping generalizations may leave all too many questions open, especially since there is no space whatever to develop the theoretical presuppositions. Even so, it seems difficult to avoid some concept overriding enough to embrace both the representational and the nonrepresentational functions of mimesis and to relate these to its discursive and its nondiscursive forms, inside and outside the theater, then and now. As distinguished from the poststructuralist use of the same term (which, at least in the work of René Girard, tends to isolate the conflictual element in nonrepresentational mimesis, its primordial pattern of instinctive action, rivalry and victimage), the proposed concept of *Aneignung* or appropriation is open to the multiple functions and hybrid forms of mimesis in the Elizabethan theater. At the same time, the seeing together of these differing modes of mimesis makes it possible not to divorce the notion of either representation or ritual from some more comprehensive idea of the connectedness of social, economic, and cultural productions. What, in the last resort, this points to is a reconsideration of mimesis according to which the production, reception, and interpretation of drama can theatrically and theoretically be used so as to redefine and revitalize a cultural "purpose of playing" – a purpose much larger and less rationalistic than Hamlet's own definition allows.

Notes

1. See, e.g., the essays by Jacques Derrida, Philippe Lacoue-Labarthe, Bernard Pautrat, and others, collected in *Mimésis des articulations* (Paris, 1975); the work of René Girard, from *Deceit, Desire, and the Novel*, tr. Yvonne Freccero (Baltimore, 1965) to *Violence and the Sacred*, tr. Patrick Gregory (Baltimore, 1977); and related studies, such as Cesareo Bandera, *Mimesis conflictiva* (Madrid, 1975). Although these do not refer to the studies of contemporary classical scholars, work in this field is undoubtedly relevant, at least since Hermann Koller, *Die Mimesis in der Antike* (Bern, 1954), who, arguing for a "close link between mimesis and the dance," has shown that *mimos* and all terms derived from it "originally have their home only in the cultic sphere, in the orgiastic cult" (12, 119). For the critique of "representation," see the well known work of Jacques Derrida, Michel Foucault, and the main stream in poststructuralist criticism; for a challenging restatement of the problem of "representation," see the editor's Preface to *Allegory and Representation: Selected Papers from the English Institute*, ed. Stephen J. Greenblatt (Baltimore, 1981), vii–xiii.
2. In their critique of these positions, poststructuralist critics share some common ground with recent Marxist reconsiderations of the mirror concept, as in the suggestive collection of studies, ed. Dieter Schlenstedt, *Literarische Widerspiegelung: Geschichtliche und theoretische Dimensionen eines Problems* (Berlin, 1981).
3. It is easier, therefore, and perfectly plausible, for A. D. Nuttall, in *A New Mimesis: Shakespeare and the Representation of Reality* (London, 1983), to provide a defense of the representational content of Shakespearean mimesis, so that the "essence" of the "new mimesis" is defined as "the reconciliation of form with veridical or probable representation" (181).
4. See, in this connection, the Epilogue, "Text and history, 1984," to the expanded edition of my *Structure and Society in Literary History* (Baltimore, 1984), 267–323. In a recent article I have attempted to make some historicizing counterproposals ("'Appropriation' and modern history in Renaissance prose narrative," *New Literary History*, XIV (Spring 1983), 459–95).
5. *William Lambarde and Local Government: His "Ephemeris" and Twenty-nine Charges to Juries and Commissions*, ed. Conyers Read (Ithaca, 1962), 80.
6. All Shakespeare quotations, except those from *Hamlet* (see note 11), are taken from *The Complete Works*, ed. Peter Alexander (London, 1951).
7. I have discussed the form and function of these nonrepresentational modes of madness and topsy-turvydom at some length in my *Shakespeare and the Popular Tradition in the Theater*, ed. Robert Schwartz (Baltimore, 1978).

8. Geoffrey H. Hartman, *Saving the Text: Literature – Derrida – Philosophy* (Baltimore, 1981), 121.

9. Cf. René Girard, *"To Double Business Bound": Essays on Literature, Mimesis, and Anthropology* (Baltimore, 1978), vii: "If one individual imitates another when the latter appropriates some object, the result cannot fail to be rivalry or conflict."

10. Philippe Lacoue-Labarthe, "Typographie," in Sylviane Agacinski, Jacques Derrida *et al.*, *Mimesis des articulations*, 246. I have used (and slightly modified) the translation of one section of this essay, "Mimesis and truth," *Diacritics* (March 1978), 21.

11. *Hamlet*, III. ii. 1–24. All quotations from *Hamlet* henceforth in this text follow the Arden Shakespeare edition, ed. Harold Jenkins (London, 1982).

12. This synthesis has been amply documented, from P. W. Biesterfeldt, *Die dramatische Technik Thomas Kyds* (Halle, 1936), and Wolfgang Clemen, *Die Tragödie vor Shakespeare* (Heidelberg, 1955), to Michael Hattaway, *Elizabethan Popular Theatre: Plays in Performance* (London, 1982).

13. The latter aspect was strikingly explored in Benno Besson's production of *Hamlet* (Volksbühne, Berlin, 1977), when Hamlet faced an impatient First Player who appeared almost bored by Prince Hamlet's advice.

14. Jenkins, Arden edn, 479.

15. Roy W. Battenhouse, "The significance of Hamlet's advice to the players," in *The Drama of the Renaissance: Essays for Leicester Bradner*, ed. Elmer M. Blistein (Providence, 1970), 26.

16. For the social background against which, in the words of Bacon, "there being more scholars bred than the State can prefer and employ," see L. C. Knights, *Drama and Society in the Age of Jonson* (Harmondsworth, 1963), 268 ff.

17. There is throughout *Hamlet* a complex use of *platea* and *locus* conventions, in the sense that the former tend to be associated with the nonrepresentational, the latter with the representational functions of mimesis; see *Shakespeare and the Popular Tradition in the Theater*, 73–85, 215–24, where I have discussed the spatial and dramaturgic implications of "impertinency" (esp. 130 ff.).

18. See D. M. Bevington, *From "Mankind" to Marlowe: Growth of Structure in the Popular Drama of Tudor England* (Cambridge, Mass., 1968), who has first drawn attention to the practical implications of the leading actor assuming the role of Vice as director.

19. Cf. Anne Righter, *Shakespeare and the Idea of the Play* (London, 1962), 158–64 and *passim*.

20. For the passage added in Q_1, see Jenkins's Arden edition, 499; all this, of course, is based on the assumption that Q_1, "deriving from performance, lacks a direct manuscript link with what the author wrote" (19).

21. As John Dover Wilson noted, Shakespeare "gets his audience to laugh, quite as often *with* his characters as *at* them" (*Shakespeare's Happy Comedies* (London, 1962), 23 ff.). I have attempted to develop this further in "Laughing with the audience: *The Two Gentlemen of Verona* and the popular tradition of comedy," (*Shakespeare Survey*, 22 (1969), 35–42).

22. Joseph Hall, *Virgidemiarum* (1597); cited by W. J. Lawrence, "On the underrated genius of Dick Tarleton," *Speeding up Shakespeare* (London, 1937), 31.

23. For a more detailed discussion of the concept, see the article cited in note 4, which refers the concept of "appropriation" or *Aneignung* to Karl Marx, *Grundrisse: Foundations of the Critique of Political Economy*, tr. Martin Nicolaus (New

York, 1973). More recently, I have attempted to discuss and view together "History, appropriation, and the uses of representation," in a forthcoming collection of essays, *The Aims of Representation: Subject, Text, History,* ed. Murray Krieger (1985).

15

MARGARET W. FERGUSON

Hamlet: letters and spirits

"The letter killeth," said Saint Paul (2 Cor. 3:6). His words can serve as an epigraph – or epitaph – to my essay, which approaches some broad questions about the genre of Shakespearean tragedy by exploring the connections between certain techniques of wordplay in *Hamlet* and a process of dramatic literalization that is associated, in this play, with the impulse to kill. In the early part of the play, Hamlet frequently uses language to effect a divorce between words and their conventional meanings. His rhetorical tactics, which include punning and deliberately undoing the rhetorical figures of other speakers, expose the arbitrariness, as well as the fragility, of the bonds that tie words to agreed-upon significations. His language in dialogues with others, though not in his soliloquies, produces a curious effect of *materializing* the word, materializing it in a way that forces us to question the distinction between literal and figurative meanings, and that also leads us to look in new ways at the word as a spoken or written phenomenon. Hamlet's verbal tactics in the early part of the play – roughly through the closet scene in Act III – constitute a rehearsal for a more disturbing kind of materializing that occurs, with increasing frequency, in the later part of the drama. This second kind of materializing pertains to the realm of deeds as well as to that of words; in fact it highlights the thin but significant line that separates those realms, while at the same time it reminds us that all acts performed in a theater share with words the problematic status of representation. This second type of materializing might be called *performative*,[1] and since in *Hamlet*, in contrast to the comedies, it almost always results in a literal death, it might also be described as a process of "incorpsing" – to borrow a term that is used once in *Hamlet* and nowhere else in Shakespeare's corpus.

Hamlet begins his verbal activity of materializing words with the first line he speaks: "A little more than kin, and less than kind" (I. ii. 65).[2] With this riddling sentence, spoken aside to the audience, Hamlet rejects the social and linguistic bond that Claudius asserted when he addressed Hamlet in terms of their kinship: "But now, my cousin Hamlet, and my son" (I.ii.64). Hamlet not only refuses to be defined or possessed by Claudius's epithets, the second of which confuses the legal relation of stepson with the "natural" one of son; he also refuses to accept the principle of similarity that governs Claudius's syntax, which here, as elsewhere, employs the rhetorical figure of *isocolon*: balanced clauses joined by "and."[3] Claudius's isocolonic style is also characteristically oxymoronic: opposites are smoothly joined by syntax and sound, as for instance in these lines from his opening speech:

> Therefore our sometime sister, now our queen,
> Th'imperial jointress to this warlike state,
> Have we, as 'twere with a defeated joy,
> With an auspicious and a dropping eye,
> With mirth in funeral and with dirge in marriage,
> In equal scale weighing delight and dole,
> Taken to wife.
>
> (I.ii.8–14)

Hamlet's remark "A little more than kin, and less than kind" unbalances the scale Claudius has created through his rhetoric – a scale in which opposites like "delight" and "dole" are blandly equated. Hamlet's sentence disjoins what Claudius has linked; it does so through its comparative "more" and "less," and also through the play on "kin" and "kind" which points, by the difference of a single letter, to a radical difference between what Claudius seems or claims to be, and what he is. The pun on the word "kind" itself, moreover, works, as Hamlet's puns so often do, to disrupt the smooth surface of another person's discourse. Hamlet's pun, suggesting that Claudius is neither natural nor kindly, is like a pebble thrown into the oily pool of the king's rhetoric. As Lawrence Danson observes in *Tragic Alphabet*, Hamlet's puns challenge Claudius's "wordy attempts at compromise" by demanding "that words receive their full freight of meaning."[4] If the puns work to increase semantic richness, however – the Elizabethan rhetorician George Puttenham characterized the pun or *syllepsis* as "the figure of double supply"[5] – they do so by driving a wedge between words and their ordinary meanings. The pun, Sigurd Burckhardt argues, characteristically performs "an act of verbal violence. . . . It asserts that mere phonetic – i.e., material, corporeal – likeness establishes likeness of meaning. The pun gives the word as entity primacy over the word as sign."[6]

If Hamlet's punning wit makes an oblique attack on Claudius's rhetorical penchant for "yoking heterogeneous ideas by violence together" – to borrow the phrase Dr Johnson used in a similar attack on what he felt to be indecorous conceits – Hamlet is, of course, attacking much more than

Claudius's rhetorical style. For Claudius has yoked not only words but bodies together, and it therefore seems likely that Hamlet's style reflects his (at this point) obscure and certainly overdetermined desire to separate his uncle from his mother. His dialogue with Polonius in II.ii offers further support for my hypothesis that Hamlet's disjunctive verbal techniques constitute not only a defense against being entrapped by others' tropes but also an aggressive, albeit displaced, attack on the marriage union of Gertrude and Claudius. By the time Hamlet speaks with Polonius, of course, he has not only had his worst suspicions about the king confirmed by the Ghost, but has also met with a rebuff from Ophelia, a rebuff dictated by Polonius's and Laertes' suspicions. It is no wonder, then, that his rhetoric is now directly deployed against the very idea of fleshly union. "Have you a daughter?" he asks Polonius (II.ii.182), and goes on to draw Ophelia into his morbid train of thought, which has been about the sun's power to breed maggots in the dead flesh of a dog. "Let her not walk i'th' sun," he says, echoing his earlier statement, in the opening scene with Claudius, "I am too much in the sun" (I.ii.67). The echo hints that Ophelia is already in some sense Hamlet's double here: both are endangered by the sun which is an emblem of kingly power, and both are also endangered – though in significantly different ways – by Hamlet's terrible burden of being a biological son to a dead king and a legal son to Claudius. As if dimly aware that his own way of thinking about Ophelia is tainting her with maggoty conceptions about sonship, Hamlet says to her father, "Conception is a blessing, but as your daughter may conceive – friend, look to't" (II.ii.184–6). It is at this point that Hamlet strikes yet another rhetorical blow against union in the realm of discourse: "What do you read, my lord?" asks Polonius. "Words, words, words," Hamlet replies. "What is the matter, my lord?" Polonius persists. "Between who?" is the perverse, ungrammatical, and fascinating reply, not an answer but, characteristically, another question. In this peculiar dialogue Hamlet disjoins words from their conventional meanings both rhetorically and thematically; in so doing, he breaks the social contract necessary to ordinary human discourse, the contract which mandates that there be, in Roman Jakobson's words, "a certain equivalence between the symbols used by the addressor and those known and interpreted by the addressee."[7]

In his first answer, "Words, words, words," Hamlet deliberately interprets Polonius's question literally; in his second reply, however, he does something more complicated than substituting a literal sense for a figurative one: he points, rather, to the problem that has always plagued classical theories of metaphor, which is that a word or phrase may not *have* a single, "literal" sense.[8] And it seems strangely appropriate that Hamlet should expose the problem of distinguishing between multiple – and perhaps equally figurative – meanings through the example of the word *matter* – a word that appears 26 times in the play, more than in any other by Shakespeare, in locutions ranging from Gertrude's acerbic remark to Polonius, "More matter with less art" (II.ii.95), to Hamlet's poignant comment to Horatio in the last act: "Thou wouldst not think how ill all's here about my heart; but it is no matter" (V.ii.208–9).

As is apparent from even a cursory examination of the play's manifold uses of this word, the relation between matter and spirit, matter and art, matter and anything that is "no matter," is altogether questionable for Hamlet; he is therefore quite accurate in presenting matter as an obstacle to unity of opinion: "Between who?" suggests only that any definition of matter will be a matter for dispute. Hamlet has indeed effectively disjoined this word from any single conventional meaning we or Polonius might want to give it; and it is no accident, I think, that Hamlet's rapier attack on the word "matter" foreshadows the closet scene in which he both *speaks* daggers to his mother and literally stabs Polonius, mistaking him, as he says to the corpse, "for thy better." In this scene, the concept of matter is linked to that of the mother by a pun that marries Shakespeare's mother tongue to the language known, in the Renaissance, as the *sermo patrius*: the language of the Church fathers and also of the ancient Romans.[9] "Now, mother, what's the matter?" asks Hamlet at the very outset of the closet scene (III.iv.7), and this query makes explicit an association of ideas already implied by a remark Hamlet made to Rosencrantz: "Therefore no more, but to the matter. My mother, you say –" (III.ii.315–16).

As we hear or see in the word "matter" the Latin term for mother, we may surmise that the common Renaissance association between female nature in general and the "lower" realm of matter is here being deployed in the service of Hamlet's complex oedipal struggle.[10] The mother is the matter that comes between the father and the son – and it is no accident that in this closet scene Hamlet's sexual hysteria rises to its highest pitch. Dwelling with obsessive, disgusted fascination on his mother's unseemly passion for her second husband, Hamlet appears to be struggling with his own feelings about her body even as he argues for his dead father's continuing rights to her bed. Hamlet's act of stabbing Polonius through the curtain, which occurs almost casually in the middle of the tirade against Gertrude's lust, seems only to increase his passionate desire to make her *see* her error in preferring Claudius to her first husband. For Hamlet, however, the problem of seeing a genuine *difference* between his original father and the man Gertrude has called his father assumes enormous significance at precisely this juncture in the drama; immediately before Hamlet refers to Claudius as a "king of shreds and patches," the Ghost appears, or rather reappears, with a dramatic entrance that allows the phrase "king of shreds and patches" to refer to the Ghost as well as to Claudius. As if to underscore the fact that Hamlet's dilemma here is a hermeneutic as well as an ethical one, Shakespeare has him address the Ghost with the pregnant question, "What would your gracious figure?" (III.iv.105). If Claudius is a figure of the father, so is the Ghost; according to what standard of truth, then, is Hamlet to distinguish between them?

Shakespeare gives this problem a further turn of the screw, as it were, by making the Ghost invisible and inaudible to Gertrude. Like the governess in Henry James's tale, who sees the ghostly figure of Miss Jessell when the "gross" housekeeper does not, Hamlet is forced to confront and deny the possibility that the Ghost may be a figment of his own imagination. He, and the audience, must at least fleetingly experience a conflict between the evidence provided by their eyes and ears and Gertrude's statement that she perceives "nothing." And even if this scene's stage directions confirm the Ghost's existence and support Hamlet's argument that what he has seen is not, as Gertrude insists, a "bodiless creation" of "ecstasy," we may well not feel entirely easy about giving credence to Hamlet here; after the Ghost exits, Hamlet declares to Gertrude that his "pulse" keeps time just as "temperately" as hers does (III.iv.142). Then, having claimed to be no less (but also no more) sane than is the woman whose perceptions we have just been forced to discount, Hamlet proceeds to promise that "I the matter will re-word, which madness / Would gambol from." The relation between the "matter" of the Ghost and the matter Hamlet will "re-word" in the ensuing passionate dialogue with Gertrude remains deeply mysterious.

By stressing the epistemologically doubtful status of the Ghost, we can usefully supplement the classic psychoanalytic explanation for why Hamlet defers performing the deed of revenge. That explanation, outlined by Freud in a famous footnote to the *Interpretation of Dreams* and elaborated by Ernest Jones, suggests that Hamlet obscurely knows that in killing Claudius he would be satisfying his repressed oedipal desire to be *like* Claudius, who has become a king and husband by killing the elder Hamlet.[11] Jacques Lacan, in his brilliant, albeit elliptical, essay on "Desire and the interpretation of desire in *Hamlet*," speculates that Hamlet's invectives against Claudius in the closet scene are an example of *dénégation*, that is, the words of dispraise and contempt are indications of repressed admiration.[12] Building on both Freud and Lacan, we might read Hamlet's frantic efforts to draw a clear epistemological distinction between his father and Claudius as a defense against his perception of an excessive degree of *likeness* between himself and Claudius, or, more precisely, between his desires and Claudius's. In fact, the distinctions Hamlet draws between Claudius and Old Hamlet seem no less questionable, in their hyperbole, than the distinction he draws between himself and his mother when, alluding to the simple moral system of medieval religious drama, he calls her a vice and himself a virtue. A parallel dualistic oversimplification informs his sermon-like speech on the pictures of the two kings, "The counterfeit presentment of two brothers," as he calls them:

> See what a grace was seated on this brow,
> Hyperion's curls, the front of Jove himself,
> An eye like Mars to threaten and command,
> A station like the herald Mercury
> New-lighted on a heaven-kissing hill
>
> (III. iv. 55–9)

He doth protest too much, methinks, in this plethora of similitudes designed, as he says, to make his mother relinquish that passion which is blind to difference. Hamlet's own passion, we might say, is making him blind to similarity. His description of his father's incomparable virtue hardly accords with what the Ghost himself said to his son when he lamented having been "Cut off even in the blossoms of my sin" and "sent to my account / With all my imperfections on my head" (I. v. 76–9). Nor does it accord with what Hamlet himself said in III. iii, where he described his father dying with "all his crimes broad blown, as flush as May" (81).

Hamlet's doubts about his father's character, about the Ghost's status as a figure, and about his own relation to both his father and Claudius, constitute one reason why he cannot resolve the matter of his mother or his revenge. Another and related reason is that he is too filled with disgust at female flesh to follow the path Freud describes for those who eventually emerge, however scarred, from the oedipal complex. That path leads to marriage with a woman who is not the mother. In Hamlet's case, the obvious candidate is Ophelia, whom Hamlet actually seems to prefer to his mother in the play within the play scene. "Come hither, my dear Hamlet, sit by me," says Gertrude, and Hamlet replies, "No, good mother, here's metal more attractive" (III. ii. 108). The metaphor is misogynistically reductive – and ominously allied to Hamlet's pervasive concern with debased currency; nonetheless, for a moment it seems that he may find in Ophelia a matter to replace his mother. "Lady, shall I lie in your lap?" he asks, and when she says no, taking him literally, he specifies his meaning, offering to lay in her lap only that part of him which houses the higher faculties: "I mean, my head upon your lap?" "Ay, my lord," she answers; but he twists her affirmation by indicating that his head is filled with thoughts of her – and his – lower parts: "Do you think I meant country matters?" he asks, punning on the slang term for the female genitals. "I think nothing, my lord," Ophelia replies; and Hamlet once again bawdily literalizes her words: "That's a fair thought to lie between maids' legs" (III. ii. 110–17). While his speeches in this dialogue seem like an invitation to sexual union (in one sense he is enticing her to realize that the matter between *his* legs is not nothing but something), the final effect of this exchange, as of all the encounters between Ophelia and Hamlet we see in this play, is to separate her from him, to push her naive love away and reduce her to incomprehension of what he later calls his "mystery." Hamlet's relation to

Ophelia seems aptly epitomized a little later in this scene, when he leaves off interpreting the tropical ambiguities of the *Mousetrap* play being presented before them to say to her, "I could interpret between you and your love if I could see the puppets dallying" (III. ii. 241–2). The role of the interpreter who stands *between* others and their loves is the role he has at once had thrust upon him by fate and which he chooses to continue to play. It is dangerous to suggest that he had any alternative, for the play notoriously foils critics who think themselves ethically or intellectually superior to this tragic hero.[13] Nonetheless, I would like to argue that the play does provide a critical perspective on Hamlet, a perspective that implies a questioning of the genre of tragedy itself more than a moral critique of the hero as an individual subject.

The critical perspective I hope to trace does not result in our feeling that Hamlet *should* have done something else at any point in the play; rather, it heightens our awareness that the drama itself is the product of certain choices which *might have been different*. Like many students of Shakespeare, I have often felt that certain of his plays strongly invite the audience to imagine how the play would go if it were written according to a different set of generic rules. Certain turns of plot are made to seem somehow *arbitrary*, and the effect of such moments is to shift our attention from the story-line to the invisible hand manipulating it; we are reminded that the dramatist's decisions about his material are *not* wholly preordained. A strange sense of potentiality arises at such moments; we enter a metadramatic realm where movements of plot and characterization no longer seem simply given or "necessary." The death of Mercutio in *Romeo and Juliet* is an example of the kind of moment I have in mind; it seems so accidental, so unmotivated, that we may well wonder how the play would have turned out had he been allowed to live. The play *could* have been a comedy – as Shakespeare later explicitly indicated by including a parody of it in Act V of *A Midsummer Night's Dream*. Shakespeare's tendency to blur generic boundaries throughout his career has often been remarked; but critics have not, to my knowledge, related this phenomenon to the peculiar way in which Shakespearean tragedy, in contrast to Greek or classical French examples of the genre, seems so often to imply a questioning of the necessity of casting a given story *as* tragedy.

The critical perspective on Hamlet – or on *Hamlet* as a "piece of work" – begins to emerge, I think, with the first death in the play, the stabbing of Polonius in the pivotal closet scene of III. iv. Here we see a darker, literalized version of Hamlet's verbal technique of separating others' words from their conventional meanings. That technique was dissociative but also semantically fecund; now, however, a spirit is definitively separated from its body, which becomes mere matter. "It was a brute part of him to kill so capital a calf," Hamlet had punningly remarked apropos of Polonius's fate when he played Julius Caesar in a university theatrical (III. ii. 104); now, by killing Polonius, Hamlet makes the earlier insult seem prophetic; he "realizes" it, transforming the old man into a sacrificial calf on another stage. This performative mode of materializing a figure, with its grim effects of tragic irony, is what I want to call "incorpsing."

Although the play raises all sorts of questions about the boundary between speaking and doing, in the closet scene there is no doubt that Hamlet passes from speaking daggers to using them. But he has stabbed Polonius only through a curtain – yet another figure for that position of "in betweenness" Hamlet himself is structurally bound to occupy. That curtain may also be seen, I think, as a material emblem not only for Hamlet's ignorance of Polonius's identity, but also for his inability to pursue a certain ethical line of interpreting the meaning of his deed. Hamlet does not inquire very deeply either here or later, when he kills Rosencrantz and Guildenstern, into the meaning of his action. This seems odd, since he has shown himself so remarkably capable of interrogating the meaning of his *inaction*. There is a thinness, even an uncharacteristic patness, to his response to his killing of Polonius: "For this same lord / I do repent," he says, adding, "but heaven hath pleas'd it so, / To punish me with this and this with me, / That I must be their scourge and minister" (III. iv. 174–7). It seems to me that the play questions this kind of self-justification, supplementing if not altogether invalidating Hamlet's view of himself as a divinely appointed "scourge." The questioning occurs most generally through the play's scrutiny of kingship; kings, like divinely appointed "scourges," may easily abuse their power by seeing themselves as heavenly instruments, beyond the authority of human laws. Shakespeare, I would argue, invites us to see that one meaning of Hamlet's "incorpsing" activity is that through it he becomes more and more like a king – or, perhaps, like a playwright. Indeed, with the killing of Polonius – the "rat" Hamlet mistakenly takes for the king he had already symbolically caught in the *Mousetrap* play – Hamlet takes a crucial step towards occupying the place of the king as the play defines it: not in terms of an individual, but in terms of a *role* associated both with the power to kill and with the tendency to justify killing with lines of argument unavailable to lesser men. Horatio darkly suggests this in V. ii. Hamlet has just described how he disposed of Rosencrantz and Guildenstern. "They are not near my conscience," he says:

> 'Tis dangerous when the baser nature comes
> Between the pass and fell incensed points
> Of mighty opposites.

> (V. ii. 60–2)

"Why, what a king is this!" Horatio ambiguously exclaims or queries. Does he refer to Hamlet or to Claudius? It doesn't much matter, Shakespeare seems to say: a king is one who thinks himself capable of literally disposing of whatever comes between him and his desires.

It is no accident that Hamlet kills Rosencrantz and Guildenstern by means of a forged letter. For Claudius's letter ordering the king of England to kill Hamlet, Hamlet substitutes a letter ordering the king to kill Rosencrantz and Guildenstern. He seals that letter with his father's ring, the signet or sign of royal power; Claudius of course possesses a copy of this ring, and it is worth noting that there is no difference between the *effect* of Claudius's copy and that of the original seal. Both have the power to order instant death. Communication among kings in this play would, indeed, appear to be a grim illustration of Saint Paul's dictum that the letter killeth. The play suggests, however, that it is not only the letter, but the desire to *interpret* literally, to find one single sense, that leads to murder. The Ghost that appeared "In the same figure like the King that's dead" commands Hamlet to take action by means of several equivocal and mutually contradictory phrases, including "bear it not," "Taint not thy mind," and "Remember me" (I.v.81, 85, 91); even when he reappears to whet Hamlet's almost blunted purpose, all the Ghost commands is "Do not forget" (III.iv.110). So long as Hamlet remains perplexed by the multiple potential meanings of these commands, he remains in a realm where destruction of meanings goes hand in hand with the creation of new ones: the verbal and hermeneutic realm of his puns. Unyoking words from their conventional meanings is not the same thing as unyoking bodies from spirits. In coming to resemble Claudius, Hamlet is driven to forget this distinction, and Shakespeare, I think, asks us to see the cost of this forgetting. He does so by giving the audience a letter (of sorts) that invites a radically different interpretation from those which Claudius and Hamlet take from the messages they receive from mysterious places.

Shakespeare's "letter to the audience," as I want to characterize it, appears in a passage immediately following Claudius's receipt of Hamlet's letter announcing his return – naked and alone – to the shores of Denmark (IV.vii.42–5): let me try to show why the juxtaposition of passages is significant. Claudius says that he cannot understand Hamlet's letter ("What should this mean?" he asks Laertes (IV.vii.47)); but he recognizes Hamlet's "character" in the handwriting and proceeds quickly enough to give it a kingly interpretation. For he immediately tells Laertes of his "device" to work Hamlet's death in a way that will appear an accident. His response to the letter – which comes, after all, from someone he believed he had sent to the country from which no traveler returns – is eerily similar to Hamlet's response to the Ghost's message from the land of the dead. Like Hamlet, Claudius wonders about the ambiguity of the message: "is [the letter] some abuse?" he asks Laertes (IV.vii.48), echoing Hamlet's earlier question to himself about whether "The spirit that I have seen" is or is not a devil that "perhaps . . . / Abuses me to damn me" (II.ii.596, 599). Also like Hamlet, although much more quickly, Claudius chooses a single interpretation of the message, finding in it an incentive to kill. It hardly seems to matter whether the message comes from a spirit or a letter: the interpreter's *decision* about its meaning creates the deadliness. But in the passage that follows, Shakespeare offers an oblique criticism of the kind of interpretive decision that the kings or would-be kings make in this play. He does so by using Claudius as the unwitting spokesman for a greater king, the one who will really win the duel in the final scene. This is the king whom Richard II describes in Act III of his play:

> within the hollow crown
> That rounds the mortal temples of a king,
> Keeps Death his court, and there the antic sits
> Scoffing his state and grinning at his pomp,
> Allowing him a breath, a little scene,
> To monarchize, be fear'd, and kill with looks;
> Infusing him with self and vain conceit,
> As if this flesh which walls about our life
> Were brass impregnable.
>
> (*Richard II*, III. ii. 160–8)

With wonderful irony, Shakespeare has Claudius metaphorically describe this king of kings while *thinking* he is pursuing his own aims – devising his own plot – by manipulating Laertes' competitive spirit to transform his rage against Claudius for Polonius's death into anger against Hamlet. "Two months since," Claudius says,

> Here was a gentleman of Normandy –
> I have seen myself, and serv'd against, the French,
> And they can well on horseback, but this gallant
> Had witchcraft in't. He grew unto his seat,
> And to such wondrous doing brought his horse
> As had he been incorps'd and demi-natur'd
> With the brave beast. So far he topp'd my thought
> That I in forgery of shapes and tricks
> Come short of what he did.
>
> (IV. vii. 81–9)

"A Norman was't?" Laertes asks, and then, in one of the subtlest non-recognition scenes in all of Shakespeare, Laertes tells us the Norman's name: "Upon my life, Lamord" (91).[14] The spirit behind these letters from the text of the Second Quarto is invisible to Laertes and Claudius; it was also invisible to the compilers of the First Folio, who spelled the Frenchman's name "Lamound," and to eighteenth-century editors like Pope and Malone; the former gave the name as "Lamond," the latter, citing the phrase which describes the character as "the brooch and gem of all the nation," suggested "Lamode," fashion.[15] But I contend that Shakespeare meant us to hear or see the word "death" in and through the letters of this name; "Upon my life,

Death," is the translation we are invited to make[16] – and for those who are uncertain of their French but willing to suspect that puns which depend on mere changes of letters have metaphorical significance, Shakespeare provides an English pun in the word "Norman," which is all too close for comfort to the phrase used by the gravedigger in the next scene: "What man dost thou dig it for?" Hamlet asks. "For no man, sir," is the equivocal reply (V.i.126–7).

The play offers other intratextual clues to the identity of "Lamord." Laertes' phrase "Upon my life, Lamord," echoes a phrase Horatio used in his discussion of the Ghost in I.i:

> Let us impart what we have seen tonight
> Unto young Hamlet; for *upon my life*
> *This spirit*, dumb to us, will speak to him.
>   (I.i.174–6; my italics)

Horatio here unwittingly exposes the same eerie truth that Laertes does in Act IV: the "spirit" of Death, whether in the figure of the Ghost or in the figure of Lamord, sits upon the lives of all the characters in the play. And the scene which introduces Lamord seems deliberately designed not only to make Death's past and future presence manifest, but to link it, ominously and obscurely, to the playwright's own activities of "forging shapes," of persuading, and of creating elegiac song: immediately after Claudius successfully persuades Laertes to envenom his sword so that if he "galls" Hamlet in the duel "It may be death" (146–7), the queen enters with news of Ophelia's fate of being pulled, by her garments, from her "melodious lay / To muddy death" (181–2).

In the description of the mysterious Norman, Shakespeare paradoxically insists on the presence of Death by animating the dead metaphor in the common phrase "upon my life"; he also creates a new adjective, "incorpsed," which editors (and the *OED*, citing this line as the first use of the term) gloss as "made into one body," but which may also evoke the image of a dead body if we hear the Norman's name as "Death." The lines make us "see" Death, as it were, in a strangely materialized and emblematic figure: that of the rider sitting on – and controlling – the horse that traditionally represents human passion and ambition: "A horse, a horse, my kingdom for a horse," Richard III famously cries, when he is about to lose the powerful vitality that animal symbolizes.[17] The figure of Lamord sitting on his horse as if he were "incorps'd and demi-natur'd / With the brave beast" is richly evocative, reminding us, as Harry Levin suggests, both of the apocalyptic image of Death as a rider on a "pale horse" (Revelation 6:8), and of Hamlet's broodings on the inherently double or centaur-like nature of man, the angel and beast, the "beauty of the world" and the "quintessence of dust" combined into one "piece of work" (II.ii.307ff.).[18]

The description of Lamord, which I would like to see as Shakespeare's figurative letter to the reader, is somber and mysterious, a *memento mori* admonition. But it contrasts in a curious way with the other messages and admonitions in this play; for there is all the difference in the world between a message that asks us, with the paradoxical temporality of literature and dream, to *remember* our own future death, and messages that ambiguously incite characters to kill and thereby to forget, as it were, the potential future of another. It seems to me significant, therefore, that Shakespeare uses the trope of personification – the animation of inanimate things – to describe Lamord. A premonitory and admonitory figure he certainly is – but how interestingly different from the literalized *memento mori* that appears in the next scene, in Yorick's skull. I do not think Hamlet grasps the meaning of Yorick's skull very completely because he so quickly forgets its implications for the fate of kings. Although seeing the skull leads him to brood on the idea that great men such as Alexander and Caesar finally become, like commoners, no more than dust to stop a bunghole, in the very next scene (V. ii. 58–62) we find Hamlet still thinking of *himself* as a "mighty opposite" in a kingly war that makes humble men like Rosencrantz and Guildenstern irrelevant to conscience. Paradoxically, the death drive in Hamlet seems too strong to allow him to understand either a graphic *memento mori* such as Yorick's skull or the more unusual, figurative one offered to the audience (but not to Hamlet) in the Lamord passage. For truly to understand a *memento mori*, one must have at least some love of life – on earth or beyond. And Hamlet lacks this love; he was speaking truly when he told Polonius that there was nothing he would prefer to lose more than Polonius's company "except my life, except my life, except my life" (II. ii. 216–17).[19] It is therefore appropriate that, in the description of Lamord that Hamlet can neither read nor hear, Shakespeare asks us to remember not only death, but also love and life – particularly the life of Hamlet as Ophelia remembers it from a time before the play began. Lamord, Laertes admiringly says, is "the brooch indeed / And gem of all the nation" (IV. vii. 92–3); the phrasing and rhythm recall Ophelia's description of Hamlet as "Th'expectancy and rose of the fair state, / The glass of fashion and the mould of form" (III. i. 154–5).

The implied parallel between Lamord and Hamlet – not the gloomy and disheveled prince we see throughout most of the play, a man obsessed with a sense of sexual impotence, but rather a prince made present to us only through the mediation of Ophelia's memorializing description – this parallel suggests that there is yet another way of interpreting Lamord's name and symbolic significance. If one listens closely to his name, one may hear in it a pun not only on Death but also on Love – there is, after all, only the slightest difference in pronunciation between the French "la mort" and "l'amour"; and the Latin *amor* is contained within the Norman's name. French Renaissance poets often punned on "l'amour" and "la mort" in ways that suggest the two forces are no less "demi-natured" than Lamord and his horse.[20]

In a play as concerned as this one is with problems of translation, it seems quite plausible that Shakespeare would pun bilingually here no less richly than he does in the bawdy "French lesson" scene of *Henry V*. It also seems plausible that he would be particularly interested in puns that strike the reader's eye even more than the listener's ear; *Hamlet* is after all a play that broods on the relation between elite and "general" audiences, and also on the relation between written texts and dramatic performances of them.[21] The play on Lamord's name suggested by the Second Quarto in any case invites those of us who read *Hamlet* now, knowing all the problems presented by the existence of its different textual versions, to imagine the playwright asking of himself a question similar to the one Horatio voices in Act V, apropos of Osric's inability to understand Hamlet's parody of the inflated courtly style Osric himself uses: "Is't not possible to understand in another tongue?" (V.ii. 125). Horatio's question, like so many questions in this play, is left unanswered. But even if most of Shakespeare's later readers and editors have *not* understand the other tongue, or tongues, spoken by the text in the Lamord passage, that passage is nonetheless significant as a kind of window that allows us briefly to look out from the dark and claustrophobic world of *Hamlet* to another verbal universe, one whose metaphysical economy is less depressed than the one we see in *Hamlet*. The description of Lamord, often cut in production and apparently so irrelevant to the play's plot that it is sometimes described as a "personal allusion" on Shakespeare's part,[22] seems to me a significant digression from the world of tragedy itself. The language of this passage is strangely foreign to *Hamlet* because here letter and spirit are joined in a message that insists on the union of life and death but does not present that union as a horror. For Hamlet, questioner of tropes and incorpser of bodies, all unions are tainted with poison, like the literal "union" (the pearl) in the cup Claudius prepares for Hamlet in the final scene. After Gertrude has mistakenly drunk from that cup and Claudius has been wounded with the envenomed sword, Hamlet ironically offers the poisoned vessel to Claudius, asking bitterly, "Is thy union here? / Follow my mother" (V.ii. 331–2).

There is a different perspective on unions in the personification of Lamord. Shakespeare explores that perspective more fully in some of his later plays, notably the romances; one might indeed see the passage on Lamord as a kind of prophecy of Shakespeare's later career, when he experimented with a genre characterized by "wondrous" escapes from potentially tragic plots. In the romances, and in a play like *Antony and Cleopatra* which blurs the boundary between tragedy and romance, we find a vision of the relation between death and life that sharply contrasts with the tragic vision represented in *Hamlet*. Characters like Antony, Florizel (*The Winter's Tale*) and Ferdinand (*The*

Tempest) inhabit verbal universes in which the verb "to die" often has a double meaning; and the playwright himself exploits the theatrical analogue to this pun by reminding us, as he does conspicuously in *Antony*, that actors, like lovers, may die many times and come again to life.[23] Antony's marvelous dialogue with Eros envisions death as a dissolving of boundaries that is more erotic than terrible, and that may well be compared to the image of Lamord "incorps'd and demi-natur'd" with his horse. "Thou hast seen these signs, / They are black vesper's pageants," Antony tells Eros after describing to him the various forms clouds take; he goes on to conjure an image that anticipates Prospero's famous "cloud-capp'd towers" speech in *The Tempest* (IV.i. 148ff.). Antony says:

> That which is now a horse, even with a thought
> The rack dislimns, and makes it indistinct
> As water is in water.
>
> (IV. xiv. 9–11)

Such a way of conceiving death allows for the possibility of new shapes rising from the dissolution of old ones; death is acknowledged but also, one might say, embraced, in a romance vision similar to the one incarnated in a dialogue in Act IV of *The Winter's Tale*. Speaking of the spring flowers she lacks (for the pastoral world of Shakespearean romance is never an Eden of timeless spring), Perdita says that if she had such flowers she would use them on her lover, "To strew him o'er and o'er." "What, like a corpse?" he asks, and she replies:

> No, like a bank, for love to lie and play on:
> Not like a corpse; or if – not to be buried,
> But quick, and in mine arms.
>
> (IV. iv. 130–2)

Here again is language like that in the Lamord passage, which speaks of something "incorps'd" and lively at once, the quick and the dead "demi-natur'd." In such visions there is a kind of sublime punning, an equivocation that holds life and death in solution or delicate balance. "We must speak by the card or equivocation will undo us," Hamlet says in the graveyard scene (V.i.133–4). Shakespeare, I think, infuses this statement with an irony Hamlet cannot see; for Hamlet is undone, and undoes others, not because he equivocates, but because he inhabits a world where equivocation tends, as if by a fatal entropy, to become "absolute for death." The play, however, renders its own generic drive toward death just equivocal enough to make us question the rules of tragedy.

Notes

I am grateful to Mac Pigman for his helpful comments on an earlier version of this essay. I am also grateful to the many friends and strangers who listened to this paper and criticized it constructively when it was presented in various forms at Wellesley, Smith, Vassar, Bennington, Williams and Mount Holyoke colleges, and at Brown and The Johns Hopkins universities.

1. I borrow the term "performative" from J. L. Austin, *How To Do Things With Words* (1962), 2nd edn (Cambridge, Mass., 1975), 5 and *passim*. Austin, however, notoriously seeks to exclude from his discussion the type of performative utterance that interests me here, namely that which occurs on a stage or in a literary text. Such performatives, he writes, "will be *in a peculiar way* hollow or void" (22, Austin's italics).

2. All quotations from *Hamlet* and other Shakespeare plays are from the New Arden editions, general editors Harold F. Brooks, Harold Jenkins and Brian Morris (London and New York). The Arden *Hamlet*, ed. Harold Jenkins, was published in 1982.

3. See Stephen Booth's excellent discussion of the syntactic and rhetorical devices Claudius uses to achieve "equation by balance"; "On the value of *Hamlet*," in *Reinterpretations of Elizabethan Drama*, ed. Norman Rabkin (New York, 1969), esp. 148–9.

4. Lawrence Danson, *Tragic Alphabet: Shakespeare's Drama of Language* (New Haven and London, 1974), 27.

5. See George Puttenham's *The Arte of English Poesie*, ed. Gladys Willcock and Alice Walker (Cambridge, 1936), 136. "Syllepsis" is the classical trope that corresponds most closely to the modern notion of the pun – a term that did not appear in English until the eighteenth century, according to the *OED*. Oswald Ducrot and Tzvetan Todorov define syllepsis as "the use of a single word that has more than one meaning and participates in more than one syntactic construction"; they cite as an example Falstaff's remark, from *The Merry Wives of Windsor*, "At a word, hang no more about me; I am no gibbet for you" (*Encyclopedic Dictionary of the Sciences of Language*, tr. Catherine Porter (Baltimore, 1979), 278). I am indebted for this citation and for my general understanding of punning tropes to Jane Hedley's unpublished essay on "Syllepsis and the problem of the Shakespeare sonnet order."

6. Sigurd Burckhardt, *Shakespearean Meanings* (Princeton, 1968), 24–5. Burckhardt's comment is cited in part by Danson, op. cit., 27, n. 2.

7. Roman Jakobson and Morris Halle, *Fundamentals of Language* (The Hague, 1956), 62; cited by Danson, op. cit., 27, n. 3.

8. See, e.g., Paul de Man's discussion of Locke's condemnation of *catachresis*, the trope that most notoriously dramatizes the difficulty of grounding a theory of figurative language in a concept of referential correspondence between words and "reality"; "The epistemology of metaphor," in *On Metaphor*, ed. Sheldon Sacks (Chicago and London, 1979), 11–28. Locke's condemnation of catachresis, in *The Essay Concerning Human Understanding*, eventually "takes all language for its target," de Man argues, "for at no point in the course of the demonstration can the empirical entity be sheltered from tropological deformation" (19–20).

9. On Latin as a *sermo patrius*, see my *Trials of Desire: Renaissance Defenses of Poetry* (New Haven and London, 1983), 24, and Leo Spitzer, "Muttersprache und Muttererziehung," in *Essays in Historical Semantics* (New York, 1948), 15–65.

10. See Ian Maclean, *The Renaissance Notion of Woman* (Cambridge, 1980), for a survey of Renaissance authors who adopted the Aristotelian scheme of dualities "in which one element is superior and the other inferior. The male principle in nature is associated with active, formative, and perfected characteristics, while the female is passive, material, and deprived" (8). See also Linda Woodbridge, *Woman and the English Renaissance: Literature and the Nature of Womankind, 1540–1620* (Urbana and Chicago, 1984), esp. ch. 3. It seems likely that an association between baseness, "matter," and his mother is at work even earlier in the play, when Hamlet vows that the Ghost's "commandment all alone shall live / Within the book and volume of my brain, / Unmix'd with baser matter. Yes, by heaven! / O most pernicious woman!" (I.v. 102–5). Cf. Avi Erlich's comments about this passage in *Hamlet's Absent Father* (Princeton, 1977), 218.

11. Freud's famous discussion of Hamlet as a "hysteric" whose guilt about his own repressed oedipal wishes prevents him from taking vengeance "on the man who did away with his father and took that father's place with his mother" was originally published as a footnote to ch. 5 of *The Interpretation of Dreams* (1900); from 1914 onward the passage was included in the text. See *The Standard Edition of the Complete Psychological Works of Sigmund Freud*, ed. James Strachey *et al.*, 4 (London, 1953), 264–6. See also Ernest Jones, *Hamlet and Oedipus* (Garden City, 1949). But see also, for a critique of the "Freud–Jones" interpretation and a discussion of other psychoanalytic readings of *Hamlet*, Theodore Lidz, *Hamlet's Enemy: Madness and Myth in "Hamlet"* (New York, 1975), esp. 9–13, 184–6.

12. Jacques Lacan, "Desire and the interpretation of desire in *Hamlet*," tr. James Hulbert, French text ed. Jacques-Alain Miller from transcripts of Lacan's seminar, in *Literature and Pyschoanalysis, The Question of Reading: Otherwise*, ed. Shoshana Felman (*Yale French Studies*, 55–6 (1977), 11–52). The mention of *dénégation* occurs on p. 50; my explanation of the term draws on the translator's note 6. I should observe, however, that Lacan's analysis departs from Freud's, or rather claims to "shed light on what Freud [had to] . . . leave out" (48), by interpreting the play with reference to the Lacanian theory of the "phallus." The fundamental reason why Hamlet cannot raise his arm against Claudius, Lacan argues, is that "he knows that he must strike something other than what's there" (51). That "something other" is the phallus, the symbolic object which, for Lacan, signifies "the law of the father," and which cannot be mastered by the individual subject because it is an *effect* of repression and of one's insertion into a cultural system of meaning. "[O]ne cannot strike the phallus," Lacan asserts, "because the phallus, even the real phallus, is a *ghost*" (50).

13. Many critics have succumbed to the temptation to reproach Hamlet for incompetence (Bradley) or for possessing "a moral sensibility inferior to our own," as Helen Gardner characterizes T. S. Eliot's rebuke to Hamlet for "dying fairly well pleased with himself" despite the fact that he has made "a pretty considerable mess of things" ("The stoicism of Shakespeare and Seneca," cited in Gardner's useful survey of the problems critics have encountered in trying to find ethical or logical "consistency" in the drama; see her chapter on "The historical approach: *Hamlet*," in *The Business of Criticism* (Oxford, 1959), 35–51).

14. The Norman's name is spelled "Lamord" in the Second Quarto and in many modern editions of the play, e.g. the Arden, the Signet, the Riverside; the entire passage is absent from the First ("Bad") Quarto.

15. See the variants and notes for IV. vii. 93 in the New Variorum *Hamlet*, ed. H. H. Furness, 5th edn (Philadelphia, 1877), 1, 363. The Variorum itself prints the name as "Lamond."

16. Although most modern editors who use the Second Quarto's spelling of the name do so without explaining their choice, Harold Jenkins in the New Arden edition does comment on his decision, suggesting that "the name of the 'wondrous' messenger (91) is a presage of fatality" and is most plausibly interpreted as a play on "La Mort" (see his note to IV. vii. 91, p. 369, and his longer note about the passage on 543–4). To the best of my knowledge, Harry Levin is the only other modern commentator who has devoted much attention to the passage; in *The Question of Hamlet* (New York, 1959), Levin discusses the "easily possible slip of typography or pronunciation" that would make "La Mort" into the Second Quarto's "Lamord" (95).

17. The common Renaissance allegorization of the horse as a symbol for those passions which need to be controlled by reason (figured in the rider or driver) frequently harks back to Plato's image of the soul as a charioteer with two winged horses (*Phaedrus*, 246–8). Shakespeare uses the horse as a figure for uncontrolled anger in 2 *Henry IV*, I. i. 9–11, and again in *Henry VIII*, I. i. 133.

18. See Levin, op. cit., 95; see also Harold Jenkins's editorial comment (op. cit., 544) that the description of Lamord recalls the image of Claudius as a satyr (I. ii. 140) and "kindred animal images, even while the horseman, in contrast with the satyr, is invested with a splendour of which no touch is ever given to Claudius."

19. Cf. Lacan's remarks on Hamlet's rejection of Ophelia once she becomes, in his eyes, "the childbearer to every sin"; she is then "the phallus, exteriorized and rejected by the subject as a symbol signifying life" (Lacan, op. cit., 23).

20. My favorite example, for which I am indebted to Joseph Shork, of the University of Massachusetts at Boston, is the following:

> Amour en latin faict amor;
> Or donc provient d'amour la mort,
> Et par avant, soulcy qui mord,
> Deuils, plours, pieges, forfaitz, remords.

Stendhal uses this *blason* as an epigraph to chapter 15 of *Le Rouge et le Noir*. I have been unable to locate a Renaissance source for this epigraph and it may of course have been composed by Stendhal himself; nonetheless, "se non è vero, è ben trovato." Its play on "mordre" as "to bite" makes it a particularly apt gloss on the Lamord passage, since one editor of *Hamlet*, Edward Dowden, connects the Second Quarto's Lamord with the French *mords*, a horse's bit. For simpler examples of wordplay on love and death in sixteenth-century French poetry, see *Poètes du XVIe siècle*, ed. Albert-Marie Schmidt (Paris, 1953), 725 (Jodelle's *Les Amours*, Sonnet 35), and 827, 823, 820 (poems from Philippe Desportes's *Les Amours d'Hippolyte*).

21. For whatever reasons – one possibly having to do with the complex publication and production history of *Hamlet* in Shakespeare's own lifetime – the play emphasizes the difference between written scripts and actors' versions of them in a way unique in Shakespeare's canon; see, e.g., Hamlet's remark to the Player in II. ii. 430–1 apropos the speech that "was never acted" ("'twas caviare to the general") and his later directive, again addressed to the Player, that "your clowns speak no more than is set down for them" (III. ii. 38–9). The play is also unusually full of references to books, tablets, letters, and forgeries of written texts; some critics have suspected that Hamlet's letter to Ophelia (II. ii. 109ff.) is a forgery by Polonius. For a discussion of the theme of writing in the play, see Daniel Sibony, "*Hamlet*: a writing effect" (*Yale French Studies*, 55–6 (1977), 53–93). On other passages in the text that contain bi- and trilingual puns, see Lidz, op. cit., 23–5.

22. As Harold Jenkins notes (Arden *Hamlet*, 369), a number of editors have suggested a "personal allusion" in the passage to the cavalier in Castiglione's *The Courtier* named Pietro Monte (rendered by Hoby in his Tudor translation as Peter Mount; cf. the Folio's "Lamound"). I do not dispute the idea of an esoteric allusion; I am simply arguing what can never be definitively proved, that an allusion to Death is more plausible.

23. See, for examples of erotic puns on "die," *Antony and Cleopatra*, I. ii. 138–42 and IV. xv. 38–9; *The Tempest*, III. i. 79–84.

16

TERENCE HAWKES

Telmah

1 Looking backwards

It begins without words. A man walks out onto the stage and takes up his position, evidently as a sentry. Another man, also evidently a sentry, follows shortly after him. Approaching the first man, the second suddenly halts, seems apprehensive and afraid. The long military spear he is carrying, the partisan, is quickly brought into an offensive position. That movement – before a word is spoken – immediately pushes the action forward: it enters a different dimension. A mystery has been posited (why are the sentries nervous, why do they make elementary mistakes of military discipline?) and a story starts to unfold.

It ends without words. Two dead bodies are taken up. They are carried ceremonially off by a troop of soldiers, among them four captains, to martial music, after which there is a "peal of ordnance." This noise, music, the cannon, also forwards the action. It implies a new, ordered world of proper, military discipline and principled yet firm political rule that will now replace a disordered society riven by betrayal and murder.

At the beginning, it is immediately noticeable that the military are not in complete control: they get things, fundamental things, wrong. Barnardo's challenge (and the play's first line) "Who's there?" is uttered, as Francisco immediately points out, correcting him, by the wrong sentry. The password, "Long live the King" is "wrong" – we know that a king has recently not lived long, and that another incumbent will soon cease to live.

At the end, similar misconceptions abound. Again, it is Horatio who gets it wrong. We know, from what we have seen, that the story which he proposes to recount to the "yet unknowing world" –

> So shall you hear
> Of carnal, bloody, and unnatural acts,
> Of accidental judgments, casual slaughters,
> Of deaths put on by cunning and forc'd cause,
> And, in this upshot, purposes mistook
> Fall'n on th'inventors' heads
>
> (V. ii. 385–90)[1]

– is not really the way it was. It was not as simple, as like an "ordinary" revenge play, as that. His solemnity – "All this can I / Truly deliver" – mocks at the subtleties, the innuendoes, the contradictions, the imperfectly realized motives and sources for action that have been exhibited to us. We are hardly surprised when Hamlet's own potentialities are summed up by Fortinbras:

> he was likely, had he been put on,
> To have prov'd most royal
>
> (V. ii. 402–3)

but they must, surely, wring a tiny gasp of disbelief at the very least from us. Nobody, so far as we have seen (and of course Fortinbras has not seen what we have seen), was likely to have proved less royal. Fortinbras's own claim to authority is decisively undermined by this poor judgment, which must strike us as misconceived, mistaken, wrong. The "friends" to this present ground, the "liegemen" to this latest Dane (he is of course "wrong" even in that, being a Norwegian), may well find the future just as bleak as their mistaken predecessors.

At the beginning, the action is overshadowed by war: by the "fair and warlike form" (the Ghost) who dominates it even in his absence. There is much talk of preparation for war.

At the end, the warlike form of Fortinbras also hangs over the action in his absence: he finally obtrudes heralded by a "warlike noise." Military rule, by a foreigner, is what lies in store for the Danish state. The war promised at the beginning has not happened, but at the end the results are the same as if it had.

At the beginning a dead king's presence overhangs the action and is evoked by the nervousness of the sentries. At the end a dead king's presence overhangs the action, and is evoked by those final cannons, whose sound has been associated with him throughout.

There is even a mirror reflection of phrases. At the beginning, Barnardo comments, "How now, Horatio? You tremble and look pale" (I. i. 56). At the end, Hamlet's words echo to a larger audience, "You that look pale and tremble at this chance" (V. ii. 339).

It would be wrong to make too much of "symmetries" of this sort, and I

311

mention them only because, once recognized, they help however slightly to undermine our inherited notion of *Hamlet* as a structure that runs a satisfactorily linear, sequential course from a firmly established and well defined beginning, through a clearly placed and signaled middle, to a causally related and logically determined end which, planted in the beginning, develops, or grows out of it.

Like all symmetries, the ones I have pointed to suggest, not linearity, but circularity: a cyclical and recursive movement wholly at odds with the progressive, incremental ordering that a society, dominated perhaps by a pervasive metaphor of the production line, tends to think of as appropriate to art as to everything else.

If we add to this the judgment that the beginning of *Hamlet* is, in a quite perplexing sense, an ending (the spear's movement forces us to look back to events that have already occurred: the Ghost presupposes a complexity of happenings that lead to its current ghostliness), and that the ending in effect constitutes a beginning (the cannon at the end makes us look forward to the new order of Fortinbras, as much as back: Fortinbras's future rule is clearly presaged as the play ends), the complexity of the whole business begins to appear.

We can even ask, as amateurs in playhouse dynamics, and in respect of the experience of a live audience in the theater, when does the play *effectively* begin? Is it when the first sentry walks out onto the stage? Or has the play already begun in our mind's eye as we enter the theater, leave our house, get up on that morning, buy our ticket some days/weeks ago? In our society, in which *Hamlet* is embedded in the ideology in a variety of roles, the play has, for complex social and historical reasons, always already begun. And onto its beginning we have always already imprinted a knowledge of its course of action, and its ending.

And when, then, does it effectively end? When the dialogue stops and when the soldiers carry the bodies off and the music and the explosion of the cannons is heard? Not really, for there follows applause, and then that complex of revisionary ironies, which we group together under the heading of the "curtain call."

This is the ultimate Pirandellian moment which any play reaches: the final moment of closure in all senses in which, significantly, precisely the question of the nature of closing is raised. Of course, it also nominates that part of the play which is closed to critical discussion: nobody ever talks about it.[2] Yet the question raised is crucial. When *does* the play close? When its "action" stops? But does not that include, at least to some degree, the curtain call (which, of course, the actors rehearse)? For at this point the actors appear before us only partly as their "real" selves. They remain partly, and significantly, still "in character," retaining mannerisms, perhaps, of the characters they have been playing. Who are they, then, at this point? Hamlet is not the prince (for he is dead), but he is certainly not the actor who played the prince either. He does not laugh or caper about as a man might who has scored (in the soccer fashion) a success. He may smile, wanly, as befits one recently slain; he may take (ruefully?) the hands of his no less "dead" opponent Claudius; he may even embrace the long-dead Ophelia. Is not this still acting? (The actor "playing" himself-as-actor). Is not this part of the action? It is the part that our applause, that nondiscursive aural kind of closure, creates for us. It is the point at which we assume control, for can we not now make Hamlet go or stay for a longer or shorter time, make him smile, frown, even laugh? It is the point, in short, at which we see the "edge" of the play before it disappears entirely.

The modern curtain call is of course very firmly part of the production: fully rehearsed in all its complicated entrances and exits. This in itself gives us a sense of the force of the modern director's feeling that he must *seal* finally and inescapably the "interpretation" he has thrust on and through the play. Yet of course the curtain call cannot be thus simply nailed down, any more than the play can be thus simply sealed up and made subject to the director's will, however hard he tries. In a way that makes it representative of the play at large, the curtain call slips from under the director's fingers to generate its own wider and wilder implications. Here, most significantly, any apparent movement in one direction of the play halts, and it begins to roll decisively in the opposite direction (if only towards the next performance, when its "beginning" will emerge from these smiling actors). In short, the sense of straight, purposive, linear motion forward through the play – the sense required by most "interpretations" of it – evaporates at the curtain call, and we sense an opposing current.

In so far as that current connects decisively with elements or aspects of the play already noticed, in so far as its force seeks to roll the play backwards, reinforces its recursive mode, makes it, as it were, move only unwillingly and haltingly forward, constantly, even as it does so, looking over its own shoulder, then I propose to recognize it and, for the sake of convenience and argument, to name it in relation to *Hamlet*. I call it *Telmah*: *Hamlet* backwards.

In search of *Telmah*, we can begin by noticing the extent to which looking backwards, re-vision, or reinterpretation, the running of events over again, out of their time sequence, ranks, in fact, as a fundamental mode of *Hamlet*. *Subsequence, posteriority*, these are the effective modes of the opening, generating phrases like "has *this thing* appear'd *again* tonight," "this dreaded sight *twice seen of us*," "Thus *twice before*, and jump at this dead hour . . . hath he gone by our watch," and so on, which eventually provoke the great retailing of past events offered by Horatio as preface to the Ghost's second appearance:

> our last King,
> Whose image even but now appear'd to us,
> Was as you know by Fortinbras of Norway,
> Thereto prick'd on by a most emulate pride,
> Dar'd to the combat; in which our valiant Hamlet . . .
> Did slay this Fortinbras, who, by a seal'd compact
> Well ratified by law and heraldry
> Did forfeit, with his life, all those his lands
> Which he stood seized of.
>
> (I.i.83–92)

This leads to the full story of Young Fortinbras and so, by backward-looking implication, brings in, from behind, Hamlet:

> Now, sir, young Fortinbras,
> Of unimproved mettle, hot and full,
> Hath in the skirts of Norway here and there
> Shark'd up a list of lawless resolutes
> For food and diet to some enterprise
> That hath a stomach in't, which is no other,
> As it doth well appear unto our state,
> But to recover of us by strong hand
> And terms compulsatory those foresaid lands
> So by his father lost. And this, I take it,
> Is the main motive of our preparations,
> The source of this our watch, and the chief head
> Of this post-haste and rummage in the land.
>
> (I.i.98–110)

Then, as a sort of climax of this revising, there is Claudius's great revisionary proposal, his reinterpretation of the past which leads up to his own present position:

> Though yet of Hamlet our dear brother's death
> The memory be green, and that it us befitted
> To bear our hearts in grief, and our whole kingdom
> To be contracted in one brow of woe,
> Yet so far hath discretion fought with nature
> That we with wisest sorrow think on him
> Together with remembrance of ourselves.
> Therefore our sometime sister, now our queen,
> Th'imperial jointress to this warlike state,
> Have we, as 'twere with a defeated joy,
> With an auspicious and a dropping eye,
> With mirth in funeral and with dirge in marriage,

In equal scale weighing delight and dole,
Taken to wife. Nor have we herein barr'd
Your better wisdoms, which have freely gone
With this affair along. For all, our thanks.
Now follows that you know young Fortinbras,
Holding a weak supposal of our worth . . .

(I. ii. 1–18)

Throughout, it seems to me, the audience of *Hamlet* might legitimately feel that it is being buttonholed, cajoled, persuaded by participants in the play to look back, to "revise," to see things again in particular ways, to "read" or interpret them along specific lines and to the exclusion of others. It is a procedure notoriously mocked by Hamlet himself, at the expense of Polonius, in a famously deconstructive moment:

Hamlet: Do you see yonder cloud that's almost in the shape of a camel?
Polonius: By th' mass, and 'tis – like a camel indeed.
Hamlet: Methinks it is like a weasel.
Polonius: It is backed like a weasel.
Hamlet: Or like a whale.
Polonius: Very like a whale.

(III. ii. 367–73)

and easily its most memorable manifestation occurs when the Ghost buttonholes the prince with a peculiarly insistent version of the murder:

Brief let me be. Sleeping within my orchard,
My custom always of the afternoon,
Upon my secure hour thy uncle stole
With juice of cursed hebenon in a vial,
And in the porches of my ears did pour
The leperous distilment, whose effect
Holds such an enmity with blood of man
That swift as quicksilver it courses through
The natural gates and alleys of the body,
And with a sudden vigour it doth posset
And curd, like eager droppings into milk,
The thin and wholesome blood. So did it mine,
And a most instant tetter bark'd about,
Most lazar-like, with vile and loathsome crust
All my smooth body.

(I. v. 59–73)

These slow-motion "action replays" of past events become a feature of the play. It seems constantly to "revise" itself in this way, and this serves to pull

315

back against any "forward" progressive movement which it might otherwise appear to instigate.

On a larger scale, a series of insistent thematic rhythms seems to run counter to or – better word – syncopate with those apparently fostered by the play's sequential development. The death of fathers, which Claudius stresses as a "common theme" – one which has reason's backing in his assertion "this must be so" –

> But you must know your father lost a father,
> That father lost, lost his
>
> (I.ii. 89–90)

– nevertheless begins to bulk disconcertingly large. It is almost a case of paternal overkill: by the middle of the play our attention has been forcefully drawn to the death of no fewer than *five* fathers: King Fortinbras; King Hamlet; Polonius; Achilles; and Gonzago, the Player King. In four of the cases an avenging son presents himself: Fortinbras, Hamlet, Laertes, Pyrrhus. The pattern seems to push Hamlet in his role as revenger into the foreground. But then notice the countervailing pattern hinted at by and available within the same structure: that of the dead father's brother, who, as *uncle* to the son, controls and redirects the son's revenging energies. The clearest case is that of Young Fortinbras, whose uncle Norway has succeeded to the throne, whereupon he reintegrates the displaced Young Fortinbras into the society. This rhythm is underscored when Claudius tries to perform exactly the same operation with Hamlet: as uncle who has taken over the throne, he tries famously to reintegrate the displaced Hamlet into the society. And it is underscored again, when, the operation having failed with Hamlet, Claudius assumes the avuncular role in respect of Laertes after Polonius's death and, again famously, redirects his revenging energy and integrates him into the society. In short, I am suggesting that there is an "avuncular" function covertly at work in *Hamlet*, activated by the common theme of the death of all these fathers.

The avuncular role seen in opposition to the paternal one becomes, in my view, an insistent aspect of the play. It derives of course from, and plays consistently on, the traditional European notion of the avunculate: the father stands as a figure of stern authority, the uncle as a figure of laxity and good humor. This is the disposition that Claudius abrogates (Hamlet's bitter description of him as "my uncle-father" reinforces that) and it is a transgression as great as the one collaterally made by Gertrude. European culture permits the transformation wife-mother, but forbids, or is deeply suspicious of, the transformation mother-wife, since that raises the specter of incest.[3] In becoming an "aunt-mother" and so a wife, Gertrude's sexuality is underlined, and this accordingly brings from Hamlet the gibe about "incestuous sheets."

The insistent quality of this aspect of the play acts, it seems to me, as a disruptive element in *Hamlet*, because it serves to promote Claudius. Its "catchy" pulse pulls constantly at the attention, and draws it away from the prince. Claudius ceases to be the simple stage-villain described by the Ghost and required by the smoothing-over process of interpretation that linear progressions demands. He has many more than one role, and these are complex, manifold: he is brother (even the primal brother, Cain, as he himself suggests), father in a legal and political sense to Hamlet, lover and later husband to Gertrude, murderer of King Hamlet, monarch, and political head of the state. In a sense, all these roles are situated within his enormously forceful role of uncle, on the basis of which his opposition to Hamlet is determined. He is, as the play terms him, no simple villain, but Hamlet's "mighty opposite," and that mightiness constantly tugs back, recursively, against the smooth flow of a play that bears, perhaps surprisingly, only the prince's name. It is not insignificant that, at that play's most recursive moment, in the performance of another play, the murderer (Lucianus) is clearly and coolly presented as a nephew, murdering his uncle. In this play within the play, right at the center of *Hamlet*, *Telmah* disconcertingly surfaces.

The Mousetrap marks Hamlet's most recursive moment: the point at which time runs most obviously backwards, and where the play does not just glance over its shoulder, so much as turn fully round to look squarely at the most prominent action replay of them all. More than a play within a play, it offers a replay of a replay: the Ghost's revised account of the murder, fitted out with actions. Equally, in so far as *The Mousetrap* is designed decisively to generate events that will forward the action of *Hamlet*, it also firmly looks towards the future. It functions, as Hamlet himself says, "tropically": that is, as both trope or metaphor, and as the "tropic" or turning point of *Hamlet* the play. For *Hamlet* to operate, the past has here to be causally fused to the future: *Hamlet*'s linear progression depends on that, and the prince himself has made it a condition of his own future actions. The Ghost's account of the events leading up to King Hamlet's murder are here to be tested by means of asking an audience at the play to interpret them in a particular way.

Hamlet himself is confident: he has written part of the script and he is "as good as a chorus" in interpreting it. Rarely can someone involved in a play have been so convinced that, in its linear, sequential unfolding, its single, unequivocal meaning will receive ready, interpreted acknowledgment. Hamlet the prince, like the play which bears his name, seems committed, purposive, moving inexorably to a predetermined end. Like *Hamlet*, confirming its enclosing presence perhaps, the play within the play begins without words. And then, suddenly, it all goes wrong. *The Mousetrap* becomes "tropical" indeed. *Hamlet* "turns" decisively. It turns into *Telmah*.

2 To the Sunderland station

The scene now shifts to a train proceeding from Leeds to Sunderland one Saturday evening in November 1917.

On that train, a man is opening his mail. Among his letters he finds a square envelope containing the issue of the *Modern Language Review* (Vol. XII, No. 4) for October 1917. Leafing through it, he finds himself attracted to a particular article and "all unconscious of impending fate," as he puts it, begins to read.

The effect, to say the least, is odd. In fact, he later uses the term "overwhelming" and speaks of the experience as capable of throwing "any mind off its balance." The man was the scholar and critic John Dover Wilson, then aged 36. The article was by W. W. Greg and it was entitled "Hamlet's hallucination."

The thrust of Greg's article lies in his clear perception that something goes badly wrong with the prince's plans right at the beginning of *The Mousetrap*. Claudius fails to make any response to that initial and vital "action replay," the dumb-show. The "full significance" of this, Greg argues, has never been appreciated. After all, the dumb-show presents the stark details of Claudius's supposed crime, in more or less exactly the form retailed by the Ghost. Claudius's failure to respond means, quite simply, that the Ghost has failed the test, organized by Hamlet himself, to establish its veracity. There is no doubt, of course, that Claudius has murdered King Hamlet. The doubts are as to the mode and methods of the act – and in this respect the Ghost is clearly revealed, Greg says, to fall short as an "objective" reporter. He has not given Hamlet true information. The "orthodox view" of the play, which requires an objective truth-bearing Ghost, with Claudius properly indicted by its testimony as the dastardly poisoning villain of the story, ignores or tries to think "around" the dumb-show. It argues, say, that the king and queen are in close conversation at the time and so pay no attention to what is going on. This explanation, says Greg, "is indeed a lame one": it treats the play as "history," not drama. Such critics inquire "why Hamlet behaved in a ridiculous way, when the question they should have asked was why Shakespeare did – or whether he did." He adds, remarkably for 1917, "this tendency is particularly prominent in the work of A. C. Bradley."

For Greg, the "extraordinary nature" of the dumb-show needs to be grasped. If we do so, we can see how genuinely upsetting Claudius's negative response to it is. Its effect is to "promote" Claudius: to make him more intriguing, his actions and his motives more complex: to make him a *victim* of the Ghost's malicious reportage as much as a villain in terms of the way the play is usually seen: to make him genuinely, as the play terms him, no simple mustache-twirling criminal, but Hamlet's "mighty opposite"; an impressive figure of potentially tragic stature whose mightiness tugs back, recursively, against the smooth flow of the play that bears only the prince's name. On the basis of the orthodox Hamlet-centered interpretation of the play, Claudius's response to the dumb-show "not merely threatens the logical structure of one of the most crucial scenes of the play, but reduces it to meaningless confusion." As a result, Greg concludes, "we have to choose between giving up Shakespeare as a rational playwright, and giving up our inherited beliefs regarding the story of *Hamlet*."

More than 60 years later, something of the panache of Greg's argument still communicates itself to us, though its potential as light reading for a Yorkshire Saturday night and Sunday morning might perhaps be a matter for dispute.

What cannot be disputed is its effect on Dover Wilson. I have described this as odd: a better phrase might be "seriously disturbing," even "mind-blowing." He himself describes it as "an intensely felt experience" which resulted in "a state of some considerable excitement." It filled him, he reports, with "a sort of insanity," and cast upon him, in his own words 18 years later, "a spell which changed the whole tenor of my existence, and still dominates it in part." Give up Shakespeare as a rational playwright indeed! Give up our inherited beliefs! Having read the article "half a dozen times before reaching Sunderland," an almost Pauline sense of mission seems to have descended upon him: "from the first [I] realized that I had been born to answer it."

Why such a heated response to an article in a learned journal? And why – perhaps more interestingly – is it recorded in such detail 18 years later, as part of the prolegomena to Dover Wilson's *What Happens in Hamlet*? We might, of course, pick up the not-quite-covert hint that the response is itself engagingly Hamlet-like. Dover Wilson describes what he calls his own "spiritual condition" at the time as "critical, not to say dangerous, a condition in which a man becomes converted, falls in love, or gives way to a mania for wild speculation." The war had its pressures, we are given to understand, and it perhaps did not seem inappropriate – it might even seem appealing – that a personality so highly charged might experience a reaction to such a situation which could be, as another critic was to put it of Hamlet, "in excess of the facts as they appear."

Of course, a lot depends on how the facts are made to appear. And just as a rather different *Hamlet – Telmah –* can be detected struggling beneath – or with – that play, so a rather different explanation of Dover Wilson's response may be heard rustling uneasily on the edge of any half-hint of the prince-like nature of its author's entirely winsome "insanity."

We can begin with the fact that, in November 1917, the war was not the only source of deep-seated disturbance in the world. In fact we could point out that, on any of the Saturdays in that month, news of the impending or actual Bolshevik revolution in Russia was likely to have been competing with news from the fronts. We have Dover Wilson's own statement that "I found it difficult to concentrate upon anything unconnected with the War" and even his comment that, spending a lot of his time in trains, "the hours of travel were mostly occupied in reading the newspapers."

A glance at the newspapers of November 1917 confirms that the Bolshevik action received wide coverage, and one could reasonably assume Dover Wilson's awareness of the events from that. On Saturday, November 3, *The Times* reported "Persistent rumours in Petrograd of the imminence of armed action by the Maximalists [i.e. Bolsheviks] whose object is to seize the supreme power" (6). The coup actually took place on Wednesday–Thursday, November 7–8 (by the Russian calendar, this was October 25–6). On Friday, November 9, extensive reports appeared in *The Times*: "Anarchy in Petrograd: Power Seized by Lenin," with editorial comment of a predictable nature: "the most extreme party in the Soviet appears to be in power . . . it is assuredly not the authentic voice of Russia." By Saturday, November 10, what *The Times* was then calling "The Lenin Revolution" was fully reported, together with an extensive account of what the headlines termed "Siege of the Winter Palace," and on both Saturday, November 17, and Saturday, November 24, there appeared lengthy reports headed "Civil Strife in Petrograd" and "Russia's Starving Armies," etc. It would have been difficult, in fact, for a newspaper reader to be unaware of these events.

However, it adds a dimension to the picture, and gives something of an edge to what we may presume to be the *quality* of Dover Wilson's awareness, if we take into account the nature of the mission on which he was currently engaged: his reason, that is, for being on that particular train at that particular time.

Dover Wilson's main employment then was as a school inspector of the Board of Education, stationed at Leeds. But, in common with other inspectors, he was also from time to time used in some war work: specifically, as an inspector for the Ministry of Munitions. The reason he was traveling to Sunderland had to do with that work, and with a particular crisis concerning it. "Some trouble," as he decorously puts it, "had arisen with local trade-union officials" in Sunderland, and Dover Wilson had been urgently dispatched there to sort it out.

It is worth very briefly reminding ourselves that the Ministry of Munitions presented at that time an unusual and, to some, a rather dangerous spectacle in terms of British labor relations. The pressures of the war (including the arrival of women workers) had created a situation in which, to use A. J. P. Taylor's words, the local shop stewards "were often revolutionary socialists . . . some of them were opposed to the war." This meant that they found themselves permanently in conflict with "official" and conservative trade-union policy, since they represented a much wider working-class interest in the face of it. Ministers such as Lloyd George and, by 1917, Churchill were forced to work "hand in hand with the revolutionary shop stewards," despite "growls of protest" from the unions.[4]

For "trouble" to occur at any time in the munitions industry was obviously bad enough. Negotiations at local level with what were later indeed called "Bolshevik" shop stewards[5] must have been, if you will pardon the expression, a potentially explosive business. Such trouble occurring in November 1917 would certainly have had a capacity for uncontrolled detonation more than sufficient to generate a "critical, not to say dangerous" condition (you will have noted Dover Wilson's submerged metaphor of impending combustion) in a man about to be ignited by a copy of the *Modern Language Review*.

Insurrection was in the air. On the first day of the Bolshevik coup (November 7), speaking, by chance, in the House of Lords, the Marquess of Salisbury had warned that "The governing classes hitherto had been inclined to regard the working class as a sort of dangerous animal of enormous strength and great potential violence, which it was necessary to be very civil to, but never to trust."[6] In short, the revolutionary proposals of Greg's article on *Hamlet* must have fallen into a powder-keg of a mind already in some degree prepared to be "blown" into "a sort of insanity" by them just as, in the wider context towards which the Leeds–Sunderland train seemed to be speeding, certain events were already shaking the world.

Before dismissing this view as one which makes far too much out of a mere coincidence of dates, certain other aspects of what is really rather a complex situation should be borne in mind. First, it is Dover Wilson himself who gives us all the facts, as it were compulsively, in a "letter" entitled "The road to Elsinore, being an epistle dedicatory to Walter Wilson Greg," which prefaces his major and highly influential book *What Happens in Hamlet* (1935). The apparently immodest, unreserved commitment to total exposition of that book's title lends its own confessional, bean-spilling air to the letter, and vice versa.

The literary device of the publicly printed letter has always, of course, exploited means of communication generated by its paradoxical mode. As a document whose standing is both private and public at the same time, it "means" both by what it is seen to offer, in confidence, and by what it is seen to withhold, in public. It operates, that is to say, both directly, by intimate revelation, and indirectly, by evident obfuscation and suppression. The two methods of signifying are equated and intimately involved. What it says and what it does not say, its utterances and its silences, are both meaningful: each is an aspect of the other. In *this* letter, the overt commitment is to the whole truth. Greg is told: "you may have guessed something of this, but you cannot know it all." The letter will thus tell all. It will explain "the origin and purpose of this book," take us to the final originary source of what happened before *What Happens in Hamlet* happened, and thus lead us, in effect, to the root cause of its writing. That origin is precisely, specifically, and insistently dated in a spirit of "classic realism": "It begins some time in the November of 1917. . . . I reached home one Saturday evening to find an urgent telephone message awaiting me." The related, concomitant silence, however, is no less insistent. There is absolutely no mention before or after of the Bolshevik revolution.

I think we can regard that silence as resonant, and not simply because of the interest of the revolution itself, or because of any potential connection, however oblique, between it and Dover Wilson's current journey (Sunderland lacks a Winter Palace, but things have to start somewhere). It could be seen as finally a matter of discourse. The discourse of literary criticism in Britain and America, then and now, tends to exclude the area of politics as not overtly appropriate to itself and its purposes. It would seem literally unreasonable for a literary critic to take such issues on board as, no doubt, it seems unreasonable for me to do so right now.

But in fact, the truth is that Dover Wilson had to hand, and was perfectly capable of using, another discourse designed exactly for that purpose. There is, it seems to me, great significance in respect of the way discourses operate in the fact that he makes no mention of the Bolshevik revolution. For it means that no mention is made of it, no connection drawn between it and his present highly emotional state, on the part of a man who had lived within the Russian Empire (in Finland) for three years, who by his own account had become, on his return to Britain, "a well known public lecturer" on the subject of Russia, who was currently, as he writes to Greg, making "fitful and unsuccessful attempts to learn Russian," and who on more than one previous occasion had written coolly, seriously, and at length about exactly this possibility of revolution in Russia and its likely consequences.

In 1906, Dover Wilson's article on "The aims and methods of the Social Revolutionary Party in Russia" appeared.[7] It begins by making my central point for me: that a revolution in Russia (he is referring of course to the revolution of 1905) must be an event of considerable significance for western Europe, and that there can be no excuse for any suppression of awareness of it:

> The newspapers have been undeniably generous in the space devoted to the "Russian Revolution," and no Englishman has any excuse for being ignorant of the fact that, from one end to the other of the great eastern plain of Europe which we agree to call Russia, a gigantic civil war is now being waged – a war which must to a large extent determine the destinies not only of Russia, but also of Europe as a whole.

The piece goes on to make what, even to my entirely unsophisticated eyes, appears as a somewhat over-simple analysis of Russia's political structure. "Russia possesses only two revolutionary factions of any real importance: the Social Revolutionaries and the Social Democrats." But, naive or not, the future reader of Greg's revolutionary proposals concerning *Hamlet* leaves us in no doubt that, of those factions, the program of the Social Revolutionaries is infinitely preferable to that advanced by the Social Democrats. The latter, being "founded on the theories of a German doctrinaire," can have no success in the face of the former, whose Fabian mode especially recommends it and ensures, for Dover Wilson, that it finds its basis in "real Russian institutions." The future of the country thus "clearly lies with the Social Revolutionaries," a situation confirmed by the fact that the wretched Social Democrats had recently split into two parties, the Minority and the Majority, thus demonstrating their hopelessness. These two factions could confidently be consigned to outer darkness and forgotten. The Social Revolutionaries, whose policy of terrorism Dover Wilson explains, condones and approves (he says it seems to be having "a distinctly beneficial result"), win his support, for "the future of the country lies with them."

Everybody makes mistakes, and a man who has espoused the cause of the Social Revolutionary party so wholeheartedly – even to the extent of condoning its commitment to terrorism – and who has so roundly dismissed the claims of the competing Social Democrats, whether Menshevik (as the minority group was called) or Bolshevik (as the majority group was called), a man who has uttered so confidently, might reasonably and significantly fall silent on the subject.

In fact, Dover Wilson committed himself yet again to the same issue in 1914. Writing in a piece called "Russia and her ideals,"[8] he offers, in his own words, to correct prejudices: to look Russia "straight in the eyes, that we may hope to catch a glimpse of her soul." The glimpse reveals, he assures us, a deep craving for order, arising out of a constant struggle for self-preservation. Autocracy comes almost naturally to be the only form of government for such a society: "A State whose very existence is perpetually at stake, for whom discipline is the primary need, has really no choice but to place itself in the hands of an imperator, a Caesar, a Tsar." As a result, autocracy in Russia is best seen as "part of religion itself," with the tsar as God's "representative upon earth." Anything more complex, he concludes, would only puzzle the Russians, for tsardom is more than autocracy in their case; it is theocracy. And he adds, with the confidence of one who has gazed "straight in the eyes" of the "teeming millions," "As both it is intensely representative of the national mind and character."

The principle of autocracy, he continues, is thus the only principle that mind and that character can understand, and it would therefore be wrong to countenance any disturbance of it. Autocracy, he assures us, in 1914

> still has a long life before it and much work to perform in Russia. It is therefore wiser to face the facts and to recognize that the Tsardom is after all Russia's form of democracy. . . . it is the kind of government the people understand and reverence, and it is their only protection against the tyranny of an aristocratic clique. . . . when the will of the autocrat is clearly and unmistakably expressed, it has always been found to correspond with the needs of the people.

Those who asked "How wrong can you be?" of Dover Wilson's 1906 article are partly answered here. You can be *much* wronger. But the piece is certainly not without interest on another level. World-picture fanciers will already have recognized in it a version of what, by the time of the second world war, had become a standard British response to national crisis: the construction of long-past, green, alternative worlds of percipient peasants, organic communities, festivals, folk art, and absolute monarchy to set against present chaos. Dover Wilson's revised Russian World Picture of 1914 has developed, since his essay of 1906, features which surface regularly in our century as part of a recurrent siege mentality. It thus has much more than a coincidental resemblance to E. M. W. Tillyard's well known war-effort, *The Elizabethan World Picture* of 1943. A discourse which, seeking for the final, confirming presence of authority, nominates the linchpin of the political structure as "God's representative on earth" is clearly heard in both.[9] Each represents, less an accurate picture of the world it purports to describe, than an intimate, covert measure of its author's fears about the fallen world in which he currently lives, and in the face of which he has constructed a peculiarly English Eden.

But it is not just a question of getting it wrong, wronger, or wrongest. The point is that the decided modification in Dover Wilson's views about Russia which takes place between 1906 and 1914, moving from an early commitment to Fabianism, to a subsequent rejection of it in favor of Tsarism, represents a serious narrowing of options, a growing sense of urgency, and a harder and harder line. And it is thus a modification which, given the previous confidence about insights into "national mind and character," must have lent the *actual* events of November 1917, when they occurred, the quality of a nightmare; turning them into a horror of such proportions that perhaps no overt response to them was possible. (His later embarrassment over his writings on Russia is evident in his autobiography: "I could not prophesy," he admits, "a portent like Lenin who arrived in 1917.")

This is what I mean when I say that the absence of any mention of the Bolshevik revolution in Dover Wilson's account of his train journey strikes me as significant. What it signifies is of course that the Bolshevik revolution *is* in effect being responded to, coped with in that "intensely felt experience," that "spell which changed the whole tenor of my existence," and that "sort of insanity" provoked by Greg's article on *Hamlet*.

Greg's attack, after all, is on the smooth surface of the play seen as the product of Shakespeare the "rational playwright," but effectively, of course, created by an "orthodox" interpretation which seeks for unity, progression, coherence, and, if possible, sequential ordering in all art, as part of a ruthless and rigorous process of domestication. There is no obvious way of placating Greg's objections to that sort of *Hamlet*, for they constitute a frontal assault on what he terms the "inherited beliefs" – that brand of literary tsarism –

which reinforce and sustain it. And the assault is certainly not Fabian in character. It is directly, violently Bolshevik.

Dover Wilson's defense took various forms. There was an immediate diagnostic response to the editor of the *Modern Language Review* in the form of a postcard dispatched upon alighting from the train at Sunderland, which went so far as to nominate Greg as an unwitting agent of the arch-revolutionary himself: "Greg's article devilish ingenious but damnably wrong," it twinkled, and offered a rejoinder, which duly appeared. There followed two major salvoes: the edition of *Hamlet* prepared by Dover Wilson for the New Cambridge Shakespeare in 1934 – a series of which, provoked into editorship by Greg's article, he says, he had become general editor in 1919 – and the book *What Happens in Hamlet*, which purports to release him from thrall to the problem, by telling all. Those interested in the details of his argument can pursue them there. Suffice it to say that I do not myself find them convincing, so much as replete with the charm and ingenuity of the truly desperate. To suggest that Claudius does not notice the dumb-show, engaged as he is in conversation with Polonius and Gertrude, seeks to "naturalize" the situation out of existence. The further suggestion that the players (a burlesque of Edward Alleyn and Shakespeare's rivals the Lord Admiral's Men) constitute a kind of surly trade union, engaged in a dispute with their temporary boss, Hamlet, which provokes an unlooked-for work-to-rule, resulting in an unauthorized dumb-show as embarrassing to Hamlet as it is ineffective in respect of Claudius, so nearly proves my own point for me that I hesitate to use it, although connoisseurs will find it on pp. 153–63 of *What Happens in Hamlet*.

But if these salvoes represent Dover Wilson's defense against Bolshevism in its specifically displaced Shakespearean form, it is possible also to suggest that the same battle was subsequently taken up on on a broader front by the same combatant. Two years later, in May 1919, a departmental committee was appointed by the president of the Board of Education to investigate what was termed "the teaching of English in England." Its terms of reference were:

> To inquire into the position occupied by English (Language and Literature) in the educational system of England, and to advise how its study may best be promoted in schools of all types, including Continuation Schools, and in Universities and other Institutions of Higher Education, regard being had to:
> (1) the requirements of a liberal education;
> (2) the needs of business, the professions, and public services; and
> (3) the relation of English to other studies.

The Committee's chairman was Sir Henry Newbolt, and prominent among its members was John Dover Wilson.

Many things have been said about the Newbolt Report, as the published findings of the Committee became known. The first thing to stress is that it was widely influential. It sold, in Dover Wilson's words, "like a best-seller," and it can be said to have effectively shaped the nature of "English" as the academic subject we know today. Its "spiritual" father is Matthew Arnold, its "spiritual" son F. R. Leavis. Its two central concerns – more or less overt – are related political ones: social cohesion in the face of potential disintegration and disaffection; and nationalism, the encouragement of pride in English national culture on a broader front. The common coin of its discourse is generated by concepts we have already encountered: those of "national mind and character." English, in this light, is presented as "the only basis possible for a national education," being not merely the medium of our thought, but "the very stuff and process of it. It is itself the English mind." An education based on English would thus have a "unifying tendency," acting as an antidote to the divisiveness, the "bitterness and disintegration" of a class-dominated society. It would heal one of the major causes of "division amongst us": the "undue narrowness of the ground on which we meet for the true purposes of social life" (without specifying what those might be). Recognizing that we are "not one nation but two," the study of English is capable of bridging, if not closing, the "chasm of separation," the "mental [sic] distances between classes." Offering a "bond of union between classes," it would "beget the right kind of national pride."[10]

The Committee was in effect responding to the sort of view promoted, oddly enough, by the Welshman Lloyd George, when the war ended. Speaking at Manchester in September 1918, he had put the case that

> The most formidable institution we had to fight in Germany was not the arsenals of Krupps or the yards in which they turned out submarines, but the schools of Germany. They were our most formidable competitors in business and our most terrible opponents in war. An educated man is a better worker, a more formidable warrior, and a better citizen.[11]

The Education Acts of 1918 (the Fisher Act) and 1944 (the Butler Act) are testimony to the fact that in Britain the threat of external disruption is usually the parent of educational change: certainly, by 1919, events outside the United Kingdom had evidently carried a clear enough message to ministers within it. If there was a breathless hush in the close of Europe, it was not inappropriate that a committee chaired by Sir Henry Newbolt (for it is he) should be urging us, through the study of English language and literature, to "play up, play up, and play the game."

Members of the committee were allotted areas of special concern; and among those assigned to Dover Wilson, he later tells us, was the one which appears in the report as Sections 232–8, "Literature and the nation." The thrust of these pages (252–60) is that teaching literature to the working class is a kind of "missionary work" whose aim is to stem the tide of that class's by then evident disaffection. The missionary to Sunderland clearly sees that workers need to be embraced into the larger way of British life, and he leaves us in no doubt that this is a matter "involving grave national issues" to which the committee has given "much anxious thought" (252).

Workers, such "thought" urges, ought to feel that there is a national culture to which they can belong, and literature is offered as an instrument for promoting social cohesion in place of division. Its political role is quite clear:

> Literature, in fact, seems to be classed by a large number of thinking working men with antimacassars, fish-knives and other unintelligible and futile trivialities of "middle-class culture," and, as a subject of instruction, is suspect as an attempt "to side-track the working-class movement." We regard the prevalence of such opinions as a serious matter, not merely because it means the alienation of an important section of the population from the "confort" and "mirthe" of literature, but chiefly because it points to a morbid condition of the body politic which if not taken in hand may be followed by lamentable consequences. For if literature be, as we believe, an embodiment of the best thoughts of the best minds, the most direct and lasting communication of experience by man to men, a fellowship which "binds together by passion and knowledge the vast empire of human society, as it is spread over the whole earth, and over all time," then the nation of which a considerable portion rejects this means of grace, and despises this great spiritual influence, must assuredly be heading to disaster.[12]

As another member of the committee put it, "Deny to working class children any common share in the immaterial and presently they will grow into the men who demand with menaces a communism of the material."[13]

The specter of a working class, demanding material goods with menaces, losing its national mind, besmirching its national character, clearly had a growing capacity to disturb after the events of 1917, particularly if that class, as Dover Wilson writes in the Newbolt Report, sees education "mainly as something to equip them to fight their capitalistic enemies. In the words of one young worker 'Yes, what you say is all right – but will that sort of stuff bring us more bread and cheese?'" To Dover Wilson – and to many others subsequently – the solution lay quite clearly in the sort of nourishment that English literature offered: the snap, crackle and pop of its roughage a purgative force of considerable political power – not because it has a direct influence on what Dover Wilson (and others) called "the social problem," but because of its indirect influence on what they certainly did not call ideology, but which is clearly signaled as such in the report's references to a general, indeed a national, "state of mind." If the "state of mind" is oriented wholly towards the "social problem," the result is an unhealthy imbalance:

This state of mind is not a new thing in history, and even goes back as far as Plato. It finds a parallel in the contempt for "poets, pipers, players, jesters and such-like caterpillars of the commonwealth" expressed by puritans of the 16th and 17th centuries, and in the hostility towards the "culture of capitalism" now prevalent in Bolshevist Russia.[14]

That hostility, that Bolshevism, is apparently best met by strengthening the character, through massive doses of poetry administered by a solicitous education system:

> we believe that, if rightly presented, poetry will be recognized by the most ardent social reformers as of value, because while it contributes no specific solution of the social problem it endows the mind with power and sanity; because, in a word, it enriches personality.[15]

Personality! The very word is like a bell. The ideological position this signals – the commitment to individualism as a long-term solution to the social problem – is a familiar one, and it remains the long-term position from which most teaching of literature is still mounted. Its political, economic, and social implications are clearly spelled out in the Newbolt Report, and most clearly in those parts of the report that we know were written by Dover Wilson. The impulse generating that position, the stimulus to which it is a considered response, lies in the events which took place in Russia in November 1917, and the subsequent sense of betrayal on the Allies' part in the face of the consequent German spring offensive of 1918 which nearly won the war for the Kaiser.

My point is a simple one. Dover Wilson's response to Greg's article on that train to Sunderland in 1917 is an excellent example of the sort of interaction between literary interpretation and political and social concerns that always obtains, but normally remains covert in our culture. Confronted by what I have called a manifestation of *Telmah* – i.e. by the disruption of the normally smooth and, in terms of individual "personality" (Hamlet's or Shakespeare's), explainable surface of a text that our society has appropriated as a manifestation of great (and thus reassuring) art – he replies with a vigor and an emotionally charged nervous energy appropriate to it as what in fact it must have seemed to be: an attack or an offensive mounted against the structure of civilization as we know it – in short, an attack on our ideology. Dover Wilson's sensitivity to overt political attacks – manifested in his articles on revolutionary Russia – fuels his response to *Telmah*, which he rightly senses as potentially revolutionary in ideological terms. Today *Hamlet*, tomorrow the world! We might in passing note (as Dover Wilson himself does, recalling the astonishing output by J. M. Robertson, E. E. Stoll, L. L. Schucking and others in the 12 months of 1919) that "For some reason or other, the War acted as a stimulus to the study of *Hamlet*."[16]

As a member of the Newbolt Committee, as we have seen, he insists on the proper, controlled study of literature as essential to a society wishing to avoid the alien barbarities of Bolshevism and to preserve the "national mind and character," i.e. the integral and coherent structures of a British way of life. Years later, writing on the work of the Workers' Educational Association classes, he comments that, but for them, "the abysmal disillusion that followed the end of the First World War ... might well have resulted in revolution." *Telmah*'s proposed reversal, its up-turning, topsy-turvy mode (in which the Ghost of one's fathers is not to be trusted), would undoubtedly have come hard to one whose very name invokes the clear, defining boundaries of an established island culture. *Telmah*'s threatened incursion would therefore have to face the determined opposition of those impregnable white cliffs, and the forces assembled – indeed, symbolized by – the figure of Sir Henry Newbolt.

Names, after all, are invested with potency. Dover Wilson's autobiography is in fact entitled *Milestones on the Dover Road*[17] and thus half humorously hints at his own eponymic standing whilst memorializing his role as defender of the British national mind, character, and culture. His article of 1914, in favor of Tsardom, is naturally anonymous. His earlier piece of 1906, with its efforts to bury Bolshevism, nevertheless offers an appealing recognition of the literally topsy-turvy function of revolution which I have tried weakly to hint at in my formulation of the name *Telmah*. Confronting Bolshevism, Dover Wilson unwittingly becomes its Greg. For what does that article do but argue that the specter which is haunting Europe is certainly one not to be trusted? It would be nice to report that an intimate and deeply personal sense of revolution and reversal accompanied these efforts to heap oblivion on Bolshevism. I can, and do. The article is signed, not John Dover Wilson, but Wildover Johnson.

It would also be nice to conclude by turning back, now, to the play. But in a very serious sense, which I hope to have made clear, we cannot do so. There is no unitary, self-presenting play for us to turn back to, and I have no intention of turning myself inside out like Wildover Johnson in pursuit of a smoothed-over (or smooth Dover) interpretation of it that can then be offered, gift-wrapped, as the truth. That kind of "appeasement" of the text can be said to have its own political analogues. And indeed ... "Dear Dr Dover Wilson," begins a missive from Birmingham dated June 7, 1936:

> I expect you will be rather surprised to get a letter from me as we have not been "introduced." But as we are both public characters perhaps we may dispense with formalities. ... I can't help telling you what immense pleasure I have had out of *What Happens in Hamlet*. I had asked for it as a Christmas present, and when it duly appeared I sat up several nights into the small hours reading it. ... When I had finished it, I did what I don't think I have ever done before with any book: I immediately read it all over again! And that won't be the last time of reading.[18]

The letter was signed "Neville Chamberlain."

In short, I am not going to suggest that we can approach *Hamlet* by recognizing *Telmah*, or that *Telmah* is the real play, obscured by *Hamlet*. That would be to try to reconcile, to bring to peace, to *appease* a text whose vitality resides precisely in its plurality: in the fact that it contradicts itself and strenuously resists our attempts to resolve, to domesticate that contradiction. I am trying to suggest that its contradiction has value, in that a pondering of some of the attempts that have been made to resolve it, to make the play speak coherently, within a limited set of boundaries, reveals the political, economic, and social forces to which all such "interpretation" is respondent, and in whose name it is inevitably, if covertly, made.[19] I am not suggesting an "alternative" reading of *Hamlet*, because that would be to fall into the same trap. I offer my title of *Telmah* as what it is: a sense of an everpresent potential challenge and contradiction *within* and *implied by* the text that we name *Hamlet*. In this sense, *Telmah* coexists with, is coterminous with *Hamlet*, in a way that must strike us, finally, as impossible. A thing, we are taught, cannot be both what it is and another thing. But that is precisely the principle challenged by *Telmah*. The notion that it cannot coexist with *Hamlet* marks the limit, I suggest, of the Eurocentric view of "sense," of "order," of "presence," if you like, and of "point of view." That Eurocentricity lies behind, and validates, a limited notion of "interpretation" which will allow us to have *Hamlet* in various guises, and which will also, as an alternative, allow clever and sophisticated interpreters to have, say, *Telmah*. But it will not allow us to have both, because that would explode our notion of the single and unified "point of view" whose "authority," as that term suggests, derives from its source, the author.

And yet, to conclude, we only have to step beyond the shores of Europe to encounter a quite different notion of interpretation which will allow exactly what I propose: the sense of a text as a site, or an area of conflicting and often contradictory potential interpretations, no single one or group of which can claim "intrinsic" primacy or "inherent" authority, and all of which are always ideological in nature and subject to extrinsic political and economic determinants.

The abstract model I reach for is of course that of jazz music: that black American challenge to the Eurocentric idea of the author's, or the composer's, authority. For the jazz musician, the "text" of a melody is a means, not an end. Interpretation in that context is not parasitic but symbiotic in its relationship with its object. Its role is not limited to the service, or the revelation, or the celebration, of the author's/composer's art. Quite the reverse: interpretation *constitutes* the art of the jazz musician. The same unservile principle seems to me to be appropriate to the critic's activity.[20] Criticism is the major, in its largest sense it is the *only*, native American art. Complaints about America's lack of original creativity in the arts miss this point. Responding to, improvising on, "playing" with, re-creating, synthesizing, and interpreting "given" structures of all kinds, political, social, aesthetic, these have historically constituted the transatlantic mode in our century and before it, to an extent that might now force us to recognize that criticism makes Americans of us all.

My emblem for this will be that critic – for in these terms Fortinbras is one – who enters at the end of *Hamlet* and speaks, in his analysis of it, in the voice of *Telmah*:

> Let four captains
> Bear Hamlet like a soldier to the stage,
> For he was likely, had he been put on,
> To have prov'd most royal; [*pause; then, turning to Claudius*]
> and for *his* passage,
> The soldier's music and the rite of war
> Speak loudly for him.
> Take up the bodies. Such a sight as this
> Becomes the field, but here shows much amiss.
> Go, bid the soldiers shoot.
>
> (V. ii. 400–8)

The equation which that particular inserted intonation permits between what the play itself calls "mighty opposites," Hamlet and Claudius, effectively turns what we call *Hamlet* momentarily into what I have been terming *Telmah* – or, no less effectively, it allows each to be seen at that moment in its most intimate involvement with the other. As the trumpets sound, the moment belongs to Fortinbras, that speculative instrument, in the tonal, or musical, or intonational quality of whose utterance these extremes meet. It is not inappropriate finally – it is not even surprising – that within his name (since my paper has spoken so much of nomenclature) we should just discern, if we ponder it, the name of the greatest black American jazz trumpeter.

Notes

A shorter version of this essay appeared in *Encounter*, LX, 4 (April 1983), 50–60.
  1. Quotations and line references are taken from the Arden edition of *Hamlet*, ed. Harold Jenkins (London, 1982).
  2. Until recently. See Bert O. States, "Phenomenology of the curtain call" (*Hudson Review*, XXXIV, 3 (Autumn 1981), 371–80).
  3. I am guided here by Edmund Leach's excellent account in his *Culture and Communication* (Cambridge, 1976), 74–5.
  4. A. J. P. Taylor, *English History 1914–45* (Oxford, 1965), 39.
  5. Ibid., 40.
  6. *The Times*, November 8, 1917, 12.

7. J. Dover Wilson, "The aims and methods of the Social Revolutionary Party in Russia" (*The Independent Review*, XI (1906), 137–50).
8. J. Dover Wilson, "Russia and her ideals" (*The Round Table*, V, 17 (1914), 103–35).
9. In 1914, together with R. W. Seton-Watson, Alfred L. Zimmern and Arthur Greenwood, Dover Wilson contributed to a volume called *The War and Democracy* (London, 1914). In a chapter devoted to a comprehensive overview of Russia he wrote of "the grand simple life they lead in the fields, a life of toil indeed but of toil sweet and infinitely varied." The Russians, he claims, have achieved democracy, have virtually realized all the principles of liberty, fraternity, equality (191), and indeed can be said to have "discovered the secret of existence" (205).
10. *The Teaching of English in England* (The Newbolt Report) (London, 1921), 21–2.
11. Cit. Margaret Mathieson, *The Preachers of Culture: A Study of English and its Teachers* (London, 1975), 69–70.
12. *The Teaching of English in England*, op. cit., 252–3.
13. George Sampson, *English for the English* (Cambridge, 1921), Preface to 1925 edn, xv.
14. *The Teaching of English in England*, op. cit., 254.
15. Ibid., 255.
16. J. Dover Wilson, *What Happens in Hamlet* (Cambridge, 1935), 14.
17. J. Dover Wilson, *Milestones on the Dover Road* (London, 1969).
18. Ibid., 213–14.
19. A valuable exception to this tendency is W. W. Robson's essay, "Does the king see the dumb-show?" (*Cambridge Quarterly*, VI, 4 (1975), 303–26), which reaches similar conclusions, although by a different route. The case for a *Hamlet* of multiple viewpoints, a precursor of the plurality inherent in the great tragedies, is incisively made.
20. This point has been made and brilliantly developed by Geoffrey Hartman in *Criticism in the Wilderness* (New Haven, 1980).